Window on Freedom

Race, Civil Rights, and Foreign Affairs, 1945–1988

EDITED BY BRENDA GAYLE PLUMMER

The University of North Carolina Press | Chapel Hill and London

Designed by April Leidig-Higgins
Set in Aldus by Copperline Book Services, Inc.
Manufactured in the United States of America

The paper in this book meets the guidelines for permanence and durability of the Committee on Production Guidelines for Book Longevity of the Council
on Library Resources.

Library of Congress Cataloging-in-Publication Data
Window on freedom: race, civil rights, and foreign affairs, 1945–1988 / edited by Brendā Gayle Plummer.
p. cm. Includes bibliographical references and index.
ISBN 0-8078-2761-4 (cloth: alk. paper)
ISBN 0-8078-5428-x (pbk.: alk. paper)
1. United States—Foreign relations—1945–1989.
2. United States—Race relations—Political aspects.
3. Racism—Political aspects—United States—
History—20th century. 4. African Americans—
Civil rights—History—20th century. 5. Minori-
ties—Civil rights—United States—History—20th
century. 6. United States—Foreign relations—
Developing countries. 7. Developing countries—
Foreign relations—United States. I. Plummer,
Brenda Gayle.
E744 .W5647 2002 327.73—dc21 2002005969

Gerald Horne's essay, "Race from Power: U.S. Foreign
Policy and the General Crisis of White Supremacy,"
was originally published, in somewhat different form,
in *Diplomatic History* 23 (Summer 1999): 437–61,
and is reprinted here with permission.

cloth   07 06 05 04 03 5 4 3 2 1
paper   07 06 05 04 03 5 4 3 2 1

Window on Freedom

CONTENTS

Window on Freedom

Introduction

During Easter week in 1958, the African American civil rights and peace activist Bayard Rustin took his place at the microphone at a rally in Britain. His speech was one of the events for a planned march from the British nuclear facility at Aldermaston, Berkshire, to London's Trafalgar Square. It was a historic day for the peace movement in democratic countries, newly resurgent after years of quiescence, when Cold War fears had equated peace advocacy with treason. Rustin was the only American speaker. He shared the stage with Reverend Michael Scott, who had risked his life in South Africa opposing apartheid; the Rhodesian novelist Doris Lessing; and philosopher Bertrand Russell. British Direct Action Committee member Michael Randle later recalled that "Bayard Rustin delivered what many regarded as the most powerful speech of that Good Friday afternoon, linking the struggle against weapons of mass destruction with the struggle of blacks for their basic rights in America."[1]

Rustin's participation in the Aldermaston march placed him squarely in a venerable tradition of international activism among African Americans that dates back to the abolitionist movement. Fugitive slave and statesman Frederick Douglass was a forerunner when slavery was still legal in the United States, and those who wanted to abolish it sought support from the English and Irish working and middle classes. The black feminist journalist crusader Ida B. Wells also preceded Rustin. She traveled to England late in the nineteenth century to reveal the atrocities of lynching to a horrified British public. The experiences of Douglass, Wells, and Rustin demonstrate that the domestic campaign to defuse the destructive power of racism and realize full civil rights for racial minorities can be profoundly and richly understood in the context of competitive international relations.[2]

International antiracist and antislavery activism belongs equally to the history of the African diaspora and the history of foreign relations. By its very nature, the history of antiracist struggle breaks down barriers between historical subfields because the race concept itself, scientifically suspect, is socially compelling. To view race as a public problem is to address it as a dynamic force, capable of protean resistances, and thus able to enter history in a

Bayard Rustin took part in the April 1958 peace march from London's Trafalgar Square to Aldermaston, the site of a major British atomic facility. (Bettmann/Corbis)

variety of forms and shapes, which affect how it is incorporated in the body politic. Scholars have frequently treated race as a discrete intervention into the foreign policy process and as a single event, moment, or crisis, while ignoring its recursive potential to redefine power relationships both at home and abroad and, perhaps most important, to name that which constitutes freedom and justice in democratic society.

This collection offers a window on the salience of race in U.S. foreign and domestic relationships and in the struggle to realize full citizenship for all Americans. The project represents the collaboration of ten scholars who bring divergent perspectives to bear on the nexus of civil rights, foreign relations, and race studies. The focus is on the forty-three years between the end of World War II and the end of the second Reagan administration. The study breaks new ground along several fronts.

The voluminous historical literature created by scholars of U.S. foreign relations and foreign policy making had too frequently concerned itself exclusively with the views, motivations, and behaviors of a small policy elite. In the past, students of American diplomacy construed this elite quite narrowly as consisting of government officials and a few powerful nongovernmental figures. More recently, social scientists have widened their understanding of the constituencies that influence foreign policy making and enter history as participants. They have come to realize that U.S. foreign relations are embedded in complex social, economic, cultural, and political factors of domestic as well as foreign origin.[3] This discovery has multiple sources. It derives partially from the race relations paradigm that dominated social science research on African Americans for much of the century. The model became normative because of the widespread acceptance of Swedish social scientist Gunnar Myrdal's conclusions, as presented in his famous book, *An American Dilemma*. Once applied to international affairs, race relations promised to reduce the uncertainties accompanying such processes as decolonization, for example, by offering explanations couched in familiar domestic terms.[4] The race relations approach was challenged, however, by events as well as by interpretations that disputed its value not long after it appeared.[5] While the race relations approach offered much practical assistance in dealing with international issues, it also helped broaden awareness that race itself is a salient factor in international relations.

It has become commonplace, for example, to note that Cold War rivalries forced the United States to confront segregation and stimulated reforms on the civil rights front. We also recognize that the anticommunist crusade retarded change by linking Americanism to the racial status quo. This volume goes beyond these observations in providing a deeper understanding of how race mediated the foreign relations of the United States. Americans, including many African Americans, often resisted perceiving any common ground with persecuted minorities overseas. By treating the American experience as unique, they performed three acts of legerdemain. First, they separated it, consciously or not, from the arena of international discussion and mediation. Second, and as a consequence, they had to assume that Jim Crow was only a minor fault in an otherwise smoothly functioning democratic system that economic growth, education, and improving communications technology would fix. Third, and most profound, they undermined the humanity of African Americans by suggesting that there was little comparability between their condition and that of the human community beyond America's shores.[6]

The enormous wealth and power of the United States after 1945 bolstered the first two of these three perspectives. The momentary elimination of foreign economic competition following World War II and the successful transition to a peacetime economy had abolished the politics of scarcity, if not scarcity itself. The informed public and its leaders predicated their thinking on the expectation of a uniquely boundless American cornucopia of productive growth, extending infinitely into the future. Prosperity would, in time, erase difference and blunt the edge of intergroup conflicts. The third perspective was abetted by racism itself: while it was essential to remove the obstacles to full civil rights for blacks, African Americans were deemed an essentially uprooted people with no reference points outside the American experience. The ills afflicting them could be removed without taking them out of the place they occupied as invisible stepchildren in the kitchen of U.S. politics. It should be realized, however, that Americans were not alone in trying to shield racial dirty linen from the eyes of the world. As Henry J. Richardson III has observed, "All major governments at the time of drafting the U.N. charter and the Universal declaration did their best to ensure, by all means known to domestic and international law, that these principles had only *international* application and carried no legal obligation on those governments to be implemented *domestically*. All tacitly realized that for their own discriminated-against minorities to acquire leverage on the basis of legally being able to claim enforcement of these wide-reaching rights would create pressures that would be political dynamite."[7]

Major powers with racial-ethnic minorities or colonial territories inhabited by people of different race were thus engaged in containment and holding operations of various kinds after the war ended. Their efforts to bridge the past and present were complicated by the new roles the postwar order imposed on them. The United States, for example, effected a transition from isolationism to globalism. The Allied triumph in 1945 laid the foundations for the rise of American hegemony and the concomitant challenge to it mounted by the Soviet bloc. Foreign critics of U.S. policy, including nationalists, communists, and others, used the prevalence of racial injustice in the United States to discredit its claims of world leadership. Officials and opinion leaders among the intelligentsia increasingly acknowledged that racial discrimination and public disorder would compromise American objectives. They called for reform in the interests of both national and international security.[8]

Breaking the habits of centuries proved hard to achieve. The subtle changes in establishment perspectives provided an opening, however, for aggressive advocates of racial equality to assert themselves. World War II enabled large numbers of African Americans to rethink their place in U.S. society. They were willing and ready for social transformation. As a community, black Americans possessed institutions—notably an independent press and mass organizations—arguably more powerful than their present-day counterparts. Black organizations joined other liberal interest groups in trying to make international commitments serve national reform agendas. Some of these activities predated the domestic struggle for civil rights. Others would later be channeled into the reservoir of political knowledge and experience subsequently tapped in the interests of domestic change.[9]

The United Nations became an early forum for contestation over human and civil rights issues. This was manifest not only in debates about the content of the Charter, but also in discussions of treaty-making powers, the role of superpowers, colonialism, the status of minorities and women, the location of UN facilities, and the character of UN personnel. The civil rights movement cloaked itself in the moral authority of international documents. It based its call for reform on principles that the United States had broadly endorsed as a major power during the war. Civil rights activists found that their own objectives sometimes meshed with, and at other times conflicted with, those of smaller states demanding equity from larger ones, and great powers hoping to score points against one another by recourse to moral arguments. The ensuing Cold War provided even greater opportunities to effect a linkage between foreign commitments and domestic obligations.[10]

Moral suasionist arguments and Cold War considerations opened a space for nongovernmental actors to have a larger impact on foreign affairs. It nevertheless remains all too common in policy circles, and among scholars who study them, to dismiss the public sector—including Congress—as ignorant and parochial, and as intrusive and disruptive interlopers in the decision-making process. A few public voices might be carefully admitted, albeit under circumstances that divorce them from the constituencies they were recruited to represent. The experience of *Ebony* magazine publisher John Johnson is illustrative. Johnson served on an advisory committee on equal opportunity in the State Department during the Kennedy years. "For the first time," he wrote in his autobiography, "I found myself in the 'area of gossip,' that informal, social-business climate where, at a club, a wedding, a dinner, or a golf outing, business deals and projections are traded by white men . . . who assume, as a matter of course, that there's nobody here but us chickens, and that everybody in the inner circle has a right to know and does."[11]

Johnson, serving on the Urban League board of directors and at other venues, had heard corporate executives discuss business "within the context of national and international affairs." Secretary of State Dean Rusk told him that the exclusion of blacks from such networks accounted for the failure to integrate the State Department as well. "After studying the data," Rusk determined "that the problem was not so much bad people as the impersonal will of a system that penalized people who were outside the area of gossip."[12] Blaming the intractability of a mechanical system bought some time for the State Department, defined the problem in a way that, if accepted, would neutralize protest, and offered the enticement of bringing a few privileged blacks into the inner circle. Such management techniques never succeeded entirely in replacing protest with accommodation or popular insurgency with summitry, but the bureaucratic articulation of race problems, particularly by broadening channels between black and white elites, helped define issues in ways that foreclosed alternative constructions of meaning and alternative courses of action.[13]

The search for a "safe" solution to America's race problem led to the publication of Myrdal's *An American Dilemma*. The study, massive for its time, had origins deep within the philanthropic establishment of interwar America. According to David Southern, author of *Gunnar Myrdal and Black-White Relations: The Use and Abuse of An American Dilemma, 1944–1969*, the initiative sprang from the Carnegie Foundation. In 1935 trustee Newton D. Baker had suggested that changing times required a fresh analysis of African Americans and their role in American life. The foundation selected Gunnar Myrdal to coordinate the resulting research project, partly because his roots in Sweden, a country without colonies or a history of fractious race relations, commended him as an objective observer of American mores. Myrdal, however, was not a complete stranger to the world of U.S. foundations. His research had been supported by Rockefeller philanthropy, and he had been a Laura Spelman Fellow. Rockefeller networks also gave him access to black scholars, who collaborated with him. Social scientists like Ralph Bunche and Charles Johnson provided him with access and insight into African American society, a segregated world that most white American social scientists could not penetrate.[14]

An American Dilemma was a high-water mark in the history of philanthropy and race relations, noted not least for Myrdal's prophecy that there would be "a redefinition of the Negro's status as a result of this war." Yet, in the coming decade, as Waldemar Nielsen has observed, "the big foundations were at the trailing edge, not the cutting edge, of change, and congressional attacks upon them in the mid-1950s . . . tended to discourage what little initiative they had been inclined to take in regard to social and racial issues."[15] The Myrdal study had nevertheless broken new ground in making what had been an insurgent viewpoint in the social sciences normative in the academy, among national civic leaders, and with parts of the educated public. Despite the work that black scholars had been producing for years, the new view of race gained legitimacy only when underwritten and rubber-stamped by a scholar anointed by mainstream academic leadership.

This collection of essays demonstrates how Myrdal's conclusions opened a window on the reworking of race in the reform agenda of the postwar years. His ideas abetted the formation of newly assertive interest groups; created political "spaces" for minority efforts to influence decision making; promoted minority contacts with foreign governments and other foreign protagonists; and, above all, legitimated a discourse that explicitly linked racial reform with the desired world order.

Racism undermined U.S. global leadership and strained its relations with countries that had a stake in achieving global racial equality. Racial discrimination in the United States also had implications for the relations between European states and their former colonies. Many of the latter tried to maintain neutralist positions regarding Cold War conflicts. Asian and African nations, carved out of the old imperial system, sought a speedy end to a colonialism that was, at the very least, racially inflected. How much reform would satisfy world opinion? Did the United States government, in distancing itself from the most egregious instances of racism, recreate a national identity that defined discrimination as merely the artifact of a discredited regional political economy? Did the government make enough progress after 1945 to convince other nations that this was so? These questions and others just as compelling are addressed in this anthology.

The scholars represented here include many pioneers in understanding the interrelations between race and U.S. foreign affairs. This historiography was made possible by a confluence of developments in other history subfields, particularly the veritable information explosion in Afro-American history over the past thirty years, the ability of social history to suggest fruitful approaches to other branches of the discipline, and the liberalization of diplomatic history, now frequently cast as the history of foreign relations. "We cannot understand the detribalization of our lives or explain it to our readers and students by concentrating heavily on policy and ignoring and downplaying the patterns of social interaction produced by contact between different peoples," two diplomatic historians, Charles R. Lilley and Michael H. Hunt, have written. "Nor can we understand the vicissitudes and follies of state power and of those who exercise it if we insist on treating culture and power as though they were largely divorced from, rather than wedded to, one another in important ways."[16]

This perspective reunites policy makers with the society from which they came and shows their vulnerability to its culture. It derives from a pluralist window on the world that examines the full range of political, social, and ideological behaviors that influence how foreign policy originates. The approach contrasts with the belief that power struggles among states nearly always fully explain the origins of foreign policy, and that policy makers stand apart from and above the prejudices and temptations of ordinary mortals. The significance of nongovernmental actors is appreciated here. The national tragedy of 11 September 2001 tells us that it is folly to ignore the potential impact of nonstate actors—and deeply held cultural, ideological, and religious convictions—on foreign affairs.

Once historians conceded the legitimacy of studying nonstate actors, and social and cultural factors in foreign relations, the subject of racial-ethnic

minorities and foreign affairs could also be examined. Historians are now re-
searching the foreign affairs interest of African Americans in specific issues,
particular epochs, and distinct areas of the world. Recent studies have appeared that focus on black radicalism,[17] the interwar through post–World
War II eras,[18] the Cold War,[19] the activities of the State Department,[20] the impact of civil rights insurgency on world affairs,[21] the independent African re-
publics,[22] Haiti,[23] Cuba,[24] decolonization and southern Africa,[25] and China
and Japan.[26] Some of this work has focused more heavily on cultural than political issues.[27] The subject of African Americans and foreign affairs has even
branched, sometimes controversially, into biography.[28] Behavioral scientists
have joined historians in taking a fresh look at how a black constituency for
international affairs has articulated itself and have applied structural analyses to the strengths and limitations of black activism in this area.[29] New scholarship that treats the engagement of other hyphenated racial-ethnic minorities is now emerging from a matrix that once centered on identity politics.[30]

Readers keyed in to events of the past decade will find that the material in
this collection, while historical, continues to help explain certain current issues. Social scientists have long held that ethnicity as a factor in foreign relations manifests itself when ethnic constituents get involved with issues affecting their countries of origin. They then tend to generate congressional
activism.[31] The interaction in the late 1980s and early 1990s between Haitian
American constituents and African American congressional representatives
exemplifies this phenomenon. The ability of the Haitian Americans, a relatively new immigrant group, to make use of the protest organizations and
elected representatives from another black ethnic group indexes the Haitian
Americans' sophistication in their ability to exploit the political system in
challenging the policies of the Clinton administration.[32]

Race and the symbolic politics of race remains America's Achilles' heel.
The former Taliban government of Afghanistan made an attempt to exploit
this in its efforts to involve the Reverend Jesse Jackson in hostage negotia-
tion. The State Department's subsequent efforts to dissuade Jackson (through
direct communication between Jackson and Secretary of State Colin Powell)
and discourage such citizen diplomacy remain consistently in character.

Recent revelations of U.S. lack of preparedness raise questions about the
level and character of U.S. missions abroad. Is there a necessary tension between a foreign service and a defense establishment that is broadly representative of the population and one that draws on traditional elites or bureaucratic legacies? Is the apparent American ignorance of other peoples and ways
of life in some way an artifact of its racial past? Did the negativity and ambivalence surrounding the official U.S. position on the September 2001 in-

ternational conference on racism at Durban, South Africa, suggest that issues regarding racism at home remain unresolved?

The extent to which the United States would commit itself to reform was a subject of self-study by elites during the World War II years. The war era sensibility was unique in its self-consciousness and intuition that it lay at the crux of pivotal future developments. In the United States, as Paul Gordon Lauren demonstrates in his essay, the public policy establishment adopted a foreign scholar's insights on race relations. *An American Dilemma* presented race as "seen from the outside" in two ways. In addition to Myrdal's own distance from the American experience, his use of black social scientists as field workers and consultants ensured that the views of marginalized practitioners would receive a hearing, however masked. America's dilemma, as old as the republic and noted by Tocqueville, became an issue during these years because it had to be explained to the world and reworked to suit a rapidly transforming society.

Lest the innocent reader believe that the 1945 watershed was achieved rapidly, smoothly, and ubiquitously, Gerald Horne has probed the sources of resistance to racial equality that persist into our time. He roots U.S. responses to the racial crises in southern Africa in U.S. frontier expansion and the white settler ethic. This is not mere speculation: he has uncovered blood ties among elites that promoted a congruence of outlook and helped to drive policy. In a broad view of twentieth-century history, Horne examines what colonized peoples and racial minorities made of racialized imperialism. Imperial Japanese ambitions, also expressed in racial terms, would serve as a substitute for colonial aspirations for freedom. The countries Japan occupied during World War II experienced profound disillusionment. Japan deployed a vicious, state-sponsored racism and a code of racial supremacy that belied its earlier emancipatory promises and blandishments. The collision of racisms that underpinned the war in what Horne has in another context called "the Black Pacific" would also trouble the peace.

Plummer's essay on "brown babies," the mixed-race orphans of occupied Germany, illustrates how, while excoriating Nazism, the Allies brought their own prejudices to bear on a society in flux. Having fought a four-year war against the most deadly and determined racist power in history, Americans collided with their own biases in constructing a postwar order. The changes they grappled with predated the Cold War Soviet challenge to U.S. hegemony. They were locked in conflict not with an Other but with themselves. The "brown babies" foreshadowed racial crises to come and limned out the contours of the initial, confused American responses. Americans had to bridge great distances in managing the public face of deeply intimate issues involving sexuality, family formation, and child rearing. The essay makes readable the invisible ink with which gender in foreign relations is often inscribed.

When the Cold War finally overtook U.S. society, it profoundly altered the political and social landscape. Its effects were felt within African American communities when pledges of anticommunist conformity on the right, and the reaffirmation of communist solidarity on the left, took priority over the civil rights agenda. Carol Anderson's essay explores the tragedy of lost opportunities attendant on the conflict between the "bleached souls" and "Red Negroes" of the time. Internecine warfare within the black leadership cadre was played out on an international stage by means of human rights petitions addressed to the United Nations. The communists of the Civil Rights Congress, NAACP liberals, and the black conservatives enlisted as apologists for the American status quo quarreled about how U.S. race relations should be judged, but all had implicitly agreed that the world had to be convinced of the justice of their respective positions. The real losers were the racial-ethnic minorities of the United States, their desire for full civil rights swallowed up for the moment in Cold War exigency.

How America explained Jim Crow and how well it did so are important parts of the story. Representation and public opinion form only one dimension, however, of the impact of race on the foreign relations of the United States. This is demonstrated in Cary Fraser's exploration of the Afro-Asian conference at Bandung, Indonesia, in 1955. Bandung preceded the wave of decolonization that swept Africa five years later. It presaged the maturation of Third World sovereignty and signaled that metropolitan countries would thereafter have to weigh the consequences of their racial policies in light of this development. Fraser makes evident that the Afro-Asian conference indexed the range of possibilities and limitations that newly sovereign countries faced in balancing the interests of their compatriots with the demands the major powers imposed on them. It was here that China debuted as a state that, although excluded from the United Nations international system, made its influence felt in Asia by extending rhetorical overtures, some of them racially inflected, to nonaligned states. In this manner, China recalls Horne's Japan, which in the interwar years provided useful metaphors for those opposing the racial imperialism of the Atlantic powers. Bandung served simultaneously as a proxy and a guide for African countries and African minorities in the diaspora to articulate a broad prescriptive agenda for the future.

The Afro-Asian conference in 1955 intersected chronologically with domestic events that lent urgency to the international dimensions of racial issues. News media worldwide extensively reported *Brown II*, the Supreme Court's second decision on school integration, which provided vague instructions for making desegregation operational. Other widely publicized incidents of the year included the Montgomery bus boycott and the lynchings respectively of George Lee, Lamar Smith, and fourteen-year-old Emmett Till in Mississippi. Each racial embarrassment created difficulties for U.S. propagandists. Each also served as a measure of growing, organized resistance to racial integration and a reciprocal determination to make it a reality.

Increasing civil rights insurgency incurred opposition from committed segregationists. The first *Brown v. Board of Education* decision of the previous year had led them to create the Citizens Councils, devoted to supposedly nonviolent resistance to desegregation. Hostility toward the South in the national and international press toughened their stance. Segregationists did not articulate a fully developed position on international affairs, as Thomas Noer points out in his essay. They did, however, create an intriguing postcolonial counterdiscourse that not only issued a challenge to the civil rights movement but also reprised the foundations of white settler claims to racial hegemony in southern Africa. In the 1960s and early 1970s, Alabama governor George Wallace was the main interpreter and promoter of "the foreign policy of the white resistance."

Readers in Delhi, Lagos, or Stockholm could find in their newspapers ample record of misdeeds in distant parts of the rural United States. It was difficult for U.S. embassies and the United States Information Agency to convince the global public that these were isolated incidents, however, when diplomats from Asian and African countries faced discrimination in the heavily traveled Maryland-Washington-Virginia corridor.[33] Michael Krenn considers the negative consequences of denying public accommodations, services, and housing to foreign envoys on racial grounds. He addresses the remedies that the State Department applied, which included involving local authorities in voluntary desegregation efforts by appealing to their patriotism. Krenn's conclusions contrast the State Department's difficulties with local Jim Crow and its own reluctance to desegregate the Foreign Service and other divisions. Insofar as the State Department failed to endorse the objectives of the civil rights movement, Krenn argues, its sincerity would always be questioned and the effectiveness of its reform efforts limited.

Mary L. Dudziak takes up the question of representation in her essay. Birmingham provided perhaps the most repellent imagery of the civil rights era. Photographs of the snarling German shepherds and fire hoses used against demonstrators were flashed around the world. The United States faced major damage control. In the midst of it all, however, it found unexpected allies in the African states. The explanation is that even as early as the Bandung Conference of 1955, many nonaligned states wished to remain just that. Moderate leaders hoped that racial extremism and reckless imperialist actions from the West would not coerce them into an undesired opposition and force them to accede to leftists or radical nationalists at home. American racial violence thus put them on the spot, and they hoped that U.S. policy makers would develop ways of defusing and explaining it that would let everyone save face.[34]

Dudziak writes about the early 1960s, when color served to both differentiate African Americans from others in U.S. society and bind them as a racial-ethnic group with distinct interests to define and defend. While elements of the civil rights movement's strategies and tactics have been incorporated in the struggles of other U.S. ethnic minorities, not all groups have interpreted the stakes in the same way. Lorena Oropeza describes how early Mexican American activists consciously and deliberately suppressed a view of Mexican Americans as a racial minority to ease assimilation. They correctly saw race as the great divider in American life and hoped to sidestep it by emphasizing similarity rather than difference. Mexican American communities traditionally sought military service to demonstrate their Americanness and promoted an ethnic persona "premised upon a white, masculinist, and militaristic citizenship."

This changed when black insurgency began bearing fruit, particularly expanding entitlements under the economic programs of President Lyndon B. Johnson's Great Society. Impoverished Mexican American communities in the Southwest and West found themselves excluded from these benefits and began to question the bases of earlier strategies and tactics, including the unquestioning acceptance of military obligation. This policy review among Mexican Americans coincided with the Vietnam War and led not only to a redefinition of how they could best press for civil rights and civil entitlements but also to a redefinition of who they were.[35]

The valorization by many youth of an Amerindian racial heritage at odds with the amorphous whiteness of the acculturative ideal played a major role in Chicano antiwar dissidence. Dissidence also involved a reassessment of ethnicity and nationality as well as race. Mexico would not be simply the country from which Mexican Americans had originally come and against which they defined themselves. The Mexican presence north of the Rio Grande, in the lands referred to as Aztlán, antedated the U.S. republic. The idea of Aztlán is powerful because it simultaneously embraces Mexico yet sets the inhabitants of its northernmost regions apart from both Mexico and the United States, simultaneously confirming allegiance and difference. Oropeza's essay is a reminder that the intersection of race and foreign affairs in the United States involves more than black and white. Contrary to some popular assumptions, Mexican Americans did not simply derive their political strategies from African American models. They confronted race on a terrain unique to their experience and interpreted it accordingly. Future scholarship will reveal the full scope of America's dilemma as research on non–African American racial-ethnic groups continues.

By 1970, when antiwar dissidence crested in the United States, social movement experience had become widespread in domestic society. The liberal view of race as inscribed by Gunnar Myrdal was now normative. Few people openly defended racism or challenged the doctrine of racial equality. The toleration and practice of racism continued but had to be carried on in the absence of respectable arguments. In this climate of liberalism and growing sophistication among activists, the antiapartheid movement found itself directly confronting the historic U.S. cooperation with the blatantly repressive and exploitative South African regime. Donald R. Culverson's essay examines the movement's successes as part of a growing global interdependence based on consensus formed by common experience.

By the 1980s, changes in American life, precipitated in large part by what activists had earlier achieved, created opportunities to address apartheid effectively. The demographic base for movement participation grew, and modes of protest came to closely resemble the more familiar practices of conventional charities and mainstream civic organizations. Technological change in communications made increased citizen involvement possible. Activists began paying attention to marketing strategies and employing the tactics of "normal politics" that they once eschewed. Antiapartheid supporters worked with sympathetic members of Congress, organized boycotts of South Africa by celebrities, and placed pressure on institutional investors. Culverson's essay is an analysis of a contemporary antiapartheid movement that benefited from the antiracist struggles of the past.

Just as the scholarship of Gunnar Myrdal provided a starting point for academic inquiry into the racial nexus of foreign and domestic affairs, the life of Bayard Rustin opens a window on how that nexus shaped social practice and helped order a single career. After the Aldermaston march, Rustin continued his distinguished career as a peace and civil rights activist. In late 1959, his Committee for Non-Violent Action teamed up with the British Direct Action Committee in planning a march from Accra, Ghana, to a French nuclear installation in the Sahara, 2,000 miles to the north. Here, they protested nuclear proliferation and the introduction of weapons research to Africa. The groups enjoyed the tacit approval of local governments that opposed nuclear weapons and testing but lacked the power to confront France directly. The French army stopped the marchers on the Upper Volta frontier, but Rustin had helped link disarmament to African desires for neutrality and peaceful development. He used his organizational skills on behalf of African independence in 1962 when Kenneth Kaunda, head of the Zambian United National Independence Party, persuaded him and members of the World Peace Brigade to organize a march from Tanzania to Zambia. Kaunda meanwhile would call a coordinating Zambian general strike. Marchers set out in March and awaited Kaunda's instructions to enter Zambia. Kaunda, however, struck a deal with the British and called the protest off.[36]

It is as the organizer of the 1963 March on Washington that Rustin is most often remembered. He nevertheless continued to mingle his networks and associations in all the institutions and movements with which he was associated. He maintained a long-term relationship as correspondent with the *Baltimore Afro-American*, which kept him in touch with African American public affairs interests and provided him a conduit to a black newspaper-reading audience. When Martin Luther King Jr. traveled to Europe in 1964 to accept his Nobel Peace Prize, Rustin went with him and arranged for him to stop in London and address a fund-raiser for the British peace movement. It is thus ironic that Rustin subsequently criticized King for the linkage he made between the civil rights and antiwar movements. "I would consider the involvement of civil rights organizations as such in peace activities distinctly unprofitable and perhaps even suicidal," he told the *Amsterdam News*. Yet Rustin had been making such linkages all his life.

One of his biographers, Jervis Anderson, observes that "earlier in his career, Rustin had combined civil rights and peace activism. But if that had been pointed out to him later, he might have said that, unlike Dr. King, he wore membership caps in both movements and was the principal leader of none." This, of course, was more than a little disingenuous. Rustin did not support the war in Vietnam. Instead, he opposed radicals' endorsement of North Vietnamese and Viet Cong military objectives, and the communist ideology that he believed had filtered into New Left ranks. Rustin's liberal vision of society looked conservative to the rebels of the period. His condemnation of the spring 1969 student takeover of Cornell University's administration building earned him a letter of praise from Gunnar Myrdal, whose own liberal orthodoxy would soon be challenged. Rustin felt that the energies activists poured into antiwar demonstrations and displays of armed militancy drained away support for social welfare programs at home. His position also reflects the shifting ground on which social movements stood during the late 1960s. The era witnessed multiple challenges to the personalist leadership styles of men like King and the paradoxical ascension of skilled and experienced, if less visible, activists like Rustin himself.[37]

The civil rights movement in the 1960s was a net competitor with other movements for scarce resources, members, and political space. Reformers might share common perspectives but remain unable for practical reasons to consolidate their work. While many African Americans could sympathize with antiwar and peace movement aims, there was little to choose among them. As Rustin noted, there would be no groundswell of black participation in the peace movement because of the priority that blacks assigned to daily problems of racial justice and poverty in the United States. As it stood, African Americans had through example energized other reform efforts without experiencing reciprocal benefits. Peace movement activists should consider devoting more time to securing racial justice, he thought.[38]

The linkages that Rustin believed problematic (although he made them himself) became not only easier to sustain in the late twentieth century, but impossible to avoid. It has become a truism that media exposure during the civil rights movement intensified the vulnerability of authorities and quickened public support for change. We are now in an age where "bearing witness" is made more effective by advancements in the same media. The possibility of making connections and forging alliances among movements is abetted by the increasing globalization of communication. Communications technology as a tool is most accessible to those exploiting it for profit, but it remains possible for racial-ethnic communities and governments alike to use the media to bring their issues to a world public. As the United States Information Agency and the State Department discovered, showing off U.S. minority cultures to a world audience can enhance national prestige.[39]

In the 1960s and 1970s, cultural diplomats added rhythm and blues to their repertory. What people of color experience, and their cultural practices, can also be interpreted, commodified, and marketed. This is a noticeable component of the international sale of such items as clothing, music, and that chimera, style. The marketing of minority subcultures for economic or political gain may be seen as a co-optative strategy that erases conflict by blurring identities. Yet that commercialization relies for its success on maintaining the tension between difference, as represented by people of color, and conformity. Rather than discounting the salience of race, the marketplace reaffirms, and glamorizes, difference. From the perspective of the nexus of race and foreign affairs, the global marketplace ensures that race will continue to inflect international relations for the foreseeable future.

Reciprocally, the instantiation and reiteration of race in American history has been a central factor in the creation of foreign policy knowledge, opinions, and objectives among African Americans and perhaps other racial-ethnic minorities. In the 1945–88 period, black Americans' goals evolved as the consensus about the national interest broke down and changes occurred in how domestic society managed race. The significance of race in U.S. relations with other powers was gradually revealed in an epoch that curiously merged ascendancy and decline.

Notes

1. Randle, quoted in Jervis Anderson, *Bayard Rustin: Troubles I've Seen* (Berkeley: University of California Press, 1998), 215. See also Richard Taylor, *Against the Bomb: The British Peace Movement, 1958–1965* (Oxford: Clarendon Press, 1988); Lawrence S. Wittner, *Rebels against War: The American Peace Movement, 1933–1983* (Philadelphia: Temple University Press, 1984).

2. For the activities of black abolitionists abroad, see Richard Blackett, *Building an Anti-Slavery Wall: Black Americans in the Atlantic Abolitionist Movement, 1830–1860* (Baton Rouge: Louisiana State University Press, 1983); Richard Blackett, "Pressure from Without: African Americans, British Public Opinion, and Civil War Diplomacy," in *The Union, the Confederacy, and the Atlantic Rim*, ed. Robert E. May (West Lafayette, Ind.: Purdue University Press, 1995); James Walvin, ed., *Slavery and British Society, 1776–1846* (Baton Rouge: Louisiana State University Press, 1982); James Walvin, *England, Slaves, and Freedom, 1776–1838* (Jackson: University Press of Mississippi, 1986). For the antilynching movement abroad, see Alfreda M. Duster, ed., *Crusade for Justice: The Autobiography of Ida B. Wells* (Chicago: University of Chicago Press, 1970).

3. Examples of earlier approaches include Alfred O. Hero, "American Negroes and U.S. Foreign Policy, 1937–1967," *Journal of Conflict Resolution* 13 (1969): 220–51; Milton D. Morris, "Black Americans and the Foreign Policy Process: The Case of Africa," *Western Political Quarterly* 25 (1972): 451–63; Jake Miller, *The Black Presence in American Foreign Affairs* (Washington, D.C.: University Press of America, 1978); Kenneth Longmeyer, "Black American Demands," *Foreign Policy* 60 (1985): 3–17.

4. Harold Isaacs, "American Race Relations and the United States Image in World Affairs," *Journal of Human Relations* 10 (1962): 266–80; Harold Isaacs, "Race and Color in World Affairs," *Foreign Affairs* 47 (Jan. 1969): 235–50; Harold Isaacs, "World Affairs and U.S. Race Relations," *Public Opinion Quarterly* 22 (Fall 1958): 364–70; George W. Shepherd and Tilden J. LeMelle, *Race among Nations* (Lexington, Mass.: Heath Lexington Books, 1970); Tilden J. LeMelle, "Race, International Relations, U.S. Foreign Policy, and the African Liberation Struggle," *Journal of Black Studies* 3 (Sept. 1972): 95–109.

5. Ronald Segal, *The Race War* (London: Jonathan Cape, 1966); Locksley Edmondson, "The Challenge of Race: From Entrenched White Power to Rising Black Power," *International Journal* 24 (Autumn 1969): 693–716; Locksley Edmondson, "The Internationalization of Black Power: Historical and Contemporary Perspectives," *Mawazo* 1 (Dec. 1968): 16–30.

6. African American engagement with foreign affairs seemed minimal and unimportant to many scholars, particularly behaviorists, who assumed that deficits in education and institutional resources had stunted black interest. Anthony Orum, "A Reappraisal of the Social and Political Participation of Negroes," in *Perspectives on Black America*, ed. Russell Endo and William Strawbridge (Englewood Cliffs, N.J.: Prentice-Hall, 1970), 42–60; Marvin E. Olsen, "Social and Political Participation of Blacks," *American Sociological Review* 35 (1970): 682–97; Harold Wolman and Norman C. Thomas, "Black Interests, Black Groups, and Black Influence in the Federal Policy Process," *Journal of Politics* 32 (1970): 875–97; Allan Kornberg, Elliot J. Tepper, and George J. Watson, "The National Elections and Comparative Positions of Negroes and Whites on Policy," *South Atlantic Quarterly* 67 (1968): 405–18; Hero, "American Negroes and U.S. Foreign Policy, 1937–1967"; John Kosa and Clyde Z. Nunn, "Race, Deprivation, and Attitude toward Communism," *Phylon* 25 (1969): 337–46.

7. Henry J. Richardson III, "Black People, Technocracy, and Legal Process: Thoughts, Fears, and Goals," in *Public Policy for the Black Community*, ed. Marguerite Ross Barnett and James A. Hefner (Port Washington, N.Y.: Alfred Publishing, 1976), 179.

8. Channing Tobias, *World Implications of Race* (New York: n.p., 1944); James L. Roark, "American Black Leaders: The Response of Colonialism and the Cold War," *African Historical Studies* 4, 2 (1971): 253–70; Mary L. Dudziak, "Desegregation as a Cold War Imperative," *Stanford Law Review* 41 (Nov. 1988): 61–120; Brenda Gayle Plummer, *Rising Wind: Black Americans and U.S. Foreign Affairs, 1935–1960* (Chapel Hill: University of North Carolina Press, 1996).

9. Richard M. Dalfiume, "'The Forgotten Years' of the Negro Revolution," *Journal of American History* 55, 1 (1968): 90–106; Nancy Weiss, *Farewell to the Party of Lincoln: Black Politics in the Age of FDR* (Princeton: Princeton University Press, 1983); Barbara Dianne Savage, *Broadcasting Freedom: Radio, War, and the Politics of Race, 1938–1948* (Chapel Hill: University of North Carolina Press, 1999). On the black press specifically, see Richard L. Beard and Cyril E. Zoerner II, "Associated Negro Press: Its Founding, Ascendancy and Demise," *Journalism Quarterly* 46 (Spring 1969): 47–52; Patrick Scott Washburn, *A Question of Sedition: The Federal Government's Investigation of the Black Press during World War II* (New York: Oxford University Press, 1986).

10. Committee on Africa, the War, and Peace Aims, *The Atlantic Charter and Africa from an American Standpoint* (New York: n.p., 1942); L. D. Reddick, "Africa: Test of the Atlantic Charter," *Crisis* 50 (July 1943): 202–4, 217–18; U.S. Senate, Committee on Foreign Relations, *Hearings on the Charter of the United Nations*, 79th Cong., 1st sess., 9–13 July 1945; Bert Lockwood Jr., "The UN Charter and U.S. Civil Rights Litigation: 1946–1955," *Iowa Law Review* 69 (1984): 901–56; Robert L. Harris Jr., "Racial Equality and the United Nations Charter," in *New Directions in Civil Rights Studies*, ed. Armstead L. Robinson and Patricia Sullivan (Charlottesville: University Press of Virginia, 1991), 126–48; Paul Gordon Lauren, "First Principles of Racial Equality: History and the Politics and Diplomacy of Human Rights Provisions in the United Nations Charter," *Human Rights Quarterly* 5 (Winter 1983): 1–26.

11. John Johnson, *Succeeding against the Odds* (New York: Warner Books, 1989), 244.

12. Ibid., 244, 245.

13. For the State Department's struggles with desegregation both within and outside its own halls, see Michael L. Krenn, *Black Diplomacy: African Americans and*

the State Department, 1945–1969 (Armonk, N.Y.: M. E. Sharpe, 1999); Renee Romano, "No Diplomatic Immunity: African Diplomats, the State Department, and Civil Rights, 1961–1964," *Journal of American History* 87 (Sept. 2000): 546–80.

14. David W. Southern, *Gunnar Myrdal and Black-White Relations: The Use and Abuse of An American Dilemma, 1944–1969* (Baton Rouge: Louisiana State University Press, 1987), 1, 4–5, 49, 50; Ralph Bunche to Willard Z. Park, 5 Dec. 1938, 1938 correspondence file, Ralph Bunche Papers, University of California, Los Angeles; Jackson Davis's memo of interview with Charles Dollard, 24 Apr. 1941, General Education Board Papers, Rockefeller Archive Center, Sleepy Hollow, N.Y.

15. Southern, *Gunnar Myrdal*, 49; Waldemar A. Nielsen, *The Big Foundations* (New York: Columbia University Press, 1972), 344.

16. Charles R. Lilley and Michael H. Hunt, "On Social History, the State, and Foreign Relations: Commentary on the Cosmopolitan Connection," *Diplomatic History* 11 (Summer 1987): 247, 246; Michael Hunt, "Internationalizing U.S. Diplomatic History: A Practical Agenda," ibid. 15 (Winter 1991): 1–11; Anders Stephanson, "Diplomatic History in the Expanded Field," ibid. 22 (Fall 1998): 595–603.

17. Gerald Horne, *Communist Front? The Civil Rights Congress, 1946–1956* (Cranbury, N.J.: Associated University Presses, 1988); Penny Von Eschen, *Race against Empire: Black Americans and Anticolonialism, 1937–1957* (Ithaca: Cornell University Press, 1997). See also an earlier work, Hollis R. Lynch, *Black American Radicals and the Liberation of Africa: The Council on African Affairs, 1937–1955* (Ithaca: Cornell University Press, 1978). Yohuru R. Williams, "American Exported Black Nationalism: The Student Nonviolent Coordinating Committee, the Black Panther Party, and the Worldwide Freedom Struggle, 1967–1972," *Negro History Bulletin* 60 (July–Sept. 1997): 13–20.

18. Danny Duncan Collum, ed., *African Americans in the Spanish Civil War: "This Ain't Ethiopia, but It'll Do"* (New York: G. K. Hall, 1992); Plummer, *Rising Wind*; Michael L. Krenn, "'Their Proper Share': The Changing Role of Racism in U.S. Foreign Policy since World War One," *Nature, Society, and Thought* 4, 1–2 (1991): 57–79; Carol Anderson, "From Hope to Disillusion: African Americans, the United Nations, and the Struggle for Human Rights," *Diplomatic History* 20 (Fall 1996): 531–63.

19. Dudziak, "Desegregation as a Cold War Imperative"; Mary L. Dudziak, *Cold War Civil Rights: Race and the Image of American Democracy* (Princeton: Princeton University Press, 2000); Gerald Horne, *Black and Red: W. E. B. Du Bois and the Afro-American Response to the Cold War* (Albany: SUNY Press, 1986).

20. Krenn, *Black Diplomacy*; Romano, "No Diplomatic Immunity."

21. Mary L. Dudziak, "The March on Washington at Home and Abroad," paper presented at the conference on African Americans and the Age of American Expansion, 1898–1998, Pennsylvania State University, 26–28 Mar. 1998; Cary Fraser, "Crossing the Color Line in Little Rock: The Eisenhower Administration and the Dilemma of Race," *Diplomatic History* 24 (Spring 2000): 233–66.

22. William R. Scott, *The Sons of Sheba's Race: African Americans and the Italo-Ethiopian War, 1935–1941* (Bloomington: University of Indiana Press, 1993); Joseph E. Harris, *African American Reactions to War in Ethiopia, 1936–1941* (Baton Rouge: Louisiana State University Press, 1994); Elliott P. Skinner, *African Americans and U.S. Policy toward Africa, 1850–1924: In Defense of Black Nationality* (Washington, D.C.: Howard University Press, 1992).

23. Brenda Gayle Plummer, "The Afro-American Response to the Occupation of Haiti, 1915–1934," *Phylon* 43 (June 1982): 125–43.

24. Carlos Moore, *Castro, the Blacks, and Africa* (Los Angeles: University of California, Center for Afro-American Studies, 1988); Rosemari Mealy, *Fidel and Malcolm X: Memories of a Meeting* (Melbourne: Ocean Press, 1993); Brenda Gayle Plummer, "Castro in Harlem: A Cold War Watershed," in *Rethinking the Cold War: Essays on Its Dynamics, Meaning, and Morality*, ed. Allen Hunter (Philadelphia: Temple University Press, 1998), 133–53; Van Gosse, "The African-American Press Greets the Cuban Revolution," in *Between Race and Empire: African-Americans and Cubans before the Cuban Revolution*, ed. Lisa Brock and Digna Castañeda Fuertes (Philadelphia: Temple University Press, 1998), 266–80.

25. Thomas Noer, "Truman, Eisenhower, and South Africa: The 'Middle Road' and Apartheid," *Journal of Ethnic Studies* 11 (Spring 1983): 75–104; Thomas Noer, *Cold War and Black Liberation: The United States and White Rule in Africa, 1948–1968* (Columbia: University of Missouri Press, 1985); Thomas Borstelmann, *Apartheid's Reluctant Uncle: The United States and Southern Africa in the Early Cold War* (New York: Oxford University Press, 1993); Robert Kinloch Massie, *Loosing the Bonds: The United States and South Africa in the Apartheid Years* (New York: Doubleday, 1997).

26. Ernest Allen Jr., "Satokata Takahashi and the Flowering of Black Messianic Nationalism," *Black Scholar* 24, 1 (1994): 29–31; Reginald Kearney, *African American Views of the Japanese: Solidarity or Sedition?* (Albany: SUNY Press, 1998); Marc Gallicchio, *The African American Encounter with Japan and China* (Chapel Hill: University of North Carolina Press, 2000).

27. Brock and Castañeda Fuertes, *Between Race and Empire*.

28. John David Cato, "James Herman Robinson: Crossroads Africa and American Idealism, 1958–1972," *American Presbyterian* 68 (Summer 1990): 99–107; Randall Robinson, *Defending the Spirit: A Black Life in America* (New York: Dutton, 1988); Karin L. Stanford, *Beyond the Boundaries: Reverend Jesse Jackson in International Affairs* (Albany: SUNY Press, 1997); Brian Urquhart, *Ralph Bunche — An American Life* (New York: W. W. Norton, 1993); Charles P. Henry, *Ralph Bunche: Model Negro or American Other?* (New York: New York University Press, 1999).

29. J. Craig Jenkins and Craig M. Eckert, "Channeling Black Insurgency: Elite Patronage and Professional Social Movement Organizations in the Development of the Black Movement," *American Sociological Review* 51 (Dec. 1986): 812–29; Brenda Gayle Plummer and Donald R. Culverson, "Black Americans and Foreign Affairs: A Reassessment," *Sage Race Relations Abstracts* 12 (Feb. 1987): 21–31; Brenda Gayle Plummer, "Evolution of the Black Foreign Policy Constituency," *TransAfrica Forum* 6 (Spring–Summer 1989): 67–81; John David Skrenty, "The Effect of the Cold War on African American Civil Rights: America and the World Audience, 1945–1968," *Theory and Society* 27 (1998): 237–85.

30. J. Jorge Klor de Alva, "Aztlán, Borinquen and Hispanic Nationalism," in *Aztlán: Essays on the Chicano Homeland*, ed. Rudolfo A. Anaya and Francisco Lomelí (Albuquerque, N.Mex.: Academia/El Norte Publications, 1989), 135–71; Julie Leininger Pycior, *LBJ and Mexican Americans: The Paradox of Power* (Austin: University of Texas Press, 1997); Lorena Oropeza, "Antiwar Aztlán: The Chicano Movement Opposes U.S. Intervention in Vietnam," in this volume.

31. Lawrence H. Fuchs, "Minority Groups and Foreign Policy," in *American Ethnic Politics*, ed. Lawrence H. Fuchs (New York: Harper and Row, 1968): 152–53; Charles Mathias, "Ethnic Groups and Foreign Policy," *Foreign Affairs* 59 (Summer 1981): 975–78; Locksley Edmondson, "Black America as a Mobilizing Diaspora: Some International Implications," in *Modern Diaspora in International Politics*, ed. Gabriel Sheffer (London: Croom Helm, 1986), 164–211.

32. Jake Miller, "Black Legislators and African-American Relations," *Journal of Black Studies* 20 (1979): 245–26; Gilburt Loescher and John Scanlan, "Human Rights, U.S. Foreign Policy, and Haitian Refugees," *Journal of Interamerican Studies and World Affairs* 26 (1984): 313–56; Michel S. Laguerre, *American Odyssey: Haitians in New York City* (Ithaca: Cornell University Press, 1984); Brenda Gayle Plummer, *Haiti and the United States* (Athens: University of Georgia Press, 1992), 201–2, 222.

33. Frenise A. Logan, "Racism and Indian-U.S. Relations, 1947–1953," *Pacific Historical Review* 54 (Feb. 1985): 71–79; Romano, "No Diplomatic Immunity."

34. Dudziak, *Cold War Civil Rights*, 169–83.

35. Lorena Oropeza, "La batalla está aquí: Chicanos Oppose the War in Vietnam" (Ph.D. diss., Cornell University, 1996).

36. Taylor, *Against the Bomb*, 156–66; Jervis Anderson, *Bayard Rustin*, 219–21, 235.

37. Jervis Anderson, *Bayard Rustin*, 193, 275, 291–98, 302, 319–20. On the inability of King and the Southern Christian Leadership Conference to make significant parts of their program effective in the North and West, and the waning ability of established leaders to sway the opinions of both working-class and middle-class black people, see ibid., 303–4; James R. Ralph, *Northern Protests: Martin Luther King Jr., Chicago and the Civil Rights Movement* (Cambridge: Cambridge University Press, 1993); Gerald Horne, *Fire This Time: The Watts Uprising and the 1960s* (New York: Da Capo Press, 1997), 298–300.

38. Bayard Rustin, *Down the Line: The Collected Writings of Bayard Rustin* (Chicago: Quadrangle Books, 1971), 167–68.

39. On the uses and implications of black music for cultural diplomacy, see S. Frederick Starr, *Red and Hot: The Fate of Jazz in the Soviet Union, 1917–1980* (New York: Oxford University Press, 1983); Von Eschen, *Race against Empire*; Krin Gabbard, "Louis Armstrong's Life as a Man," *Chronicle of Higher Education*, 30 June 2000, B9–10; Donald R. Culverson: "From Cold War to Global Interdependence: The Political Economy of African American Antiapartheid Activism, 1968–1988," in this volume.

Seen from the Outside

The International Perspective
on America's Dilemma

There are times in life when others may see us far better from the outside than we see ourselves from within. They can apply a certain objectivity, distance, broader perspective, freshness, and honesty that we are not always able or willing to produce on our own. They can often see through the rationalizations, excuses, self-willed naiveté, or myths that we create about ourselves. Sometimes they are free to speak out when we feel compelled by social conformity or existing power to remain silent. For these reasons, outsiders can often perceptively evaluate our strengths and weaknesses, including the level of commitment we have to our stated values, based not on our words but rather on our actions. This can happen when we are examined as individuals as well as groups. It can occur when foreign observers, like the Swedish social economist Gunnar Myrdal, view the broader character, values, and behavior of our nation as a whole.

Outside observers have long been fascinated with America. Its experiments with the principles and practices of freedom in a new land attracted foreign attention from the very beginning.[1] Outsiders came to see—and to scrutinize—the emerging nation, its people, and their values. One of the greatest and shrewdest of these was Alexis de Tocqueville. Tocqueville, who took full advantage of his foreign status, was simultaneously descriptive, analytical, complimentary, critical, and prophetic, seeing qualities in the nineteenth-century United States that many others either missed or chose to ignore.[2] Given his powers of observation, his honesty, and his concern with humanity, it is hardly surprising that Tocqueville's insightful analysis, *De la démocratie en Amérique*, would quickly fix upon the problem of race. Indeed, an entire chapter devoted to this subject began with these cautionary words: "The absolute supremacy of democracy is not all that we meet with in America." Tocqueville described the superior position and power accorded to "the white or European" and the blatant subjugation imposed upon "the Negro and the Indian." "Both of them," he observed, "occupy an inferior rank in the country they inhabit; both suffer from tyranny." Struck by the striking anomaly between the rhetoric of democracy and actual practice, he concluded that "we should almost say that the European is to the other races of mankind what man is to the lower animals;—he makes them subservient to his use; and when he cannot subdue, he destroys them. Oppression has, at one stroke, deprived the descendants of the Africans of almost all the privileges of humanity."[3]

Tocqueville's conclusions resembled those of other contemporary foreign visitors. His compatriot and traveling companion, Gustav de Beaumont, wrote a book entitled *Marie, ou l'esclavage aux Etats-Unis*, which focused entirely upon America's dilemma. Beaumont noted that Americans "who have perfected the theory of equality" nevertheless failed to heal what he called "the great canker": racial injustice in a supposedly democratic society. "I see," he has his major character say tragically, "in the midst of a civilized Christian society, a class of people for whom that society has made a set of laws and customs apart from their own; for some, a lenient legislation, for others a bloody code; on one side, the supremacy of law, on the other, arbitrariness; for the whites the theory of equality, for the blacks the system of servitude; two contrary codes of morals: one for the free, the other for the oppressed; two sorts of public ethics: these—mild, humane, and liberal; those—cruel, barbaric, and tyrannical."[4] Similarly, when the political philosopher John Stuart Mill reviewed the work in translation, *Democracy in America*, he observed that despite the rhetorical claims of equality, in the United States "the aristocracy of skin" obviously "retains its privilege."[5]

These conclusions were reaffirmed a century later by a visitor whose observations would also deeply influence American self-reflection. Indeed, the impetus for Gunnar Myrdal's sojourn and research in the United States came from Americans themselves. Beginning in 1935 the Carnegie Corporation became extremely interested in the continuing and painful problem of race and democracy in the United States. It decided to sponsor a comprehensive study that would collect, analyze, and interpret information about the status of blacks in America. Interestingly, this philanthropy determined that the way to achieve the best possible results would be to invite a researcher from abroad to conduct a study. "There was no lack of competent scholars in the United States who were deeply interested in the problem and had already devoted themselves to its study," it carefully explained, "but the whole question had been for nearly a hundred years so charged with emotion that it appeared wise to seek as the responsible head of the undertaking someone who could approach his task with a fresh mind, uninfluenced by traditional attitudes or by earlier conclusions." The Carnegie board wanted a foreigner "of high intellectual and scholarly standards but with no background or traditions of imperialism which might lessen the confidence . . . as to the complete impartiality of the study and the validity of its findings." The task before them, in the insightful words of historian Walter A. Jackson, was in "finding a Tocqueville."[6] With precisely this objective in mind, they selected a young Swede named Gunnar Myrdal to come to the United States and conduct a study of race and democracy.

Like Tocqueville before him, Myrdal began by traveling, viewing the nature and manifestations of the problem with his own eyes. Beginning in 1938, he visited government offices, universities, schools, churches, factories, and plantations, speaking as he went with politicians, police officers, teachers, preachers, journalists, workers, and sharecroppers, among many others. Assisted by a team of scholars, including African American social scientists, and other authorities, he sought to collect as much information as possible. As he observed, listened, and read, and as he began to write his long manuscript, Myrdal was increasingly struck by one fundamental fact: the stark contrast between the glorious ideals of liberty and equality on the one hand, and blatant racial prejudice and discrimination on the other. When he published his monumental study in 1944, he accordingly selected a thoughtful, troubling, and revealing title that still provokes discussion to this day: *An American Dilemma: The Negro Problem and Modern Democracy*. After many years, twenty-five printings, and two anniversary editions, no book, before or since, has ever had as much an impact upon how race in America is viewed. After several years of carefully studying the inalienable rights enunciated in the Declaration of Independence and Bill of Rights, the tragic history of slavery and segregation, racial violence and intimidation, and the complex intersection of economic, social, political, and cultural factors, Myrdal concluded that America's finest values received only "lip service" where race was concerned. "From the point of view of the American Creed the status accorded the Negro in America represents nothing more and nothing less than a century-long lag of public morals," he wrote. "In principle the Negro problem was settled long ago; in practice the solution is not effectuated. The Negro in America has not yet been given the elemental civil and political rights of formal democracy, including a fair opportunity to earn his living, upon which a general accord was already won when the American Creed was first taking form. And this anachronism constitutes the contemporary 'problem' both to Negroes and to whites."[7]

Myrdal understood from the beginning that the publication of his book would draw widespread attention to the race problem. He clearly anticipated that within the United States some would welcome his observations, but that he would also provoke hostility, generate strong opposition, alienate friends, and force people to confront an issue that they would prefer to ignore. "The

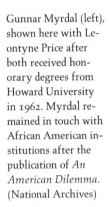

Gunnar Myrdal (left), shown here with Leontyne Price after both received honorary degrees from Howard University in 1962. Myrdal remained in touch with African American institutions after the publication of *An American Dilemma*. (National Archives)

reading of this book must be somewhat of an ordeal to the good citizen," he reflected.[8] Yet Myrdal was addressing a foreign audience as well. When the horrors of World War II exposed the raw power of racial hatreds as never before,[9] people around the world had many reasons to observe carefully how a great power would actually resolve race conflicts. Myrdal's sponsors understood this. As the president of the Carnegie Corporation acknowledged in the foreword to *An American Dilemma*: "The eyes of men of all races of the world over are turned upon us to see how the people of the most powerful of the United Nations are dealing *at home* with a major problem of race relations."[10]

Americans from their origins had been a self-conscious people. As John Winthrop wrote in one famous sermon while crossing the Atlantic Ocean: "For we must consider that we shall be as a city upon a hill. The eyes of all people are upon us, so that if we shall deal falsely with our God in this work we have undertaken . . . we shall be made a story and a by-word throughout the world."[11] The statement evoked a dynamic and democratic nation, bursting with energy, guided by a spiritual compass, and free from the trappings of a feudal past, monarchical privilege, government oppression, class divisions, and intolerance that plagued other, less fortunate countries. Winthrop's America was an unfettered, shining land of opportunity whose free people and egalitarian society aroused respect, admiration, and the desire to emulate in others. Outsiders like Tocqueville and Myrdal seriously challenged these perceptions and expectations. The public prominence given to their stark criticism of racial mores augured things to come, especially as the U.S. role in global affairs continued to intensify.

While international criticism of racial discrimination was a muted subtheme in U.S. relations with other countries early in the twentieth century,[12] it was increasingly heard after World War II. Its unequaled military might, economic strength, human resources, and inspiring promises about democratic values and human rights played critical roles in enabling the United States to win the war and shape the peace. When San Francisco hosted the 1945 conference on peace and security, the United States took pride in welcoming the statesmen and other dignitaries from around the globe to one of its own cities, where it could display its many achievements for the world to see. The assembled delegates certainly observed some of the best but, to the shock and embarrassment of their hosts, they also observed, read about, or heard personally from representatives from the African American community some of the worst aspects of discrimination. W. E. B. Du Bois and Walter White of the National Association for the Advancement of Colored People (NAACP), M. W. Johnson from Howard University, Mary McLeod Bethune from the National Council of Negro Women, and Edgar Brown of the National Negro Council attended the conference as either official consultants in the case of the NAACP officials and Bethune or as unofficial observers. African American activists present in San Francisco described in meetings, in the press, and on street corners the pernicious consequences of racial prejudice and discrimination at home.[13] At the same time, they watched the official U.S. delegation resist the inclusion of any meaningful provision in the United Nations Charter that spoke to the issue of nondiscrimination and racial equality.[14] In this setting, foreign delegates could readily see with their own eyes and report to their home governments their personal and professional observations about the American racial conundrum.[15]

These concerns only grew worse as domestic events during 1945 unfolded before the world. Just when U.S. representatives in San Francisco proclaimed with great fanfare their support of freedom and opposition to discrimination of any kind, southern Democrats allied with Republicans in Congress to filibuster the Fair Employment Practices Commission to death. To black ex-servicemen just returning from a war ostensibly fought to defend democracy, such a blow seemed particularly vicious. Many had believed in the double-V campaign, "victory over the Axis abroad and victory over racial discrimination at home,"[16] and were in no mood to live again in the racially segregated society to which they returned. Within a year, race riots erupted in major cities like Philadelphia as well as smaller ones like Columbia, Tennessee, and Athens, Alabama. The Ku Klux Klan publicly announced its revival at an Atlanta meeting. In Mississippi, Senator Theodore Bilbo declared that the "white primary" election would remain in force forever and that whites should use "any means at their command" to keep blacks from the polls.[17] Outside observers and foreign delegations visiting the United States could read newspaper accounts or see newsreels depicting these highly visible manifestations of racial bias and discrimination for themselves.

Racial conflict also attracted the particular attention of Asian, African, and Latin American visitors. During World War II they had looked to the United States as the "arsenal of democracy" and listened intently to President Franklin Roosevelt's proclamations about human rights and the evils of Nazi racism. They had heard President Harry Truman supporting the principle of nondiscrimination in the United Nations Charter. Jim Crow laws, lynching, race riots, and other public displays of blatant prejudice aroused deep disappointment and bitterness. India numbered among the first and most outspoken of Asian critics. Its press began to hammer steadily on the race theme with headlines like "Treatment of Negroes a Blot on U.S." Editors described discrimination as "shameful manifestations of racial intolerance." U.S. diplomats abroad watched these attacks with alarm, describing the attention given to America's dilemma as nothing short of an "obsession" among overseas observers.[18]

As the United States moved increasingly to the forefront of world affairs, assuming the leadership of the West in the emerging Cold War contest, it drew considerable attention to itself, thereby exposing its domestic practices as never before in its history. The results could be seen immediately. Italians learned from Rome's daily *Unità* that "in the land of the Four Freedoms thirteen million Negroes struggle against American racial discrimination."[19] Mexicans, through the pages of *El Universal*, *La Prensa*, and *El Nacional*, Chinese through *Ta Kung Pao*, Argentineans through *Epoca*, Filipinos through the *Manila Chronicle*, Haitians through *La Nation* and *La Phalange*, and Iraqis through *Al Yaqdha*, among many others, read similar stories.[20] The *Fiji Times & Herald* published a major article entitled "Persecution of Negroes Still Strong in America," which informed its readers that "the United States has within its own borders, one of the most oppressed and persecuted minorities in the world today."[21] The *Bombay Chronicle* and the *Bombay Sentinel* contrasted the Americans' fight against Nazi race doctrines during the war and their defense of the same beliefs at home.[22] In the Soviet Union, *Trud* provided glaring details of recent lynchings in the South, while *Pravda* reported that "the Constitution of the U.S. guarantees to all citizens equal rights before the law; however, the Negro population, consisting of 13,000,000 people, actually does not have these rights. Racial discrimination continues to exist in all its forms and in all branches of the economy and culture of the country."[23] To support this claim, the newspaper correctly cited the number of states where African Americans recently had been deprived of freedom of speech, forced to attend segregated schools, prevented from using public facilities equally with whites, prohibited from entering into mixed marriages, and, in some cases, lynched. Intense and unrelenting criticism from outsiders, particularly those from the Soviet Union, effectively held up a magnifying glass and invited the rest of the world to look through it and see the United States at its worst.

To compound the difficulty, some of the most stinging rebukes came from close friends and allies. The British wire service, Reuters, for example, frequently reported U.S. racial conflicts. The respected *Manchester Guardian* published detailed accounts of Klan activities. Readers often reacted with indignation. The U.S. Embassy in London received more than 300 communications of protest against racial discrimination, a number of which contained several hundred signatures. Three members of the House of Commons sent a telegram directly to President Truman urging him to protect the basic human rights of all Americans.[24] Chinese friends like Ambassador Wellington Koo frequently addressed the issue of racial equality.[25] In Greece, Helen Vlachos wrote a scathing essay in the newspaper *Kathimerini* relating her exposure to racial prejudice on a recent stateside visit. Interestingly, a U.S. diplomat in Athens reporting on this article to the Department of State noted that Vlachos generally had been "well disposed with respect to the American people and their institutions and in harmony with the basically friendly attitude the author has always shown toward the United States." He concluded that her comments "should therefore be regarded, not as stemming from any anti-American bias, but as the author's frank reaction to what she regards as a deplorable situation."[26]

At times attacks from the outside could be expected, especially if they came from Cold War enemies looking for ways to exploit vulnerabilities. On other occasions, the United States found itself caught off guard. The U.S. role as the host country to the United Nations, for example, brought many nonwhite Secretariat staff members to New York. Their own governments usually carefully selected these individuals because of their impressive personal accomplishments. Yet, when they arrived in the United States, they suddenly found themselves for the first time in their lives unable to rent or purchase housing solely because of their skin color. Official delegates from Africa,

Asia, and Latin America similarly were shocked to discover that while traveling around the country on official business, or even visiting the nation's own segregated capital city, they actually might be refused service in restaurants or be barred from hotels because of their race. Soviet criticisms could sometimes be dismissed or rationalized away as exaggerated propaganda, but these personal insults to distinguished outsiders were another matter. Once victimized by racial prejudice themselves, foreign visitors saw racism firsthand, often forming painful, bitterly hostile, and lasting impressions. They did not passively accept the result. They instead reported these incidents to their own governments and often lodged serious, formal complaints against the United States itself. In New Delhi the *National Call* printed headlines reading: "Foreign Diplomats in Washington Also Face Color Bar."[27] An official from Haiti furiously returned home after having been denied accommodations in Biloxi, Mississippi, for "reasons of color," and explained to a U.S. official: "You can see how I would not wish to visit your country soon again."[28]

In this setting, Washington policy makers found themselves and their country not only supremely embarrassed but also faced with what one described as an "extremely dangerous" development in the global competition for the hearts and the minds of all uncommitted, nonwhite peoples. They came to understand that discrimination could no longer be considered a purely domestic matter, as in the past. This assessment weighed heavily on President Harry Truman's decision to create the special President's Committee on Civil Rights, composed of distinguished citizens. The committee turned to the Department of State for specific information on how racial discrimination at home affected U.S. foreign policy abroad. Secretary of State George C. Marshall responded by warning that "the foreign policy of a nation depends for most of its effectiveness, particularly a nation which does not rely upon possible military aggression as a dominant influence, on the moral influence which that nation exerts throughout the world. The moral influence of the United States is weakened to the extent that the civil rights provided by our Constitution are not fully confirmed in actual practice."[29] The department's legal adviser was equally candid. "Irrespective of what the U.S. obligation may eventually prove to be with regard to human rights [under the United Nations Charter]," he wrote, "it must be realized that as a leading member of the international community, *the eyes of the world will be upon the United States.*"[30]

Such attention to problems of race, of course, did not center exclusively on the United States. Indeed, the experience of racism during World War II included Nazi genocide, revealed in shocking detail during the Nuremberg war crimes trials. After the war, apartheid, a newly virulent racial policy in South

Africa, emerged. The perpetuation of colonial empires, immigration exclusion by white nations, and the continuing legacy of centuries of racial slavery
and exploitation propelled racism to the forefront as a global issue of the first
magnitude. Many nonwhite, non-Western peoples who continued to suffer
the consequences of racism saw it as an issue of critical importance that they
determined to raise on every possible occasion. They did so at the United Nations, a body pledged to advance the cause of international human rights
without discrimination based upon race. The UN provided a forum for protest against discrimination and a focal point for pressure to eliminate it. During the very first year of its existence all the Asian and African and most of
the Latin American delegations united to force explicit debate on the ramifi-
cations of racial discrimination. They considered the race issue a "burning
question," a "vital" issue of "immense importance," and as "one of the most
important questions which the conscience of this august Assembly must
face."[31]

This growing and determined international attention[32] confirmed to W. E. B.
Du Bois that the world had finally acknowledged his famous prediction made
years before that "the problem of the twentieth century is the problem of the
color line—the relation of the darker to the lighter races of men in Asia and
Africa, in America and the islands of the sea."[33] He took great comfort in the
fact that so many others could now see this problem and were now unwilling
to let governments continue to use national sovereignty as a cover to protect
themselves from outside scrutiny. Many Americans viewed the vigor with
which the United Nations tackled the race issue with alarm and hoped that
the foreign gaze could somehow be diverted from U.S. conditions, but Du
Bois went out of his way to attract it. In an effort to deliberately focus international attention on racial oppression, the indefatigable and nearly eighty-
year-old Du Bois worked with the NAACP in preparing a petition to submit
to the United Nations. He supervised the writing of a remarkable 155-page
report to the world community that described in detail the long history of
racial segregation in the United States and the denial of basic legal rights to
African Americans. The petition called on UN members to honor their obligations under the Charter concerning the promotion of basic human rights
for all.

News of this explosive document began to leak. NAACP Executive Secretary Walter White noted that newspapermen "from all over the world"
wanted to obtain advanced copies of the petition. "The matter cannot be kept
secret," he wrote, "so great is the interest."[34] Secrecy, of course, was the fur-
thest thing from Du Bois's mind. Indeed, when he submitted it to the United
Nations in October 1947, he did so in the full light of the widest possible

publicity and media coverage. He entitled the petition "An Appeal to the World: A Statement on the Denial of Human Rights to Minorities in the Case of Citizens of Negro Descent in the United States of America and An Appeal to the United Nations for Redress."[35] Du Bois declared in his accompanying public statement that he spoke on behalf of 14 million African American citizens and passionately asserted: "This protest, which is open and articulate, and not designed for confidential concealment in your archives, is a frank and earnest appeal to the world for elemental Justice against the treatment which the United States has visited upon us for three centuries. . . . It is to induce the nations of the world to persuade this nation to be just to its own people that we have prepared and now present to you this document. . . . We hand you this documented statement of grievances, and we firmly believe that the situation pictured here is as much your concern as ours."[36]

The NAACP realized the full implications of its project. "The eyes and the ears of the chancelleries of the world will be focused upon this petition," the association declared, accurately conjecturing that "this question then, which is without doubt primarily an internal and national question, becomes inevitably an international question, and will in the future become more and more international."[37] Many Americans reacted with acute embarrassment or vehement anger, while foreign journalists, sensing that they were witnessing an extremely important event, provided widespread publicity.[38] Delegates anxious to press the issue of race in an international forum, especially those from African and Asian countries, took it up as their own, offering to provide whatever official assistance might be necessary to pursue the case further.[39] Moreover, and of particular significance to the politics and diplomacy of the emerging Cold War, the Soviet Union and its communist allies eagerly seized upon the petition as a source of mortification for the United States that could be exploited to enormous advantage. This forced Attorney General Tom Clark to admit that he and the country stood before the world "humiliated."[40]

Foreign reactions subsequently weighed heavily upon the thinking of the President's Committee on Civil Rights. Its members came to understand that, under the harsh glare of global opinion, the racial equality issue could no longer be treated simply as a domestic matter. As a result, they determined to make bold recommendations, and their famous and uncompromising 1947 report, *To Secure These Rights*—whose title was taken from the Declaration of Independence—is still described as "one of the most outspoken and impressive documents of all time bearing upon human rights."[41] The report outlined the tragic record of racial discrimination in the United States, the constitutional guarantees for equal protection under the law, the new obligations for nondiscrimination under the Charter, and the influence of world opinion. "Throughout the Pacific, Latin America, Africa, the Near, Middle, and Far East," it warned, "the treatment which our Negroes receive is taken as a reflection of our attitude toward all dark-skinned peoples" and plays "into the hands of Communist propagandists. . . . The United States is not so strong, the final triumph of the democratic ideal is not so inevitable that we can ignore *what the world thinks* of our record." The President's Committee on Civil Rights called forcefully for the prohibition of state voting rights' restrictions based upon race, a federal law against lynching, an end to segregation in education, a fair employment act prohibiting discrimination, and denial of federal aid to any state that refused to comply. These measures, committee members declared, should be directed toward one ultimate goal: "The elimination of segregation based upon race, color, creed, or national origin from American life."[42]

As the Cold War escalated, as Asian and African nations acquired greater self-confidence within the United Nations system, and as newly independent states emerged from collapsed colonial empires, the number of foreigners weighing in on race and the intensity of their views increased. A Ceylonese diplomat reported that Jim Crow attracted far more attention than any other single subject. Reports from Athens, Bombay, Manila, Mexico City, Moscow, Shanghai, and many other cities around the world confirmed the same story. As the U.S. mission in Accra noted, Ghanaian papers had little interest in international news, with one notable exception: racial prejudice and discrimination against blacks in the United States.[43] Eleanor Roosevelt, simultaneously serving on the board of directors of the NAACP and as the U.S. representative on the United Nations Commission on Human Rights, witnessed the same phenomenon. "Anyone who has worked in the international field," she noted with sorrow and frustration, "knows well that our failure in race relations in this country, and our open discrimination against various groups, injures our leadership in the world. It is the one point which can be attacked and to which the representatives of the United States have no answer." A New Zealander who watched her in this painful setting concluded that America, with its "Negro problem," "sets her representatives an almost impossible job when it comes to matters of principle."[44]

Through time the task became even more difficult. Outside observers watched with shock and anger as the Eisenhower administration fired the much admired Eleanor Roosevelt from her position as chair of the Commission on Human Rights and announced to the world that it would not abide "foreign interference" in its "domestic affairs" and would not become a party to any human rights treaty ever approved by the United Nations.[45] They listened to radio broadcasts of southern officials who, despite the *Brown v. Board of Education* decision outlawing racially segregated schools, proclaimed publicly that they would never support integration. They read newspaper accounts of the 1955 Montgomery, Alabama, bus boycott, initiated after seamstress and longtime civil rights activist Rosa Parks refused to give up her seat to a white passenger as required by city ordinance because of her race. They saw images, via the expanding medium of television, of a high school, bombed by a Clinton, Tennessee, mob. Foreign nationals witnessed federal troops being sent to Little Rock, Arkansas, to protect young black students from harm by unruly rioters, and tobacco-chewing police chiefs sending out dogs to attack brutally civil rights protesters. They observed as the federal government revoked the passports of activists Du Bois and Paul Robeson, and witnessed efforts to smear the reputation and ruin the career of African American UN official Ralph Bunche. The State Department directed U.S. diplomats abroad to interfere with Latin American concert venues for African American jazz singer and dancer Josephine Baker because of her outspoken statements on discrimination.[46]

Foreign representatives spoke openly at the United Nations about American racial prejudice and segregation. The subject was also broached during such special international meetings as the Asian-African conference convened at Bandung, Indonesia, and then the All-African Peoples' Conference in Accra, Ghana.[47] Disapproval of U.S. racial customs was so strongly expressed that even Secretary of State John Foster Dulles found himself forced to apologize to diplomats who found themselves discriminated against and to admit that discriminatory practices were "ruining our foreign policy."[48]

Africans and Asians heard, and then repeated, the story that when then vice president Richard Nixon attended the independence celebrations in Ghana, he turned to his black neighbor at the dinner table to ask, "How does it feel to be free?" The reply came: "I wouldn't know. I am from Alabama."[49] Much of the world read accounts of four African American students being refused service at a lunch counter in Greensboro, North Carolina, during 1960 and then beginning a "sit-in" of protest. Foreign observers watched intently when in May 1961 black and white foes of segregation organized a "freedom ride" throughout the South to test the effectiveness of federal regulations that prohibited discrimination in interstate transportation, only to be assaulted by mobs who set their bus on fire. Their vocal criticisms and observations forced yet another secretary of state, Dean Rusk, to confront the same inextricable connection between domestic and foreign policies as his immediate predecessors and admit that "the biggest single burden that we carry on our backs in our foreign relations in the 1960s is the problem of racial discrimination."[50]

If foreigners have unique qualifications to observe behavior in other countries, it must also be acknowledged that they possess deficiencies as well. Whatever original insights and fresh perspectives they may bring to a subject, outside observers simply cannot be as well informed as those who have spent years of their lives developing a specialized expertise, or who live with a problem on a daily basis. As Myrdal himself confessed before embarking on the study that led to *An American Dilemma*, he knew little about race in America and had never before traveled in the South. His contacts with black Americans had been limited to elevator operators, hotel housekeepers, and redcaps in train stations.[51] Similarly, foreign representatives posted to Washington, D.C., or to the UN in New York often experienced the U.S. racial climate for the very first time with their diplomatic assignment. They frequently arrived with oversimplified impressions rather than with specific facts. Foreign correspondents who covered racial issues for their own national papers often found themselves rotating in and out of various countries, including the United States, and were never able to develop fully any special knowledge about U.S. conditions. They knew little about the actual history of race relations, domestic politics, regionalism, or the mechanics of federalism.

Perhaps no observers, however objective they might want or try to be, ever come to a problem involving human behavior without a degree of bias, preconception, or predisposition. Expectations thus tend to confirm experiences.[52] While the Carnegie Corporation sought out Myrdal as a "wholly objective and dispassionate" man to conduct its race study, for example, he had been a prominent Social Democrat in the Swedish parliament and held strong opinions about the nature of politics and the state, and the capacity of society to enact change.[53] The aliens who commented on America's dilemma after World War II and during the Cold War often came from countries with their own histories of racial and ethnic persecution. They saw reflected in the American experience their own bitter legacies of conquest, slavery, and exploitation.[54] As she watched decolonization unfold before her eyes at the United Nations, Eleanor Roosevelt wrote: "An age-old sore had come to light and I felt the weight of history for which the nations of the Western world are now to be called to account." The intensity of feeling among delegates from Asian and African countries, she continued, came from their belief "that we, because our skins are white, necessarily look down upon all peoples whose skins are yellow or black or brown. This thought is never out of their minds."[55] Those who struggled for racial equality in one part of the world could identify with similar struggles elsewhere and, in the words of one commentator, believe that they all shared "one common problem—*color*."[56]

Not all foreigners who looked upon America's dilemma remained mere passive observers. Some became serious activists in their own right. Myrdal and many of his collaborators, like Ralph Bunche, strongly believed in racial equality and wanted to induce reform by creating a work of "practical significance."[57] Activism in the UN took the form of ensuring that the issue of race appeared prominently on the international agenda. Committed delegates wrote explicit provisions against racial discrimination into major declarations and treaties. These included the groundbreaking Universal Declaration on Human Rights, the Convention on the Prevention and Punishment of the Crime of Genocide, the Declaration on the Granting of Independence to Colonial Countries and Peoples, the Declaration on the Elimination of All Forms of Racial Discrimination, and the landmark International Convention on the Elimination of All Forms of Racial Discrimination with its enforcement mechanism, among others.[58]

Individual foreign leaders might express solidarity with the U.S. struggle for civil rights through symbolic gestures. Vijaya Pandit, the sister of Nehru and Indian ambassador who served for a year as the president of the UN General Assembly, for example, participated in events sponsored by the NAACP, National Council of Negro Women, and the Congress of Racial Equality. Presidents Kwame Nkrumah of Ghana, William Tubman of Liberia, Gamal Abdel Nasser of Egypt, Sekou Touré of Guinea, and Emperor Haile Selassie of Ethiopia, among others, visited Harlem in New York City while attending UN sessions and strongly encouraged African Americans in their fight for racial dignity and equality. The Kenyan leader, Oginga Odinga, personally met with members of the Student Nonviolent Coordinating Committee while visiting Atlanta, Georgia. Diplomats attended the massive rally at the Lincoln Memorial in 1963 to lend their support and to hear Martin Luther King Jr. deliver his famous speech, "I Have a Dream."[59] Some maintained contact with King and Malcolm X, stressing their solidarity and support of African American aspirations.[60]

Outsiders, it should be noted, might also have other objectives and other agendas. They may focus their comments and criticisms on a particular problem in another country not necessarily for the purpose of resolving it, but rather to win the approval of third parties, to deflect attention from sensitive issues at home, or to embarrass a political enemy. The Soviet Union and Fidel Castro's Cuba, for example, quickly discovered the political advantages of exploiting America's Achilles' heel in the global Cold War competition. They could shine a glaring spotlight on their chief adversary and, with little effort, point out U.S. hypocrisy for the world to see.[61]

Foreign critics also risked falling prey to the classic human tendency to see the mote in the eye of others while ignoring the beam in their own. The problem of race and democracy in America was certainly not a mere speck, but many nations suffered from their own problems of racial prejudice and discrimination and engaged in some guilt projection. Countries as different as Australia and Panama imposed immigration restrictions based on race. Several European nations still harbored troublesome racist and anti-Semitic neofascist organizations. The racial violence in Little Rock, Arkansas, in 1957 was roughly contemporaneous with the Notting Hill race riots in Britain and the Sharpeville Massacre of blacks in South Africa. Racial conflict confronted indigenous peoples around the world. These included the Aborigines and Torres Straits Islanders in Australia, the Maori in New Zealand, the Uygur and Hui in China, the Ainu in Japan, the Dayaks in Malaysia, the Papuans in Indonesia, the Andamans in India, the Basarwa in Botswana, the Inuit and Metis in Canada, and the Amerindians in Mexico, Peru, and Guatemala. America's critics could be accused of practicing a double standard in racial matters if they focused attention on U.S. conditions while ignoring those in their own countries.[62]

Yet, despite these considerations, foreigners' observations more often than not proved accurate. For various reasons, foreigners knew racial prejudice and discrimination when they saw it and were not afraid to say so. Their pointed commentaries and the political consequences that flowed from them opened a window on challenges facing the United States in the postwar era.

Many who struggled for racial equality in the United States enthusiastically welcomed outsiders' opinions because they gave additional and often significant weight to the substantive argument and the political momentum being generated against racial prejudice and discrimination in the presumed land of the free. As Ralph Bunche told his listeners at a huge protest rally for racial dignity and equality: "In the UN we have known from the beginning that secure foundations for peace in the world can be built only upon the principle and practice of equal rights and status for all peoples, respect and dignity for all men. The world, I can assure you, is overwhelmingly with us."[63]

When Myrdal's An American Dilemma was published, W. E. B. Du Bois described it as "monumental" and "unrivaled." The book received accolades from African Americans as diverse as E. Franklin Frazier, Richard Wright, Adam Clayton Powell Jr., and Martin Luther King Jr. National publications commended its sophisticated "analytical probing by a sharp-eyed foreigner" and described it as "incisive, persuasive, and brilliant."[64] Civil rights activists were encouraged by a study emanating from the social science establishment that appeared to endorse their cause.

Yet others angrily resented outsiders passing judgment on the United States and its values. They saw such commentators as Myrdal as agitators and enemies, fumed at their criticisms, challenged their assumptions, contested their methodologies and motives, and complained bitterly about the presumed threat they posed to national sovereignty. Senator James Eastland of Mississippi introduced a resolution calling for an investigation of Myrdal, accusing him of being part of a worldwide communist conspiracy and a propagator of "alien ideologies." Other segregationists described him contemptuously as the "notorious Swedish Communist," the "Red psychologist," the "alien anthropologist," and the "foreign expert."[65] Governor Herman Talmadge of Georgia complained bitterly that the nation was too preoccupied with international opinion. "Who cares what the Communists say!" he shouted. "Who cares what *Pravda* prints!" This attitude became increasingly pronounced as the UN General Assembly evolved into a majority of "colored peoples" determined to place the issue of race high on the international agenda.[66] This development helped galvanize members of the Ku Klux Klan, John Birch Society, and White Citizens Councils into opposition to the UN. Among elected officials, Dixiecrats, members of the House Un-American Activities Committee, and the right wing of the Republican Party proved responsive to anti-internationalist arguments made by segregationists.

Whether gratefully and enthusiastically praised or vehemently condemned, the foreign observers who viewed America's dilemma from the outside made several critical contributions to the civil rights movement. Within the United States, they gave immediate hope and encouragement to African Americans in the fight for equality by confirming that others perceived the same conditions and that those who struggled were not alone. More broadly, they figuratively held up a mirror and turned it toward the faces of Americans in order to expose the contrast between the stated principles of democracy and actual racial practices. They forced many white Americans to look at themselves and see what others saw. The observations of outsiders helped to make white racism significantly less morally and politically respectable at home and contributed to what has been called the "war against bigotry."[67]

For a work of social science research, *An American Dilemma* sold remarkably well. Copies went to schools, universities, the armed forces, government agencies, churches, and civil rights groups. Reviews appeared in newspapers, professional journals, and popular magazines such as *Life, Time,* and *Saturday Review,* which in turn broadly circulated liberal ideas about race across the country. *An American Dilemma* directly influenced President Truman's decision to integrate the armed forces and establish the President's Committee on Civil Rights. Its conclusions shadowed the workings and reports of the U.S. Civil Rights Commission; and the Supreme Court's decisions in *Shelley v. Kraemer,* challenging the enforceability of restrictive covenants based on race, and *Brown v. Board of Education,* outlawing racially segregated schools.[68]

The Justice Department filed numerous amicus curiae briefs in major civil rights cases, repeatedly and explicitly acknowledging the influence of foreign opinion. "[T]he hostile reaction," stated one brief, "among normally friendly peoples, many of whom are particularly sensitive in regard to the status of non-European races is growing in alarming proportions. In such countries the view is expressed more and more vocally that the United States is hypocritical in claiming to be the champion of democracy while permitting practices of racial discrimination here in this country."[69]

Every secretary of state and U.S. representative to the United Nations during these years, regardless of partisan affiliation, conceded the role that outside opinion on race played in wreaking havoc with U.S. foreign policy abroad. President Eisenhower admitted that his decision to send federal troops to Little Rock in order to desegregate Central High School in 1957 was heavily influenced by the opinions of outsiders and the eyes of the world. The four African American college students who challenged segregation by sitting down at the lunch counter in Greensboro, North Carolina, explicitly acknowledged that they had been inspired by foreign supporters like Myrdal and Mohandas Gandhi, as did others actively involved in the forefront of the civil rights movement. International outcry generated by television and newspaper coverage of the 1963 Birmingham crisis with its scenes of protesters, many of them women and children, being viciously bitten by police dogs and injured by high-pressure fire hoses, similarly played a significant role in forcing President John F. Kennedy to place civil rights higher on his political agenda.[70]

In 1964 President Lyndon B. Johnson signed a civil rights act that enlarged federal power to protect voting rights, provided open access for all races to public facilities, accelerated the pace of school desegregation, and ensured equal job opportunities in business and unions. In explaining the factors that led to the successful passage of this legislation, Martin Luther King Jr. openly paid tribute to the support given by foreigners, gratefully declaring that their views and criticisms of America's dilemma played a significant role in advancing civil rights. "The world is now so small in terms of geographic proximity and mutual problems," King said, "that no nation should stand idly by and watch another's plight." King praised those governments that used their influence "to make it clear that the struggle of their brothers in the U.S. is part of a worldwide struggle."[71]

In reciprocal fashion, African Americans aided their own cause by an ability to make careful, if sometimes invidious, comparisons. "Today the Negro looks beyond the borders of his own land and sees the decolonization and liberation of Africa and Asia," King intoned. "He sees colored peoples, yellow, black, and brown, ruling over their own new nations. He sees colored statesmen voting on vital issues of war and peace at the United Nations at a time when he is not even permitted to vote for the office of sheriff in his local county."[72]

From the earliest years of the nation to the present, the observations of outsiders have played a significant role in shaping how Americans view themselves. Perhaps nowhere is this more evident than in the debate over democracy and race during the years between the 1944 publication of Myrdal's book and the Civil Rights Act of 1964. Indeed, at the time he wrote, Myrdal accurately observed that the American dilemma had "acquired tremendous international implications. . . . The situation is actually such that any and all concessions to Negro rights in this phase of the history of the world will repay the nation many times, while any and all injustices inflicted upon them will be extremely costly." "History," he wrote, "is never irredeemable, and there is still time to come to good terms" with the issue of race and democracy. Myrdal believed that the task ahead contained elements of both danger and promise in that "the Negro problem is not only America's greatest failure but also America's incomparably great opportunity for the future." If it could successfully bring about racial equality and integrate African Americans into its democracy, he predicted, the "century-old dream of American patriots, that America should give to the entire world its own freedoms and its own faith, would come true."[73] As Myrdal anticipated, world opinion helped Americans move closer toward realizing this dream in the years that followed. Although one might have wished that policy makers would respond more forcefully to moral imperatives than to outside pressure, the fact remains that international judgments greatly contributed to the movement for racial equality in the United States by variously embarrassing, prodding, pressuring, and encouraging its citizens finally to begin the work of perfecting freedom.[74]

Notes

1. Among early examples, see Alexander Hamilton, *Gentleman's Progress* (1744), ed. Carl Bridenbaugh (Chapel Hill: University of North Carolina Press, 1948); Gottlieb Mittelberger, *Journey to Pennsylvania* (1756), ed. Oscar Handlin and John Clive (Cambridge, Mass.: Harvard University Press, 1960); Andrew Burnaby, *Burnaby's Travels through North America* (1775), ed. Rufus Wilson (New York: Wessels, 1904); Marquis de Chastellux, *Travels in North America in the Years 1780, 1781, and 1782*, 2 vols., ed. Howard Rice Jr. (Chapel Hill: University of North Carolina Press, 1963); Francisco de Miranda, *The New Democracy in America: Travels of Francisco de Miranda in the United States, 1783–84*, ed. John Ezell (Norman: University of Okla-

homa Press, 1963), among others. For a late nineteenth-century example, see James Bryce, *The American Commonwealth*, 2 vols. (London: Macmillan, 1889).

2. For excellent discussions of the background, context, and meaning of his journey with Gustave de Beaumont through the United States, see James T. Schliefer, *The Making of Tocqueville's Democracy in America* (Chapel Hill: University of North Carolina Press, 1980); George Wilson Pierson, *Tocqueville in America* (Baltimore: Johns Hopkins University Press, 1996).

3. Alexis de Tocqueville, *Democracy in America*, 2 vols., trans. Henry Reeve (New York: Schocken, 1961), 1:393, 394–95.

4. Gustave de Beaumont, *Marie, or Slavery in the United States*, trans. Barbara Chapman (Stanford: Stanford University Press, 1958), 216, 73, 214, 230–31.

5. John Stuart Mill, review of *Democracy in America*, *London Review*, July 1835, as reproduced in Tocqueville, *Democracy in America*, xii. Mill also commented in this context that "the aristocracy of sex" retained its privileges as well.

6. Frederick P. Keppel, president of the Carnegie Corporation, in the foreword to Gunnar Myrdal, *An American Dilemma: The Negro Problem and Modern Democracy*, 2 vols. (New York: Harper and Brothers, 1944), 1:vi; Walter A. Jackson, *Gunnar Myrdal and America's Conscience* (Chapel Hill: University of North Carolina Press, 1990), 10–35.

7. Jackson, *Gunnar Myrdal and America's Conscience*, 24.

8. Ibid., xix.

9. For more discussion, see Paul Gordon Lauren, *Power and Prejudice: The Politics and Diplomacy of Racial Discrimination*, 2nd ed. (San Francisco: Westview/Harper-Collins, 1996); and John Dower, *War without Mercy: Race and Power in the Pacific War* (New York: Pantheon, 1986).

10. Frederick P. Keppel, in Myrdal, *An American Dilemma*, 1:viii.

11. John Winthrop, "A Model of Christian Charity" (1630), in *The Puritans in America: A Narrative Anthology*, ed. Alan Heimert and Andrew Delbanco (Cambridge, Mass.: Harvard University Press, 1985), 91, and based upon the biblical text of Matthew 5:14–15.

12. Criticism, for example, was particularly intense after Woodrow Wilson thwarted the Japanese attempt to secure a racial equality clause in the Covenant of the League of Nations, the riots and bloodshed of the "Red Summer" of 1919, and the Scottsboro case of the 1930s when nine black boys were accused of raping two white women. See Lauren, *Power and Prejudice*, 100–107; Dan Carter, *Scottsboro* (Baton Rouge: Louisiana State University Press, 1979); and James Goodman, *Stories of Scottsboro* (New York: Vintage, 1994).

13. See "Two Noted Negroes Here Seek a World without Bias," *San Francisco Chronicle*, 1 May 1945; "Prominent Negroes to Speak," *San Francisco Chronicle*, 4 May 1945; and Brenda Gayle Plummer, *Rising Wind: Black Americans and U.S. Foreign Affairs, 1935–1960* (Chapel Hill: University of North Carolina Press, 1996), 125–65.

14. 501.BD Human Rights/11-1349, Record Group (RG) 59, Records of the Department of State, National Archives (NA), Washington, D.C.; Lauren, *Power and Prejudice*, 157–68; and Robert L. Harris Jr., "Racial Equality and the United Nations Charter," in *New Directions in Civil Rights Studies*, ed. Armstead L. Robinson and Patricia Sullivan (Charlottesville: University Press of Virginia, 1991), 126–48.

15. Among many examples, see Britain, Public Record Office, Foreign Office, General Correspondence 371/50703 (PRO/FO); "World Organization: Racial Equality

and Domestic Jurisdiction," 4 June 1945, PRO/FO, 371/46324; and External Affairs (EA), series 2, and the Peter Fraser Papers dealing with the San Francisco Conference, National Archives of New Zealand, Wellington.

16. George Padmore, *Pan-Africanism or Communism* (New York: Roy, 1956), 290. See also Carol Anderson, "From Hope to Disillusion: African Americans, the United Nations, and the Struggle for Human Rights, 1944–1947," *Diplomatic History* 20 (Fall 1996): 531–63.

17. Theodore Bilbo, as cited in Ronald Segal, *The Race War* (New York: Bantam, 1967), 229. His statement was in direct response to *Smith v. Allwright*, in which the Supreme Court ruled that the Democratic Party in Texas could not prohibit blacks from voting in primary elections.

18. "Treatment of Negroes a Blot on U.S.," *Sunday Standard* (Bombay), 8 July 1945; and "Shameful Act," *Morning Standard* (Bombay), 16 Oct. 1945. See also Frenise A. Logan, "Racism and Indian-U.S. Relations, 1947–1953: Views in the Indian Press," *Pacific Historical Review* 54 (Feb. 1985): 71–79; Howard Donovan to Secretary of State, 11 July 1945, dispatch no. 2169, 811.4016/7-1145, RG 59, NA.

19. *Unità*, 15 Mar. 1946, enclosed in 811.4016/3-1846, RG 59, NA.

20. See *La Prensa*, 27 July 1946; *Epoca*, 14 Mar. 1946; *Al Yaqdha*, 5 June 1946; and *Manchester Guardian*, 21 June 1946; clippings in boxes 4650 and 4651, RG 59, NA.

21. "Persecution of Negroes," *Fiji Times & Herald*, enclosed in dispatch no. 96 from American Consul General (Suva) to Secretary of State, 27 Dec. 1946, 811.4016/12-2746, RG 59, NA.

22. "Off My Chest," *Bombay Chronicle*, 18 June 1946; and "American Race Prejudice," *Bombay Sentinel*, 18 June 1946.

23. *Trud*, 23 Aug. 1946, a copy of which is enclosed in dispatch no. 355, Restricted, from Crawford to Secretary of State, 26 Aug. 1946, 811.4016/8-2646, RG 59, NA; *Pravda*, 17 Nov. 1946. See also *Izvestia*, 11 Oct. 1946.

24. For archival evidence about British reactions to U.S. race issues, see, for example, 811.4016/1-1647, 811.4016/2-647, 811.4016/6-2546, and 811.4016/9-1246, RG 59, NA; and PRO/FO, 371/67600, 371/67601, 371/67606, 371/67610, and 371/72806.

25. Wellington Koo Papers, Rare Book and Manuscript Library, Columbia University, New York.

26. Ibid.; dispatch no. 775, 811.4016/7-2248, RG 59, NA.

27. See, for example, "U.N. Secretariat Staff Fear Racial Discrimination," *Morning Standard*, 26 July 1947; and "No Hope," *Free Press Journal*, 26 July 1947; 811.4016/5-847, RG 59; box 78 generally, in Records of the U.S. Mission to the United Nations, RG 84, NA. "Foreign Diplomats in Washington Also Face Color Bar," *National Call*, 8 Jan. 1949.

28. François Georges, as cited in American Embassy (Port-au-Prince) to Robert F. Woodward, Department of State, 18 Nov. 1947, 811.4016/11-1847, RG 59, NA.

29. Memorandum from Harley Notter to Dean Rusk, 1 May 1947, 501.BD Human Rights/4-447; letter from George C. Marshall to Robert Carr, 28 July, 501.BD Human Rights/6-547, RG 59, NA.

30. Letter from Charles Fahy to Robert Carr, restricted, 17 June 1947, 501.BD Human Rights/4-2447, RG 59, NA (emphasis added).

31. United Nations, General Assembly, Official Records, *Plenary Meetings of the General Assembly, Verbatim Record, 23 Oct.–16 Dec. 1946* (Flushing Meadow, N.Y.: United Nations, 1947), 953ff.

32. For efforts during 1946, see ibid.; United Nations, General Assembly, *Official

Records, Joint Committee of the First and Sixth Committees, Summary Record (Flushing Meadow, N.Y.: United Nations, 1947), 1–8; U.S. Mission to the United Nations, box 78, file "Discrimination, Race: Union of South Africa," RG 84, NA; and Resolution 44 (I), "Treatment of Indians in the Union of South Africa," 8 Dec. 1946, in United Nations, General Assembly, *Official Records, Resolutions, 1946* (Lake Success, N.Y.: United Nations, 1947), 69.

33. W. E. B. Du Bois, as cited in United Nations, Centre against Apartheid, *International Tribute to W. E. B. Du Bois* (New York: United Nations, 1982), 48.

34. Walter White to Eleanor Roosevelt, 20 Oct. 1947, in Eleanor Roosevelt Papers, box 3766, Franklin D. Roosevelt Library, Hyde Park, N.Y.

35. The text of the petition can be found in the W. E. B. Du Bois Papers, reel 86, Petitions, frames 1490–1545, Manuscript Division, Library of Congress (LC), Washington, D.C.

36. "Statement of Dr. W. E. B. Du Bois to the Representatives of the Human Rights Commission and Its Parent Bodies," 23 Oct. 1947, in Du Bois Papers, reel 60, Correspondence, frame 1079, LC; "Discrimination, Race: US, 1947," Records of the U.S. Mission to the United States, box 78, RG 84, NA.

37. Report by H. H. Smythe of the NAACP entitled "Afro-Americans Petitioning the United Nations for Equal Rights," in Du Bois Papers, reel 60, Correspondence, frames 708–9, LC.

38. See the report entitled "Press Reaction to the N.A.A.C.P. United Nations Petition," in Du Bois Papers, reel 60, Correspondence, frames 788ff., LC; clippings, box 4651, RG 59, NA; "Discrimination against Negroes," *Free Press Journal* (Bombay), 28 Oct. 1947.

39. H. H. Smythe to Cedric Dover, 3 Nov. 1947, in Du Bois Papers, reel 60, Correspondence, frame 787, LC.

40. Tom Clark, as cited in Gerald Horne, *Black and Red: W. E. B. Du Bois and the Afro-American Response to the Cold War* (Albany: SUNY Press, 1986), 80.

41. Hersch Lauterpacht, *International Law and Human Rights* (New York: Garland, 1973), 157–58.

42. United States, President's Committee on Civil Rights, *To Secure These Rights* (Washington, D.C.: U.S. Government Printing Office, 1947), 111, 147–48, 166 (my emphasis).

43. P. Jester to Secretary of State, 22 Jan. 1948, and E. T. Smith to Secretary of State, 14 May 1948, 811.4016/1-2248, RG 59, NA.

44. Eleanor Roosevelt, "My Day," syndicated column, 9 Feb. 1948, and Agnes McIntosh to Peter Fraser, 16 Aug. 1948, EA/2, File 108/23/1(1), National Archives of New Zealand.

45. "United States Policy Regarding the Draft United Nations Covenants on Human Rights: The 1953 Change," in United States, Department of State, *Foreign Relations of the United States, 1952–1954* (Washington, D.C.: U.S. Government Printing Office, 1979), 3:1536–81; John Foster Dulles, "The Making of Treaties and Executive Agreements," *Department of State Bulletin* 28 (20 Apr. 1953): 591–93.

46. See Plummer, *Rising Wind*, 195–97; and Mary Dudziak, "Josephine Baker, Racial Protest, and the Cold War," *Journal of American History* 81 (Sept. 1994): 543–70.

47. See Republic of Indonesia, *The Asian-African Conference* (New Delhi: Information Service of Indonesia, 1955), which provides the official transcripts of the speeches and final communiqué of the Bandung Conference.

48. John Foster Dulles, telephone conversation with Attorney General Brownell, 24 Sept. 1956, Telephone Calls Services, John Foster Dulles Papers, Dwight D. Eisenhower Presidential Library, Abilene, Kans.

49. See Hugh Tinker, *Race, Conflict, and the International Order: From Empire to United Nations* (London: Macmillan, 1977), 84.

50. Dean Rusk, as cited in Harold Isaacs, *The New World of Negro Americans* (New York: John Day, 1963), 19. For more on the broader context of the Cold War, see the excellent book by Mary Dudziak, *Cold War Civil Rights: Race and the Image of American Democracy* (Princeton: Princeton University Press, 2000).

51. See David W. Southern, *Gunnar Myrdal and Black-White Relations: The Use and Abuse of An American Dilemma, 1944–1969* (Baton Rouge: Louisiana State University Press, 1987), 5.

52. For a more recent example, see Brian Magee, "O Brave New World," *Guardian Weekly*, 7 Oct. 1990, 22–23.

53. Walter Jackson, *Gunnar Myrdal and America's Conscience*, is particularly good on this point. See also Nikhil Pal Singh, "Culture/Wars: Recoding Empire in an Age of Democracy," *American Quarterly* 50 (Sept. 1998): 486–87; Rogers M. Smith, "Beyond Tocqueville, Myrdal, and Hartz: The Multiple Traditions in America," *American Political Science Review* 87 (Sept. 1993): 549–66; and Ann-Sofie Kälvemark, *More Children of Better Quality? Aspects of Swedish Population Policy in the 1930s* (Uppsala: Almqvist & Wiksell, 1980), 52ff.

54. See, among others, DAG-1, 5.1.3, Papers of the Secretary General [Hammarskjöld Papers], box 4, and DAG-1/5.2.7, Papers of the Secretary General [Thant Papers], boxes 2 and 3, United Nations Archives, New York; Immanuel Geiss, *Panafrikanismus: Zür Geschichte der Dekolonisation* (Frankfurt am Main: Europäische Verlagsanstalt, 1969); and Cheik Anta Diop, *Nations nègres et culture* (Paris: Editions africaines, 1955).

55. Eleanor Roosevelt, *India and the Awakening East* (New York: Harper and Brothers, 1953), xiii and 115.

56. C. Eric Lincoln, "The Race Problem and International Relations," *New South* 21 (Fall 1966): 13–14.

57. Southern, *Gunnar Myrdal and Black-White Relations*, 30.

58. For more discussion, see Lauren, *Power and Prejudice*, 178–250; Paul Gordon Lauren, *The Evolution of International Human Rights: Visions Seen* (Philadelphia: University of Pennsylvania Press, 1998), 205ff.; and Marc Bossuyt, *L'interdiction de la discrimination dans le droit international des droit de l'homme* (Brussels: Bruylant, 1976).

59. I am indebted to former ambassadors Frank Corner from New Zealand and Henri Sekyi from Ghana for sharing their personal experiences and observations on these points. An excellent discussion also can be found in Plummer, *Rising Wind*, 219–21, 249, 273–85. See also Clayborne Carson, *In Struggle: SNCC and the Black Awakening of the 1960s* (Cambridge, Mass.: Harvard University Press, 1981), 134.

60. Malcolm X, *The Autobiography of Malcolm X* (New York: Grove Press, 1965).

61. 501.BD Human Rights, box 2257, RG 59, NA; *Morgantown Post*, 15 Oct. 1947: Du Bois Papers, reel 60, Correspondence, frames 787–89, LC; *Congressional Record*, 80th Cong., 2nd sess., 1948, 4270–71; "Second Class Citizens," *New Statesman and Nation*, 3 Apr. 1948; "Washington's Color Bar," *Ceylon Observer*, 21 May 1949.

62. Lauren, *Power and Prejudice*, 295–301, 313–14; and Carl Rowan, *The Pitiful and the Proud* (New York: Random House, 1956), 154–56.

63. Ralph Bunche, as cited in Brian Urquhart, *Ralph Bunche — An American Life* (New York: W. W. Norton, 1993), 439.

64. "W. E. B. Du Bois," *Phylon* 5 (1944): 118–24; Southern, *Gunnar Myrdal and Black-White Relations*, 227–32; and Walter Jackson, *Gunnar Myrdal and America's Conscience*, 245–49; "U.S. at War," *Time*, 7 Feb. 1944; and Gerald Johnson, in *New York Herald Tribune Weekly Book Review*, 13 Aug. 1944.

65. See Southern, *Gunnar Myrdal and Black-White Relations*, 127, 156, 174–75; and *Congressional Record*, 84th Cong., 1st sess., 1955, 101, part 5: 6963–64. Eastland's denunciation of Myrdal came in response to the Supreme Court having cited *An American Dilemma* in the *Brown* decision.

66. Herman Talmadge, *You and Segregation* (Birmingham, Ala.: Vulcan Press, 1955), vi; Lauren, *Power and Prejudice*, 178–83, 210ff.

67. Southern, *Gunnar Myrdal and Black-White Relations*, 109.

68. Ibid., 71, 101–50.

69. Brief for the United States as amicus curiae in *Brown*, 347 U.S. 483 (1954), as cited in Mary Dudziak, "Desegregation as a Cold War Imperative," *Stanford Law Review* 41 (Nov. 1988): 111, a particularly fine discussion of these briefs. See also Bert Lockwood Jr., "The United Nations Charter and United States Civil Rights Litigation, 1946–1955," *Iowa Law Review* 69 (May 1984): 901–56.

70. Lauren, *Power and Prejudice*, 201, 204, 207, 220, 241, 244; Dudziak, *Cold War Civil Rights*; Dwight Eisenhower, 24 Sept. 1957, as cited in John Hope Franklin and Isidore Starr, eds., *The Negro in the Twentieth Century: A Reader on the Struggle for Civil Rights* (New York: Vintage Books, 1967), 290; Pat Watters, *Down to Now: Reflections on the Southern Civil Rights Movement* (New York: Pantheon, 1971), 73; Carl M. Brauer, *John F. Kennedy and the Second Reconstruction* (New York: Columbia University Press, 1977), 234, 240–41, 247.

71. Winthrop Jordan and Leon Litwack, *The United States* (Englewood Cliffs, N.J.: Prentice-Hall, 1987), 763; Martin Luther King Jr., as reprinted in James Washington, ed., *A Testament of Hope: The Essential Writings and Speeches of Martin Luther King, Jr.* (San Francisco: HarperCollins, 1991), 364.

72. Martin Luther King Jr., 15 Mar. 1965, in Washington, *A Testament of Hope*, 183.

73. Myrdal, *An American Dilemma*, 2:1015, 1018, 1021.

74. The problem of race and democracy in the United States and the debate over the nature of the "American dilemma" persists, as is documented in such works as C. Eric Lincoln, *Race, Religion, and the Continuing American Dilemma* (New York: Hill and Wang, 1999); and Paul Sniderman, Philip Tetlock, and Edward Carmines, eds., *Prejudice, Politics, and the American Dilemma* (Stanford: Stanford University Press, 1993).

Race from Power
U.S. Foreign Policy and the General Crisis of White Supremacy

Explicit doctrines of racial supremacy are in bad odor nowadays, particularly among foreign policy elites; such retrograde ideas are viewed widely as the justly neglected relic of a long forgotten era. That epoch has its archaeologists in the proliferating critical studies of the "construction of whiteness."[1] These studies have posed a profound question: how was it that those who had fought in Europe—English versus Irish, French versus German, Russian versus Pole, Serb versus Croat, even Jew versus Gentile—were, on arrival on these shores, suddenly reconstructed as "white," and provided real or imagined privileges based on "white supremacy"? We define white supremacy here as the belief in the right of those of European heritage to dominate all others.[2] Some studies have noted that in addition to providing a cohesive identity for diverse European immigrants, "whiteness" and white supremacy had the added advantage of providing a convenient rationale for seizing the resources and labor of darker peoples who were presumed to be "inferior": that is "race" ("whiteness") was derived from "power," and "power" was derived from "race."

In spite of the richness of these studies, few place the construction of whiteness in the context of U.S. foreign policy, in spite of the highly relevant global context. At the very least, whiteness and white supremacy provided an alternative to the ethnic identities that had so often plunged Europe into war. Additionally, whiteness studies have generally not included Africans—as opposed to African Americans—in their understanding of the construction of whiteness, nor have they comprehended that the closing of the frontier in North America and the final defeat of Native Americans led directly to an assault on the "frontier" in Africa. Whiteness studies, broadly speaking, have neglected to perceive Asia, and notably the ascendancy of Japan after its 1905 defeat of Russia, as a central factor in the evolution of white supremacy.

One cannot begin to understand U.S. foreign policy during the past century without contemplating race and racism, or understand the ebb and flow of race and racism in this nation without contemplating the global context. If, as some have suggested, "class struggle" is the motive force of history, this insight should be complemented with the idea that relations, or struggles, between and among nations is the locomotive of history and the leading factor determining the advance and retreat of white supremacy. The evolution of white supremacy and the accompanying construction of race has not been a static process. The discrediting of fascism as a result of the Holocaust, the civil rights movement in the United States, and the antiapartheid movement in South Africa were among the epochal events that precipitated a basic reconsideration of racial supremacist ideas. The ability of nations as various as Japan and the Soviet Union to make U.S. tacit or explicit support for white supremacy a liability for Washington also helped neutralize the force of racist ideologies and policies.

While the horrors of Nazi Germany may have discredited racism as a respectable belief system, and the Cold War might have forced a reconsideration of the cost of maintaining a white supremacist society, it should be remembered that the atomic bombs the United States detonated during World War II fell on Asia, not Europe. In spite of the bluster and tension in the Moscow-Washington relationship, the United States did not go to war with the Soviet Union but instead wreaked havoc on Korea, Vietnam, Grenada, Panama, and Iraq, among other states. This reality should alert us to the fact that official nostrums notwithstanding, disarticulated notions of white supremacy did not disappear after 1945.[3]

The history of the American West might seem at first an odd place to look for the origins of white supremacy in U.S. relations with other powers. More is embedded in the history of the West, however, than the saga of the conquest of native peoples and the mock diplomacy that accompanied much of it. The frontier also engendered political, social, and cultural values and institutions that carried the United States from the farms and ranches of its heartland directly to imperial adventures among exotic lands and peoples. The biography of one quintessential westerner, Frederick Russell Burnham, provides a unique view of the historical evolution of racial domination.

Burnham was born on an Indian reservation in Minnesota. He later followed the frontier west as it was closing in Arizona and California, while gaining a well-deserved reputation as an "Indian fighter." He sailed for southern Africa in 1893 in search of a new frontier. Burnham joined Cecil Rhodes's war against King Lobengula in the country that eventually was called Rhodesia. An avowed advocate of what he called "white supremacy," he was quick to compare the wars that led to the expropriation of Native Americans to the war that led to the dispossession of the Africans.[4] For Burnham, the defeat of darker peoples, be they in North America or Africa, was an inevitable process.

In June 1893 Burnham noted the increasing number of settlers arriving in Matabeleland, soon to be christened Southern Rhodesia. "The American element is growing and bids fair to be [a] controlling one here inside five years." He envisioned a replay of what had occurred in the U.S. West, the eviction of indigenous people, followed by resettlement with immigrants from the Pan-European world. In words that would have resonated in the U.S. South, Burnham confided that the "one great stumbling block" to progress in that African colony was "the presence of the nigger." Burnham's brother-in-law did not "blame the whites for wanting to kill the nigs."[5]

Burnham was one among many Americans who were instrumental in furthering the imperial project of Cecil Rhodes, a mission in which any whites of "goodwill" and possessing sufficiently strong character were welcome to participate. In Cecil Rhodes's Africa, racial identity prevailed over national identity. Particular imperial identities meant much less in a developing colony in which a shared whiteness trumped specific traditions of colonial rule. Arguably, Rhodes would not have been as successful in his exploits were it not for the timely assistance of his U.S. supporters.[6] Just as whiteness served in the United States to neutralize preexisting tensions between the English and Irish, or Serbs and Croats, the same construction in Africa helped reconcile John Bull and Uncle Sam.

The whiteness that was defined in the United States as the opposite of a negative blackness was used by colonial authorities in southern African settler societies to police the frontier between "barbarism" and "civilization." The shrewdest policy makers sensed the synchrony between the U.S. frontier and African colonization. As Burnham recounted his meeting with Winston Churchill early in the twentieth century, the future prime minister "questioned me sharply and minutely on my early life among the Indians and made me recount almost step-by-step every contact I had ever had with any enemy along the wide frontier from Texas to California."[7] Burnham, who eventually returned to the United States and became a wealthy oil baron, was also friendly with Theodore Roosevelt, who had traveled extensively in Africa. The U.S. president believed that Cecil Rhodes's project in "Matabeleland represented a great and striking conquest for civilization."[8]

Burnham's experiences reveal the cosmopolitanism embedded in the civilizing mission of white supremacy. Empire builders compared notes across continents and peoples. The African American intellectual W. E. B. Du Bois recognized the global range of this problem and asserted almost 100 years ago that "the problem of the twentieth century is the problem of the color line." This NAACP founder did not limit this formulation to "black-white" relations as understood in the United States. Du Bois continued forcefully in words that too often have been forgotten: that the dilemma of color "included the relation of the darker to the lighter races of men [*sic*] in Asia and Africa, in America and the islands of the sea."[9] Today's dialogues on race often seem a retreat from the more expansive racial discourse of a century ago, which insisted on its worldwide dimensions. Du Bois's approach is inherently more appropriate when considering U.S. foreign policy and the question of white supremacy together.

Du Bois was not the only observer who linked color with a sense of impending change caused by the colonizing activities of European powers. Soviet social scientists often referred to what they termed the "general crisis of capitalism." The phrase was intended to suggest that with the Bolshevik Revolution of 1917 a fatal breach in the capitalist system had been made, and the system was undergoing an inevitable and inescapable decline. As one Soviet textbook put it, "Under conditions of the general crisis of capitalism, this system is no longer able to keep peoples in subjugation, and one after another they throw off the yoke of capital."[10] The conviction that capitalism's "general crisis" would emancipate the colonies, which were mostly in Africa and Asia and endured a heavily racialized form of economic exploitation, was implicit in these words.

The events of 1989 and the subsequent collapse of the Soviet Union have raised serious questions about the viability of this theory of capitalism's "general decline." What has gone largely unnoticed in the wake of the communist recessional, however, is the concomitant general crisis of white supremacy that in the past assured the world domination of Europe-descended peoples and the return of Asia to a preeminent position in the global economy. Jeffrey Sachs and Steve Radelet recently spoke to this question in the journal *Foreign Affairs*:[11]

> Beginning in the early 1500s, for more than four centuries now, the West has been ascendant in the world economy. With but 14 percent of the world's population in 1820, Western Europe and four colonial offshoots of Great Britain (Australia, Canada, New Zealand, and the United States) had already achieved around 25 percent of world income. By 1950, after a century and a half of Western industrialization, their income share had soared to 56 percent, while their population share hovered around 17 percent. Asia, with 66 percent of the world's population, had a meager 19 percent of world income, compared with 58 percent in 1820. In 1950, however, one of the great changes of modern history began, with the growth of many

Asian economies. By 1992, fueled by high growth rates, Asia's share of world income had risen to 33 percent. This tidal shift is likely to continue, with Asia reemerging by the early 21st century as the world's center of economic activity.

The authors dismiss the Asian economic recession of the late 1990s as "not a sign of the end of Asian growth but rather a recurring—if difficult to predict—pattern of financial instability that often accompanies economic growth."

Even if one does not accept every aspect of these analysts' bold predictions, it is apparent that the ascent of Asia augurs a fundamental change in the global economy that will have a corresponding impact on diplomatic relations. Sachs and Radelet unintentionally return us to the days of yore when race was perceived not solely as a domestic issue but as a question of global proportions. These analysts' prognostication may come as a shock at the end of the twentieth century, but it might not have surprised those who lived at the end of the nineteenth century.

The war of 1898 with Spain, which can fairly be said to have marked the beginning of U.S. preeminence, led to a robust debate in the United States about the theory and praxis of white supremacy. The decision to intervene in the internal affairs of Hawaii, a few years before, created a similar exchange of views: should the United States gamble its racial patrimony by gobbling up an island kingdom of unassimilable "natives,"[12] or should it step in on behalf of the white settlers precisely to preserve white supremacy? The annexation of Hawaii and the war against Spain as fought in the Caribbean and the Philippines were both heavily inflected by race.

The use of African American troops to impose the U.S. diktat in the Philippines, Cuba, and Puerto Rico provides an example. Black soldiers, falsely believed to have greater immunity than whites to tropical diseases, served with great ambivalence in the Spanish-American War. Doubly alienated by Jim Crow at home and the civilizing mission in the tropics, the African American soldier exploded the respective categories of victim and colonizer. It became increasingly difficult to launch wars with soldiers of color in the vanguard.[13] The era of the "Splendid Little War" synchronized with the intensification of lynching, the legalization of segregation as a national standard by the Supreme Court, and the forcible ouster of African Americans from positions of political power throughout the South.[14] Historian Rayford W. Logan called the 1890s the nadir of African American political power.[15] This low point also coincided with the extensive colonization of Africa by means of open warfare and so-called punitive expeditions.

The defeats being inflicted on peoples of color throughout the world had as their objective not only military conquest but demographic displacement.

The turn of the twentieth century, if a nadir for blacks, was a golden age for those who espoused a policy of out-breeding those they considered to be of lesser race. Theodore Roosevelt, president from 1900 through 1908, admired some of the most notorious white supremacists of his time, including those who were preoccupied with the future of the "white race" and feared what was called "race suicide." Roosevelt and other elite eugenicists worried that people of European descent were a global minority whose relatively low birth rates portended even steeper declines. White men and women should be "eager lovers," he thought, in order to arrest this development.[16] Roosevelt's friendship with Madison Grant, one of the leading racial theorists of that era, indicated the seriousness of his beliefs.[17]

Madison Grant's coterie included the influential eugenicist Lothrop Stoddard. Unlike many Americans today who speak of race solely in the domestic context, Stoddard viewed race as a worldwide problem. "The first real challenge to white world supremacy," he wrote, "was the Russo-Japanese War of 1904." As a result of an Asian nation's victory over a European power, Stoddard argued, "throughout Asia and even in Africa, races hitherto resigned or sullenly submissive began to dream of throwing off white control." The United States, one of Europe's "white outposts," was central to reversing this "rising tide of color."[18] U.S. strategic interests in the Pacific were thus held to have an implicit racial content.[19]

Like Du Bois, Stoddard saw race as the fundamental problem of the twentieth century and not as simply a "black-white" issue. Instead, writing in the midst of World War I, he admitted, "There is no immediate danger of the world being swamped by black blood. But there is a very imminent danger that the white stocks may be swamped by Asiatic blood." A triumphant Japan marked the "beginning of the ebb." Sadly, Stoddard recalled, "the legend of white invincibility was shattered, the veil of prestige that draped white civilization was torn aside, and the white world's manifold ills were laid bare for candid examination."[20] Grant, who wrote the introduction to his friend's text, confessed that he, too, was riveted by the "conflict between the East and the West—Europe and Asia," which had "lasted for centuries, in fact, it goes back to the Persian Wars." For his part, Stoddard worried deeply that World War I, which was "from the first the White Civil War," would "gravely complicate the course of race relations" and undermine the ability of Europe and Euro-America to resist the advance of the darker peoples.[21]

During this era, W. E. B. Du Bois's thinking ironically dovetailed in part with that of these racial theorists. He looked at the world problem of race, however, from the other end of the telescope. The defeat of Russia by Japan, Du Bois thought, awakened among Euro-Americans a "fear of colored revolt against white exploitation." Japan's victory fomented an enduring fear among many Euro-Americans but made Du Bois an enduring admirer of that country.[22] From the white supremacist perspective, there was justifiable concern about Russia's defeat. The Japanese success "electrified the atmosphere in India. It shattered the illusion of European invincibility."[23]

Having proved itself in the field of war, Japan proceeded after World War I to assert a claim for the racial equality of nations at the Versailles peace conference in 1919. President Woodrow Wilson, a southern Democrat, viewed the Japanese proposal to insert a racial equality clause into the charter documents of the League of Nations with more than mild concern. A fierce debate took place on the Japanese "equality of nations" resolution. The U.S. delegation feared the resolution's consequences for immigration to California as well as its implications for the racially stratified society that had developed across North America.[24] The import of race was by now not confined to the southern states. The United States was now not only an Atlantic nation but a Pacific one as well.

African Americans, waging at the time the beginnings of the battle for full civil rights, perceived Japan as a useful instrument in their own challenge to racial domination. Japan's very existence as a modern capitalist state in Asia called into question the essential premises of white supremacy and, as a consequence, was viewed as a threat to the United States. After World War I, the legendary black labor leader A. Philip Randolph "concluded that Japan, plus the power of other free nations 'combined with an international league of workingmen' could effectively pressure the Western powers."[25] Randolph backed up his rhetoric by joining black nationalist leader Marcus Garvey and others at the home of one of the nation's few black women millionaires, C. J. Walker, to form the International League of Darker Peoples in 1919. The short-lived league had arranged a New York meeting with a visiting Japanese publisher and editor to seek Tokyo's assistance in raising the question of racial equality at Versailles. Tellingly, the league not only encompassed those of African descent but those of Asian—particularly Japanese—descent as well.[26]

Activists in the African diaspora began to play upon dissension between Washington and London on the one hand and Tokyo on the other to their own advantage. Both British and U.S. military intelligence took careful note of an editorial in Garvey's newspaper, *Negro World*, which said as much: "With the rising militarism of Asia and the standing militarism of Europe one can foresee nothing else but an armed clash between the white and yellow races. When this clash of millions comes, an opportunity will have presented itself to the Negro people of the world to free themselves. The next war will be between the Negroes and the whites, unless our demands for justice are recognized. With Japan to fight with us we can win such a war."[27] Eliminating the more egregious aspects of white supremacy was increasingly seen in Washington as a question of national security, though this forced march away from the power of race was often cloaked in the guise of morality.

Japanese newspapers carried editorials condemning lynching of African Americans in the Deep South. A visiting delegation of Japanese filmmakers praised black protest of the racist feature film *Birth of a Nation* (1915). Many African Americans had come to see Tokyo as an ally.[28] Japan's perspective on African Americans reflected its approach to Africa as well. Tokyo recognized that the aching Achilles' heel of the European powers—and their cousins in Washington—was their practice of white supremacy in Africa and else-where, which allowed Japan to portray itself more readily as a viable alter-native to European colonialism and U.S. hegemony. Indeed, competition in Africa was a salient factor in the rapid deterioration of relations between Japan and Britain during the first half of the twentieth century.[29] The Japa-nese effort to incorporate racial equality into international law at Versailles was ultimately foiled by President Wilson's crude parliamentarianism, with the collusion of Britain.[30]

Challenge to white supremacy came from another unexpected place. The Bolshevik Revolution contributed to the general crisis of white supremacy by making ethnic, national, and racial allegiances secondary to class struggle. President Wilson feared the impact of communist ideology on the black troops who "returning from abroad would be our greatest medium in conveying bolshevism to America." The president was as deeply concerned with "whites" as with "reds."[31] Lothrop Stoddard and Madison Grant also glimpsed early the implications of the Bolshevik Revolution for white supremacy. Grant saw "Asia in the guise of Bolshevism with Semitic leadership and Chinese execu-tioners . . . organizing an assault upon western Europe." Stoddard saw Lenin as "a modern Jenghiz Khan plotting the plunder of a world." Bolshevism, he exclaimed, was "in fact, as anti-racial as it is anti-social" and "thus reveals it-self as the arch-enemy of civilization and the race. Bolshevism is the rene-gade, the traitor within the gates, who would betray the citadel. . . . There-fore, Bolshevism must be crushed out with iron heels, no matter what the cost."[32] For the nascent U.S. intelligence community, Bolshevism further complicated the challenges mounted by black radicalism. Early in 1919 one harried U.S. intelligence agent argued that African American radicalism aimed at a "combination of the other colored races of the world. As a colored move-ment it looks to Japan for leadership; as a radical movement it follows Bol-shevism and has intimate relations with various socialistic groups throughout the United States."[33] Official Washington found this multihued specter quite disturbing.

The Soviet potential attracted a number of leading African American intellectuals, including Jamaican American poet Claude McKay, W. E. B. Du Bois, Shirley Graham Du Bois, Paul Robeson, Langston Hughes, and Claudia Jones.[34] It made inroads in Africa by pledging to assist anticolonial movements.[35] Here, the Japanese communist Sen Katayama played a pivotal role. He assisted in organizing communist parties in Japan, Mexico, Canada, and the United States, eventually being elected to the leading body of the Moscow-based Communist International. In 1928 Katayama helped formulate the official communist position on the "Negro Question," including the "right of Negroes to self-determination in the Southern States." The Comintern pledged to support African American efforts to defeat segregation and third-class citizenship.[36]

Americans found the Japanese more intimidating as empire builders than communists. The United States declared war on Japan following the 7 December 1941 attack on Pearl Harbor. In 1942 a number of African American nationalists, including Elijah Muhammad, were arrested because of their pro-Japanese sympathies. Even Roy Wilkins, the moderate leader of the NAACP, conceded that the catastrophe at Pearl Harbor was caused in part by the tendency among many Euro-Americans to despise anyone not regarded as "white." Folklore emerged about a black sharecropper who told his white boss during the war, "By the way, Captain, I hear the Japs done declared war on you white folks."[37] U.S. elites realized not only that African Americans might be less than enthusiastic about going to war against Japan but—worse—that they might harbor a subversive "fifth column."

Black dissidents were not alone in ascribing a racial character to the conflict. Former president Herbert Hoover viewed the military landscape in 1942 through the lens of white supremacy. "When the Japanese take Burma, China and organize the forces of the discontent in India," he warned,

> we are looking in the face of something new. . . . The white man has kept control of Asiatics by dividing parts of them against the other and generally establishing an arrogant superiority. Universally, the white man is hated by the Chinese, Malayan, Indian and Japanese alike. . . . Unless [Japanese] leadership is destroyed, the Western Hemisphere is going to confront this mass across the Pacific. Unless they are defeated, they will demand entry and equality in emigration . . . and there will be in twenty-five years an Asiatic flood into South America that will make the Nazis

look like pikers. . . . And we will have to go through with it until we have destroyed [Japan]. That may take a million American lives and eight or ten years, but it will have to be done.[38]

A considerable percentage of the "million American lives" to be sacrificed would be black. Many blacks wondered why they should give their lives to protect and preserve white supremacy. The same question was being asked in different ways across the globe. In India a nationalist movement had begun to grow rapidly after World War I. The British government dispatched Sir Stafford Cripps to an Indian National Congress gathering in Delhi in an attempt to enlist support for the British war against Japan. The quid pro quo was a form of independence. "This is a postdated cheque on a crashing bank," Mahatma Gandhi commented.[39]

World War II, inter alia, represented a true crisis of white supremacy. Washington and London found it ever more difficult to explain why it was necessary to make sacrifices to defeat systems of racial domination devised in Tokyo and Berlin, while racialized systems of oppression were maintained at home. World War II compelled these great powers to undertake a "race" away from the "power" that the more outlandish versions of white supremacy represented. American eugenicists and other racists had influenced Nazi ideology, but even racial conservatives realized that doctrines of racial and ethnic superiority, left unchecked, could lead to a holocaust of unimaginable proportions.[40]

Although the praxis of "white supremacy" was castigated officially and eroded substantially during the Cold War, it was not extinguished altogether but buttressed by an aggressive anticommunism that had the advantage of being—at least formally—nonracial. Anticolonialism sought to overturn the racial oppression and underdevelopment characteristic of imperialist society.[41] In turn, the benefits of colonial exploitation could be best defended in this new era by interpreting anticolonial sentiment as "communist."[42] The red tag slowed down independence movements and, not coincidentally, gave white supremacy a new lease on life.

The U.S. battle against white supremacy had unique characteristics. Mary Dudziak is largely correct in asserting that "desegregation" was a "Cold War imperative."[43] Without slighting the heroic contribution of those who participated in the civil rights movement, it must be recognized that the international community played a substantial role in compelling the nation to disavow the more outrageous aspects of racism. Washington could not credibly charge Moscow with human rights violations when minorities at home were so horribly treated. International pressure was felt directly and powerfully during the 1957 school desegregation crisis in Little Rock. In retrospect, it is clear that President Dwight D. Eisenhower's decision to commit troops to that Arkansas racial tinderbox was motivated considerably by his sensitivity to the damage inflicted on the U.S. image abroad.[44] At the same time, growing antiracism made it more difficult for Washington to openly maintain the customary cozy relationship with its allies in South Africa and Rhodesia.[45]

While the domestic struggle against Jim Crow was the most salient racial issue confronting Americans during the 1950s, Africa became the center of the struggle against white supremacy once segregationist resistance was weakened by middecade. The Soviets were quick to ally themselves with national liberation movements. During the decisive stages of the Algerian Revolution, they "supplied free to the People's Liberation Army . . . 25 thousand rifles, 21 thousand machine guns and sub-machine guns, 1300 howitzers, cannons and mortars, many tens of thousands of pistols and other weapons. Over 5 million rubles' worth of clothes, provisions and medical supplies were supplied to Algeria by Soviet social organizations alone. Hundreds of wounded from the Algerian Liberation Army were saved and treated in the Soviet Union. Soviet wheat, sugar, butter, conserves, condensed milk, etc., streamed into Algeria."[46] Similar assistance was provided by Moscow to those fighting colonialism and other forms of exploitation in Indo-China, Southern Africa, and Cuba, which also had a substantial population of African descent. Assistance to those fighting racialized systems of oppression was no small factor in sparking the economic and political crisis that led to the USSR's collapse.

Many Americans felt such aid violated the basic norms of "peaceful coexistence" and "détente," though without Soviet aid, Asians, Africans, and Cubans would have had more difficulty confronting their opponents. Critics of this "Third World"–Moscow alliance continually asserted that their opposition was not based on an outdated devotion to white supremacy but rather to the Cold War creed of anticommunism. Southern Rhodesia, the colony that Frederick Russell Burnham had helped to found decades earlier, effectively illustrates the fate of white supremacy during an era when that doctrine had little legitimacy outside the settler regimes. Despite official bromides, racist thinking continued to exert a powerful influence on U.S. foreign policy, even when it was not disguised in the finery of newer anticommunist doctrine.

Dean Acheson, secretary of state during the Truman administration, was in his words "present at the creation" of the Cold War. His anticommunist credentials were impeccable and he was a member in good standing of the U.S. elite. In his communications, however, many of them public, he revealed that white supremacy was no negligible factor in explaining his support for the minority regimes in Southern Africa. His exchanges with Sir Roy We-

An antiapartheid demonstration in Dar-es-Salaam, June 1965. South African refugees, wearing Ku Klux Klan costumes, link repressive regimes in southern Africa with U.S. racism. (Bettmann/Corbis)

lensky, a prominent statesman and member of the Rhodesian ruling class, illustrate the continuing influence of this doctrine as late as the 1970s.

In 1965 Southern Rhodesia had refused to accede to the winds of change blowing through the continent and declared a unilateral declaration of independence in defiance of the worldwide movement toward decolonization. To Roy Welensky, the implications of President Richard Nixon's 1971 opening to China were just as portentous for white supremacy as for the conventional balance of power between the West and communist powers. "We Whites seldom appreciate the extent to which the Black and the Brown man order their thinking on how strong or weak they think one is," he informed Acheson, "and it is, therefore always unwise to start off on a basis they think one is afraid of them. This may sound childish to you Dean, but I've lived all my life where the Whites have been outnumbered many times. I don't know the Yellow man, but I'm told that he is even more concerned about his dignity and face-saving than the Black man and will always interpret our casual ways as being weak."[47] Acheson mulled over this, telling his interlocutor, "I still cling to Bret Harte's aphorism, 'That for ways that are dark And for tricks that are vain The Heathen Chinese is peculiar.' But no more so than the heathen Japanese."[48]

Welensky, Acheson, and many other leaders from the Pan-European world were not simply driven by anticommunism during the Cold War—they were also driven by white supremacy. If a Pan-African ideal surfaced in the midst of the Cold War, a revived Pan-Europeanism arose to counter it. The failure to completely mask racism in the guise of anticommunism has roots that historians have not completely explored. "Roots" is indeed the operative word here because, while U.S. investors perceived that they had a material stake in maintaining the bounty of cheap labor and minerals that white supremacy had delivered,[49] quite a few elite Americans literally had kith and kin in southern Africa. They avidly supported their relatives' attempts to preserve minority rule and forestall the possibility of Europeans' being overrun by African "hordes."

Ian Smith, prime minister of the illegal Rhodesian regime, had an uncle who was "well established in the United States." When he met then secretary of state Henry Kissinger, Smith observed that "like me," the diplomat's wife was "conservative by nature, had Scottish blood . . . and believed that we had much in common."[50] President Lyndon Baines Johnson was "very interested" in the Baines School in Bulawayo and wondered if the surname reflected a familial relationship. He could trace this branch of his family back to 1741 only and did not know if this meant that he too had relatives in Rhodesia.[51] A. R. W. Stumbles, a former speaker of the Rhodesian parliament, like many leading Rhodesians, was born in South Africa but had two ancestors who were independently related to George Washington. The "W" in his name stood for Washington.[52] Angus Graham, who served as Rhodesia's minister of external affairs and was one of its leading white supremacists, proudly told Dean Acheson of the "letter" he received from "Mrs. Nora Acheson, a Canadian who married my mother's cousin, Patrick Acheson."[53] Evidently, Graham was related to the former U.S. secretary of state.[54] Chester Crocker, the architect of "constructive engagement" with the apartheid regime in South Africa during the 1980s, also had intimate Rhodesian ties. His wife and in-laws hailed from that country. When he visited Rhodesia in 1979, with the war for national liberation still raging, he discussed President Jimmy Carter's fear of losing black votes if he were not sufficiently tough with Rhodesia. Dr. Crocker reassured his white hosts that the United States was "a white majority government . . . not a black majority [government]."[55] The implication was that a GOP administration could seek dialogue with the white minority government rather than condemn it, partly because a Republican president would have minimal dependence on minority voters.[56]

Crocker had a point. Whiteness, if not white supremacy, was rarely distant from the machinations of U.S. opinion molders, even when racist thinking was officially renounced. The United States had been founded as a bastion of white supremacy, and this principle had not been eradicated in the twentieth century, despite substantial antiracist activism at home and abroad. There were many reasons for this, including the blood ties that bonded influential Americans to relatives in the white settler states. Leaders of these minority regimes enjoyed a sentimental advantage in certain high-powered Washington circles that helped to preserve white supremacy as an element of U.S. foreign policy.

For much of the twentieth century, race was an international concern for U.S. foreign policy makers, even if it was seldom acknowledged publicly. In the first fifty years, Japan was rarely distant from calculations about the global implications of the concept. During the Cold War, however, Japan became a U.S. ally and its ability and desire to attract disgruntled African Americans searching for leverage against their own government disappeared. In Japan itself, the Cold War policy of anticommunism undercut the antiracists of the left while providing leverage to those Japanese who were the ideological descendants of the "antiwhite" thinkers of the interwar and World War II eras.[57] When the Soviet Union collapsed, the adhesive that had bound many of the Japanese right, and certain Chinese elites, to the United States gave way. A troubling eruption of racialist thought appeared in its stead that has also been reflected in other important parts of Asia.[58]

Racialist discourse emerged in Malaysia in the 1990s. Mahatir Mohamad, prime minister of Malaysia, collaborated with Shintaro Isihara, a leading Japanese conservative, on a recent book, *The Voice of Asia: Two Leaders Discuss the Coming Century*. They raise intriguing questions about the future of "race" and "white supremacy" in the twenty-first century. Mohamad and Isihara align themselves with Lenin in associating European hegemony with the age of imperialism. (Mohamad, ironically, benefited directly from a protracted Cold War campaign spearheaded by London and assisted by Washington that routed the left in his country.)[59] "Western civilization," the authors state, "was built on war" and "Europeans and Americans are still dreaming of past glory." Asia, as an economic powerhouse, "presents a more serious threat to the West than even militaristic Japan did earlier this century." The Gulf War was no more than another expression of white supremacy. "If the United States can get away with this—peddling arms throughout the Middle East, intervening militarily to protect its supply of oil, and arm-twisting Japan to foot the bill—then the white race still rules the world." These writers believed it "impossible to communicate with Americans as well as we do with

Asians." Why? "Color is one reason . . . the perception that white people are better than colored people." They pointedly observe that it may "take a cataclysmic event" to "shake the great majority of Americans out of their hubris and self-righteousness" and suggest that "we may have to form an Asian united front against Americanization."[60] This overt hostility to the United States, and especially to Euro-Americans, was not lessened by the financial crisis that gripped Japan, Malaysia, and its neighbors at the end of the twentieth century but instead has seemed to spread.[61]

No identifiable U.S. constituency would align itself with this perspective today, as black nationalists did in the interwar years. The Cold War took its toll on African Americans, forcibly diminishing internationalist—if not race-conscious—thinking among them.[62] Black communities have come to recognize that the civil rights concessions they received, particularly affirmative action, heavily depended on a Cold War dispensation that has evaporated, while newly minted racists posit ever more sophisticated versions of white supremacy.[63] Who is to say how U.S. minorities may react in the future to more aggressive assertions of racism? Perhaps they may feel compelled to align with "antiwhite" Asians, as some once aligned with Soviet communists. The decline of the socialist project and the retreat of solidarity based on class make such a prospect less farfetched than it may appear at first glance. The moment could be imminent when a forced "race" from the "power" that white supremacy was thought to provide will seem prudent. The brusque reassertion of racial thinking in Asia has materialized just as the quality of U.S. relations with both China[64] and Japan are declining. It is strategically impractical to maintain prickly relations with both of these Asian giants simultaneously, though the incivility of white supremacy makes it difficult to forge subtle distinctions between and among "nonwhites." Simultaneously, warnings from the intelligentsia of a "clash of civilizations" bear an eerie resemblance to the racial ruminations of Lothrop Stoddard and Madison Grant a century ago.[65] As ever, the contours of race in this nation will be shaped by developments in the global arena and, it appears, U.S. foreign policy will continue to be shaped by racial considerations. We are experiencing the preliminary stages of a general crisis of white supremacy that may conclude with a basic reordering of concepts of "race" that have been, in turn, fundamentally derived from "power."[66]

Notes

1. Richard Delgado and Jean Stefancic, eds., *Critical White Studies: Looking behind the Mirror* (Philadelphia: Temple University Press, 1997); Michelle Fine, Lois Weis, Linda C. Powell, and L. Mun Wong, eds., *Off White: Readings on Race, Power and*

Society (New York: Routledge, 1997); Susan Gubar, *Racechanges: White Skin, Black Face in American Culture* (New York: Oxford University Press, 1997); Toni Morrison, *Playing in the Dark: Whiteness and the Literary Imagination* (Cambridge, Mass.: Harvard University Press, 1992); Ruth Frankenberg, *White Women, Race Matters: The Social Construction of Whiteness* (Minneapolis: University of Minnesota Press, 1993); Joe L. Kincheloe, Shirley R. Steinberg, Nelson M. Rodriguez, and Ronald E. Chennault, eds., *White Reign: Deploying Whiteness in America* (New York: St. Martin's Press, 1998); Mike Hill, ed., *Whiteness: A Critical Reader* (New York: New York University Press, 1997); Ian F. Haney López, *White by Law: The Legal Construction of Race* (New York: New York University Press, 1996); Eric Lott, *Love and Theft: Blackface Minstrelsy and the American Working Class* (New York: Oxford University Press, 1993); David R. Roediger, *The Wages of Whiteness: Race and the Making of the American Working Class* (London: Verso, 1991); Noel Ignatiev, *How the Irish Became White* (New York: Routledge, 1996); Grace Elizabeth Hale, *Making Whiteness: The Culture of Segregation in the South, 1890–1940* (New York: Pantheon Books, 1998); Theodore Allen, *The Invention of the White Race*, vol. 1, *Racial Oppression and Social Control* (London: Verso, 1994); Elvi Whittaker, *The Mainland Haole: The White Experience in Hawaii* (New York: Columbia University Press, 1986).

2. See, for example, George Frederickson, *White Supremacy: A Comparative Study in American and South African History* (New York: Oxford University Press, 1981); John Cell, *The Highest Stage of White Supremacy: The Origins of Segregation in South Africa and the American South* (New York: Cambridge University Press, 1982); Clifton C. Crais, *White Supremacy and Black Resistance in Pre-Industrial South Africa: The Making of the Colonial Order in the Eastern Cape, 1770–1865* (New York: Cambridge University Press, 1992).

3. White supremacy is hardly an exclusively U.S. phenomenon. See, for example, Alice L. Conklin, *A Mission to Civilize: The Republican Idea of Empire in France and West Africa, 1895–1930* (Stanford: Stanford University Press, 1997); Allison Blakely, *Blacks in the Dutch World: The Evolution of Racial Imagery in a Modern Society* (Bloomington: University of Indiana Press, 1993); Frances Winddance Twine, *Racism in a Racial Democracy: The Maintenance of White Supremacy in Brazil* (New Brunswick: Rutgers University Press, 1998); Gretchen Fitzgerald, *Repulsing Racism: Reflections on Racism and the Irish* (Dublin: Attic Press, 1992); Panikos Panayi, ed., *Racial Violence in Britain, 1840–1950* (Leicester: Leicester University Press, 1993); Jay Kinsbruner, *Not of Pure Blood: The Free People of Color and Racial Prejudice in Nineteenth-Century Puerto Rico* (Durham: Duke University Press, 1996).

4. Frederick Russell Burnham, *Scouting on Two Continents* (Bulawayo, Rhodesia: Books of Rhodesia, 1975), 218; Frederick Russell Burnham, *Taking Chances* (Prescott, Ariz.: Wolfe, 1994). See also Mary Bradford and Richard Bradford, eds., *An American Family on the African Frontier: The Burnham Family Letters, 1893–1896* (Niwot, Colo.: Roberts Rinehart Publishers, 1993); Arthur Keppel-Jones, *Rhodes and Rhodesia: The White Conquest of Zimbabwe, 1884–1902* (Kingston, Ont.: McGill-Queen's University Press, 1983); and Dane Kennedy, *Islands of White: Settler Society and Culture in Kenya and Southern Rhodesia, 1890–1939* (Durham: Duke University Press, 1987).

5. Frederick Russell Burnham to Madge Blick, June 1893; Frederick Russell Burnham to Josiah Russell, circa 1894; Blanche Blick Burnham to Blick family, 6 Feb. 1894; John Blick to parents, 16 Oct. 1894, in Bradford and Bradford, *An American Family on the African Frontier*, 65, 133, 121, 176, 268.

6. Maurice Heany, one of the biggest businessmen in "Rhodesia," was a cousin of Edgar Allen Poe who also fought Native Americans in the West before crossing the Atlantic. Coleman Joseph, born in Philadelphia, built Bulawayo's first synagogue. See Eric Rosenthal, *Stars and Stripes in Africa* (Cape Town: National Books, 1968), 7, 15, 37, 176. Mining engineers from the United States, like John Hays Hammond and Gardner Williams, pioneered in developing gold mines in the region. Bradford and Bradford, *An American Family on the African Frontier*, xi. See also R. W. S. Turner, "American Links with Early Days of Rhodesia," *Rhodesia Calls* 55 (May–June 1969): 4–13.

7. Burnham, *Taking Chances*, 266.

8. William N. Tilchin, *Theodore Roosevelt and the British Empire: A Study in Presidential Statecraft* (New York: St. Martin's Press, 1997), 24.

9. W. E. B. Du Bois, *The Souls of Black Folk* (Boston: Bedford Books, 1997), 45.

10. O. W. Kuusinen and C. P. Dutt, *Fundamentals of Marxism-Leninism*, 2nd rev. ed. (Moscow: Foreign Languages Pub. House, 1963), 317. See also Fenner Brockway, *The Colonial Revolution* (New York: St. Martin's Press, 1973); Fedor Mikhailovich Leonidov, *Racism — An Ideological Weapon of Imperialism* (Moscow: Progress Publishers, 1965); H. R. Cowie, ed., *Imperialism and Race Relations* (Melbourne: Nelson, 1986).

11. Steven Radelet and Jeffrey Sachs, "Asia's Reemergence," *Foreign Affairs* 76 (Nov.–Dec. 1997): 44–59. See also Janet Abu-Lughod, *Before European Hegemony: The World System, A.D. 1250–1350* (New York: Oxford University Press, 1989).

12. Thomas Osborne, *"Empire Can Wait": American Opposition to Hawaiian Annexation, 1893–1898* (Kent, Ohio: Kent State University Press, 1981); Joseph A. Fry, *John Tyler Morgan and the Search for Southern Autonomy* (Knoxville: University of Tennessee Press, 1992); Richard H. Miller, ed., *American Imperialism in 1898: The Quest for National Fulfillment* (New York: Wiley, 1970); Christopher Lasch, "The Anti-Imperialists, the Philippines and the Inequality of Man," *Journal of Southern History* 24 (Aug. 1954): 319–31; David Healy, *U.S. Expansionism: The Imperialist Urge in the 1890s* (Madison: University of Wisconsin Press, 1970); Julius Pratt, *Expansionists of 1898: The Acquisition of Hawaii and the Spanish Islands* (Baltimore: Johns Hopkins Press, 1936); Sylvester K. Stevens, *American Expansion in Hawaii, 1842–1898* (Harrisburg: Archives Publishing Company of Pennsylvania, 1945). I am grateful to Eric Love for helping to shape my thinking on this period.

13. Piero Gleijeses, "African Americans and the War against Spain," *North Carolina Historical Review* 23 (Apr. 1996): 184–214. See also Willard B. Gatewood Jr., *Black Americans and the White Man's Burden, 1898–1903* (Urbana: University of Illinois Press, 1975); Willard B. Gatewood Jr., *"Smoked Yankees" and the Struggle for Empire: Letters from Negro Soldiers, 1898–1902* (Urbana: University of Illinois Press, 1971); George P. Marks, ed., *The Black Press Views American Imperialism (1898–1900)* (New York: Arno Press, 1971); Igor Dementyev, *USA: Imperialists and Anti-Imperialists: The Great Foreign Policy Debate at the Turn of the Century* (Moscow: Progress Publishers, 1979); Hazel M. McFerson, *The Racial Dimensions of American Overseas Colonial Policy* (Westport, Conn.: Greenwood Press, 1997); Alexander Deconde, *Ethnicity, Race, and American Foreign Policy: A History* (Boston: Northeastern University Press, 1992); and Melvin Small, *Democracy and Diplomacy: The Impact of Domestic Politics on U.S. Foreign Policy, 1789–1994* (Baltimore: Johns Hopkins University Press, 1996).

14. Ida B. Wells-Barnett, *Crusader for Justice: The Autobiography of Ida B. Wells* (Chicago: University of Chicago Press, 1970); Ida B. Wells, *Southern Horrors and*

Other Writings: The Anti-Lynching Campaign of Ida B. Wells, 1892–1900 (Boston: Bedford Books, 1997); and Nell Irvin Painter, *Standing at Armageddon: United States, 1877–1919* (New York: W. W. Norton, 1987).

15. Rayford W. Logan, *The Negro in American Life and Thought: The Nadir, 1877–1901* (New York: Dial Press, 1954).

16. Thomas G. Dyer, *Theodore Roosevelt and the Idea of Race* (Baton Rouge: Louisiana State University Press, 1980), 165, 17. See also George Sinkler, *The Racial Attitudes of American Presidents from Abraham Lincoln to Theodore Roosevelt* (Garden City, N.Y.: Doubleday, 1972); Fritz Hirschfield, *George Washington and Slavery: A Documentary Record* (Columbia: University of Missouri Press, 1997). The connection between race and gender supremacy is explored in such works as Jessie Daniels, *White Lies: Race, Class, Gender and Sexuality in White Supremacist Discourse* (New York: Routledge, 1997); Gail Bederman, *Manliness and Civilization: A Cultural History of Gender and Race in the United States, 1880–1917* (Chicago: University of Chicago Press, 1995); Glenda Gilmore, *Gender and Jim Crow: Women and the Politics of White Supremacy in North Carolina, 1896–1920* (Chapel Hill: University of North Carolina Press, 1996); Ann Laura Stoler, *Race and the Education of Desire: Foucault's History of Sexuality and the Colonial Order of Things* (Durham: Duke University Press, 1995); Zillah R. Eisenstein, *Hatreds: Racialized and Sexualized Conflicts in the 21st Century* (New York: Routledge, 1996); and Jacinth Samuels, *The Sound of Silence: Racism in Contemporary Feminist Theory* (Ottawa: National Library of Canada, 1991), microform.

17. See Madison Grant, *The Passing of the Great Race or the Racial Basis of European History* (New York: C. Scribner, 1916).

18. Lothrop Stoddard, *Clashing Tides of Color* (New York: C. Scribner's Sons, 1935), 9, 54.

19. See also navalist Alfred Thayer Mahan's earlier argument that Hawaii should be annexed as a counterweight against menacing Asian powers. "Shall [Hawaii] in the future be an outpost of European civilization," he asked plaintively, "or of the comparative barbarism of China[?]" *New York Times*, 31 Jan. 1893.

20. Lothrop Stoddard, *The Rising Tide of Color against White Supremacy* (New York: Scribner's, 1920), 153.

21. Ibid., v, vi, xxiii, 301.

22. W. E. B. Du Bois, *Dusk of Dawn: An Essay toward an Autobiography of a Race Concept* (New York: Schocken, 1968), 232.

23. R. P. Dua, *The Impact of the Russo-Japanese (1905) War on Indian Politics* (New Delhi: S. Chand, 1966), vii, viii.

24. Frank Lyon Polk to Roland Sletor Morris, 21 Apr. 1919, in Arthur Link, ed., *The Papers of Woodrow Wilson*, vol. 57 (Princeton: Princeton University Press, 1987), 570–71. See also Henry P. Frei, *Japan's Southward Advance and Australia: From the Sixteenth Century to World War II* (Honolulu: University of Hawaii Press, 1991).

25. Judith Stein, *The World of Marcus Garvey: Race and Class in Modern Society* (Baton Rouge: Louisiana State University Press, 1986), 50.

26. Robert Hill, ed., *The Marcus Garvey and Universal Negro Improvement Association Papers*, vol. 1 (Berkeley: University of California Press, 1983), 345.

27. Ibid., 404.

28. Reginald Kearney, "Afro-American Views of the Japanese, 1900–1945" (Ph.D. diss., Kent State University, 1991). Claude Clegg, *An Original Man: The Life and Times of Elijah Muhammad* (New York: St. Martin's Press, 1997). See also George W. Shepherd Jr., *Racial Influences on American Foreign Policy* (New York: Basic Books,

1970); Arnold Shankman, *Ambivalent Friends: Afro-Americans View the Immigrant* (Westport, Conn.: Greenwood Press, 1982).

29. Richard Albert Bradshaw, "Japan and European Colonialism in Africa, 1800–1937" (Ph.D. diss., Ohio University, 1992), 15. See also Shinya Sugiyama, *Japan's Industrialization in the World Economy, 1859–1899: Export Trade and Overseas Competition* (London: Athlone Press, 1988); Kweku Ampiah, "British Commercial Policies against Japanese Expansionism in East and West Africa, 1931–1935," *International Journal of African Historical Studies* 23 (1990): 619–41; Peter Lowe, *Great Britain and the Origins of the Pacific War: A Study of British Policy in East Asia, 1937–1941* (Oxford: Clarendon Press, 1977).

30. David Hunter Miller diary entry, 30 Jan. 1919, in Link, *The Papers of Woodrow Wilson*, vol. 54, p. 379. See also Phil Hammond, ed., *Cultural Difference, Media Memories: Anglo-American Images of Japan* (London: Cassell, 1997); Robert Lansing, *The Peace Negotiations: A Personal Narrative* (Boston: Houghton Mifflin, 1921), 243–56.

31. Dr. Grayson diary entry, 9 Mar. 1919, in Link, *The Papers of Woodrow Wilson*, vol. 55, p. 471. See also Theodore Kornweibel Jr., *"Seeing Red": Federal Campaigns against Black Militancy, 1919–1925* (Bloomington: University of Indiana Press, 1998).

32. Kornweibel, *"Seeing Red"*; Stoddard, *The Rising Tide of Color*, xxxi, 219, 221.

33. Stoddard, *The Rising Tide of Color*, xxxi, 219, 221; Kornweibel, *"Seeing Red,"* 81.

34. Karl G. Yoneda, "The Heritage of Sen Katayama," *Political Affairs* 14, 3 (Mar. 1975): 38–57. See also Hyman Kublin, *Asian Revolutionary: The Life of Sen Katayama* (Princeton: Princeton University Press, 1964); Wayne Cooper, *Claude McKay: Rebel Sojourner in the Harlem Renaissance: A Biography* (Baton Rouge: Louisiana State University Press, 1987); Tyrone Tillery, *Claude McKay: A Black Poet's Struggle for Identity* (Amherst: University of Massachusetts Press, 1992).

35. Philip S. Foner, *The Bolshevik Revolution: Its Impact on American Radicals, Liberals and Labor* (New York: International Publishers, 1967); Allison Blakely, *Russia and the Negro: Blacks in Russian History and Thought* (Washington, D.C.: Howard University Press, 1986); Daniel Mason and Jessica Smith, eds., *Lenin's Impact on the United States* (New York: NWR, 1970).

36. Yoneda, "The Heritage of Sen Katayama"; Kublin, *Asian Revolutionary*; Cooper, *Claude McKay*; Tillery, *Claude McKay*.

37. John Dower, *War without Mercy: Race and Power in the Pacific War* (New York: Pantheon, 1986), 175–76. See also Robert O. Ballou, *Shinto, the Unconquered Enemy: Japan's Doctrine of Racial Superiority and World Conquest* (New York: Viking, 1945); Russell Braddon, *Japan against the World, 1941–2041: The 100-Year War for Supremacy* (New York: Stein & Day, 1983); Willard H. Elsbree, *Japan's Role in South-East Asian Nationalist Movements* (Cambridge, Mass.: Harvard University Press, 1953); Akira Iriye, *Power and Culture: The Japanese-American War, 1941–1945* (Cambridge, Mass.: Harvard University Press, 1981); V. G. Kiernan, *The Lords of Humankind: Black Man, Yellow Man and White Man in an Age of Empire* (Boston: Weidenfeld & Nicolson, 1969); John J. Stephan, *Hawaii under the Rising Sun: Japan's Plan for Conquest after Pearl Harbor* (Honolulu: University of Hawaii Press, 1984); Hugh Tinker, *Race, Conflict and International Order: From Empire to United Nations* (New York: St. Martin's Press, 1977); and Rubin Francis Weston, *Racism in U.S. Imperialism: The Influence of Racial Assumptions on American Foreign Policy, 1893–1946* (New York: Columbia University Press, 1972).

38. Walter LaFeber, *The Clash: A History of U.S.-Japanese Relations* (New York: W. W. Norton, 1997), 217.

39. Richard Storry, *Japan and the Decline of the West in Asia, 1894–1943* (London: Macmillan, 1979), 4. See also Bradford A. Lee, *Britain and the Sino-Japanese War, 1937–1939* (Stanford: Stanford University Press, 1973); Gunter Bischof and Robert L. Dupont, eds., *The Pacific War Revisited* (Baton Rouge: Louisiana University Press, 1997).

40. Stefan Kühl, *The Nazi Connection: Eugenics, American Racism, and German National Socialism* (New York: Oxford University Press, 1994); Lawrence Le Blanc, *The United States and the Genocide Convention* (Durham: Duke University Press, 1991); and Frank Chalk and Kurt Jonassohn, *The History and Sociology of Genocide: Analyses and Case Studies* (New Haven: Yale University Press, 1990).

41. Walter Rodney, *How Europe Underdeveloped Africa* (Washington, D.C.: Howard University Press, 1981); Amilcar Cabral, *Return to the Source: Selected Speeches* (New York: Monthly Review Press, 1974); Samora Machel, *Samora Machel, An African Revolutionary: Selected Speeches and Writings* (London: Zed, 1985); Kenneth Kaunda, *Zambia Shall Be Free: An Autobiography* (London: Heinemann, 1963); and Kwame Nkrumah, *Neo-Colonialism: The Last Stage of Imperialism* (New York: International Publishers, 1966).

42. Robert J. McMahon, *Colonialism and Cold War: The United States and the Struggle for Indonesian Independence, 1945–1949* (Ithaca: Cornell University Press, 1981); Sean Kelly, *America's Tyrant: The CIA and Mobutu of Zaire* (Lanham, Md.: American University Press, 1993); William Roger Louis, *Imperialism at Bay, 1941–1945: The United States and the Decolonization of the British Empire* (Oxford: Clarendon Press, 1977); H. W. Brands, *The Specter of Neutralism: The United States and the Emergence of the Third World, 1947–1960* (New York: Columbia University Press, 1989); David N. Gibbs, *The Political Economy of Third World Intervention: Mines, Money, and U.S. Policy in the Congo Crisis* (Chicago: University of Chicago Press, 1991); Richard D. Mahoney, *JFK: Ordeal in Africa* (New York: Oxford University Press, 1983); Kwame Nkrumah, *The Challenge of the Congo* (New York: International Publishers, 1967); and Stephen Weissman, *American Foreign Policy in the Congo, 1960–1964* (Ithaca: Cornell University Press, 1974).

43. Mary L. Dudziak, "Desegregation as a Cold War Imperative," *Stanford Law Review* 41 (Nov. 1988): 61–120.

44. Azza Salama Layton, "International Pressure and the U.S. Government's Response to Little Rock," *Arkansas Historical Quarterly* 56 (Autumn 1997): 257–72. See also the definitive article on this subject by Mary Dudziak, "The Little Rock Crisis and Foreign Affairs: Race, Resistance, and the Image of American Democracy," *Southern California Law Review* 70 (Sept. 1997): 1641–1716.

45. Penny Von Eschen, *Race against Empire: Black Americans and Anticolonialism, 1937–1957* (Ithaca: Cornell University Press, 1997); Brenda Gayle Plummer, *Rising Wind: Black Americans and U.S. Foreign Affairs, 1935–1960* (Chapel Hill: University of North Carolina Press, 1996); Robert Weisbord, *Ebony Kinship: Africa, Africans and the Afro-Americans* (Westport, Conn.: Greenwood Press, 1973); Jake C. Miller, *The Black Presence in American Foreign Affairs* (Washington, D.C.: University Press of America, 1978); Lewis V. Baldwin, *Toward the Beloved Community: Martin Luther King, Jr. and South Africa* (Cleveland: Pilgrim Press, 1995); Gerald R. Gill, "Afro-American Opposition to the United States' Wars of the Twentieth Century: Dissent, Discontent and Disinterest" (Ph.D. diss., Howard University, 1985); Austin M. Chakaodza, *International Diplomacy in Southern Africa: From Reagan to Mandela* (London: Third World, 1990); and Patrick J. Furlong, *Between Crown and*

Swastika: The Impact of the Radical Right on the Afrikaner Nationalist Movement in the Fascist Era (Hanover, N.H.: Wesleyan University Press, 1991).

46. "Stenogram: Meeting of the Communist Party of the Soviet Union and the Chinese Communist Party, Moscow, 5–20 July 1963," *Cold War International History Project*, no. 10 (Mar. 1998): 175–82.

47. Sir Roy Welensky to Dean Acheson, 30 July 1971, Dean Acheson Papers, box 34, Sterling Memorial Library, Yale University, New Haven, Conn. For a fuller exploration of the U.S.-Rhodesian axis, see Gerald Horne, "Gangsters, 'Whiteness,' Reactionary Politics and the U.S.-Rhodesian Connection," *Southern Africa Political and Economic Monthly* 9, 2 (1995): 31–34. See also Gerald Horne, *From the Barrel of a Gun: The U.S. and the War against Zimbabwe, 1965–1980* (Chapel Hill: University of North Carolina Press, 2001).

48. Dean Acheson to Sir Roy Welensky, 7 Oct. 1971, Acheson Papers. Sir Roy had a virtual obsession with China: "I heard the announcement that China had put her first satellite into orbit. I noticed our newspapers this morning treated it as almost a minor event—I consider it one of the most serious bits of news I have listened to for a long time!" Sir Roy Welensky to Dean Acheson, 27 Apr. 1970, Acheson Papers.

49. Robert Kinloch Massie, *Loosing the Bonds: The United States and South Africa in the Apartheid Years* (New York: Doubleday, 1997); Thomas Borstelmann, *Apartheid's Reluctant Uncle: The United States and Southern Africa in the Early Cold War* (New York: Oxford University Press, 1993); Janice Love, *The U.S. Anti-Apartheid Movement: Local Activism in Global Politics* (New York: Praeger, 1985).

50. Ian Smith, *The Great Betrayal: The Memoirs of Ian Douglas Smith* (London: Blake, 1997), 24, 202.

51. Juanita Roberts to Kevin Lee, 24 Apr. 1966, National Security File, Country File, Rhodesia, box 97, Lyndon Baines Johnson Papers, Johnson Library, Austin, Tex.

52. A. R. W. Stumbles, *Some Recollections of a Rhodesian Speaker* (Bulawayo, Rhodesia: Books of Rhodesia, 1980), 171.

53. Angus Graham to Dean Acheson, 1 July 1968, Acheson Papers.

54. Dean Acheson to Angus Graham, 23 July 1968, ibid.

55. *Sunday Mail* (Rhodesia), 10 June 1979.

56. Kevin Phillips, *The Emerging Republican Majority* (New Rochelle, N.Y.: Arlington House, 1969); Dan T. Carter, *From George Wallace to Newt Gingrich: Race and the Conservative Counter-Revolution, 1963–1994* (Baton Rouge: Louisiana State University Press, 1996).

57. Michael Schaller, *The American Occupation of Japan: The Origins of the Cold War in Asia* (New York: Oxford University Press, 1985); Myles I. C. Robertson, *Soviet Policy toward Japan: An Analysis of Trends in the 1970s and 1980s* (New York: Cambridge University Press, 1988); Charles E. Ziegler, *Foreign Policy and East Asia: Learning and Adaptation in the Gorbachev Era* (New York: Cambridge University Press, 1993).

58. Frank Dikotter, ed., *The Construction of Racial Identities in China and Japan* (Honolulu: University of Hawaii Press, 1997); Frank Dikotter, *The Discourse of Race in Modern China* (Stanford: Stanford University Press, 1992); Alf Hiltebeitel and Barbara Miller, eds., *Hair in Asian Cultures: Context and Change* (Albany: SUNY Press, 1997); Benjamin Schwartz, *In Search of Wealth and Power: Yen Fu and the West* (Cambridge, Mass.: Belknap Press of Harvard University Press, 1964); Yoshino Kosaku, *Cultural Nationalism in Japan* (London: Routledge, 1992); Cullen T. Hayashida, "Identity, Race and the Blood Ideology of Japan" (Ph.D. diss., University of

Washington, 1976). Despite the paucity of Jewish people in Japan, there has been a persistent strain of anti-Semitism in that nation and, to an extent, in the region. See David G. Goodman and Masanori Miyazawa, *Jews in the Japanese Mind: The History and Uses of a Cultural Stereotype* (New York: Free Press, 1995); David Kranzler, *Japanese, Nazis and Jews: The Jewish Refugee Community in Shanghai, 1938–1945* (New York: Yeshiva University Press, 1976); James R. Ross, *Escape to Shanghai: A Jewish Community in China* (New York: Maxwell Macmillan International, 1994); and Ernest G. Heppner, *Shanghai Refugee: A Memoir of the World War II Jewish Ghetto* (Lincoln: University of Nebraska Press, 1993).

59. Robert Jackson, *The Malayan Emergency: The Commonwealth's Wars, 1948–1966* (New York: Routledge, 1991); Donald W. Hamilton, *The Art of Insurgency: American Military Policy and the Failure of Strategy in Southeast Asia* (New York: Praeger, 1998); Edgar O'Ballance, *Malaya: The Communist Insurgent War, 1948–1960* (London: Faber and Faber, 1966); Richard Stubbs, *Hearts and Minds in Guerrilla Warfare: The Malayan Emergency, 1948–1960* (New York: Oxford University Press, 1989); Robert Thompson, *Defeating Communist Insurgency: The Lessons of Malaya and Vietnam* (New York: Praeger, 1966).

60. Mahatir Mohamad and Shintaro Isihara, *The Voice of Asia: Two Leaders Discuss the Coming Century* (Tokyo: Kodansha International, 1995), 22, 29, 53, 90, 98, 134.

61. *Far Eastern Economic Review*, 19, 26 Mar. and 2 Apr. 1998.

62. See generally Gerald Horne, *Fire This Time: The Watts Uprising and the 1960s* (Charlottesville: University of Virginia Press, 1995).

63. Gerald Horne, *Reversing Discrimination: The Case for Affirmative Action* (New York: International Publishers, 1992); Joe L. Kincheloe, Shirley R. Steinberg, and Aaron D. Gresson III, eds., *Measured Lies: The Bell Curve Examined* (New York: St. Martin's Press, 1996).

64. See, for example, Michael Pillsbury, ed., *Chinese Views of Future Warfare* (Washington, D.C.: National Defense University Press, 1997); Richard Bernstein and Ross H. Munro, *The Coming Conflict with China* (New York: A. A. Knopf, 1997); Ezra Vogel, *Living with China: U.S.-China Relations in the 21st Century* (New York: W. W. Norton, 1997); Daniel Burstein and Arne De Keijzer, *Big Dragon: China's Future: What It Means for Business, the Economy and the Global Order* (New York: Simon and Schuster, 1998); Nicholas Kristof and Sheryl WuDunn, *China Wakes: The Struggle for the Soul of a Rising Power* (New York: Vintage, 1995); Edward Gargan, *China's Fate: A People's Turbulent Struggle with Reform and Repression, 1980–1990* (New York: Doubleday, 1990); Kenneth Lieberthal, *Governing China: From Revolution through Reform* (New York: W. W. Norton, 1995).

65. Samuel P. Huntington, *The Clash of Civilizations and the Remaking of World Order* (New York: Simon and Schuster, 1996).

66. Peter Ratcliffe, ed., *"Race," Ethnicity and Nation: International Perspectives on Social Conflict* (London: UCL Press, 1994); Robert Miles, *Racism after "Race" Relations* (New York: Routledge, 1993); Anthony Marx, *Making Race and Nation: A Comparison of the United States, South Africa and Brazil* (New York: Cambridge University Press, 1998).

Brown Babies

Race, Gender, and Policy
after World War II

"Brown babies," a euphemism the black press popularized, were the children born of European women and African American soldiers during the World War II era. Their confused civil status, mixed-race identity, and urgent material needs engaged the complex intersection of race and gender as it unfolded after 1945. Brown babies were born as regimes of racial domination toppled in Europe and Asia, and as racist ideologies lost credibility in the United States. U.S. legal segregation survived the Third Reich, but the seeds of its demise had already germinated by war's end. Existentially at the margins of the postwar experience, mixed-race war orphans embodied the conflicts over fundamental meanings that so characterized the age. This essay examines these children's place in the broader context of postwar decision making and demonstrates the intimate relationship between their plight and American designs for the future, two subjects generally treated as entirely separate in historical scholarship.

By 1945 the army had already circumscribed the status of mulatto children yet to be born. In the European Theater of Operations (ETO), commanding officers could veto or approve GI marriages on their own discretion. Few black soldiers were allowed to marry British and Italian women, for example, even when they had fathered their children.[1] Commanding officers likewise blocked interracial marriages in Germany, where some 1,500 brown babies were born. The brass's interest in racial endogamy took priority over the welfare of children as they sought to preserve proprietary attitudes toward women and the racist and sexist social divisions maintained in peacetime at home. The brown babies' story captures the United States at an important time of transition, before contemporary attitudes naturalized the practice of interracial adoption and when the public perceived mixed-race children as novelties.

In the 1940s and 1950s, mixed-race families were uncommon objects of curiosity and disapproval. The initial military response toward the brown babies involved secrecy and suppression. Social workers, including the sympathetic, joined U.S. Army authorities in trying to quiet the issue, claiming that black newspapers in the United States were cheaply sensationalizing it. At a time when African American public opinion endorsed maximum black participation in the armed forces, some civilian leaders and military officials alike feared the brown baby could become a tar baby: boomeranging, achieving domestic notoriety, and lending credence to those who advocated black troop reductions in Europe.[2]

Brown babies remained mostly invisible to mainstream audiences, but their popularity with African American readers as human-interest stories kept them in print. Racial transgression was the key to the fascination they generated, as were the interracial exploits of black soldiers in Europe generally. The unusual circumstances of war and occupation provided opportunities for African Americans to thumb their noses at Jim Crow prohibitions, and black readers enjoyed accounts of how this was done.[3] Sympathy among black Americans for mixed-race war orphans was not, however, a foregone conclusion. In the slavery era, white men sired most mulattoes in socially mismatched relationships that reflected the inferior status of the black mother in particular and of all black persons in general. After emancipation, both whites and blacks continued to associate first-generation mulattoes with bastardy. Although the customary U.S. practice of hypodescent—a law in some southern states—made anyone with visible African ancestry black, African Americans did not necessarily believe that all mulattoes shared a broadly conceived African American ethnic culture or inhabited its psychological milieu. It is telling that, as late as 1959, authorities found it difficult to place abandoned American-born mulatto orphans with either black or white parents.[4]

Military policy placed obstacles in the path of normalizing family life for mulatto children born overseas of black fathers and white mothers. Some of these unions were essentially exchange agreements motivated by crisis, where the destitution of one partner encountered the comparative power and opportunism of the other. U.S. policy toward Germany shortly after its defeat in 1945 was initially harsh, although substantially moderated over the course of the occupation period. Military authorities decided that the German population, as a whole responsible for choosing and sustaining the Nazi regime, should enjoy no priority in the distribution of food and health resources. Only after the needs of the liberated countries were addressed would German living standards be allowed to rise.[5]

Hunger motivated many European women at the end of the war to seek intimate relationships with foreign soldiers. Cynthia Enloe suggests that privation can be understood as a form of coercion. "A military base," Enloe writes, is "a package of presumptions about male soldiers' sexual needs and about the local community's resources for satisfying those needs."[6] The power relationships created from the circumstances of the occupation eroticized German destitution and defeat through submissive and prostituted women. Ute Frevert characterizes the "borderline between rape and prostitution" in the Western zones of occupation as "a fluid one: many American and British soldiers paid for their pleasures in cigarettes, chocolate and bread." A population on the brink of starvation, in early 1947 taking in, on average, 850 calories a day, often condoned the illicit relations between Allied soldiers and local women, both married and single. The Nazi instrumentalist view of women also helped prepare the ground that exigency fertilized.[7]

Army officials did not leave the regulation of sexual relations between soldiers and women in occupied countries in wartime to chance. Monitoring prostitution and other sexual relations was a military necessity that, in Enloe's words, "required explicit American policy-making." How did military authorities regulate, and condone, what they claimed to oppose?[8] Although brown babies were born in Britain[9] and Italy as well as Germany, Germany's unique history and former status as an adversary provide a distinctly privileged view of the intersections of race and gender. Military leaders from a country where race governed social relations—the United States—were confronted by a nation where race had also played a powerful role in constructing the identity of its recently defeated government. How did U.S. officials negotiate these rocky shoals at a historical moment when both nations faced multiple social and political challenges?

In any war, personal relationships, whether romantic or commercial, develop between occupiers and nationals. In Germany, although ranking U.S. officers usually viewed interracial relationships negatively, they pursued policies that, given the cultural imperatives they shared with enlisted men, made such relationships inevitable. Men who served in World War II, regardless of rank, tended to assume that all soldiers would seek sexual outlets. The solution to the problem of interracial sex should then be providing acceptable partners for black soldiers.

The U.S. military was never completely candid about the roles played by female USO workers and by "Government Girls," the thousands of women civilians recruited to white-collar positions during the war. Ostensibly, these were "nice girls" with whom soldiers could socialize, nonprostitutes who provided an alternative to commercial sex.[10] For the black GIs in Germany, however, no African American equivalents existed at first. The military resisted hiring black women civilians to staff the many clerical positions that the occupation government had created. Segregation decreed that black and white Government Girls could not room together, and residences were available only for the whites. The lack of housing for female African American stenographers and clerks meant that they could not be stationed in Germany, adding another twist to the contradictions surrounding race and gender. Even though many U.S. officers believed that contact with women was an important perquisite for soldiers, black soldiers were thus cut off from both "respectable" and tawdry social outlets.[11]

Government disapproval of both interracial sexual liaisons *and* the presence of black women illustrates how official thinking about race and sex contradicted itself. Another example is white American reluctance to strip defeated German *men* of their racial privileges. The army initially tried to avoid assigning black troops to police work that would elevate them to positions of authority over Germans. Although the desire to respect local sensibilities provided the pretext, it should be noted that, in many parts of the United States at the time, black police officers had limited authority over white civilians, which typically prevented them from making arrests across the color line. Marcus H. Ray, aide to the secretary of war and adviser on matters related to black soldiers, found army policy in this matter indefensible. "To accept the prejudices of the German people as a reason for nonutilization of the American soldier who happens to be nonwhite," he wrote, "is to negate the very ideals we have made a part of our reeducation program in Germany."[12] Ray might have also argued that it defeated the purpose of the war itself, including the massive propaganda campaign that had been mounted against Nazi racism.

The exaggerated high status of American white women as compared with German women in the U.S. zone of occupation also reflects contradictions in U.S. thought and practice. German women did not receive in identical measure the skin and gender privileges that they would have had as white women in America. As citizens of a nation with whom the United States had engaged in bitter and protracted war, they were, in the early years of the occupation, particular targets of hostility from a high command that tacitly encouraged sexual exploitation. This included the creation by a *Stars and Stripes* cartoonist of a buffoonish female character, Veronica Dankeschön ["thank you very much"], referred to as V. D., with acronymic reference to sexually transmitted disease. The plump, hapless Veronica wore the plain braids of the Nazi era and a skirt hemmed with swastikas.[13] Her stereotype enhanced a climate that made possible U.S. military "vice raids" to punish women who clearly were not prostitutes.

In an illustrative incident in Coburg, the Office of the Military Government of the United States (OMGUS) strained its relations with local German leaders after MPs detained "many prominent women of the city, including the Burgermeister's daughter, the wives of prominent businessmen, etc." According to official reports, "they were picked up as they left the opera, stores, etc." Only unaccompanied women were arrested; those with GI escorts were spared. The Coburg raid reneged on an agreement that OMGUS had made to consult German authorities and to refrain from taking women into custody during hours when "respectable" women were on the street.[14] Both occupiers and nationals thus enforced the distinction between "good" and "bad" women.

As a result of its violation of tacitly understood rules, the Coburg raid demonstrates the contours of a bureaucratic control system. U.S. officials, with the acquiescence of local authorities, had first created a double standard. Then, using public health as a rationale, they proceeded to obliterate the standard. The epidemic rate of sexually transmitted diseases among the troops and the creation of an emergency around that statistical fact provided a pretext for the erasure of German women's respectability.

The improbable vice raids were probably intended in part to harass the German population and were especially directed toward humiliating women. Apart from the embarrassment of the arrest itself, it was often followed by coerced physical tests for venereal disease. "Patients" complained of rough treatment, doctors who examined them vaginally using cold and dirty specula, and an ethos where medical attendants could be bribed to provide written proof of negative results. In the spring of 1947 authorities conducted a "surprise medical examination" of women working in an OMGUS cafeteria in Bavaria. The German employees and the community at large disbelieved the diagnosis that eleven of the workers, including an elderly woman, had gonorrhea, and demanded that a German physician reexamine them. Some thought the examination a ploy to fire women who would be replaced by girlfriends of some of the U.S. officers. When the supposedly infected women refused treatment, they were forcibly hospitalized, where a second culture tested negative.[15]

The venereal disease problem in the U.S. military, the ostensible reason for these measures, had a racial angle. Infection rates among black troops in some units were as high as six or seven times that of whites, and the high rate had played a major role in the postwar decision to demobilize large numbers of black troops. MPs disproportionately targeted for arrest those German women who dated black GIs, claiming that they had been shown to have higher rates of infection than those who dated white Americans.[16] During the latter years of the occupation, military authorities toned down the Veronica Dankeschön persona as well as the vice raids, ultimately finding both counterproductive. Dwight P. Griswold, director of OMGUS Internal Affairs and Communications Division, disapproved of these tactics. "Mass examinations of civilian women and so-called 'vice raids' conducted solely to discover cases of venereal disease," he held, "are unsound and hazardous to ideological objectives in Germany." Griswold believed them "wasteful of time and facilities." "Unit commanders . . . conducting venereal disease control activities outside of prescribed channels" hampered German efforts to control sexually transmitted disease among civilians. The brass came to recognize that this modus operandi did not pay off in reducing the infection rate or identifying more than 20 percent of the local women believed to be carriers.[17]

The militant approach to vice, generally discredited by the late 1940s, nevertheless persisted when interracial sex was involved. In the Rhineland-Palatinate, local authorities punished most severely women accused of prostituting themselves to black men. In Kreuznacht, a black soldier and a German woman were arrested when they could not prove that they were engaged in a serious relationship because they did not have the permit required of engaged couples. When the soldier, in his fiancée's company, later asked his commanding officer for a marriage application, the incredulous CO asked the prospective bride why she would wed a black man. Indignant, the GI berated his superior, which only earned him a demotion.[18]

In Birkenfeld, a woman was charged with prostitution for allowing black soldiers to buy her a drink. Local authorities resented the fact that blacks subject to segregation laws in their own country had so much freedom in Germany. According to Maria Höhn, when German civilians were no longer hungry after 1951, their friendliness toward black soldiers diminished. When Germany regained sovereignty in 1955, criminal prosecutions of interracial friendships increased substantially while white Americans romantically involved with Germans were left alone. A curtain of white endogamy was drawn over such relationships while "Veronica Dankeschön" was now defined and prosecuted as a woman who slept with blacks. Such associations, more than ever defined as illicit, were driven into lower-class neighborhoods more likely to be targeted by police.[19]

On the American side, racial prejudice could drive hostility toward German women and black men alike. A group of German women boarded the army transport USS *Henry Gibbins* in spring 1949. The Carrie Chapman Catt Foundation had invited them to the United States to study democratic institutions. The army housed them "next to the stokers' quarters" in an unheated stateroom. The women had to walk through the black crews' berths to get to their lavatory and were forced to eat the leftovers of American passengers and use their soiled napkins. Black sailors, who felt sorry for them, slipped them fresh food and water on the sly. The character of the official disrespect shown here is revealing; it would have been unthinkable to house middle-class white American women in the bowels of a ship next to low-

ranking black troops with whom they would be forced into physical contact
on such an intimate level. In the context of U.S. racial conventions and stereo-
types of the period, the berth assignment was an open invitation to the black
soldiers to rape these unwanted passengers. The black GIs got the message
and stood it on its ear—instead extending courtesies to the unlucky passengers.[20] Military propaganda and practice thus helped create an image of the
immoral and unworthy German woman that contrasted sharply with that of
the good American wife, presumably waiting patiently and virtuously at
home. Race played a vital role in this construction.

Germany's former adversary status influenced all relationships between
Americans and Germans during the occupation. Contemporary observers believed that most of the children GIs fathered in Germany were born to married women whose husbands were absent. Early estimates of the numbers of
such babies ranged from 30,000 to 52,000, of which some 3,000 were believed
to be mulattoes. Germans joked that, in case of another war, the United States
would not need to send any more soldiers, just new uniforms. Children sired
by white Americans could often slip through the cracks of the German nationality law's insistence on "blood," their legitimacy contested only by returning husbands. Black infants could not disappear into German society in
this way and presented a prima facie case of bastardy.[21]

The vanquished Third Reich's commitment to racism provided an ironic
note. From the standpoint of Nazi eugenics, the brown babies were part of what
the war had been fought to prevent. As conditions deteriorated in Germany
by mid-April 1945, Himmler tried to barter concentration camp prisoners'
lives for Allied pledges that the SS would be treated like ordinary prisoners
of war and that black soldiers would not be among the army of occupation.[22]
Allied policy making reflected awareness of such antiblack sentiments in Germany. John R. McCloy, assistant secretary of war, wondered if the Office of
War Information and the Bureau of Public Relations should prepare Germans
"for the possible use of Negro troops as components of the occupation force."
Lieutenant General Thomas T. Hardy, assistant chief of staff, saw black troop
deployment as "governed entirely by operational needs" and saw no need to
consult the locals. Hardy believed a special campaign to orient Germans to
the black presence would "lead to unfortunate publicity in the United States."
He advised against any such initiative.[23]

The concern over black troops as occupiers had a history that predated
Himmler. After the Allied victory in World War I, France and Belgium had
sent colonial troops to Germany. The foreign garrisons at that time included
Africans, Arabs, and Vietnamese, much to German chagrin. All the German
political parties except the Socialists signed a parliamentary petition calling

for the withdrawal of these armies of color on racial purity grounds. A small number of mulatto children were born as a result of this occupation. Hitler, after coming to power in 1933, moved slowly on the question of mixed-race Germans. For the next four years, certain mulattoes were courted. May Opitz writes: "In consideration of foreign policy interests, caution was exercised not to allow the abuse of Africans and Afro-Germans to go beyond certain bounds. A note of warning from the Foreign Office stated: 'Let us not forget, now that the accusations against Germany over the Jewish question are beginning to abate somewhat, that we must not allow the colored question to provide new substance to the enemy propaganda in the struggle against the new Germany.' In order not to antagonize foreign diplomats traveling to Germany and thereby jeopardize trade relations, a campaign was even begun against xenophobia." At first, German officials perceived certain resident blacks as potentially valuable intermediaries should Germany once again become a colonial power in Africa. By the late 1930s, however, this view yielded increasingly to those who favored extermination and sterilization.[24]

Following the Allied conquest of Italy in 1943, German propaganda had emphasized to Italians the racial dangers that a black American military presence presented. A notable propaganda poster depicted a drunken, leering GI with one simian arm around the waist of the chaste, marble Venus de Milo, on which he had placed a $2 price tag. Planning for the occupation of Germany envisaged the United States, Soviet Union, and Britain providing most of the garrisons. The Big Three did not want to exclude France for political reasons but were not enthusiastic about its participation, having learned that the Free French were readying 175,000 French and 275,000 French African troops in Africa.[25]

African Americans did participate in the Rhineland occupation, where they encountered hostility from local officialdom and the press. Firmly associated with crime, vice (both heterosexual and homosexual), and venereal disease in the eyes of the police and sectarian welfare agencies, black soldiers had a poor reputation. Infractions committed by anonymous American soldiers were routinely attributed to blacks, without proof. German newspapers exaggerated the number of blacks, as they had done in the previous war.[26] Racial distinctions and the preservation of white skin privilege would be a point of friction in postwar race relations.

In Giessen, black labor units were made to work alongside POW labor gangs, both supervised by white Americans. Similar problems occurred in the United States as well. At Camp Andrews in Maryland, black women PX workers were fired and replaced by German POWs hired at sixty cents a day. Stories abound of the favorable treatment of ex-Nazis in public accommodations and other facilities.[27] What this meant to patriotic black veterans was explained by one of them to Ollie Harrington. "You fought, if you are a Negro veteran, to tear down the sign 'No Jews Allowed' in Germany, to find in America the sign 'No Negroes Allowed.' You fought to wipe out the noose and the whip in Germany and Japan, to find the noose and the whip in Georgia and Louisiana. One veteran put it to me this way: 'I got through fighting in the E.T.O.,' he said, 'and now I've got to fight in the S.T.O.' I asked, 'What's the S.T.O.?' He said, 'Haven't you heard? The Southern Theater of Operations, U.S.A.'"[28]

While the Grand Alliance did not ban black troops as Himmler wished, it made futile efforts to discourage fraternization between black Allied troops and German citizens. Petra Goedde has argued that the initial military policy that prohibited fraternization between German nationals and occupying U.S. troops was widely flouted because most social contacts among Germans and American soldiers involved women. The scarcity of German men in the civilian population and the perception of women as not only relatively harmless but helpless and in need of protection led to what Goedde calls the "feminization of Germany" in the minds of soldiers and policy makers alike.[29] Once tamed, little separated Germany from an Americanization that some Germans and Americans alike thought desirable. The activities of women in this feminized nation were of political interest to those concerned about Germany's future. "Public discourse in the media and among social critics," Katherine Pence writes, "often made the Americanizing transformation of women's bodies, women's identities, and women's role in German society a site for voicing anxieties about the reconstruction of the German state and civil society within an American alliance."[30] From a race-conscious perspective, Germany, once feminized and Americanized, was now subject to the peculiar racial taboos that infected sexual relations in U.S. culture.

As of 9 August 1947, the U.S. Army had not approved any applications from black soldiers who wished to marry German women. This did not prevent sexual liaisons from developing, however, and the number of mulatto children steadily rose.[31] Reporter William Nunn, on an army-sponsored tour of the ETO, described the improvised communities that resulted. "Now that the sun has brought warm weather to Bavaria . . . Munich . . . Frankfort . . . Mannheim and other sections thickly populated by Negro soldiers . . . the streets adjoining and approaching Kasernes where Negro troops are stationed, are rendezvous for many attractive Frauleins wheeling carriages bearing their sons and daughters. The girls appear to be happy and jubilant."[32]

Black journalist Cliff MacKay also took a sanguine view. "The tan babies at present are unquestionably the most healthy in Germany, for the simple reason that they are the best fed," he wrote. "It is not an uncommon sight to see these mothers walking up and down in front of colored military posts at mess time, waiting for the fathers of their children to bring out food no other Germans can enjoy." The underground economy worked in their favor. According to MacKay, "A soldier can secure care for a child and mother for a whole week for one package of cigarettes, currently valued on the black market at 80 marks."[33]

Neither reporter focused on what worried less casual observers. What would happen to these army dependents once the GIs left Germany? No one at the time predicted the intensity and longevity of the standoff between the Soviets and the West that wrecked the Grand Alliance. It was reasonable to assume that the military occupation would end after a specified time and that connections forged in the interim would consequently be altered. Close examination had already revealed that German women with mulatto children received a different response in their own communities when no Americans were present, and that charities did not give them the same consideration as other needy Germans. Nunn heard rumors about "brown babies" being killed, sold, and displayed in carnivals. Such stories revived fears of Germany's all-too-recent Nazi past. Even if such tales were exaggerations, how would Germany's mulatto children be socialized? How would they assimilate into German society and what future would they have? The number of children who were not cared for by their birth mothers further clouded the matter. One group lived in an orphanage in Frankfurt where many were reportedly afraid of black adults.[34]

A strong current of opinion among African Americans favored fathers' assumption of responsibility. Reporter Ollie Stewart criticized black GIs who abandoned their children and girlfriends. GIs were quick to respond that they faced the major problem, as in Britain, of surmounting the obstacles to expatriation, including the army's initial ban on all German-American marriages and, subsequently, its continued prohibition of interracial marriages.[35] In spite of these difficulties, many black soldiers bucked the trend. According to statistics of the German Association for Public and Private Assistance, 9 to 10 percent of all U.S. soldiers paid child support. Within that group, black soldiers constituted 25 percent of those making payments.[36]

In June 1946 an act of Congress permitted GIs to bring home prospective "war brides" during fiscal year 1946–47 on ninety-day visitors' visas, but the army did not permit its enactment until December of that year. It then created stipulations designed to delay and restrict these unions. Even unit commanders often failed to understand the complicated rules. Only GIs with less than six and more than three months left to serve could apply to marry a German national. Permissions routinely took three months to process, and often the soldier was shipped out before the papers came through. Even the successful applicants had difficulties. Prospective immigrants still had to run a gauntlet of medical examinations, denazification certification, character examination by a cleric, clearance by intelligence officials, and approval by a joint travel-security agency. They then faced the expense and scarcity of travel during a period when nonmilitary transport remained restricted.[37]

The degree of scrutiny that newly constituted German-American families faced regarding their moral fitness and political conformity was an extension of pacification policies and eerily echoed the certification policies of the Third Reich. The opposition to paternal adoption reinforced the status boundaries between conquerors and the vanquished. Needy mothers who could not marry the fathers of their children had no recourse but to apply for charitable assistance. U.S. military archives are filled with "Dear Jane" letters in which officials inform German women that they cannot help them.[38] The stringent rules derived from the extraterritorial rights that the United States bestowed upon itself. The terms of the occupation dictated that German courts, which ruled on adoptions of all children born in Germany of a German mother, did not have jurisdiction over Americans. Neither could "a competent court" simply expatriate German-born orphans for adoption in the United States because the State Department would not issue visas for orphans lacking a determination of paternity. Those courts, however, could not determine that an American had fathered a child by a German woman without the permission of the military government.[39]

In an age when legitimacy held considerable social weight, the army had made every mixed-race child of a black serviceman *necessarily* a bastard. In so doing, it ironically replicated slavery-era principles that guaranteed the anonymity of mulattoes' fathers. Policy made history repeat itself in yet another respect. The shedding of paternal responsibility was a proxy for the shedding of national responsibility. This abdication went all the way to the top. As early as February 1945, when Eleanor Roosevelt approached her husband about brown babies in England, FDR had replied, "I think this is a British problem—not American."[40]

Race posed other obstacles to family constitution. Military judges relied on the laws of the various states to determine whether a proposed union could be approved and compiled the relevant statutes for their own use. Racial record keeping on marriages began in 1947. German courts followed this example. The Allies, having struck down the Nuremberg laws and made explicit reference to the abrogation of the 1935 "Law for the Protection of German Blood and German Honor," oddly found themselves reapplying such legislation in the American zone of occupation where the German courts followed suit.[41] The Legal Affairs Division's correspondence suggests that it took racial identification seriously in matters of both marriage and adoption. A soldier from a state where interracial marriages were illegal would have his application to marry outside his race rejected. That Americans were not bound to remain in the states where they lived before the war did not seem to dawn on anyone.[42] Additionally, as one military official noted in reply to a German agency's inquiry, "the adoption laws of some of the states of the U.S.A. require that a colored child can only be adopted by a colored adopter and a white child only by a white adopter."[43] Texas and Louisiana forbade the adoption of a child by a prospective parent of different race. South Carolina restricted the adoption of children born out of wedlock *and* limited the inheritance rights of those who did find adoptive parents. This hypocrisy was not lost on the Germans, and it fed into an indigenous racism that never disappeared.

Legal difficulties and tacit understandings about race and sex, inflected by the bitterness of wartime, helped delay the beginning of positive responses to mixed-race orphans among African Americans. Just as the episode aboard the USS *Henry Gibbins* underscored the use of race as a marker of subordination, under certain circumstances blacks could "borrow" the identity of the white American conquerors. A *Baltimore Afro-American* feature story described black officers who retained German house servants at thirty dollars a month. The article's accompanying photograph showed a humble German maid serving dinner to a black military man and his wife. In addition to the reversal of German fortunes that the story highlighted, the employment by blacks of white servants also stood customary American race relations on their head and inverted the traditional subservience of black women to white women. From the German domestic's perspective, such jobs commanded vastly higher wages than they could otherwise make, even if some of their compatriots regarded maids who worked for blacks as little better than prostitutes.[44]

Pittsburgh Courier reporter William Nunn, investigating the brown baby question in 1948, found that black servicemen's wives did not sympathize with the mixed-race orphans or their German mothers. The war had enabled the African American army wife to be an honorary white vis-à-vis Germans. She could discuss the "servant problem" in Germany just as glibly as any other American housewife. "A white epidermis here is just nothing at all," journalist J. A. Rogers observed of European society a few years later. "The masses are poor and color doesn't help. In America it's only the presence of the Negro that gives any value to a white skin."[45] With such unpromising beginnings, what would explain why the black public came to register a concern about the children that black soldiers had left behind in Europe? Here is a case where official policy, evolving cultural attitudes, and large-scale social change collide.

Black Americans shared the ethos of the time. The war had created the terms of citizenship. Society had wanted warriors and defense workers; now the site of production of good citizens had shifted to the family. Blacks were as ready as whites to return to a domesticity once seen as subversive of the war effort and now hailed as the next correct thing to do.[46] Americans renewed their interest in child rearing as the troops came home, a concern reflected in the surging birthrate. Adoption became an increasingly attractive option for infertile couples as the public interest in parenting began to neutralize earlier reservations about the practice. The large numbers of Asian orphans created by World War II and the Korean War also provided an opportunity to link adoption to Cold War concerns. Destitute children could become a destabilizing factor in the power relations between the Eastern and Western blocs. "I have returned from overseas with the realization that the Communists care enough to make very successful capital of democracy's failures," wrote the founder of the Christian Children's Fund. This Richmond, Virginia–based social service agency supported foreign orphanages because of "the strong conviction that we Americans can not close our eyes or stop our ears to the cry of a hungry child anywhere in the world."[47]

There was so much demand for young children that by 1947 a domestic black market in white infants had developed. In the course of the late 1940s many state legislatures changed their adoption laws to require licensing for agencies, establishing conditions under which parental rights could be terminated, guardianship constituted, and the like.[48] The end of racial segregation among adoption agencies also became a practical possibility for the future. In New York City, revised Department of Welfare regulations withdrew city financial support to institutions and agencies that discriminated against black children. Some social workers persisted in the view that black children were unadoptable, and non-tax-supported, private organizations continued to set their own standards. Government's expanding role in child welfare, however, foreshadowed integrationist policies in the coming era.[49]

Black communities and organizations shared this natalist enthusiasm. The New York Urban League began an "Adopt a Child Project." Photographs of children were featured more frequently in black newspapers, which paid substantial attention, for example, to the Fultz quadruplets of Madison, North Carolina. Multiple births, unassisted then by drugs, were rare, and pictures of the Fultz girls, born in 1946, provided ample human interest during the years of their infancy and toddlerhood.[50] The unprecedented prosperity of the late 1940s for blacks and the sense of optimism attendant on the end of the war also facilitated a *black* baby boom. Like whites, blacks who either could not conceive offspring of their own or wished to enlarge their families through adoption became more aware than previously of the orphan pool.

Rickie Solinger, in her study of teenage, out-of-wedlock pregnancy in the 1950s, has indicated that white girls were much more likely than black ones to place their children for adoption. Indeed, pregnancy and childbirth for the unwed teenage mother of white middle-class origin was often shrouded in secrecy and shame.[51] While a similar sense of shame affected many black unwed mothers, black families were comparatively more accepting of such offspring and more likely to keep them within the family. The scarcity of black children as subjects for adoption, then, was not only a product of the disinterest of whites in adopting nonwhite children but also a result of such children's relative acceptance in black communities and consequent unavailability. Adoption of foreign nonwhite children was still rare among whites, although some liberal social workers advocated it. The domestic shortage of orphans consequently made the adoption of brown babies a possibility for black Americans.[52]

It is important to note that some of the racial barriers challenged during the late 1940s involved direct assaults on white social exclusiveness. Unlike the era of *Brown v. Board of Education*, with its comparatively impersonal focus on the desegregation of institutions and facilities, the 1940s faced such intimate issues as marriage, residence, and family formation head on. In most instances, World War II had been the enabler. The legality of interracial marriages, which the Supreme Court would ultimately decide in a 1967 case, *Loving v. Virginia*, became a heated issue during this period. Military leaders partially ducked it by assigning the few black soldiers with white wives to posts outside the South. Snafus did occur, as in the case of one couple posted to Dixie in error. The unlucky pair went to jail following their attempt to rent off-base housing.[53] Other challenges to housing practices, in the wake of the 1948 Supreme Court cases *Shelley v. Kraemer* and *Hurd*, resulted from the domestic effects of the war.

The Cold War conflicts that developed between the United States and the USSR after World War II came rapidly to a head in Germany, culminating in the circumstances that led to the Berlin airlift of 1948. The Soviets had been criticized in the Western press for their dogged unwillingness to cooperate on numerous matters. One of these was the refusal to permit Soviet war brides to join British and American husbands. The Soviet press in turn was more than happy to rake the United States over the coals for its Jim Crow racial practices regarding soldier marriages, which could not be defended as being in the interests of U.S. national security.[54] The new U.S. vulnerability over racial matters abetted subtle transitions across the social spectrum.

By the end of the 1940s, for example, a notable change in attitude about brown babies began occurring among African Americans. The desire by the child welfare establishment to break down black reservations about adopting foreign mulattoes played a part. Social worker and Urban League official Lester Granger believed that "the state of mind of the Negro community" "would have to [be] built up to accept" it. The black press was a major catalyst in developing such favorable opinion. It had received a warm response to its "human interest" features on the orphans and favored their stateside adoption.[55] Culturally and politically supported desires for family formation and growth among African Americans in the postwar years probably played the determining role. English-born mulatto children of black GIs were easier to accept. Britain had been a wartime ally and language barriers did not exist. As early as 1946 a group of African American women in Chicago had sent "care packages" to children in British orphanages whom they wished to bring to the United States. British adoption law foiled the effort, but it demonstrated that attitudes were changing.[56]

African American newspapers were at the height of their influence during the World War II era. Policy makers from the departments of Justice, State, and War monitored them nervously for fear that black sedition and unrest would compromise the Allied effort. Little escaped the attention of would-be censors and those hoping to deflect black dissatisfaction. Officials regularly clipped such leading periodicals as the *Pittsburgh Courier, Baltimore Afro-American,* and *Chicago Defender* with an eye to what these papers were saying about war-related subjects. The habit continued during the German occupation. Articles about brown babies circulated among military commanders and social workers alike. The questions the black public asked forced Children's Bureau officials and others to think about the future that these orphans would have.[57]

If the brown babies were not brought to America, they would grow up in Germany. A group of American social welfare professionals discussed this possibility in early 1951. Comprising an ad hoc committee that represented such diverse organizations as the Child Welfare League of America, the National Association for the Advancement of Colored People (NAACP), the Displaced Persons Commission, and the Catholic Committee for Refugees, among others, these officials took up the question at a New York meeting. A representative from the Church World Service had contacted the Venezuelan government, which expressed interest in taking the children. He acknowledged that the option would entail "sending children into a land where they would be entirely strange to the native stock." The Brooklyn Catholic Interracial Council committee member dismissed such expatriation as "tantamount to evasion of the problem." The best solution, the committee ultimately agreed, would be one that would not put the burden of placing the orphans on an economically beleaguered black community alone and would view the brown babies "as children, as a human problem, and not involving the race and color of the child."[58]

The Children's Bureau, a federal agency with origins in the movement to suppress child labor, had interested itself in the brown baby question since the early postwar years. It shared the views of the private agencies and tried to widen the circle of responsibility for war orphans to include the State Department, the High Commissioner for Germany, and the Displaced Persons Commission. Its director, Katherine Lenroot, "felt strongly that the responsibility for some of these international situations rested with a public agency." Children's Bureau officials tacitly communicated disapproval of the War Department's refusal to provide GIs' mailing addresses to women they were believed to have impregnated. The only responsibility the War Department assumed was that of forwarding mail from jilted wives and girlfriends. As a result of pressure from both private and governmental social service organizations, the departments of State and War concluded a verbal agreement whereby the State Department would assume responsibility for answering the many letters federal agencies were receiving from abandoned, divorced, and exploited foreign women. Public oversight did not permit executive departments charged with making war or overseeing the restoration of peace to distance themselves completely from the messy consequences of troop deployment during the occupations of both Britain and Germany. State Department officials found themselves participating in interagency and joint committees designed to address a problem unprecedented in its scale.[59]

The onset of the Cold War and the military standoff between the superpowers meant the continuous overseas deployment of U.S. troops. Tangled legal and domestic relationships previously associated only with the exigencies of a "hot war" would now be enduring. Yet this permanence did not dissuade federal officials from pursuing policies that made children born out of wedlock a responsibility for the host country and discouraged congressional involvement in creating special legislation for what had become an extraordinary situation. Policy makers chose not to follow Canada's World War I example, whereby Ottawa made payments to Britain for every child begot there by a Canadian soldier. Brown babies and other children of war would have to rely on the strained social services infrastructure of the countries where they were born.[60]

In 1952 an unusual partnership developed between a black army family and the *Baltimore Afro-American*. Chief Warrant Officer Oscar Grammer and his wife Mabel helped to publicize and promote adoptions of German-born mulattoes by black parents in the United States. The *Afro-American* celebrated the new parents in lavish photospreads designed to encourage others to adopt. The Grammers themselves subsequently adopted nine orphans. The law required the visas in such cases to be filed for by a recognized agency, but many private U.S. adoption agencies persisted in their refusal to handle black cases, placing the burden of work on the few. Children not admitted under the Displaced Persons Act for purposes of adoption would have to come to America under the German quota. Comparatively few brown babies made the transatlantic crossing. Proponents of transnational adoption faced another hurdle in establishing contact between American applicants and German legal guardians. Under German law, guardians retained custody until all administrative processes were concluded. German agencies were not compensated for their work with biracial children. In mid-1954, 4,000 children were awaiting transport under the Refugee Relief Act.[61]

By 1955, when the Federal Republic of Germany became fully autonomous, the oldest of the mixed-race war orphans were already attending school. They faced a hostile German social science establishment that viewed them with condescension, when it was not downright racist and based on Nazi science. Certain blacks and mulattoes had survived the Third Reich because Nazi authorities wanted to use them as an advance phalanx in Africa once Germany's former colonies had been restored. The idea briefly reemerged after the war and abruptly died.[62] Yet, the West Germany of the Adenauer years was a different place than the Third Reich. The ultimate repudiation of Nazism involved a revulsion against the American racism that made banner headlines all over the world in the 1950s. In the United States, the status of black children became a national issue through the decision of the Supreme Court in *Brown v. Board of Education*. *Brown* not only concerned education; it was also historic because it at last included black juveniles in the category "children." The sociological jurisprudence the court exercised indicated its acceptance as a valid argument that racism damaged black children. This acceptance thus acknowledged implicitly—in a manner unprecedented for U.S. law—the humanity of black children. The clash between this recognition and a century of Jim Crow social conventions, including a popular culture that depicted black children as dwarf copies of clownish black adults, embarrassed the United States in its efforts to lead the Western world.

School integration crises in the United States influenced the West German decision consciously and rationally to integrate mixed-race orphans into German society, thus depriving Cold War enemies of a race-related issue to which

German-born mulatto children at a milk bar in West Berlin, 1954. The children were taking a break from filming a movie in which they were clad in "native" costumes. (Bettmann/Corbis)

Germany's history made it particularly vulnerable. Dr. Dorothea Struwe of the Nuremberg Youth Office reminded *Ebony* magazine that "the incidents in Little Rock (Ark.) have caused much indignation in Germany. I hope that no one will ever have reason to clean up before our own door." She continued: "It is essential that our colored children can expand and develop their talents and abilities so that they will be firmly rooted in our community and will not some day constitute a source of unrest." During the era of civil rights insurgency in the United States, the German state made a concerted, conscious, and largely successful effort to integrate the brown babies into the blue-collar work force. German universities were asked to help plan the assimilation program. Their social absorption was greatly assisted by the rebounding German economy of the period that muted class and ethnic tensions. Critics subsequently complained, however, that Germans of African descent found barriers in their path when they sought to climb the socioeconomic ladder into the professions by seeking higher education or specialized training.[63]

The brown babies' saga is a tale of war that varies considerably from the official, triumphal story of the suppression of racism in the U.S. armed forces after 1945. It is also a story of how the United States sorted out the hierarchies of race, nationality, and gender during the occupation's brief "colonial moment." Most military histories of race relations during this epoch focus on the concentrated efforts of the civil rights establishment, liberal-minded policy makers, and enlightened segments of the public to make the army and other branches abandon their discriminatory treatment of the black GI. Left implicit, rather than made explicit, was how conventional thinking about race and gender could be harnessed to the accomplishment of this task. Equalization of the status of all *men* in the U.S. military required the inclusion of the African American soldier as an equal among men. Not only did this mean rating black troops above German prisoners of war and treating them accordingly, but it also entailed revising the status and roles of women—and, specifically, white women—vis-à-vis these newly appraised blacks. Questions related to fraternization and intermarriage plagued an issue that could not be simply reduced to strategic concerns. Ambivalence continued, as did, for example, the prohibition against Japanese-American marriages, still in force in 1949.[64] We are thus presented with an index of the register of changes through which transitions in racial attitudes and behavior were rung.

The black father in the postwar state is at the center of the matter. During the slavery era, black fathers had no legal authority over their offspring. Antebellum legal convention held that a slave's father was unknown to the law to protect the privileges and status of white men who wished to engage in interracial liaisons. It also denied the legitimacy of black paternity, thus undermining black men's ability to assume the same paternalist role assumed by their white congeners. This did not make things easy for black women and children, because society assigned them dependent status in any case, and its refusal to recognize black patriarchy left them without conventional protections. Responsible fatherhood, linked to citizenship and property holding, indicated civic entitlement and respectability. It marked the distinction between fathering, as a free man would, and siring, as done by a slave or an animal. During and after World War II, U.S. military authorities had considerable difficulty in recognizing the capacity and right of the African American men under their control to father. To see them as men in that sense and not as mere lusting beasts would mean envisioning them as civic persons, a leap of the imagination that the emerging civil rights movement would make possible a decade later.

It is partly for this reason that the military so strongly resisted black GI attempts to establish legitimate paternity and play the male-dominant roles that were conventional in society at large. The reflexive hostility with which

many white men viewed interracial relationships was not, as many interpreted it, instinctual. It was instead the product of a tacit, if not entirely conscious, chain of thought in which the claims of black challengers to white male
supremacy—and endogamy—were denied. In the process, the white woman
gained a symbolic, if extrinsic, status. That status could be taken away as a
penalty for transgression, as the German women's case illustrates. (German
men, however, as the POW experience indicates, were not thus punished.)
Under the circumstances, the brown babies indicated that more than simple
indiscretion had occurred. Instead, they showed that the barricades had been
breached.

Over the past fifteen years, scholars have made considerable advances in
recording the evolution of thinking and policy about race and gender, looking
at a variety of evidence ranging from popular culture to law. The post–World
War II years provide a fascinating laboratory for such study because of the
speed and complexity of transformation that U.S. society was then undergoing. Even before the Berlin airlift institutionalized the Cold War rift between
the Western powers and the Soviet bloc, race had the power to embarrass the
United States, complicate the execution of its laws and policies, confound its
most fundamental objectives, and muddle its relations with foreign powers.
The war orphans of mixed race, when visible at all, are generally treated as
footnotes to the main drama of the epoch. Caught between the old order and
the new, brown babies were both the product and the subject of policy conflict. They lay at the center of the imperatives to normalize Europe and, at
home, to reconstruct conventional home life, to define a more inclusive citizenship, and to reform racial institutions.

Notes

1. Maj. Gen. Edward F. Witsell to Dr. M. L. Ogan, 16 Apr. 1946; Gianna Del Prede
to Director of NAACP, 11 Nov. 1945; Walter White to Robert P. Patterson, Secretary
of War, 20 Dec. 1945; National Association for the Advancement of Colored People
(NAACP) Papers, part 9: Discrimination in the Armed Forces, series B, reel 15
(Bethesda, Md.: University Publications of America, 1991).

2. The League of Coloured Peoples *Newsletter* 17, no. 104, Oct.–Dec. 1948, 111,
116; Percival L. Prattis to William Nunn, 13 Mar. 1949, P. L. Prattis Papers, Moorland-
Spingarn Research Center, Howard University, Washington, D.C.

3. See, for example, "Italian Woman Weds War Vet," *Baltimore Afro-American*, 9
Aug. 1947, 11; "Affairs with Frauleins Accepted in Germany," ibid., 5 June 1948, 1,
2; "Connecticut Vet Weds Italian Girl," *Amsterdam News*, 20 Nov. 1948, 1, 3, 6;
Erich Lissner, "We Adopted a Brown Baby," *Ebony*, May 1953, 36–45.

4. Michael Omi and Howard Winant, *Racial Formation in the United States*, 2nd
ed. (New York: Routledge, 1994); Committee to Consider Possibilities and Resources
for the Immigration of a Group of German Orphans of Negro Blood, minutes of 29

Jan. 1951 meeting, p. 4, NAACP Papers, part 9: Discrimination in the Armed Forces, series B, reel 8; "The Problem of America's Brown Babies," *Ebony*, Dec. 1959, 65–72; Alice Dunnigan, *A Black Woman's Experience — From Schoolhouse to White House* (Philadelphia: Dorrance, 1974), 371–72. For similar problems affecting Eurasian orphans, see I. Evelyn Smith to Mrs. James A. Michener, 1 Oct. 1952, Children's Bureau Records, Record Group (RG) 102, National Archives and Records Administration (NA), Washington, D.C. (I am grateful to Joanne Meyerowitz for alerting me to the Children's Bureau material and providing many of the citations to that collection.)

5. "Germany: Occupation Period: Policy with Respect to Standards of Subsistence for the Civilian Population—Views of the Interdivisional Committee on Germany," 22 July 1944, State Department Documents of the Interdivisional Country and Area Committees, 1943–46, NARA Microfilm Publication T1221, reel 5 (Washington, D.C., 1979).

6. Cynthia Enloe, *The Morning After: Sexual Politics at the End of the Cold War* (Berkeley: University of California Press, 1993), 118; John Lie, "The State as Pimp: Prostitution and the Patriarchal State in Japan in the 1940s," *Sociological Quarterly* 38 (Spring 1997): 251–64.

7. Ute Frevert, *Women in German History: From Bourgeois Emancipation to Sexual Liberation* (Oxford: Berg, 1989), 258; Matthew Stibbe, "Women and the Nazi State," *History Today* 43 (Nov. 1993): 35–40. See also Anne-Marie Tröger, "Between Rape and Prostitution: Survival Strategies and Chances of Emancipation for Berlin Women after World War II," in *Women in Culture and Politics*, ed. Judith Friedlander, Blanche Wiesen Cook, Alice Kessler-Harris, and Carroll Smith-Rosenberg (Bloomington: University of Indiana Press, 1986), 97–120. For the U.S. military and prostitution in another context, see Katharine H. S. Moon, *Sex among Allies: Military Prostitution in U.S.-Korean Relations* (New York: Columbia University Press, 1997).

8. Enloe, *The Morning After*, 118; Lie, "The State as Pimp," 251.

9. For Britain, see Graham Smith, *When Jim Crow Met John Bull: Black American Soldiers in World War II Britain* (New York: St. Martin's Press, 1987); Sonya O. Rose, "Sex, Citizenship, and the Nation in World War II Britain," *American Historical Review* 103 (Oct. 1998): 1147–76.

10. See the discussion of this issue in Beth Bailey and David Farber, *The First Strange Place: The Alchemy of Race and Sex in World War II Hawaii* (New York: Free Press, 1992).

11. Francis A. Kornegay to Lt. Col. Marcus Ray, 14 Dec. 1945, Assistant Secretary of War Subject File 1940–47, Records of the Office of the Secretary of War, RG 107, NA.

12. Willie Dulaney, Raymond Jones, and Joseph D. Lewis, *Black Police in America* (Bloomington: Indiana University Press, 1996); memorandum, Secretary of War Robert P. Patterson for Deputy Chief of Staff, 7 Jan. 1947, in *Blacks in the Military: Essential Documents*, ed. Bernard C. Nalty and Morris J. MacGregor (Wilmington, Del.: Scholarly Resources, 1981), 217.

13. James P. O'Donnell, "The GI Legacy in Germany," *Newsweek*, 16 June 1947, 48.

14. Major General Frank A. Keating to Lt. General Clarence R Huebner, 12 June 1947, Reports and Programs against Venereal Disease, Prostitution, and Sex Vices, AG 726.1, Records of the Office of the Military Government (OMGUS), Records of U.S. Occupation Headquarters, RG 260, NA.

15. Edgar G. Conner to OMGUS Bavaria, n.d., Reports and Programs against Venereal Disease, Prostitution, and Sex Vices, AG 726.1, RG 260, NA.

16. Ibid.; Col. Leslie E. Babcock to Chief of Staff, 2 Dec. 1946, Ray's Field Trips, in Office of the Assistant Secretary of War, Civilian Aide to the Secretary, RG 107, NA.

17. Griswold to Chief of Staff, 6 May 1947, AG 726.1, RG 260, NA.

18. Maria Höhn, "GIs, Veronikas and Lucky Strikes: German Reactions to the American Presence in the Rhineland-Palatinate during the 1950s" (Ph.D. diss., University of Pennsylvania, 1995), 244, 250.

19. Ibid., 237, 253–57, 261; Earl F. Ziemke, *The U.S. Army in the Occupation of Germany* (Washington, D.C.: Center of Military History, United States Army, 1975), 438.

20. Freda Utley, *The High Cost of Vengeance* (Chicago: Henry Regnery, 1949), 239–41.

21. O'Donnell, "The GI Legacy in Germany," 48.

22. Robert W. Kestling, "Blacks under the Swastika: A Research Note," *Journal of Negro History* 83 (Winter 1998): 84–99.

23. Lt. General Thomas T. Hardy to John J. McCloy, 23 Sept. 1944, Negro troops–Civilian Aide, ASW 291.2, Formerly Security-Classified Correspondence of John J. McCloy 1941–45, RG 107, NA.

24. May Opitz, "African and Afro-German Women in the Weimar Republic and under National Socialism," in *Showing Our Colors: Afro-German Women Speak Out*, ed. Katharine Oguntoye, May Opitz, and Dagmar Schultz (Amherst: University of Massachusetts Press, 1992), 52. German women of mixed African and European descent have been very active in inscribing the history and consciousness of what they have chosen to call "Afro-Germans." See also Karin Obermeier, "Afro-German Women: Recording Their Own History," *New German Critique* 46 (Winter 1989): 172–80. On the World War I–era occupation, see Keith L. Nelson, "The 'Black Horror' on the Rhine: Race as a Factor in Post–World War I Diplomacy," *Journal of Modern History* 42, 4 (1970): 606–27; Reiner Pommerin, "The Fate of the Mixed Blood Children in Germany," *German Studies Review* 5, 3 (1982): 315–23; Sally Marks, "Black Watch on the Rhine: A Study in Propaganda, Prejudice, and Prurience," *European Studies Review* 13 (1983): 297–333. Katerine Oguntoye and May Opitz, "Showing Our Colours! The Testimony of Two Afro German Women," in *Invisible Europeans? Black People in the "New Europe,"* ed. Les Back and Anoop Nayak (Birmingham: AFFOR, 1993), 94–119; Opitz, "African and Afro-German Women in the Weimar Republic and under National Socialism," 50, 52.

25. "The Position of France in the Military Occupation of Germany," Country and Area Committee Report no. 133, 25 Mar. 1944, p. 2, State Department Documents of the Interdivisional Country and Area Committees, 1943–46, NARA Microfilm Publication T1221 (Washington, D.C., 1979).

26. Höhn, "GIs, Veronikas and Lucky Strikes," 117–21.

27. Including a recollection by African American historian Nathan Huggins, who, on guard duty during World War II, could only stand outside the Jim Crow restaurant where his German POW charges were being served. See David W. Blight, "In Retrospect: Nathan Irvin Huggins, the Art of History, and the Irony of the American Dream," *Reviews in American History* 22 (Mar. 1994): 12.

28. *Manuscript*, no. 22, 13 Aug. 1945; Marcus Ray to General Joseph T. McNarney, 23 Nov. 1946, Ray's Field Trips, Office of the Assistant Secretary of War, Civilian Aide to the Secretary, RG 107, NA. Col. Leslie E. Babcock, chief, Inspections Division, denied this report in Babcock to Chief of Staff, 2 Dec. 1946, in ibid.; Oliver W. Har-

rington, *Why I Left America and Other Essays* (Jackson: University Press of Mississippi, 1993), 90–91.

29. Petra Goedde, "From Villains to Victims: Fraternization and the Feminization of Germany, 1945–1947," *Diplomatic History* 23 (Winter 1999): 1–20.

30. Katherine Pence, "The 'Fräuleins' Meet the 'Amis': Americanization of German Women in the Reconstruction of the West German State," *Michigan Feminist Studies* 7 (1992–93): 83–108.

31. Hildegarde Kaiser to Jesse O. Dedmon, 7 Dec. 1946; Howard C. Peterson, Assistant Secretary of War, to Alice Rivkin, 17 May 1947; NAACP Papers, part 9: Discrimination in the Armed Forces, series B, reel 15; Douglass Hall, "Don't Disgrace Women, GI's Advised," *Baltimore Afro-American*, 9 Aug. 1947, 1, 11.

32. Clare George, *Berlin Days: 1946–1947* (London: Macmillan, 1989), 55–56; Ziemke, *The U.S. Army in the Occupation of Germany*, 321–27; William G. Nunn, "Europe's 'Brown Babies' in Dire Need of Help," *Pittsburgh Courier*, 29 May 1948, 1, 4.

33. Cliff MacKay, "How Many 'Wild Oats' Babies in Germany," *Afro Magazine*, 8 May 1948, 11. See also Frevert, *Women in German History*, 261; Maria Höhn, "Frau im Haus und Girl im *Spiegel*: Discourse on Women in the Interregnum Period of 1945–1949 and the Question of German Identity," *Central European History* 26, 1 (1993): 63–64.

34. Nunn, "Europe's 'Brown Babies' in Dire Need of Help"; Ollie Stewart, "Germany's New Problem," *Afro Magazine*, 3 July 1948, 6; "'Brown Babies' Turned into Side Show Attraction," *Pittsburgh Courier*, 17 July 1948, 7; "Brown Skinned War Babies, An Intimate Story of How These Children Are Cared for Inside Hitler's Germany Today," *Chicago Defender*, 5 Nov. 1949, magazine, 18, 21.

35. See, for example, "Ohio Claims Three 'Brown Babies,'" *Pittsburgh Courier*, 2 Mar. 1949, 11. Master Sgt. Herman Richardson to the Editor, *Sepia*, July 1952, 6.

36. May Opitz, "Afro-Germans after 1945: The So-Called Occupation Babies," in Oguntoye, Opitz, and Schultz, *Showing Our Colors*, 90.

37. Robert W. Bruce to T/Sgt. Donald H. Miller, 21 Sept. 1948, Reading File of the Chief and Deputy Chief of the Legal Affairs Division, Records of the U.S. High Commissioner for Germany, RG 466, NA; OMGUS cable, 15 Aug. 1947, Marriage Policy, AG 291.1; O'Donnell, "The GI Legacy in Germany," 49.

38. Franklin J. Potter to Fred J. Cohn, 27 Sept. 1947; Stanley H. Gaines to S/Sgt. Moe Nehrer, 27 Dec. 1950; Gaines to Lt. Col. Thomas A. Fagan, 26 Jan. 1951; Gaines to Messrs. Gelnhausern and Backer, 18 Apr. 1951; Ernest Anspach to Genoveva Strohmenger, 2 Mar. 1950, and to B. Staedter, 2 Mar. 1950, Reading File of the Chief and Deputy Chief of the Legal Affairs Division, RG 466, NA.

39. Lt. Col. J. V. Sheldon, Asst. Adj.-General, to Commanding Generals, 5 Mar. 1946, OMGUS Records, RG 260; Robert W. Bruce to Ruth Haas, 15 Dec. 1948, Reading File of the Chief and Deputy Chief of the Legal Affairs Division, box 2, NA.

40. "Illegitimacy in England Laid to U.S. Ban on Mixed Marriage," *Baltimore Afro-American*, 1 Feb. 1947, 8; "GI's English Kids Labeled 'Apes,'" ibid., 26 Apr. 1947, 3; Emory Ross to Maud Morlock, 10 Mar. 1947, RG 102, NA; Graham Smith, *When Jim Crow Met John Bull*, 209.

41. Country and Area Committee 37, 13 July 1944, "Germany: Occupation Period: Abrogation of Laws," State Department Documents of the Interdivisional Country and Area Committees, 1943–46, NARA Microfilm Publication T1221, reel 4 (Washington, D.C., 1979); Reading File of the Chief and Deputy Chief of the Legal Affairs Division, box 2, RG 466, NA. A comprehensive list of states banning intermarriage in

1945 is found in Robert L. Carter to Cpl. Cleophas J. Randall, 26 Nov. 1945, NAACP Papers, part 9: Discrimination in the Armed Forces, series B, reel 15.

42. Stanley H. Gaines to Mr. Dunn, 2 May 1951, Reading File of the Chief and Deputy Chief of the Legal Affairs Division, RG 466, NA. Franklin Potter to OMGUS, 8 Oct. 1947; Potter to Pfc. Horace Bell, 21 Oct. 1947; Potter to Minister of Justice for Hesse, 4 Nov. 1948; Stanley H. Gaines to Capt. A. R. Koval, 5 Dec. 1950; Gaines to Otto Michaelis, 7 July 1950; cable, 6 Dec. 1947, Marriage Policy; Office of the Commanding General, Memorandum, 13 Dec. 1947, Marriages Dec. (1947); Capt. Harry Ross to Commander in Chief, EUROCOM, 4 Dec. 1947, AG 291.1 Marriage Reports, RG 260, NA.

43. Robert W. Bruce to the Hessischer Landesverein, 24 Jan. 1949, Reading File of the Chief and Deputy Chief of the Legal Affairs Division, box 2, RG 466, NA.

44. Höhn, "GIs, Veronikas and Lucky Strikes," 48, 254.

45. Doug Hall, "Christmas Finds These Americans in Germany," *Afro Magazine*, 27 Dec. 1947, M-12; Nunn, "Europe's 'Brown Babies' in Dire Need of Help"; J. A. Rogers column, *Pittsburgh Courier* clipping, 1956, n.d., Tuskegee News Clipping File (Sanford, N.C.: Microfilming Corp. of America, 1976).

46. Goedde, "From Villains to Victims," 8.

47. Quoted in Christina Klein, "Family Ties and Political Obligation: The Discourse of Adoption and the Cold War Commitment to Asia," in *Cold War Constructions: The Political Culture of United States Imperialism, 1945–1966*, ed. Christian Appy (Amherst: University of Massachusetts Press, 2000), 47.

48. Manuel Kaufman to Maud Morlock, 9 Aug. 1948, RG 102, NA; "Laws Tightened to End Black Market in Babies," *Baltimore Afro-American*, 22 Mar. 1947, 9; Rickie Solinger, "Race and 'Value': Black and White Illegitimate Babies in the U.S.A., 1945–1965," *Gender & History* 4 (Autumn 1992): 348–50.

49. "New York Bans Agency Jim Crow," *Baltimore Afro-American*, 22 Mar. 1947, 9; Maud Morlock to Esther G. Levitt, 8 May 1950, RG 102, NA.

50. William S. Jackson to Jean Blackwell, 31 Dec. 1954, Schomburg Clipping File, 000,035; Urban League press release, 25 Jan. 1955, in ibid.; Bettye Cook, "Fultz Quads on Road to Long Life," *AFRO Magazine*, 24 Apr. 1947, 1, and photospread, 3; "Fultz Quadruplets Steal Show at Festival in N.C.," *Baltimore Afro-American*, 31 May 1947, 9.

51. Rickie Solinger, *Wake Up Little Susie* (New York: Routledge, 1992). See also Solinger, "Race and 'Value.'"

52. Committee to Consider Possibilities, minutes of 29 Jan. 1951 meeting, 5, NAACP Papers, part 9: Discrimination in the Armed Forces, series B, reel 8.

53. *Loving v. Virginia*, 388 U.S. 1 (1967); Lee Nichols, *Breakthrough on the Color Front*, 2nd ed. (Colorado Springs: Three Continents Press, 1993), 166. For other references to this issue, see Franklin H. Williams to James C. Evans, 22 Apr. 1948, NAACP Papers, part 9: Discrimination in the Armed Forces, series B, reel 15.

54. Elfrieda Berthiaume Shukert and Barbara Smith Scibetta, *War Brides of World War II* (Novato, Calif.: Presidio, 1988).

55. Committee to Consider Possibilities, minutes of 29 Jan. 1951 meeting, 4–5, NAACP Papers, Part 9: Discrimination in the Armed Forces, series B, reel 8; "German War Babies: Red Tape Balks Adoption of Orphan by Teacher," *Ebony*, Jan. 1951, 35–38; "German Brown Babies in the United States," *Sepia*, Feb. 1952, 52–54.

56. Beth Muller to Miss Smith, interoffice memorandum, 26 May 1948; Martha Wood's memorandum, 4 June 1948, Social Security Administration, Chicago branch, RG 102, NA.

57. Patrick Washburn, *A Question of Sedition: The Federal Government's Investigation of the Black Press during World War II* (New York: Oxford University Press, 1986); Louise Noble's report for the Federal Security Agency—Social Security Board, Nov. 1947; Beth Muller, Regional Child Representative, to Louise Noble, Chief of Field Service, Federal Security Agency—Social Security Board, 4 June 1951, RG 102, NA.

58. Committee to Consider Possibilities, minutes of 29 Jan. 1951 meeting, 5–7.

59. Maud Morlock to Miss Nutt, 1 Aug. 1946, Morlock memorandum, 17 Sept. 1946; Willard L. Thorp, Assistant Secretary of State, to Maj. Gen. Edward F. Witsell, n.d., Children's Bureau copy received 8 Jan. 1947; memorandum of Morlock's telephone conversation with J. Charnow, 24 Jan. 1947; Jane M. Hoey, "Report on Problems Arising from the Presence of United States Troops Overseas," 21 Mar. 1949; I. Evelyn Smith to Dr. Elisabeth Meyer-Spreckels, 26 July 1951, RG 102, NA.

60. Katherine F. Lenroot to Rep. Joseph R. Farrington, 31 May 1949; Frances K. Kernohan to Irene Murphy, 8 June 1949; I. Evelyn Roberts to Kiyoko Nishi, 8 May 1952, RG 102, NA.

61. *Baltimore Afro-American*, 7 Aug. 1954, 1, 6; 17 May 1958, 3; 20 June 1953, 1, 3; Evelyn Roberts to Kiyoko Nishi, 8 May 1952, RG 102, NA; Committee to Consider Possibilities, minutes of 29 Jan. 1951 meeting, 2, NAACP Papers, part 9: Discrimination in the Armed Forces, series B, reel 8.

62. Opitz, "African and Afro-German Women in the Weimar Republic and under National Socialism," 52; Opitz, "Afro-Germans after 1945," 79–100; Freda Rippy to Walter White, 15 Mar. 1953; Caroline A. Flexner to Walter White, 17 June 1953, NAACP Papers, part 9: Discrimination in the Armed Forces, series B, reel 8.

63. "Brown Babies Go to Work—1,500 Negro Youths Integrated into Germany's Work Force," *Ebony*, Nov. 1960, 98; May Opitz, "Afro-Germans after 1945," 97–108.

64. Nichols, *Breakthrough on the Color Front*, 161–68; Cpl. George D. Brown to NAACP Legal Committee, 20 Nov. 1949, NAACP Papers, part 9: Discrimination in the Armed Forces, series B, reel 15.

Bleached Souls and Red Negroes

The NAACP and Black Communists
in the Early Cold War, 1948–1952

Almost a century ago, W. E. B. Du Bois observed "that one ever feels his two-ness, an American, a Negro; . . . two warring ideals in one dark body."[1] During the early years of the Cold War, "two-ness" took on an even more complicated dimension as the American Negro and the Red Negro waged war against each other. The National Association for the Advancement of Colored People (NAACP) leadership declared its refusal to let the communists "capture . . . split and wreck the NAACP" and went after *suspected* communists with a vengeance. Walter White, the association's executive secretary, and Roy Wilkins, its chief administrator, vowed to be "utterly ruthless in clean[ing] out the NAACP, and, mak[ing] sure that the Communists were not running it."[2] While the literature on the complex relationship between African Americans and American socialists and communists continues to grow, few scholars have come to terms with the rancor that the ideological conflicts of the early postwar years engendered among blacks, and the significance of these fratricidal tensions for the character of future black insurgency.[3]

In the early 1950s the NAACP leadership was determined to put its resources, expertise, and valued name in the hands of the Truman administration and State Department to beat back damaging Soviet charges of racial discrimination in the United States. Walter White, the NAACP's executive secretary, was outraged that the U.S. government appeared impotent in countering Soviet taunts about American racism. He blasted members of the Senate for allowing the Kremlin to pump the "Third World" with "tragic distortions" about the Roman holiday lynchings and terror-filled elections in the United States.[4]

On multiple occasions, White made sure that the Truman administration knew that he was willing to refute "Soviet propaganda" about the oppressive conditions under which black Americans lived. In short, the head of the NAACP was so intent on defending his nation's honor that he was ready to misrepresent the sad state of affairs in black America. In 1951 White published a "Progress Report" on civil rights, which he encouraged Eleanor Roosevelt, chair of the UN's Commission on Human Rights, to use whenever the Soviets launched into their standard harangue about American racism. The executive secretary of the NAACP boasted in the report that the quality of life for blacks, especially in key areas like voting, housing, employment, and education, was quickly approaching that of white Americans. Although White conceded that there was still some work to be done, he deliberately "white-wash[ed]" a string of atrocities in Illinois, Florida, Texas, and Alabama. He further failed to admit that while he was applauding Hollywood for its positive portrayal of African Americans, the NAACP had launched a boycott of the *Amos 'n Andy* television show. In short, while White saw "positive gains" there were some bitter truths that he refused to acknowledge.[5]

Indeed, another brutal killing in a small southern town occurred shortly after the publication of White's "Progress Report." The stage was set two years earlier in 1949 when whites in Groveland, Florida, rampaged through the black neighborhood, burning African American children alive, yet the only screams authorities heard were those of a white woman shouting "rape." The manhunt was on, and four black men with unshakable alibis were quickly arrested. Indeed, the police killed one of them even before he arrived at the jail. In this hostile atmosphere, justice, in the words of the NAACP attorney, had "all the earmarks of a dime store criminal novel." The U.S. Supreme Court agreed, and in 1951 overturned the convictions, and demanded a change of venue to retry the defendants. Sheriff Willis McCall, while transporting two of the accused, drove into the backwoods, stopped the car, told his prisoners to get out, and then unloaded his guns into them. McCall was fully exonerated.[6]

Sensing an opportunity, Soviet foreign minister Andrei Vishinsky pounced. Is it really progress, Vishinsky asked, when the U.S. courts condone the murder and near fatal wounding of two handcuffed black men by a southern sheriff? The NAACP leadership was angered by the crime, but it was even more incensed that this latest example of southern justice would further tarnish America's carefully crafted human rights image. In spite of the fact that the bullet-riddled prisoners were NAACP clients, association board member Channing Tobias blithely ignored the lynch mob atmosphere that surrounded the case. During a press conference, he dismissed the incident as tragic but not indicative of anything important.[7]

Describing Tobias's response as "disgraceful," the Civil Rights Congress (CRC), led by William Patterson, chose a different method for dealing with Soviet charges of racial violence. The CRC, with encouragement and support from the Communist Party of the United States, determined that it would meticulously document the violence and use the United Nations to expose the depths of American racism.[8] Before the onset of the Cold War, the NAACP and the National Negro Congress had petitioned the UN on behalf of African Americans. While those earlier petitions accused the United States of violating blacks' human rights, the Civil Rights Congress charged it with genocide.[9]

The CRC's saga of lynching, segregation, and unequal education, housing, and health care repeated a story already told brilliantly in the NAACP's 1947 petition, *An Appeal to the World*. The difference was that the CRC's petition, entitled *We Charge Genocide*, set out to prove governmental intent. Patterson argued forcefully that Jim Crow was the result of a deliberate government policy to destroy African Americans. Under this grip of oppression, Patterson charged, an additional 32,000 African Americans died each year because they did not enjoy the same quality health care, jobs, education, and housing as whites. Those stressful conditions, he continued, cut the average life expectancy of blacks short by eight years. As the CRC told Eleanor Roosevelt, whether it happens relatively quickly, as in the Third Reich, or slow and steady, as in Mississippi, genocide is genocide.[10]

The State Department, of course, contended that the parameters detailed in the UN Convention on Genocide were not applicable to the United States because the United States had refused to sign the treaty. That refusal, of course, was firmly rooted in the issue of lynching. The federal government had no intention of breaching the sacred barrier of states' rights, and the southern Democrats in the Senate had made clear that the Genocide Convention was nothing more than a "back-door method of enacting federal anti-lynching legislation." State Department officials admitted that the "Southern Senators were afraid" that with a convention in place, the UN could legally go after lynchers who, despite "convincing evidence of [their] guilt," had already been acquitted by the U.S. judicial system. Such intrusion would be unwarranted, the State Department believed. While thousands of blacks had been lynched, the death toll was not high enough to constitute genocide.[11]

Patterson understood, however, that the convention did not require the complete annihilation of a group. It only required governmental intent to destroy a racial minority "in whole or in part." There was no other explanation, furthermore, for Jim Crow, southern justice, or disease-infested ghettos. The CRC's charge that the U.S. government was fully engaged in the systematic, long-term destruction of 15 million people solely because of their race was shocking, disturbing, and contained just enough truth to resonate. Patterson and William Z. Foster, chair of the U.S. Communist Party, proudly discussed the "remarkably effective weapon" the CRC had created. Because the specter of the Holocaust continued to haunt the international conscience, *We Charge Genocide* concluded, the petition strategy would have enormous "ideological . . . and organizational value" for the U.S. Communist Party.[12]

While Patterson had envisioned this strategy to evoke the greatest "ideological . . . and organizational value" for the party, he was slow to design a plan to gain the greatest impact for African Americans. This oversight simply reflected the low priority Patterson initially placed on having the petition actually reviewed by the United Nations. In fact, in talking with leftist labor leader Ben Gold, Patterson bluntly stated that it did not matter "whether" the petition was actually "placed on the [UN's] agenda . . . or not." To be sure, Patterson intended to have We Charge Genocide submitted to the UN by Paul Robeson and W. E. B. Du Bois, but that was to give the petition a certain cachet. Patterson did not send the petition to any of the delegations or to Eleanor Roosevelt until 18 December, just as the Sixth Session of the General Assembly was about to recess. He did, however, devise a way to publicize the existence of this "bitter book [of] horrors" and distribute it to communists in Eastern Europe, Britain, and France.[13]

Patterson's actions make it clear that We Charge Genocide was not about black people. Rather, it was about the complex and desperate needs of the Communist Party of the United States. Anticommunist hysteria had taken its toll on Communist organizations, and the CRC was no exception. The Civil Rights Congress was desperately in need of funds: it could barely pay its staff and its utility bills, and could not finance the legal defense needs of the jailed American Communist Party leadership, which it considered its "A-1 civil rights case." Those groups which might have been allies, the black church and organized labor, had sealed off their organizations and their bank accounts from the Civil Rights Congress. To Patterson, these groups had the money, while the CRC had the program. There had to be a way to bring the two together.[14]

The CRC sought a crisis that would overcome liberal organizations' reservations about working with communists. A case as powerful and shocking as Scottsboro some twenty years earlier, in which nine young black men were convicted of rape and received capital sentences, would help the CRC. Patterson wanted an issue that reeked of such obvious and brutal racism that a well-financed, united front, rallying behind it, could become the battering ram to free the Communist Party leadership.[15]

With We Charge Genocide, the CRC believed it had created a better issue than Scottsboro. The petition was a damning indictment that would show, as Patterson declared, that America had "plumbed to the lowest depths" of its Nazi "German counterpart."[16] Just as Munich and Auschwitz had revealed the vile nature of the Nazi regime, Patterson boasted that the petition, if effectively used, would unmask the true barbaric character of the U.S. government. The Americans' alleged use of chemical warfare against Asian troops in Korea, Patterson declared, proved as nothing else could that the "wanton

Civil Rights Congress member and Du Bois associate W. Alphaeus Hunton (right) is handcuffed to writer Dashiell Hammett as they are arrested on 9 July 1951 for contempt. They refused to give federal authorities information on bail-jumping Communist Party leaders. (Bettmann/Corbis)

murder of Negroes had been a dress rehearsal for the murder of Koreans and Chinese." Patterson hoped that the superbly crafted petition would "pollute" the air so badly with the "stink" of America's horrendous crimes, that the Europeans, who were under considerable pressure from the U.S. government to rearm West Germany and build the North Atlantic Treaty Organization (NATO), would have no choice but to "cry 'Americans . . . go home.'"[17]

We Charge Genocide, in short, was a deftly crafted Communist Party fund-raiser and foreign policy saboteur that skillfully used the plight of African Americans to advance the CRC agenda. Unfortunately, for all that it was, it was not designed to advance directly the cause of black equality. Patterson clearly stated that there was a fight beyond Negro rights "which [was] of infinitely greater importance." That was consistent with the CRC's unwavering assertion that its main mission was to free the Communist Eleven, protect the civil liberties of the U.S. Communist Party, and undermine U.S. foreign policy. In that hierarchy, black equality was important, but only as a means to an end.[18]

Columnist Drew Pearson accurately predicted Walter White's reaction to the petition. White, eager to meet the State Department's need for a loyal black face, gladly penned a stinging rebuttal to the Civil Rights Congress.[19] He sought first to undermine the credibility of the CRC by defining *We Charge Genocide* as "a gross and subversive conspiracy [by] prominent American Communists." He also impugned the research itself. White described the fifty pages of lynching and racist incidents as "alleged instances" designed to "suborn the allegiance of Negro citizens . . . to their foremost loyalty—loyalty to the United States of America."[20] After it became clear that the CRC had, in fact, meticulously verified each incident, White tried another tactic. The "facts are true," he lamented, but "like all indictments drafted by a prosecutor," *We Charge Genocide* "paint[ed] only the gloomiest picture of American democracy and the race question." White set out to present a brighter picture by celebrating the country's "phenomenal gains in civil rights." Thus, while some complained that nearly 90 percent of all U.S. soldiers charged and convicted of cowardice in the Korean War were African American or railed against the Ku Klux Klan's reign of terror in Cicero, Illinois, and Groveland, Florida, White simply chalked these incidents up to the "unfinished business of democracy."[21]

This was too much even for Roy Wilkins, who was perhaps the staunchest anticommunist in the NAACP. Although Wilkins considered the Civil Rights Congress to be nothing but the Kremlin in blackface, he nonetheless wondered how the NAACP could "'blast' a book that use[d] our records as source material." Wilkins asserted that the entire array of NAACP initiatives, including a federal ban on lynching, equal employment legislation, and an end to Jim Crow education, had as its initial starting point governmental abuse of black Americans. Only a few months earlier, Wilkins had ironically occupied the same position as Patterson when the editors of the *Atlanta Constitution* accused the NAACP of "distorting the picture" of race relations "for the propaganda effect." Wilkins's retort was simple. The picture "is bad enough. . . . Why try to paint blacker the inside of a cave?" Wilkins then went on to recount the rising rate of lynching, peonage "that [held] thousands of families in virtual slavery, school segregation, and the abuses of a deeply corrupt and vindictive court system." Given the brutal realities of the black condition, and the government's reluctance to end those brutal practices, certainly, Wilkins added, the "State Department [could] not expect that we will . . . assume the role of 'blaster' of this petition."[22]

NAACP board member Judge Hubert T. Delany was even more direct. Let the State Department do its own dirty work. The CRC had accused the U.S. government of the same atrocities that the NAACP had detailed in *An Ap-*

peal to the World. Those oppressive conditions, Delany pointed out to White, still existed. The NAACP must not give the impression that it was satisfied with the status quo and lose its reputation as "a militant organization fighting for first-class citizenship for the Negro."[23]

Undeterred, White worked feverishly to have his rebuttal in the hands of the U.S. delegation so that he could stop the *Genocide* petition before it gained momentum. Given Wilkins's and Delany's opposition, White needed a strong ally. He found it in NAACP board member Dr. Channing Tobias.[24] Tobias, who had so casually dismissed the killing and wounding of handcuffed prisoners by Sheriff McCall, was an alternate member of the U.S. delegation to the General Assembly, scheduled to meet in Paris in November 1951. He was, in the words of one State Department official, "an outstanding colored man," who could help the United States counter Soviet "propaganda" about race relations.[25] Tobias proved instrumental in getting White's searing denunciation of the CRC out of the NAACP bureaucracy and wired to the U.S. delegation in Paris, in spite of Wilkins's and Delany's objections.

Tobias was the kind of American Negro the State Department desperately needed, especially after an internal review determined that the "well documented [and] carefully presented" petition tarnished the image of the United States. Although White's statement was a useful silver bullet, it could lose its power to discredit the CRC's indictment if the finger pulling the trigger was that of John Foster Dulles or any other member of the white elite that composed the State Department's officialdom. In the tried and true strategy of getting blacks to denounce other blacks, department officials told Walter White that "it would be most desirable for some outstanding Negro leaders to be present in Paris" to refute the CRC's charges.[26] In addition to Walter White patrolling the domestic front, in Paris stood Nobel Peace Prize winner Dr. Ralph Bunche. Channing Tobias, also director of the Phelps-Stokes Fund and a YMCA executive, joined Bunche. White could count on Professor Rayford W. Logan, the executive director of the Association for the Study of Negro Life and History. Finally, attorney Edith Sampson, a black Chicagoan who had served on the U.S. delegation during the previous UN session, was also in France poised to strike. Sampson, who was not originally scheduled to be in Paris, was called in specifically to undertake a whirlwind tour of Scandinavia and undo any damage caused by the *Genocide* petition.[27] Seeing this formidable array of America's Negroes, Patterson registered his disgust that "for money and a title these Negro hirelings [would] travel the . . . world . . . preaching the glories of this bloodthirsty dollar-democracy."[28]

The State Department's American Negro show began in earnest when Tobias slammed the CRC for resorting to hyperbole and treating "isolated" incidents as if they represented a deliberate, governmental attempt to destroy African Americans. When Patterson countered that there was no other explanation for fifty pages of documented persecution culled from just the past six years, Tobias seethed. He demanded to know why Patterson did not love America enough "to write about genocide in the Soviet Union." Just "how the hell," Patterson retorted, was "a national of the USA going to interfere in USSR matters?" As Tobias launched into a recital of Soviet atrocities, Patterson challenged him to "prove it." The confrontation ended when Tobias turned and walked away. Patterson later commented that the way Tobias, Bunche, and Sampson "ran interference for the American government" showed how thoroughly they had been duped.[29]

The seeming ability of the United States to seduce black leadership at home and developing nations abroad left Patterson isolated and stymied at every turn. When he finally realized that he needed to do more than just show up in Paris with a petition, he approached first the Indian, then the Ethiopian, Egyptian, Haitian, Dominican, and finally Liberian delegations. These diplomats assured him how sympathetic they were, but let him know that, due to anticipated development aid from the United States, championing such a petition, no matter how valid, would not be diplomatically prudent. Because the needs of the U.S. Communist Party required that the Soviet Union not touch the petition, lest it be tainted with the red dye of "propaganda," that route was also closed to Patterson.[30] The situation in Paris then went from bleak to bleaker. Soon after Patterson had secured an interview with a *New York Times* reporter, the U.S. Embassy tried to seize his passport and have him deported because his presence in Paris was "not in the best interest of the United States." Ever defiant, Patterson told the embassy to "go to hell," threw his always packed suitcases in a taxi, rushed to the airport, and fled to Eastern Europe.[31]

It appeared that the CRC's attempt to create an open forum for *We Charge Genocide* was all but finished. But then came another shocking blow out of the American South. The cold-blooded murder of Samuel Shepherd and near fatal wounding of Walter Irvin had been just the latest episode of violence in a two-year reign of terror in Florida, where the president vacationed. Throughout 1949, 1950, and 1951, Jewish synagogues, Catholic churches, and black homes in white neighborhoods were bombed at will. Indeed, during this period, Florida experienced an average of one bombing every two months. By November 1951, Harry T. Moore, state director of Florida's NAACP, had had enough. Moore defiantly challenged the state to rein in the Klan and its minions and bring the cowards, including Sheriff McCall, to justice. With that last act of courage, Harry T. Moore signed his death warrant. On Christmas night, as Moore and his wife slept, the Klan detonated a bomb so powerful that it blew out half of the Moores' home and killed Harry Moore almost instantly. His wife suffered burns so horrendous that she lingered in agony for days until, mercifully, death ended her misery.[32]

It was clear that a discernible path of governmental indifference led straight from the carnage at Groveland to the charred bodies of Harry and Harriet Moore.[33] African Americans and other equally appalled citizens were enraged that the federal government could somehow marshal enormous financial and moral resources to defend the "oppressed" in Eastern Europe and Korea, but declare bankruptcy when it came to protecting the lives of black citizens in the United States. "If you can intervene in a civil war in far off Korea," one group wrote to Truman, "surely you can intervene in the war against the . . . Negro people in the United States." One man observed that "something is truly wrong when black men have a better chance on the front lines in Korea than they have in Truman's vacation paradise of Florida." Fed up with all of the government's excuses, another woman simply "demand[ed]" that Truman "get off [his] rear end and do the right thing—NOW!"[34] In short, African Americans laid the responsibility for the Moores' assassination right where it belonged: on Truman's doorstep.

The stark reality of that disturbing fact evoked a crisis in confidence in one of America's most ardent supporters, the NAACP. When news of the bombing reached Channing Tobias in Paris, he bowed down his head and sadly remarked that after all the NAACP had done to protect America's honor against the CRC, to have the Moores killed was a body blow from which the United States might never recover. State-condoned murders of civil rights workers —on the holiest of all holidays—seemed to punctuate what Patterson had said all along. Maybe one or two murders could be explained away as "isolated" incidents. But the assassination of Harry Moore and his wife was clearly the capstone on years of state-sanctioned persecution. In Tobias's words, "The American delegation [was] . . . confronted daily" with "a recital of racial violence" not only from the Soviets but also "from the nonwhite nations whose friendship we sorely need[ed]."[35]

Tobias may have focused his angst on the international implications of the murders, but the fundamental question of just what is American democracy vexed the NAACP leadership at home. Even Walter White was temporarily shaken out of his "enormous progress" realm. White told Edith Sampson that out "of the more than forty lynchings and more than twenty race riots [he had] investigated . . . this was by long odds the most cold, unjustified, and heinous one of them all." A response to the Moores' assassination by Roy Wilkins and signed by Arthur B. Spingarn, president, and Louis Wright, chair of the NAACP, reflected how profoundly the murders had unsettled the association. Harry T. Moore, they wrote President Truman, "believed in the American Declaration of Independence." He "believed in the Constitution." Moore had protested the brutal murder of a handcuffed prisoner "in the American way, with the American weapons of law and order." For believing in America, he was mercilessly killed. Worse, he was murdered by a group of cowards who had been allowed to terrorize blacks, Jews, and Catholics for years. In a desperate plea for Truman to catch just one lyncher, they ruefully concluded that "if Harry T. Moore was wrong, . . . then there is no America . . . and all the dreams we [have] preach[ed] have no meaning."[36]

As eloquent and painful as the NAACP's plea to the president may have been, Truman remained unaffected. He apparently believed that most of the howling was just more of the same, shrill communist wailing. Phileo Nash, his assistant in the minority affairs office, gently set the record straight. Nash carefully explained that in just one week, the White House had been deluged with hundreds of angry telegrams. While there were clearly some communists who complained, "as indicated by their use of the word 'genocide' . . . there [were] many [telegrams] from sincere and loyal Americans who [were] shocked by the crime and [who felt] that [the president] should do something about it personally."[37]

The CRC also responded forcefully to the murder of the Moores, refusing to allow its charge of genocide to be dismissed as hyperbole. Angie Dickerson, assistant executive secretary of the CRC, remarked that the bomb that sent Mr. and Mrs. Harry Moore to eternity was exploding for the entire world to hear.[38] CRC branches pointed to the Moores' charred remains and declared "Genocide: Exhibit A." They adroitly linked the American Embassy's attempt to seize Patterson's passport with the desperate U.S. need to keep the slaughter of African Americans hidden behind the cotton curtain.[39] The Moores' deaths rejuvenated Patterson, the Civil Rights Congress, and the CRC's sagging *Genocide* petition efforts. The Christmas bombing had simply raised the stakes. *We Charge Genocide* now had more than cachet; it had credence. The CRC reported that important countries outside the Soviet bloc had agreed to place the *Genocide* petition on the docket of the Commission on Human Rights. Shortly after this announcement, Patterson triumphantly returned to Paris.[40]

U.S. officialdom responded with alacrity. UN Commission on Human Rights chair Eleanor Roosevelt had already alerted Truman that the *Genocide* petition had "hurt [the United States] in so many little ways."[41] Patterson's reemergence in Paris could now only portend more difficulties for the U.S. delegation. It was clear that Patterson had to be removed and the damage undone. Earlier in 1951 he had dodged a "contempt of Congress" conviction because of a mistrial. Apparently, the lone African American juror was outraged that a Georgia congressman who had called Patterson "a black son-of-a-bitch" was not the one cited for "contempt," and she simply refused to find the national secretary of the CRC guilty of any wrongdoing. Because of her resolve, Patterson was free but only temporarily. Undoubtedly, his international exploits had now prompted the U.S. government to go after him again and, more important, to set the new trial date for 28 January 1952. With the new court date looming, Patterson was quickly thrown on a plane back to New York and his passport confiscated. Shortly after his arrival in the United States, however, Patterson learned that his case had been conveniently postponed, but with no passport, he could not return to Paris. The simple truth, Patterson railed, in explaining his "humiliating" treatment, was that the U.S. government "was afraid to face . . . 'charges of genocide.'"[42]

There was another "truth" the State Department wanted the world to hear and wanted Edith Sampson—not William Patterson—to tell. It was obvious why. Sampson had vowed to "link arms with the worst Dixiecrat [sic] . . . to save [her] country." At a meeting with an Indian audience, which was usually very vocal about the harsh treatment of African Americans, she gaily prattled on about the wonderful "benefits of slavery" such as "never hav[ing] to worry about unemployment . . . food, clothing, and shelter." That type of performance made her the perfect American Negro for the State Department, especially now with the Moore bombing undercutting all of the hard work done by the NAACP to discredit the *Genocide* petition. Sampson, of course, denounced the petition as nothing but the "Communists . . . spreading misinformation about the Negro" and she swore to do a "stepped-up, hard-hitting job . . . to offset the damage which ha[d] already been done [by America's] enemies."[43]

In Helsinki, Sampson praised the U.S. judicial system for its unrelenting efforts to drive the Klan out of business. She boasted to the Finns that "the KKK ha[d] disappeared" from the American scene and its leaders had been "sent to the penitentiary." She scoffed at the idea of Jim Crow and assured her audience that she did not live in a black neighborhood, worship at an all-black church, nor had she ever attended a racially segregated school. Sampson also allayed the audience's fears about the franchise. Negroes did not exercise their right to vote, she said, but there was nothing stopping them. The poll tax, she claimed authoritatively, was a relic of the past. Also a distant memory, Sampson insisted, was the grinding poverty that had consigned African Americans to the mudsills of America's economic ruts. All the Negroes she knew had big shiny, black Cadillacs, lived in $100,000 homes, and sent their children to schools that were the envy of whites. Sampson concluded this amazing speech with a ready-made explanation of both Sheriff McCall's execution of Samuel Shepherd and the Moores' hellish deaths. Those acts of violence, Sampson assured her audience, were just "the last ditch acts . . . of a small group of pathological people." As she took her final bows, Sampson earnestly swore that she had not attempted to paint a prettier picture than that which actually existed in the United States. Rather she had "simply given [them] the truth, the whole truth, and nothing but the truth."[44]

State Department officials congratulated themselves on their brilliant strategy and raved about what "an unqualified success" Sampson had been in their "carefully-planned Scandinavian speaking tour." One report asserted that "there [was] no question whatever that Mrs. Sampson's visit did a great deal to open the eyes of a good many Swedes to the fact that the days of Uncle Tom's Cabin belong[ed] to the past." Of course, that statement was difficult to reconcile with the Justice Department's analysis that "Southern Negroes . . . were treated . . . as if there had never been a Reconstruction. They lived in fear just as they had many years ago."[45]

African American leaders and the black press carefully noted Sampson's swirl of lies. One reporter for the NAACP's *Crisis* declared that Sampson's Copenhagen performance was "dishonest and . . . revolting." Sampson, he wrote, "created an observable shudder of revulsion . . . by boasting about the 'expensive black cars' and the $100,000 . . . homes which a few wealthy Negroes own." Yet, although Sampson tried to illustrate black equality in the United States by pointing to a handful of African Americans who enjoyed some success, she "failed to explain . . . how the appointment of a Negro judge improve[d] the living conditions of 14,999,999 other Negroes." In short, the reporter concluded, Sampson's "propaganda with a capital 'P' was sheer fantasy" straight out of "Cloud-Cuckoo Land."[46]

Eleanor Roosevelt "did not like the report in *Crisis* on Mrs. Sampson's speech" and made sure that Walter White knew it. Yet, a Swedish woman who had heard the speech implored White to set the record straight. Sampson's speech was "a betrayal of the Negro people" and "demonstrate[d] its venality" by totally misrepresenting the power and influence of the Ku Klux Klan. Sampson, the Swede declared, was so caught up in the Truman administration's cynical policy of "brazenly denying" the deplorable condition of blacks in the United States that she failed to use America's vulnerability in the area of civil rights to "wring from [the United States] greater justice for the Negro." The Civil Rights Congress also lambasted Sampson and predicted that after the extent of her "State Department–inspired lies" became known, she would be "so ridiculed by the masses of the Negro people that she could never again be advertised as a so-called spokesman for Negro Americans."[47]

The CRC wanted that honor for itself. Patterson had come out hard against Sampson. He had denounced the U.S. government for its sins of omission in allowing the slaughter to occur in Florida, and he had backed up that fiery defense of "Negro rights" with a petition submitted to the United Nations. Was this enough for the CRC to position itself more favorably in the African American community? Patterson certainly hoped so because the needs of the Communist Party leadership were becoming desperate. In June 1951 the Supreme Court upheld the Smith Act convictions of the Communist Eleven, and, in a frantic move to keep the government from prosecuting the party into oblivion, the remaining leadership, sensing that it was "'five minutes to midnight,' . . . disappeared into an elaborate underground apparatus." CRC was also teetering on the brink. Only a massive infusion of money and members could shore up what was now a weak and vulnerable organization.[48]

Now was the time to form the vanguard of the united front. Patterson therefore explained to a CRC colleague that the *Genocide* petition provided "great possibilities for unifying elements who . . . would not [have] move[d] in concert with us before." Patterson especially targeted the black church as a possible partner in struggle. He confided to his colleague at the National Council of American Soviet Friendship that the CRC had decided through the skillful use of the *Genocide* petition "to undertake a systematic and persistent effort . . . to raise the thinking of the Negro clergy." In wooing the church, he offered D. V. Jemison, the head of the National Baptist Convention, the position of chair of the National Committee to End Genocide. He also tried to persuade the largest black Baptist organization in the United States to issue a massive reprint of the *Genocide* petition and distribute it at the upcoming national convention of ministers.[49] The issue of African Americans' rights was the moral hook that Patterson hoped would bring church membership and financial resources to bear on the CRC's "A-1 civil rights case," the imprisonment and ongoing persecution of the Communist Party leadership. Patterson therefore directed that the CRC make "every effort . . . to use Negro History Week" to fuse the struggle to find the Moores' killers with anti–Smith Act protest and "the fight for the rights of minority political parties." In a fund-raising letter to religious and fraternal organizations, Patterson, evoking the name of *We Charge Genocide*, declared that the petition had firmly established the CRC's civil rights credentials. He insisted that with the financial support of the churches and the unions, the "offensive" begun for the "rights and human dignity of the Negroes could be enlarged . . . to destroy the Smith . . . Act."[50]

The national secretary of the CRC fully realized, however, that in order to have the united front he so desperately craved, the NAACP would have to be converted or at least neutralized. Although Patterson's previous attempts to forge some type of rapprochement with the NAACP were answered "with as rotten a statement as [Patterson] ha[d] ever seen in all [his] life," he was will-ing to try again. Was it not about time, he pleaded with the NAACP leader-ship, that we "end once and for all the pitting of Negro against Negro?"[51] The problem, however, was that Negro was not pitted against Negro. Rather, So-viet Negro was pitted against American Negro so that no one articulated the complete needs of African Americans.

The Civil Rights Congress's priorities were decidedly skewed. Although its Marxist analysis sometimes provided rapier insight into the economic con-ditions of black America, the CRC's devotion to the Communist Party hob-bled the organization's effectiveness and severely crippled the CRC's credibil-ity. As long as the CRC continued to maintain that the "A-1 civil rights case in America" was that of the Communist Eleven, it could not launch a full frontal assault on American racism and black inequality. Indeed, the CRC lead-ership openly acknowledged that its efforts to defend blacks who had been rushed to the executioner's chair were "spotty and weak."[52] It admitted that in the struggle for equal employment, the CRC was "not . . . a leader in the fight for . . . Negroes." Patterson, however, was unapologetic. While finaliz-ing the *Genocide* petition, he stated unequivocally that when it came to set-ting human rights priorities, he "put[s] first . . . the fight against the Smith Act, and *then* the fight for Negro rights."[53]

The NAACP had its own difficulties setting priorities. Just as the CRC's strength was drained by too close an alignment with the Communist Party, the NAACP's liaison with the Democratic Party proved just as debilitating. By 1948 the NAACP had allowed itself to be seduced by President Truman's cam-paign promises. In desperate need of the black vote in a highly politicized Red-baiting election, Truman whispered sweet civil rights talk into the NAACP's ear. The price of succumbing to that seduction, however, was the ouster of as-sociation cofounder W. E. B. Du Bois and the repudiation of the UN petition, *An Appeal to the World*.[54] A full three years later, the civil rights promises remained just that, promises. Although the NAACP leadership began to grumble that Truman had just strung it along, the association now had no place else to go.[55] It had ceded its leverage to play off the Democrats against the Republicans, jettisoned its international strategy, and discarded its most visionary leader. The association was, therefore, left with a very limited range of options to secure black rights. Most important, it made no use of the Declaration on Human Rights as a vehicle for black equality.

Human rights were nevertheless essential. The NAACP, as influenced by Du Bois, understood this and had attempted to wed the association's civil rights agenda to the United Nation's human rights platform. This not only included the traditional political and legal rights as enumerated in the U.S. Constitution, but encompassed a range of social, cultural, and, most important, economic rights. Then came the Cold War and the NAACP's strategy shattered. In McCarthyist America, economic equality quickly became linked with communism. This was especially evident after the UN published the Covenant on Human Rights, which, unlike the declaration, was a treaty. Southern Democrats and right-wing Republicans immediately denounced the economic and social equality sections as a Soviet Trojan horse that would corrupt the very foundation of American society. Because those rights were supposedly rooted in communist ideology, the Truman administration was averse to accepting them as part of the covenant. When the United States made it clear that it could not reconcile economic and social rights with full democracy, the NAACP, afraid of jeopardizing its legal efforts to dismantle Jim Crow, declared itself an "American organization." It discarded the now tainted human rights platform and opted to pursue the still difficult, but politically safer, civil rights strategy.[56]

This was a fateful decision. In its rush for Cold War respectability, the NAACP had allowed its Negro soul to be "bleach[ed] . . . in a flood of white Americanism."[57] The association draped itself in the flag and confined itself to a civil rights platform stripped of the economic rights necessary to overcome more than 300 years of oppression. Just as troubling, African American leftists like William Patterson embroiled themselves in the legal battles of the Communist Party and subordinated the needs of black America to the priorities of an organization more committed to the welfare of a foreign nation. The onset of the Cold War left the African American leadership struggling with "two warring ideals in one dark body."[58] African Americans were unfortunate casualties of that war.

Notes

1. W. E. B. Du Bois, *The Souls of Black Folk* (New York: New American Library, 1969), 45.

2. Resolutions Adopted by the 41st Annual Convention, 23 June 1950, part 1, reel 12, NAACP Board of Directors Meetings, 1944–53 (Washington, D.C., 1982), microfilm (hereafter NAACP); NAACP Moves to Ban Communist Activity, press release, 24 June 1950, part 1, reel 12; minutes of the Meeting of the Board of Directors, 11 Dec. 1950, part 1, reel 3; NAACP Press Releases, 24 June 1950, part 1, reel 12, NAACP.

3. Dan T. Carter, *Scottsboro: A Tragedy of the American South* (Baton Rouge: Louisiana State University Press, 1969, 1979), 51–103; Resolutions Adopted by the 41st Annual Convention, 23 June 1950, part 1, NAACP Board of Directors Meetings, 1944–53; NAACP Moves to Ban Communist Activity, press release, 24 June 1950,

part 1; minutes of the Meeting of the Board of Directors, 11 Dec. 1950, part 1; NAACP Press Releases, 24 June 1950, part 1, reel 12, NAACP. For more on the relationship between the NAACP and the Left, see Wilson Record, *The Negro and the Communist Party* (New York: Atheneum, 1971); Wilson Record, *Race and Radicalism: The NAACP and the Communist Party in Conflict* (Ithaca: Cornell University Press, 1964); James L. Roark, "American Black Leaders: The Response of Colonialism and the Cold War," *African Historical Studies* 4, 2 (1971): 253–70; John Baxter Streater, "The National Negro Congress, 1936–1947" (Ph.D. diss., University of Cincinnati, 1981); Gerald Horne, *Black and Red: W. E. B. Du Bois and the Afro-American Response to the Cold War* (Albany: SUNY Press, 1986); Gerald Horne, *Communist Front? The Civil Rights Congress, 1946–1956* (Cranbury, N.J.: Associated University Presses, 1988); Robin D. G. Kelley, *Hammer 'n Hoe: Alabama Communists during the Great Depression* (Chapel Hill: University of North Carolina Press, 1990); Gerald Horne, *Black Liberation/Red Scare: Ben Davis and the Communist Party* (Newark: University of Delaware Press, 1994); Earl Ofari Hutchinson, *Blacks and Reds: Race and Class Conflict, 1919–1990* (East Lansing: Michigan State University Press, 1995).

4. White to Senator Albert Thomas, 6 July 1950, box 1, file "Agreements with Foreign Governments, 1948–1953," NAACP Papers, Washington Bureau, Library of Congress, Washington, D.C. (NAACP/LC).

5. White to Matthew J. Connelly, 7 Sept. 1950, box 27, file "Civil Rights/Negro Affairs, 1949–52," Papers of David K. Niles, Harry S. Truman Library, Independence, Mo.; White to Harry S. Truman, 7 Sept. 1950, box 27, file "Civil Rights/Negro Affairs, 1949–52," Niles Papers; White to Truman, telegram/cross reference sheet, 11 Dec. 1950, box 545, file "OF 93 Miscellaneous—1950," Papers of Harry S. Truman: Official File (Truman: OF), Truman Library. Francis J. McConnell to Eleanor Roosevelt, 15 Oct. 1951, box 3389, file "White, Walter, 1951–52"; White to Eleanor Roosevelt, 27 Sept. 1951, box 3389, file "White, Walter, 1951–52"; Walter White, "Time for a Progress Report," *Saturday Review of Literature* (Sept. 1951), in box 3389, file "White, Walter, 1951–52," Papers of Eleanor Roosevelt, Franklin D. Roosevelt Presidential Library, Hyde Park, N.Y. "White Cites Gains in U.S. Race Relations," press release, 13 Sept. 1951, in part 2, reel 17, Papers of the Civil Rights Congress (Washington, D.C., 1989), microfilm (hereafter CRC).

6. "Report of Miss L. B. DeForest on the Rape in Groveland, Florida," 27 July 1950, box 1101, folder 1, Papers of the American Civil Liberties Union, Seely Mudd Manuscript Library, Princeton University, Princeton, N.J.; NAACP, "Groveland U.S.A.: Riots, Hate, Terror, Lynch Law, Ku Klux Klan, Night Riding, Home Burning," pamphlet, part 2, reel 19, CRC. On Groveland, see also Jack Greenberg, *Crusaders in the Courts: How a Dedicated Band of Lawyers Fought for the Civil Rights Revolution* (New York: Basic Books, 1994).

7. "What Dr. Tobias Replied to Russia's Andrei Bishinsky [*sic*]," 21 Nov. 1951, folder 42, "United Nations 1951–1952," biographical file: Channing Tobias Papers, University of Minnesota, Minneapolis.

8. William Z. Foster to William Patterson, 23 Nov. 1951; Patterson to Ferdinand C. Smith, 2 Nov. 1951; Patterson to Smith, 10 Nov. 1951, part 2, reel 2; Patterson to William Z. Foster, 16 Nov. 1951; Patterson to Pettis Perry, 26 Nov. 1951, part 2, reel 1, CRC. Patterson to Darling [Louise Patterson], 10 Dec. 1951, box 9, folder 87; draft Chapter XVII, *We Charge Genocide*, n.d., box 7, folder 53; draft *I Go to the United*

Nations, n.d., box 7, folder 47, William Patterson Papers, Moorland-Spingarn Research Center, Howard University, Washington, D.C.

9. Carol Anderson, "From Hope to Disillusion: African Americans, the United Nations, and the Struggle for Human Rights, 1944–1947," *Diplomatic History* 20 (Fall 1996): 531–63; Patterson to Oakley C. Johnson, 6 May 1952, part 2, reel 3, CRC. On human rights petitions to the United Nations see Paul Gordon Lauren, *Power and Prejudice: The Politics and Diplomacy of Racial Discrimination,* 2nd ed. (Boulder: Westview Press, 1996); Brenda Gayle Plummer, *Rising Wind: Black Americans and U.S. Foreign Affairs, 1935–1960* (Chapel Hill: University of North Carolina Press, 1996).

10. Aubrey Grossman to Friend, 15 July 1951, part 2, reel 14, CRC; Aubrey Grossman to Eleanor Roosevelt (including attached pamphlet "The Case of Willie McGee: A Fact Sheet Prepared by the Civil Rights Congress"), 9 Mar. 1951, box 3326, file "McGee, Willie, 1950–51," Roosevelt Papers.

11. "Questions and Answers on Genocide Convention," n.d., box 8, file "Genocide (folder 1 of 2)," lot file 55D429, General Records of the Department of State, Record Group 59, National Archives (hereafter RG 59); Donald C. Blaisdell, interview, Donald C. Blaisdell Oral History, Truman Library. Sandifer to Gross, memo, 14 Apr. 1948, box 8, file "Genocide (folder 1 of 2)," lot file 55D429, RG 59; "Position on Genocide Convention in ECOSOC Drafting Committee: Through Gross and Sandifer," 2 Apr. 1948, box 8, file "Genocide (folder 1 of 2)," lot file 55D429, RG 59; Durward V. Sandifer, interview, Durward V. Sandifer Oral History, Truman Library; Brien McMahon to Harry Truman, 13 July 1950, box 1699, file "2352," Truman: OF; Fisher to Rusk, memo, 19 Jan. 1950, box 8, file "Genocide (folder 1 of 2)," Lot File 55D429, RG 59.

12. "We Charge Genocide: Speech Delivered by William L. Patterson . . . to Launch the Publication of the Book," 12 Nov. 1951, box 5, folder 27, Patterson Papers; Patterson to William Z. Foster, 16 Nov. 1951, part 2, reel 1, CRC.

13. Patterson to Ben Gold, 20 Nov. 1951, part 2, reel 2, CRC; Patterson to John Adams Kingsbury, 28 Nov. 1951, reel 66, *Papers of W. E. B. Du Bois* (Sanford, N.C., 1980); Patterson to Ferdinand C. Smith, 6 Sept. 1951, and 2 Nov. 1951; Patterson to Harry Pollitt, 9 Nov. 1951; Patterson to Joseph Starobin, 26 Nov. 1951, part 2, reel 2; Elizabeth to Patterson, n.d., part 2, reel 33, CRC; Patterson to Darling [Louise Patterson], n.d., box 9, folder 87; draft Chapter XVIII, At the Palais Chaillot in Paris, n.d., box 7, folder 56; Patterson to All Delegates to the General Assembly of the United Nations, 18 Dec. 1951, box 5, folder 70, Patterson Papers; Patterson to Eleanor Roosevelt, 18 Dec. 1951, part 2, reel 2, CRC.

14. Report to the National Committee, 7 Feb. 1949, box 9, folder 51; Muriel to Leon, 13 May 1949, box 9, folder 43, Patterson Papers. Patterson to Friend, 27 Aug. 1948, part 2, reel 8; Patterson to Anne Shore, 6 Jan. 1950, part 2, reel 22; Patterson to Anderson, 25 Jan. 1950, part 2, reel 1; "Introductory Remarks Concerning the Following Organizational Plans," 17 May 1949, part 2, reel 8; Patterson to Margie Robinson, 17 Nov. 1949, part 2, reel 22; Patterson to Jack Raskin, 25 Nov. 1949, part 2, reel 27, CRC.

15. Patterson to Raskin, 4 Nov. 1948, part 2, reel 27; Patterson to Benjamin J. Davis Jr., 11 Mar. 1949, part 2, reel 1; Trenton Six Appeal to Be Argued May 16, news release, 10 May 1949, part 2, reel 13; Marcia Friedman to Friend, 13 May 1949, part 2, reel 13; Patterson to Phil Frankfeld, 19 Oct. 1949, part 2, reel 26, CRC. "Why CRC

Should Continue as a General Civil Rights Organization," 2 Jan. 1950, box 9, folder 51, Patterson Papers; Patterson to Percival Prattis, 27 Mar. 1950, part 2, reel 33; Patterson to Nancy Kleinbord, 1 May 1950, part 2, reel 24; Patterson to Ida Rothstein, 5 Jan. 1951, part 2, reel 23; sale of "We Charge Genocide" Vital: Plan of Work, ca. Nov. 1951, part 2, reel 14, CRC.

16. Patterson to Darling [Louise Patterson], ca. 10 Dec. 1951, box 9, folder 87, Patterson Papers. Patterson to C. L. Crum, 21 Aug. 1951, part 2, reel 1; Patterson to Holland Roberts, 26 Nov. 1951, part 2, reel 5, CRC.

17. "We Charge Genocide: Speech Delivered by William Patterson . . . to Launch the Publication of the Book," box 5, folder 27, Patterson Papers. Patterson to Daniel Hughes, 27 Aug. 1951; Patterson to D. N. Pritt, 28 Aug. 1951; Patterson to Joseph Starobin, 26 Nov. 1951, part 2, reel 2, CRC. Draft, "I Go to the United Nations," n.d., box 7, folder 48, Patterson Papers.

18. Patterson to George Marshall, 12 Aug. 1949, box 9, folder 43, Patterson Papers. "Major CRC Campaigns," 21 June 1949, part 2, reel 18; "Summary of Findings and Decisions of the Conference for Civil and Human Rights," 25 June 1949, part 2, reel 29; "Major CRC Campaigns," 16 July 1949, part 2, reel 11; Minutes Resident Board Meeting, 16 July 1949, part 2, reel 12, CRC. George Marshall to Patterson, Milton Wolff, and Will Hayett, 2 Nov. 1949, box 9, folder 51, Patterson Papers. "Some Suggestions for the Baltimore Conference," n.d., part 2, reel 26, CRC.

19. Drew Pearson script, 23 Nov. 1951, box 636, file "United Nations: Genocide, 1947–51"; Wilkins to Committee on Administration, memo, 20 Nov. 1951, box 636, file "United Nations: Genocide, 1947–51"; White to Wilkins, memo, 23 Nov. 1951, box 636, file "United Nations: Genocide, 1947–1951," NAACP/LC.

20. Untitled statement to John Pauker—Voice of America, 16 Nov. 1951, box 636, file "United Nations: Genocide, 1947–51."

21. Statement by Walter White Made upon Request of the U.S. State Department, n.d., box 636, file "United Nations: Genocide, 1947–51."

22. Wilkins to White, memo, 21 Nov. 1951, box 636, file "United Nations: Genocide, 1947–51"; addenda to Address by Roy Wilkins . . . in Answer to Editorial Appearing in the *Atlanta Constitution*, 26 June 1951, in part 2, reel 17, CRC.

23. Hubert T. Delany to White, 23 Nov. 1951, box 636, file "United Nations: Genocide, 1947–51," NAACP/LC.

24. John Devine, Memorandum of Telephone Conversation with Mr. Drew Pearson, 17 Nov. 1951, box 60, file "Genocide against the Negroes, 1951–52," entry 1587, RG 59.

25. Mr. Wainhouse to Mr. Hickerson, memo, 24 Apr. 1951, "General Assembly Sixth Session, US Delegation, Paris, 1951," lot file 55D429; John D. Hickerson "Memorandum for File," box 2, file "6th General Assembly," lot file 58D33, RG 59; "Dr. Tobias Named Alternate U.S. UN Delegate," 20 Sept. 1951, folder 42, "United Nations 1951–1952," Tobias Papers.

26. Derrick Bell, *Faces at the Bottom of the Well: The Permanence of Racism* (New York: Basic Books, 1992), 118; To Mr. Kohler, unsigned [John Hickerson?], 15 Nov. 1951, "Genocide against the Negroes, 1951–52," entry 1587; Hickerson to the Secretary, memo, 24 Oct. 1951, box 2, file "6th General Assembly," lot file 58D33, RG 59; Walter White to Paul Hoffman, 29 Nov. 1951, "United Nations: Genocide, 1947–51," NAACP/LC.

27. Chester S. Williams to Michael Weyl, 19 Dec. 1951, box 11, folder 231, Papers of Edith Sampson, Radcliffe College, Boston.

28. "We Charge Genocide: Speech Delivered by William L. Patterson . . . to Launch the Publication of the Book," 12 Nov. 1951, box 5, folder 27, Patterson Papers.

29. Marginalia to Darling [Louise Patterson] written on "We Charge Genocide: A Speech prepared by William L. Patterson for the . . . United Nations," Dec. 1951, Patterson Papers. Logan to White, 19 Nov. 1951; "Rayford Logan, 1950–51"; Tobias to White, 4 Dec. 1951; "United Nations: Genocide, 1947–51"; White to Tobias, 12 Dec. 1951, NAACP Papers; Logan to White, 28 Dec. 1951, box 404, file "Rayford Logan, 1950–51"; White to Mrs. G. Willard Hales, 7 Feb. 1952; "United Nations: Genocide, 1952–53," NAACP/LC. Pat [William Patterson] to Angie, Dec. 1951; Pat [William Patterson] to [Louise Patterson], n.d., part 2, reel 3, CRC; "We Charge Genocide: A Speech Prepared by William L. Patterson for the General Assembly of the United Nations, Paris France," Dec. 1951; Pat [William Patterson] to Darling [Louise Patterson], 7 Dec. 1951, and n.d.; draft Chapter XVIII, At the Palais Chaillot in Paris, box 7, folder 56, Patterson Papers. Patterson to H. H. Robnett, 1 Feb. 1952, part 2, reel 24, CRC.

30. William A. Rutherford to William Patterson, 19 Feb. 1952, part 2, reel 2, CRC. Draft "I Go to the United Nations: Contemplating the Project," n.d., Patterson Papers. Patterson to John Green, 28 Nov. 1951, part 2, reel 2; Patterson to Pettis Perry, 26 Nov. 1951, part 2, reel 1, CRC. Draft "I Go to the United Nations," box 7, folder 47, Patterson Papers. William Z. Foster to Patterson, 23 Nov. 1951, part 2, reel 2, CRC.

31. Walter Winchell broadcast, transcript, 30 Dec. 1951; draft Chapter XVIII, At the Palais Chaillot in Paris, n.d., box 7, folder 56, Patterson Papers.

32. On the Moore case, see Caroline Emmons, "'Somebody Has Got to Do That Work': Harry T. Moore and the Struggle for African American Voting Rights in Florida," *Journal of Negro History* 82 (Spring 1997): 232–43; James Ridgeway, "Murder Won't Out," *Village Voice* 36, no. 40, 1 Oct. 1991, 23–24.

33. Peter Robertson to Truman, telegram, 27 Dec. 1951, box 547, file "OF 93 Misc.—Moore Bombing," Truman: OF; Ann Lloyd to Truman, telegram, 28 Dec. 1951, box 547, file "OF 93 Misc.—Moore Bombing," Truman: OF; Leo Linder to Truman, telegram, 28 Dec. 1951, box 547, file "OF 93 Misc.—Moore Bombing," Truman: OF. Truman received over 6,000 telegrams denouncing the murders and the federal government's inability to stop the reign of terror in Florida.

34. The Teenage Club of Elizabeth to Truman, telegram, 6 Jan. 1952, box 547, file "OF 93 Misc.—Moore Bombing," Truman: OF; Joe Jacobs to Truman, telegram, 29 Dec. 1951, box 547, file "OF Misc.—Moore Bombing," Truman: OF; S. Rosenblatt to Truman, 28 Dec. 1951, box 547, file "OF Misc.—Moore Bombing," Truman: OF.

35. White to Thurgood Marshall et al., memo, 25 Jan. 1952, box 147, file "Board of Directors: Channing Tobias—General, 1950–53"; Channing H. Tobias, "Not for the Negro Alone," speech, 15 Mar. 1952, box 148, file "Board of Directors: Channing Tobias, Reaction to His Broadcast—1952," NAACP/LC.

36. White to Edith Sampson, 3 Jan. 1952, box 3, folder 72, Sampson Papers; Arthur B. Spingarn and Louis T. Wright to Truman, 27 Dec. 1951, box 10, file "Miami Bombings," Phileo Nash Papers, Truman Library (HST:Nash Files).

37. Truman to Phileo Nash, telegram, 29 Dec. 1951, box 10, file "Miami Bombings"; Phileo Nash to Truman, memo, 3 Jan. 1952, box 10, file "Miami Bombings," HST:Nash Files.

38. Angie Dickerson to Roscoe Dunjee, 14 Jan. 1952, part 2, reel 1, CRC.

39. S. L. Pullman to Truman, telegram, 28 Dec. 1951, box 547, file "OF 93 Misc.—Moore Bombing," Truman: OF; New York State Communist Party to Truman, telegram, 26 Dec. 1951, box 547, file "OF 93 Misc.—Moore Bombing," Truman: OF;

Civil Rights Congress San Francisco Chapter to Truman, telegram, 26 Dec. 1951, box 547, file "OF 93 Misc.—Moore Bombing," Truman: OF. The reference to the "cotton curtain" was earlier but infinitely appropriate; see Patterson to Albert E. Hart, 11 May 1950, part 2, reel 1, CRC.

40. "Two Non–East Bloc Countries to Seek Action by United Nations on Petition Charging U.S. government with Anti-Negro Genocide," press release, 6 Jan. 1952, part 2, reel 19, CRC; William A. Rutherford, "Patterson Defies Ban Returns to Paris," press release, 12 Jan. 1952, box 9, folder 88, Patterson Papers.

41. Eleanor Roosevelt to Truman, 21 Dec. 1951, box 4560, file "Harry S. Truman, 1949–1952," Roosevelt Papers.

42. "Patterson, CRC Head, Faces Second Trial, Jan. 28 in Washington, D.C.," press release, 21 Jan. 1952, box 636, file "United Nations: Genocide, 1952–53," NAACP Papers; no title, press release, 24 Jan. 1951, part 2, reel 42, CRC; Ferdinand Smith to William Patterson, 28 Jan. 1952, part 2, reel 2, CRC.

43. Edith Sampson to Mrs. Eugenia Anderson, 16 Mar. 1952, box 11, folder 229; "Mrs. Edith Sampson's Record of Performance at the Fifth General Assembly," n.d., box 10, folder 210, Sampson Papers. "Address by Mrs. Edith S. Sampson, Alternate U.S. Representative to the General Assembly at the Meeting of the India League Celebrating Gandhi's Birthday," press release, 1 Oct. 1950, NAACP Papers, Race Relations in the International Arena, 1940–55, part 14, reel 17 (NAACP Int'l); Chester S. Williams to Michael Weyl, 19 Dec. 1951, box 11, folder 231; Sampson to Eleanor Roosevelt, 26 Jan. 1952, box 11, folder 234, Sampson Papers.

44. "Mrs. Sampson's Speech (auspices Finnish American Society)," 14 Jan. 1952, box 11, folder 231, Sampson Papers; "Summary of Address delivered by Mrs. Edith Sampson in Stockholm, Sweden . . . on 'The Negro in America,'" 18 Jan. 1952, part 14, reel 17, NAACP Int'l; From Ernie Johnson, News Unit, Department of State, news release, Feb. 1952, part 14, reel 17, NAACP Int'l; "Statement Made in Copenhagen by Mrs. Edith Sampson . . . while visiting Mrs. Eugenia Anderson, American Ambassador to Denmark," 26 Jan. 1952, part 2, reel 5, CRC.

45. State Department memo [fragment], 5 Feb. 1952, box 11, folder 231, Sampson Papers; Eleanor Bontecou, interview, Eleanor Bontecou Oral History, Truman Library.

46. Rea Stanton to Walter White, 3 Feb. 1952, part 14, reel 17, NAACP Int'l; William Worthy, "In Cloud-Cuckoo Land," *Crisis* (April 1952): 226–30, part 14, reel 17, NAACP Int'l.

47. Rea Stanton to Walter White, 3 Feb. 1952, part 14, reel 17, NAACP Int'l; Worthy, "In Cloud-Cuckoo Land"; Eleanor Roosevelt to Walter White, 12 May 1952, box 3389, file "White, Walter, 1951–52," Roosevelt Papers; "State Dep't Charged with Hiding Its 'Overseas Propaganda' on Negroes from U.S.," press release, 11 Feb. 1952, part 2, reel 40, CRC; "Statements Made in Copenhagen by Mrs. Edith Sampson . . . while visiting Mrs. Eugenia Anderson, American Ambassador to Denmark," part 2, reel 5, CRC.

48. Edward P. Johanningsmeier, *Forging American Communism: The Life of William Z. Foster* (Princeton: Princeton University Press, 1994), 324–29; Patterson to John Daschbach, 18 Feb. 1952, part 2, reel 31; D. Quailey to Miss Block, 15 Feb. 1952, part 2, reel 2, CRC. George Marshall to Milt Wolff, n.d., box 9, folder 36, Patterson Papers; Frederick V. Field to Aubrey Grossman, 28 May 1952; Aubrey Grossman to Frederick V. Field, 9 June 1952, part 2, reel 2, CRC.

49. Patterson to Bishop J. H. Clayborn, 30 Jan. 1952, part 2, reel 1; Patterson to

H. H. Robnett, 1 Feb. 1952, part 2, reel 24; Patterson to Rev. Richard Morford, 21 Feb. 1952; Angie Dickerson to Dr. D. V. Jemison, 2 May 1952, part 2, reel 1, CRC.

50. Patterson to H. H. Robnett, 1 Feb. 1952, part 2, reel 24; Patterson to Dear Friend, Feb. 1952, part 2, reel 40, CRC.

51. Patterson to Anne Shore, 14 June 1950, part 2, reel 27; "Let us end once and for all the pitting of Negro against Negro . . . ," *Washington Afro-American*, 23 Feb. 1952, in box 636, file "United Nations—Genocide, 1952–53," NAACP Papers. Patterson to All District Leaders, Boards and Organizers, memo, 19 Feb. 1952, part 2, reel 5, CRC.

52. George Marshall to William L. Patterson, Milton Wolff, and Will Hayett, memorandum, 2 Nov. 1949, box 9, folder 51; George Marshall to Milton Wolff, memorandum, 28 Dec. 1949, box 9, folder 51, Patterson Papers.

53. "Some suggestions for the Baltimore Conference," n.d.; Patterson to D. Pritt, 28 Aug. 1951, part 2, reel 2, CRC (emphasis added).

54. Alfred Baker Lewis to Walter White, 19 Dec. 1947, box 665, file "Wallace, Henry A.—General, 1945–48"; White to Truman, telegram, 2 Feb. 1948, file "Harry S. Truman, 1946–49"; "The President Means It by Walter White," 9 Feb. 1948, file "Articles: Walter White Syndicated Column Drafts, 1948," NAACP/LC. White to David Niles, box 27, file "Civil Rights Negro Affairs, July 1947–48," Niles Papers; Channing H. Tobias to Phileo Nash, 29 March 1948, box 14, file "T (folder 1)," HST:Nash Files. Du Bois to Arthur Spingarn, 2 April 1948, box 94-20, folder 449, Arthur B. Spingarn Papers, Moorland-Spingarn Research Center, Howard University, Washington, D.C. Tobias to Truman, telegram, 27 July 1948, box 1512, file "T," Truman: OF; "Itinerary of Governor William H. Hastie: Campaign Tour for the Re-Election of President Truman," 13 Oct. 1948, box 62, file "WH Files—Political—1948—Campaign Hastie, Governor—Political Tour—Press Releases," HST:Nash Files. White to Truman, telegram, 3 Nov. 1948, box 633, file "Harry S. Truman, 1946–49," NAACP Papers; Phileo Nash to Truman, memorandum, 6 Nov. 1948, box 27, file "Civil Rights/Negro Affairs July 1947–48," Niles Papers; Charles P. Howard to Roy Wilkins, 6 Nov. 1948, box 633, file "Harry S. Truman, 1946–49," NAACP/LC.

55. Roy Wilkins to Truman, telegram, 12 Apr. 1950, box 1235, file "413 (1950–53)," Truman: OF; Walter White to David Niles, 11 June 1951, box 26, file "Civil Rights/Negro Affairs 1945–June 1947," Niles Papers.

56. Keynote Address of Roy Wilkins at 42nd Annual Convention of NAACP, 26 June 1951, part 2, reel 17, CRC.

57. Phrase taken from Du Bois, *Souls of Black Folk*, 45. The phrase was not directed at the NAACP (when the book was first written in 1903, the NAACP had not yet been founded), but its meaning superbly conveys what happened to the NAACP.

58. Du Bois, *Souls of Black Folk*, 45.

An American Dilemma

Race and Realpolitik in the
American Response to the
Bandung Conference, 1955

In December 1954 five newly independent Asian countries—Burma, Ceylon, India, Indonesia, and Pakistan—announced a plan for a conference of African, Asian, and Middle Eastern states. The ensuing 1955 Afro-Asian conference in Bandung, Indonesia, ushered in a new era of international relations as nations of color began a sustained campaign to end colonial rule in the non-European world and its corollary of white supremacy. It was the first major conference of non-European states and led to the creation of the nonaligned movement.

For the United States, this provocation by nonwhite peoples was particularly discomfiting. International attacks on white supremacy made it clear to U.S. policy makers that outside observers were assessing the domestic record on race relations. The recent Supreme Court decision in the case of *Brown v. Board of Education* provided a benchmark for measuring the distance between American performance and American promise. Washington's willingness to underwrite European imperial pretensions as well as its own status as a colonial power in the Caribbean and the Pacific was under scrutiny. America confronted a three-part dilemma provoked by its own domestic record on race, its practice of colonialism, and its tacit support of European colonial systems.

The Afro-Asian conference, often referred to in the literature simply as the Bandung Conference, brought revised perspectives on the politics of race in both domestic and foreign arenas. This essay argues that the U.S. response to the Bandung Conference provides critical insights into American efforts to manage an international system that was increasingly shaped by the politics of race and anticolonialism. The emergence of the Third World as a factor in international relations inaugurated a reevaluation of American capacity to mold the agendas in the global arena. It also had a little noted, but significant, impact upon U.S. race relations.

The State Department's response to the Bandung Conference revealed much about U.S. ideological and policy goals outside Europe. Bandung also sparked interest among prominent African Americans, most notably Adam Clayton Powell and Richard Wright.[1] Their individual decisions to attend the Bandung Conference provide some insights into the catalytic impact that Bandung had on American race relations. The foreign and domestic politics of race intersected at Bandung, an event that would prove to be a watershed in the struggle to end white supremacy and the European colonial enterprise in Asia and Africa. The politics of race at Bandung imposed limits on the U.S. capacity to influence the evolution of the international order. Racism at home and support of European colonialism abroad combined to limit the credibility of espousals of "freedom" as counterweights to the anticolonial strategies of communist states.

Asian leaders' objectives in calling a conference included exploring and advancing "common and mutual interests" among the Afro-Asian countries. The Bandung Conference would "consider problems of special interest about nationalism, racialism, and colonialism" and "view the position of the African-Asian countries and their peoples in the world today and the contributions they can make to the promotion of world peace and cooperation." Their message indicated that twenty-five other countries, including Japan, the People's Republic of China, the British colonies of Gold Coast and the Central African Federation, and both North and South Vietnam would be invited. The leaders expressed their support for the Geneva Agreement on Indochina, which they "hope[d] would be fully respected and implemented by all concerned and that there would be no outside interference which would hinder their successful implementation." The message endorsed Indonesia's position on West Irian in its dispute with the Netherlands and reiterated Asian leaders' support for "the demands of the peoples of Tunisia and Morocco for their national independence and their legitimate right to self determination."[2] The leaders clearly signaled that the newly independent Asian states were becoming active players on their own behalf in a region where the Korean War and the French struggle to control Indochina had become surrogate wars between the major European alliances and their respective Asian allies.

In contrast, the U.S. extension of its security umbrella in the region through Southeast Asian Treaty Organization (SEATO) defense agreements with Japan, Australia and New Zealand, and South Korea appeared to be an attempt to institutionalize a bipolar order in Asia that would parallel that in Europe. Efforts to create the Baghdad Pact provoked similar concerns on the part of Egypt and India. In essence, a movement to reproduce the Soviet-American conflict in Asian and Middle Eastern countries seemed to be gaining mo-

By 1960 the interest in nonalignment expressed at the Bandung Conference had produced a multiracial bloc of neutralist states whose leaders included those shown here.
From left to right: Jawaharlal Nehru of India, Kwame Nkrumah of Ghana, Gamal
Abdel Nasser of the United Arab Republic, Sukarno of Indonesia, and Marshall Tito
of Yugoslavia. (Bettmann/Corbis)

mentum in areas outside of Europe just as Western colonial controls in these
regions were being dismantled. Support for Indonesia in its dispute with the
Netherlands, the invitation to the People's Republic of China, and the public
support for the Geneva Agreement on Indochina demonstrated the desire of
these leaders to assert a greater degree of control over Asian affairs.[3]

Just as important, the invitation to China to participate in the meeting and
the exclusion of the Soviet Union and its Warsaw Pact allies, Yugoslavia and
the European neutrals, and the entire American continent from the list of invitees demonstrated the focus on issues of import to Asians and Africans. For
Asian and Arab states that achieved independence in a world dominated by
the countries of the Northern Hemisphere and were excluded from the decision-
making bodies of the United Nations, the Bandung Conference represented
a collaborative search for a vehicle to exert influence on the international order.
The decision to invite Arab and African countries to the Bandung Conference,
and the open endorsement of national self-determination by the sponsoring
countries, also indicated their willingness to take their search for allies be-

yond Asia.[4] The Bandung Conference was the first step in institutionalizing the nonaligned movement that increasingly influenced international relations after 1950, and in popularizing the notion of a "Third World" that transcended the major alliance systems. The Afro-Asian conference launched an era of growing antiracist assertiveness by people of color. Asians and Africans frequently focused on the ideologies of white supremacy that girded segregation in the United States, apartheid in South Africa, and European colonial rule in Africa, Asia, and the Caribbean.

The meeting of the leaders of the five South and Southeast Asian states at Bogor (Indonesia) in December 1954 and their joint communiqué proposing the Afro-Asian conference posed a serious dilemma for the United States. The U.S. Embassy in Djakarta, in an assessment of implications for American policy, revealed the nature of the predicament. "Contrary to earlier expectations of many," Ambassador Hugh Smith Cumming Jr. wrote, "Afro-Asian conference is apparently now about to become a reality. From one standpoint Red China has won a real victory: Short of membership in UN they have gained a forum and a potential audience which must have been beyond their expectations. This is real gain for Peking and for Ho Chi-Minh. On the other hand I think we should not be discouraged. The conference, if properly handled by our information agencies and through well-planned diplomatic action, may, I think, be used to our advantage."

The People's Republic of China (PRC), through its military support for North Korea against the United States in the Korean War and its role in helping the Viet Minh humiliate France in Indochina, had become a major constraint upon the expansion of American influence in Asia. The U.S. response to the PRC's growing power was to treat it as a "pariah" state in the hope of isolating it from its Asian neighbors and containing its influence in the region. The invitation to the PRC by the sponsoring countries cast doubt on the effectiveness of the anti-Chinese campaign.

In returning to the drawing board, Cumming highlighted two possible approaches to an event that the State Department saw as highly problematic. "We can disparage the conference: Point up the divergences of the political, religious and even racial interests of the participating countries and thus turn a cold shoulder to the whole affair." The embassy thought that strategy would only alienate Asian leaders. "It would stimulate not only Communist propaganda but would also expose the US to the false charges so frequently heard in this part of the world that we are not really interested in the attainment of full sovereign positions in world affairs by the new south and southeast Asian countries."

Cumming favored another tack. "The most useful line to be taken both diplomatically and publicity wise would be one of general sympathy, hope for the conference's success, and moderate expressions, short of condescension, of approval of this example of the growth of a sense of responsibility to and in the world of these new nations, even though we may not agree with their methods or all their aims. In other words, encourage[ment,] not discouragement." The ambassador advocated persuading such friendly countries as the Philippines, Thailand, Iran, Egypt, Iraq, "and above all Turkey to attend so that their voices may be heard."[5] Bandung was emerging as a test of American willingness to accommodate to the changing power realities in Asia, realities that envisaged the diminution of Western influence in the region. The U.S. Embassy in Djakarta clearly understood those realities, and its proposed response illustrated its realization that flexibility was a prerequisite for the continued exercise of American influence.

In a memorandum on "U.S. Asian Policy and Communist China," the State Department began to grapple directly with the implications of the Afro-Asian conference. It was becoming clear that the PRC was gaining influence among the nonaligned states. "We were sure," wrote one member of the Southeast Asia section, recalling Korean War–era contacts with the Chinese, "from our dealings with them and from Peking's propaganda that the regime was interested in a conference primarily as a sounding board and as a means to regularize its status outside the UN as long as their admission to that organization was barred. Geneva certainly increased the status and acceptability of Communist China in Asia. The Afro-Asian conference, if held without any major difficulties or disagreements would go even further along these lines."

This assessment acknowledged that Asian countries were likely to normalize their relations with China: some had already done so. The United States sought a response to the trend. "How are we going to deal with Asian governments and peoples with respect to Communist China? If it is true that there is a growing tendency to accept Communist China and to regularize relations—a tendency conceived in fear and logic—what can we do about it?"[6]

The end of the Korean War and the conclusion of the Geneva Agreement on Indochina had created a new context in Asia, one in which the Chinese presence could not be discounted by other Asian states or by extraregional actors such as the United States. Bandung served as a catalyst for the United States to rethink its relationship with the PRC as Asian opinion about China's regional role began to shift.[7] The U.S. Embassy in Tokyo communicated to Washington the extent to which the proposed meeting had redefined the Asian context. The Japanese government, according to embassy analysts, saw an invitation to the conference as a way of "enhancing its prestige in Asia.

Japanese are deeply sensitive about isolation from mainstream Asian politics, and desirous of exploiting any opportunity to reestablish Japan's status as major Asian power. . . . Furthermore, particularly if decision must be made prior to March elections, government will be under strong political pressures to attend since rejection would be viewed as contrary to 'new' foreign policy of 'independence' and increased Asian emphasis. Decision of other anticommunist Asian invitees to attend would also strengthen Japanese determination to accept invitation."[8]

While the embassy believed that the Japanese government was likely to make a decision about attending the conference only after consultation with the United States, it argued that the Japanese should be encouraged to participate so as to provide leadership for the anticommunist countries. Japan's prestige had been badly tarnished by its imperialist policies in China and Korea and by the behavior of its armed forces in areas they occupied during the 1930s and 1940s. Bandung was undoubtedly perceived by the Japanese government as an opening to other nations that could help rehabilitate its reputation in Asia. Tokyo, which had redefined itself as a pillar of the Pax Americana, seemed conscious of the changing political milieu and the opportunities it provided for reinserting itself into regional politics.[9]

Notwithstanding the increasing evidence of China's evolving status in Asia, Secretary of State Dulles seemed unwilling to make the intellectual leap of rethinking the American role in Asia. In a circular telegram to missions in Asia and Africa, Dulles made it clear that the United States feared the Bandung Conference could abet communist efforts to create divisions between noncommunist Asian governments and Washington. "In such circumstances Asian states would be exposed to eventual Communist engulfment."[10]

Dulles clearly recognized the significance of the conference for redefining Asian politics and viewed its sponsors as "dupes" of the communist powers. In a subsequent message, Dulles let it be known that the United States had tentatively decided that "if without strong-arm methods Conference could be prevented or considerable number significant countries influenced decline attend US would welcome such outcome. US would not however want to take any open action which could be considered threatening since would probably bring bad reaction." If the Afro-Asian meeting could not be sabotaged, Dulles advised that the United States would prefer that its friends participated and introduced "resolutions and amendments which would embarrass Communist China." Such actions would curtail the possibility that a hostile bloc of states would be formed.[11]

Dulles's views had been articulated at a meeting with senior officers of the State Department and his brother, CIA director Allen Dulles. In that meeting

John Foster Dulles expressed his view that "such a loose regional association with meetings from time to time could become a very effective forum, and that the idea of such regional groupings approximated the Soviet line advanced at the Berlin Conference in favor of continental groupings in Europe, Asia, and Africa with the United States excluded, then the Communist engulfment of these nations will be comparatively easy." Dulles was unwilling to concede that the Asian countries were capable of exercising autonomy in the international relations of the region. He obviously feared that such autonomy would compromise Western influence and argued that "if the nations invited to Bandung, acquired the habit of meeting from time to time without Western participation, India and China because of their vast populations will very certainly dominate the scene and that one by-product will be a very solid block of anti-Western votes in the United Nations."[12]

Dulles disliked the idea of a center of decision making in the international system that was independent of the West, whether communist-dominated or not. The prospect of India and China, the two largest Asian states, exercising leadership within the Afro-Asian grouping, despite the ideological differences between them, was too much for the secretary to bear. Dulles moreover had become fixated upon the emergence of the PRC as representative of both communist success and Asian autonomy, a precedent that a succession of U.S. administrations sought to frustrate in Vietnam from Truman through Nixon.

Dulles counted on the Arab states to help extricate the United States from its dilemma, but this hope proved short-lived. The embassy in Djakarta informed him that at a meeting in that city Arab League representatives were advocating participation and Turkey and Iran would be encouraged to participate.[13] The British and French had also decided not to discourage the presence at the meeting of noncommunist Asian states. French complaisance, however, did not extend to an African presence at the meeting. While the British were open to having Africans attend, the French were hostile to the suggestion. France claimed that African participation "made little sense either on geographical or ideological grounds." It was leery that the conference was "expected to be a developing link between Asiatics and Africans based on common attitude toward western 'whites' . . . particularly in light indications that Communist China now taking lead in promoting theme of racial antagonisms in its anti-Western propaganda."[14] French objections seemed based on the assumption that Europeans and Americans could freely coordinate their responses to Bandung but that people of color should not assume the right to convene a meeting to discuss matters of common concern. Clearly, the lessons of the demise of French imperial authority in Indochina had yet to make a lasting impact upon the French official mind.[15]

The fear of the racial implications of Bandung, as well as the growing influence of China, was not restricted to the French. The Dutch Foreign Office was reportedly

> seriously concerned at the possible results of the Afro-Asian Conference as far as Western interests are concerned. They believe that the Conference will be dominated by Communist China which will have a definite idea of exactly what it wishes to accomplish. The only question . . . is what tactics the Chinese will use, whether they will endeavor to exploit and exacerbate differences between Asiatic and African countries and the West or whether they will use reasonableness and moderation as a means of enhancing their international standing. The belief is expressed that the latter tactic would be much more dangerous and harder to combat. For example, they say, a Communist inspired resolution which expressed the sense of the Conference that Japan and Communist China should be admitted to the United Nations would be extremely difficult for Japan to oppose.[16]

Dutch Foreign Ministry officials hesitated to discourage participation because pro-Western countries could help shape conference resolutions. The PRC had changed the strategic map of Asia and the Western powers were grappling with the issue of developing counterweights to Chinese influence, among them a stronger Japan. Barely a decade after the atomic bombs dropped on Hiroshima and Nagasaki ended the Japanese displacement of Western influence in Asia, it was clear that Japan would again become a major player on that continent. The Dutch also believed that "the real danger to the West in the Conference lies in the fact that it may further a division of the world on the basis of a color line. This, in their opinion, would be extremely harmful to Western interests since the only real prospect of checking the spread of Communist influence in the Far East lies in the maintenance and development of ties between moderate Asians and the Western powers. Drawing of lines on a color basis would jeopardize these ties and facilitate Communist expansion."[17] Fear of the newly assertive world of color was proving to be contagious among the Western powers, and the PRC had become the symbol of that assertiveness that so threatened the West. Dutch government perspectives, made known following the Netherlands' postwar expulsion from Indonesia, indicated that the European states had yet to face the fact that the sun was setting on the imperial era.

The Dutch reaction also conveyed the tinge of hysteria that was creeping into Western analyses. Ever since Japan had bested Russia in 1905, the European colonial powers and the United States had been ambivalent about the emergence of an Asian state that could compete with them in the region.

Japan's defeat in 1945 had effectively diminished that threat to Western influence but the emergence of the PRC had transformed Communist China into a symbol of the potency of Asian nationalism that might yet successfully contest Western preeminence in Asia. For colonial powers such as Britain, France, and Holland, this could hasten the end of their Southeast Asian empires.

The divergences in perspective between the Western powers and the Third World states were apparent when the U.S. Embassy in Saudi Arabia, one of the most anticommunist of the Arab states, sought to raise the issue of Saudi participation. The Saudis concurred with the decision of the Arab League to participate in the Bandung Conference on condition that Israel be barred. The acting Saudi foreign minister responded bluntly to U.S. worries about the Chinese presence. "Why should you be concerned? America recognizes communism's mother country, Soviet Russia; Saudi Arabia—and now Iraq—do not."[18] The Saudi's reply implied a contradiction between U.S. readiness to recognize European communists and rejection of communists of color. The incident vividly exemplified the inability of U.S. officials to understand the explicit messages their policies conveyed about the racial and ethnic hierarchies into which they had been socialized.[19]

Further evidence of the dilemma facing U.S. policy in dealing with Bandung came from Carl Rowan, an African American correspondent for the *Minneapolis Tribune* who in January 1955 toured South and Southeast Asia under the auspices of the State Department's Exchange-of-Persons program. Rowan reported that "as he is a negro many Asians spoke freely to him, claiming that they could trust him more than 'white' Americans." The U.S. consul general in Hong Kong conveyed Rowan's views to the State Department because the black journalist "appears to have acquired a useful sampling of Asian opinion on the forthcoming Conference, and it is thought that his comments may help in planning measures which can be taken to counteract Communist influence at the Conference." The consul general's assessment of the information Rowan might impart indicated the growing suspicion with which Asians were viewing official U.S. policy. According to Rowan, his conversations with prominent Asian public figures led him to believe "that the countries of Asia would probably want to discuss three topics of common interest: 1) The evils of Western colonialism; 2) The white man's attitude of discrimination against colored peoples; and 3) The economic problems of the area." It was obvious that the politics of white supremacy had become a major factor in the evolving Asian context. The Western allies were correct in perceiving that Asian autonomy constituted a threat to the colonial order.[20]

Rowan's comments were, however, not restricted to increasing sensitivities about race. "In the countries which he had visited," he advised the consul general, "there was a strong fear of Communist China's military might. Because of this factor people were reluctant to criticize or oppose the Chinese Communists for fear they would suffer later. There was also a fear that the United States would pull out in a crisis and leave them unprotected against China." The PRC's strategic weight had become a factor, like American influence, in the Asian power calculus. As Rowan indicated, the PRC's willingness to confront the Western powers had provoked ambivalence among other Asians: "There was an emotional reaction of distrust of the white people and a certain feeling of exhilaration when an Asian army fought the United States to a standstill in Korea and defeated the West in Indo-China. There was also opposition to what they consider the 'intransigent' attitude which the United States has taken against the recognition of Communist China." Rowan believed that this ambivalence would be expressed at Bandung. His insights confirmed the evolving climate of opinion in Asia, particularly on the issue of Chinese power and the resentment of the "white supremacist" order that underlay European colonial rule.[21]

The consul general was so impressed with Rowan that he recommended that he "would probably be an excellent man to cover the Conference as a reporter. At the same time he might be able to do some excellent backstage public relations work for the United States among the delegates and observers."[22] The consul general's recommendations about Rowan's potential usefulness at Bandung undoubtedly derived from the perception that an African American was likely to be more credible in Asian eyes than a white interlocutor. The willingness of a State Department official to recommend an African American for such a role perhaps resulted from a sense that the politics of racial representation in U.S. foreign relations with the world of color was entering a new phase.[23]

Rowan did attend the Bandung Conference as a correspondent for the *Minneapolis Tribune*. CIA director Allen Dulles apparently encouraged his presence there. According to Rowan, Dulles told the *Tribune*'s editor that Rowan would have "access to the key people who will be there well beyond the access available to anyone in the foreign service."[24] The director's encouragement of Rowan's attendance signaled that senior U.S. policy makers knew that the politics of white supremacy had become an anachronism in an age of African, Arab, and Asian nationalism. Rowan's presence could also prove useful to officials who sought multiple sources of information on the evolving state of Asian opinion.[25] Rowan also met personally with Chou En-lai, a meeting about which his autobiography is rather reticent.

On 25 January 1955 senior State Department officials convened in Secretary Dulles's office to discuss the U.S. position on the Bandung Conference and draft an official position paper that would be circulated to overseas posts. During the discussion, it became clear that Dulles was leaning toward the view that "it would be preferable for friendly Asian countries to attend." In contrast, a consensus developed that an effort should be made to restrict African participation to Libya and Egypt. John Durnford Jernegan, later U.S. ambassador to Iraq, noted that the British had informed Gold Coast and Central African Federation leaders that "it would not be desirable for them to attend." He did not want the meeting to deal with "the South African problem" and hoped that joint Anglo-American pressure would persuade Libya, the Gold Coast, the Central African Federation, and Ethiopia to skip the conference. Geographical error notwithstanding, Jernegan argued that the United States should prevent the "establishment of a precedent that the Africans and the Asians should deal with outside powers as a bloc." He was particularly concerned that Ethiopia would send a "weak" delegation but was reminded by Dulles that this issue "should not be considered in an exclusively African context." The lack of sustained hostility to the communist powers or notions of racial solidarity that opposed white supremacy constituted evidence of "weakness." Clearly, racial dynamics were never far below the surface in the State Department's discussions about Bandung.[26]

Dulles's circular telegram stated that the State Department had "no illusions as to risks inherent in Conference and believes it important these be overcome by clear presentation views that fraternity of peoples must not be divided by arbitrary geographical or racial distinctions." Based on advice and reports provided by the various missions, friendly Asian states would be encouraged to accept the conference invitation. According to Dulles, "Dept adopting public position Conference is primarily concern States invited, that US recognizes Communists will attempt exploit Conference to divide these countries from their other free world friends but that other countries should be aware Communists' designs and will work for reasonable and constructive results." Bowing to the inevitable, Dulles moved toward the position that the embassy in Djakarta initially recommended. The United States should seek to use its Asian allies to influence the meeting's outcome.[27]

When it became known that Ethiopia and Liberia would attend the conference, Dulles again shifted ground and accepted his inability to prevent African participation. When the Gold Coast, still officially a British colony, decided to send a representative to Bandung, the United States again found itself confronted by evidence of a "Third World" agenda over which it had little control. This frustrated the search for a unified strategy by the alliance of colonial powers, including the United States, to contain the political aspirations of the emerging states.

Having lost two initial battles—the first, to prevent the conference being held; and the second, to limit participation to Asian states—the State Department began to formulate a strategy for influencing the deliberations and outcome of the conference. For this purpose, it used proxies and interlocutors among invitees to pursue a Washington-prescribed agenda and strategy at Bandung. The State Department hoped to fashion an anticommunist coalition of Afro-Asian states. An early indication of this goal was provided in a conversation between G. Lewis Jones, the chargé in the American Embassy in Cairo, and Mohammed Heikal, an Egyptian journalist close to Prime Minister Gamal Abdel Nasser. Jones, in an effort to influence Egyptian thinking about the recently enacted Baghdad Pact—which the Egyptians viewed with trepidation—informed Heikal that the United States would be monitoring the stances adopted by countries at the conference: "There will be the communist side and we know what they will say: there will be the anticommunist side in which, I suppose, the Turks, the Pakistanis and other friends of the West will take the lead. Everyone in the United States will follow with interest the position adopted by Egypt: after Nehru's visit they will be watching to see whether Egypt follows his lead or whether it will show itself willing to stand up and be counted with the pro-Western contingents."[28]

The attitude displayed by the chargé in Cairo was not singular and reflected an emerging consensus within the State Department about the most effective way to use the Bandung Conference to American advantage. In a summary of the department's thinking, sent to the relevant missions for use in consultations with the governments invited to Bandung, the acting secretary of state recommended that "friendly delegations" be warned against "Communist tactics" and take firm positions against "misrepresentations" coming from the communist bloc. The State Department believed the "major division in [the] Conference is between Communist countries and all others, not (as Communists will try to have it) between 'U.S. Stooges' and all others." It predicted that pro-Western countries would prevail.[29]

The assumption that an anticommunist platform provided the best option for containing the PRC's increasing influence as a major power in Asia and the wider Third World underlay administration strategy. The fear of potential Chinese diplomatic successes at Bandung fed the State Department's hope of molding its agenda and outcome. In an advisory to various missions, the State Department suggested that "while Communist countries constitute only small minority at Conference Chinese Communists may be expected exert disproportionate influence and make every effort utilize conference enhance own prestige and discredit U.S. and its allies in eyes of Asian-African nations."[30]

The State Department understood that the United States could be tainted by its alliance with the European colonial powers. According to the telegram, "Chinese communists may also be expected present selves as spokesmen for peoples struggling to free selves from subjugation by 'U.S.-supported' colonial Powers. In meeting Communist efforts exploit colonial question we believe it would be mistake try persuade our friends make issue defending position Colonial Powers (especially France), except perhaps to extent keeping record straight and pointing out number countries attending which were given independence from Western rule in past generation."[31] When faced with a criticism from the PRC on collusion with colonialism, the United States would have to adopt a strategy that minimized its vulnerability. As a counter, the State Department suggested reminding participants that the largest number of Asians under European colonial rule inhabited the Soviet Asian territories.[32]

As had been evident from the outset, the issues of colonialism and the PRC's role in Asia assumed a new dynamism within the context of the Bandung Conference. The United States wanted to straddle the issue of colonialism in a manner that would not offend its Western allies while seeking to play to the sympathies of people of color in Asia and Africa. In effect, the United States sought to be nonaligned on the issue of European colonialism while using anticommunism and Soviet "colonialism" to divide Bandung Conference attendees and contain the PRC. Unfortunately, the strategy did little to enhance the U.S. credibility among its allies, the subjects of colonial rule, or the communist states.

An early indication of the problem that would beset U.S. strategy toward Bandung came from Libya, where negotiations on the withdrawal of French forces from that country appeared to have stalled. The U.S. mission in Tripoli reported the Libyan prime minister's concern about the pace of the negotiations and his anxiety that they be concluded before the Afro-Asian conference convened. French recalcitrance could damage Western interests by making it difficult for Libya to be a moderate and accommodating presence there. Although the Libyan prime minister had an "apparently honest desire to stand up to anti-imperialist diatribes at Bandung, I fear that, unless [the] Fezzan negotiations are successfully concluded before [the] conference convene[s] (and short of US pressure this seems highly unlikely), [the] temptation to use this forum as means of turning pressure of world opinion on [the] French will be too great to resist."[33]

The United States would have to pay a price if it wanted staunch allies for its anticommunist strategy at Bandung, and that price could easily entail alienating NATO allies who were desperately seeking to cling to the remnants of empire. Colonialism, however, was not the only complication. In early March, the U.S. Embassy in Cairo reported that Nasser would attend the conference personally. The Egyptian military was increasing pressure on Nasser to adopt a stance that would distance Egypt from the United States. The Iraqi-Turkish pact was one of the catalysts for this pressure, as was the Israeli attack on Gaza on 28 February. According to the embassy in Cairo: "Since the signing of the Turko-Iraq Pact the regime has been in the process of doing exactly what the officers are now demanding: namely, formulating a new policy that is more independent and less identified with the West, particularly the United States. Pressure from the Army officers, therefore, will probably compel the regime to be less cautious and even more definite in assuming a position of independence on international matters."[34] The telegram went on to argue that Nasser's decision to go to Bandung and strengthen his relationship with the Asian countries reflected the shift in the relationship between Egypt and the United States. The Western-supported Baghdad Pact and Arab-Israeli tensions had begun to affect the orientation of Egyptian leadership. The Afro-Asian conference could potentially redefine Cairo's relationship with Washington, and not in the manner in which the Eisenhower administration had originally envisaged.

The desire to establish an anticommunist coalition in the Middle East initiated a process that the most influential Arab state began to resist. Bandung was the opening act in Egypt's rejection of a Western-dominated regional order. As in East Asia, the spillover of conflict between the major alliances into the Middle East had resulted in a search by regional states for containment. Notwithstanding indications of Egypt's shifting stance, Dulles sought Nasser's collaboration with the Turkish delegation. In a telegram to the U.S. Embassy in Cairo, Dulles advised that Nasser be encouraged to make personal contact with the Turks, since the latter were open to general discussions pertaining to both the Bandung Conference and Middle Eastern defense. Dulles emphasized that Nasser should "realize positions taken by Egypt at Conference will be widely noted by US public. In view Egyptian attitude towards Turk-Iraq Pact it would be particularly unfortunate if Egypt followed anti-Western course."[35] In hindsight, it is remarkable that, despite the clear signals Egypt gave the Western powers, Dulles would assume that Nasser would be pliable. Dulles's perceptions of U.S. leverage over Nasser and the latter's willingness to operate within the confines of a Western-inspired regional order would be shattered in later years.

Dulles's ongoing effort to shape the views of the participating countries was not restricted to Egypt. Pakistan, Thailand, the Philippines, Turkey, Japan, and Lebanon were all disposed to collaborate with the United States in fashioning an anticommunist agenda and strategy. The State Department entrusted the responsibility of coordinating the efforts of the anticommunist group at Bandung to the U.S. Embassy in Djakarta. On 2 April, Dulles advised the relevant embassies that they should brief Embassy Djakarta on "individual delegation members with whom it might usefully make contact should circumstances require." Additionally, "certain members of the Embassy staff will be unobtrusively present at Bandung to give such assistance to friendly delegates as may be deemed appropriate in the circumstances."[36]

The United States was thus participating in the Afro-Asian conference although it had not been invited. Its participation was guaranteed by its partnership with invited delegations and the use of the Djakarta Embassy as a clearinghouse to coordinate the activities of the anticommunist coalition. The scope of U.S. efforts to influence the agenda and deliberations reflected a desire to shape the international system and establish a Pax Americana. Some of the consequences of this project were revealed in a meeting between Henry Villard of the State Department and the Lebanese ambassador in Washington, Charles Malik. Villard pressed Malik to lead the Lebanese delegation to Bandung since the United States wanted to ensure strong pro-Western representation at the meeting. Malik had already seen some of the background papers that the U.S. Embassy in Beirut had used in briefing the Lebanese government.

In an exchange of views on the conference, Malik informed Villard that the roots of Bandung lay in the crises of Palestine and Korea. Faced with Western support for Israel, the Arab nations had sought to make common cause with the Asian and African states. The Korean War had provided the impetus for this collaborative process, and it advanced with British support. According to Malik, Britain in 1950–51 had encouraged the Arab, African, and Asian states to work together to moderate U.S. policy, as the latter was perceived to be extreme. The extension of American influence into the non-European world was consequently a catalyst itself for the increasing cooperation among the Asian states that led to Bandung.

Malik also expressed his concern about the potential for racial polarization that could turn into "a racial alignment against the West." Although he thought that the anticommunist coalition could counter any PRC attempt to dominate the conference, Malik acknowledged that Chinese support for an agenda in which resentment against Western racial prejudices facilitated consensus would be much more difficult to combat.[37] Malik's opinions revealed the paradox of U.S. relations with nonaligned states serving as a catalyst for "neutralist" sentiment, the very sentiment that was in many ways anathema to the American desire to assume a broader leadership role in the international system.

Villard, for his part, emphasized that the conference "might offer an opportunity for the Asians and Africans jointly to exercise a restraining influence with respect to the bellicose utterances of the Chinese Communists and thus to serve the cause of peace, as we felt there would be no war in Asia unless the Communists took the initiative."[38] Despite Washington's concern about the emergence of a Third World grouping of states, it depended on some of those states to exercise a moderating influence upon the PRC. The conference was rapidly becoming a mechanism through which the United States would engage China through friendly interlocutors, in a search for an entente in Asia. Neutralism was thus useful for opening up channels of communication, and, if effectively exploited, could serve as an instrument of containment.[39]

The thrust of U.S. strategy was reaffirmed in a conversation between Malik and Dulles, a few days after the Lebanese ambassador's meeting with Villard. Dulles expressed the view that a key American concern was whether Bandung participants could "deter the Communist Chinese from undertaking aggression" against Formosa. Dulles saw the conference as an opportunity for the PRC to assess the amenability of Asia to the forcible integration of Formosa into China. If Dulles was correct, "the question of peace or war in the Far East may be determined at the conference." Dulles also revealed his apprehension that "anti-white" sentiment in Asia could harden, with deleterious consequences. "In the past," he told Malik, "the record of the Western powers in Asia had not been without regrettable faults. There was nothing to be gained, however, by the Asian and African powers falling into the same faults, particularly the fault of racialism, in the opposite direction."[40]

The racial sensitivities occasioned by Bandung had become discomfiting for Dulles. He admitted the Western tendency to display "a sense of racial superiority" and pleaded for Asians to avoid repeating that error. Dulles knew that race was a complicating factor for U.S. foreign policy. The growing unacceptability of white supremacy had limited American effectiveness in managing the PRC. Western efforts to maintain influence in Asia and Africa were compromised by the weight of race.

Dulles's preoccupation with the PRC and the racial dynamics of the Bandung Conference showed plainly in his conversation with the British ambassador in Washington, Sir Roger Makins. Two days prior to his audience with Malik, Dulles suggested that "the question of war or peace in the Far East could be significantly affected by what happens at Bandung." He argued that "if assurances could be obtained through the Bandung Conference that the

Chinese Communists would agree to a cease-fire regarding Formosa which would leave the islands to be fought for, this would itself be a considerable contribution, although it would obviously be nowhere near as good as an over-all cease-fire such as envisaged in the draft New Zealand Resolution prepared for presentation to the UN." The secretary would urge certain friendly countries represented at Bandung to propose a cease-fire if the subject of peace or Formosa was raised.

Dulles indicated that the countries that might be asked to serve as interlocutors for American views were Pakistan, the Philippines, Thailand, Turkey, possibly Iraq, and Lebanon, if Malik were present at Bandung. The British ambassador informed him that the Foreign Office was likely to pursue a similar approach to Formosa and asked to be kept informed of which countries the U.S. government approached on the issue. Dulles promised to do so and provided a list of the targeted countries and "the tenor of our instructions."[41]

Dulles revealed to Makins his gloom over Asia. Makins's memorandum of the conversation recalled Dulles's particular dislike of Jawaharlal Nehru's militancy. The Indian prime minister had rebuked the West for supporting the Portuguese in Goa and intervening in Middle Eastern affairs. Nehru harshly criticized NATO and the Union of South Africa. One of his recent speeches seemed to call Western civilization itself into question. "With respect to Asia, the Secretary felt we were up against a bigger and more long-term problem than the details or incidents which make daily headlines in the press," Makins recorded. "In effect, he felt that there were Asian elements that were pushing for a Pan-Asian movement which would be by its very nature and concept anti-Western." Dulles expressed the hope that the British would "use their very considerable influence with certain friendly Asian countries so that both the Formosa situation and the over-all problem of pan-Asianism might not become more aggravated."[42]

Bandung had provoked a sense of uncertainty in Dulles and his despondency was linked to his growing sentiment that the international politics of race was redefining the parameters and rules of the game in the international system. In his conversations with both Malik and Makins, he sought ways to find credible interlocutors for his negotiations with the PRC on Formosa and the offshore islands. He was unsure about the level of support enjoyed by the PRC or whether the divide between the Western alliance and the world of color would shift to the disadvantage of the United States. The Afro-Asian conference was midwife to an international order in which the politics of race was an essential factor in the calculus of power. The United States had little control over the resolution of the thorny issue of race in international perspective or its impact upon the world system.

Increasing Asian autonomy had important implications for relationships within the Western alliance. A conversation between the Belgian attaché for Congo affairs in Washington and Henry Villard of the State Department revealed how Bandung was disrupting the assumptions of a European-dominated international order. The Belgian attaché, Baron Dhanis, thought the conference might prove to be a "keg of dynamite." The Belgian's biggest concern was that Bandung would adopt an anticolonial attitude. For Dhanis, "if a strong resolution were adopted attacking the so-called colonial powers, it might freeze the position of the Asian and African peoples against the Western nations in this respect and the result might be most unfortunate. While too much could not be expected any longer from Asia, if Africa were lost to the West, a most serious blow would be dealt with respect to the supply of essential raw materials and minerals. . . . It was necessary, therefore, to do everything possible to keep the African peoples in particular oriented toward Western thinking."[43]

Dhanis's argument suggested that Asian autonomy required strengthening Western and particularly European dependence on empire in Africa. It was little wonder that the Western allies had sought to prevent and/or circumscribe African participation in the Bandung Conference. The emergence of a Third World anticolonial alliance was profoundly unsettling to the Western position. The politics of race deeply informed geostrategic thought in Europe and North America, and the fears of antiwhite sentiment betrayed by Dhanis and Dulles expressed worry that Afro-Asian autonomy would mean loss of control over the international order and the hierarchy of power that informed its operations. The Belgian diplomat's views reflected Western Europe's desire for an anticommunist and anticolonial alliance in which the United States would help to buttress its pretensions in Africa and Asia. The United States, less dependent on its colonial possessions for the maintenance of its status as a major power, but committed to strengthening the NATO alliance as its primary instrument of anticommunist containment, had found itself increasingly a guarantor of European colonial authority.

It was in this context that the PRC's championship of anticolonialism limited the effectiveness of the U.S. appeal to containment outside Europe. The PRC's support for anticolonialism had proved to be of much greater relevance to Third World sensibilities than had the call for anticommunism. The failure to impress the bipolar vision that informed U.S. foreign policy upon others was particularly disconcerting to Dulles. That the strategy of indirect engagement with the PRC left the United States in a position of dependence upon intermediaries was even more problematic for the secretary of state. His discomfort arose from the fact that, for domestic audiences, direct en-

gagement with the PRC was not an acceptable option. U.S. policy was consequently held hostage to domestic politics and allowed little room for flexibility. The PRC had proved very adept at using indirect channels to exploit
openings as it had during the conferences on Korea and Indochina that had
validated its influence in both Northeast and Southeast Asia. It seemed as if
Bandung would again offer the PRC an opportunity to overwhelm U.S. efforts to contain it.

As the State Department sought to shape policy toward the Afro-Asian
conference, it found that the United States could not define the rules of the
game on this uneven playing field. Bandung ushered in a new era where the
relative comfort and certitude of the bipolar vision that applied in Europe
proved less than ideal elsewhere. The disconcerting issue of race as a dimension of international affairs, moreover, could no longer be disguised as the
destabilizing factor it was in the relationships being forged among the First,
Second, and Third Worlds.

Even as Dulles and the State Department grappled with devising an appropriate strategy for dealing with the Afro-Asian conference and the perceived
threat to America, the response among African Americans suggested the gal-
vanizing impact of the conference on people of color. Soon after the announcement of the planned conference, Congressman Adam Clayton Powell Jr., representing Harlem, wrote to the White House indicating that the United
States should send a team of U.S. representatives, both black and white, to
Bandung. "I know personally many of the chiefs of State and members of the
foreign offices of these countries, both in Africa and Asia," Powell declared,
"and I can assure you that the appearance in Indonesia at that time of American officials, both Negro and white, will be of tremendous value."[44]

Powell's recommendation that the United States send a delegation to Bandung that would be in some measure representative of the diversity of American society was a radical proposal in early 1955. The Supreme Court had
only recently handed down the *Brown* decision and Powell was undoubtedly
sensitive to the need for the United States to show that it endorsed this extraordinary step in racial reform. The State Department responded by actively attempting to discourage Powell from attending the conference, because
the conferees might construe his presence to imply official U.S. involvement.[45] Powell indicated that he was prepared to go as an American Negro
and a journalist. It was an interesting coincidence that Powell was ready to
assume this role in opposition to the State Department's views, while Carl
Rowan, a bona fide professional African American journalist, was seen as a

safer bet by the State Department and the Central Intelligence Agency. Powell was determined not to allow Washington to limit his role as a racial spokesperson. "Bandung was a pilgrimage to a new Mecca," he reminisced years later. "I was one of the pilgrims and I went because I had to. Divine compulsion had been laid upon me. I did not know what I could do. I had no idea that I would be more than an interested bystander rubbing elbows with history and breathing in the ferment of a new world. I went to Bandung knowing it could be one of the most important events of the twentieth century. I left Bandung knowing that it had been."[46]

Powell's response to the announcement of the Bandung Conference and his insistence upon attending the meeting indicated the changing mood among African Americans that flowered over the next decade as the civil rights struggle swept America.[47] His determination to breathe in "the ferment of a new world" was not singular in this regard. Richard Wright, the African American writer who had found the climate in Europe more conducive to his intellectual interests and made his home there, responded in similar fashion to Bandung.

> It was the kind of meeting that no anthropologist, no sociologist, no political scientist would ever have dreamed of staging; it was too simple, too elementary, cutting through the outer layers of disparate social and political and cultural facts down to the bare brute residues of human existence: races and religions and continents. There was something extra-political, extra-social, almost extra-human about it; it smacked of tidal waves, of natural forces. . . . And the call for the meeting had not been sounded in terms of ideology. . . . I felt that I had to go to that meeting; I felt that I could understand it. I represented no government, but I wanted to go anyhow.[48]

Bandung triggered a visceral response in Wright to the idea that people of color could create a forum and set an agenda for change that contested conventional notions of their inferiority. "I'm an American Negro; as such, I've had a burden of race consciousness. So have these people," he told his wife, explaining his decision to attend the conference. "I worked in my youth as a common laborer, and I've a class consciousness. So have these people. I grew up in the Methodist and Seventh Day Adventist churches and I saw and observed religion in my childhood; and these people are religious." Wright articulated an African American sense of identification with "the despised, the insulted, the hurt, the dispossessed—in short, the underdogs of the human race [who] were meeting." "I was a member of the Communist Party for twelve years," he wrote, "and I know something of the politics and psychology of rebellion. These people have had as their daily existence such politics.

These emotions are my instruments. They are emotions, but I'm conscious of them as emotions. I want to use these emotions to try to find out what these people think and feel and why."[49]

The geographic distance that separated Powell in the United States and Wright in Paris could not disguise the similarities in their response to Bandung. In an interesting comment on Powell's activities, Wright wrote: "The astounding aspect of Congressman Powell's appearance at Bandung was that he felt the call, felt its meaning. . . . At the very moment when the United States was trying to iron out the brutal kinks of its race problem, there came along a world event which reawakened in the hearts of its 23,000,000 colored citizens the feeling of race, a feeling which the racial mores of American whites had induced deep in their hearts. If a man as sophisticated as Congressman Powell felt this, then one can safely assume that in less schooled and more naïve hearts it went profoundly deep."[50]

As Wright suggested, Bandung evoked empathy from a cross-section of African Americans, including "Mr. Jones . . . a light brown, short, husky man who, according to American nomenclature, was 'colored.' He was a mechanic in Los Angeles. He had never in his life written a line for publication, yet, when he heard that there was going to be a 'big conference of all the colored nations on earth,' this obscure man became deeply affected. By hook or crook he persuaded a newspaper to give him credentials, and he took all of his life's savings and those of his wife and set out for Bandung."[51]

Bandung evoked empathy in Powell, Wright, and Mr. Jones, but that sense of identity with the world of color also led Paul Robeson, W. E. B. Du Bois, and Roy Wilkins to send messages of support to the conference, although they were unable to attend it. For African Americans across the political spectrum, Bandung gave notice that the white supremacist order was under siege in both the domestic and international spheres. In a 1957 speech, Martin Luther King Jr. articulated the linkage between the domestic politics of race and wider international events. He maintained that the turmoil in Asia, Africa, Hungary, Egypt, and America was "indicative of the fact that a new world order is being born and an old order is passing away."[52] King, and later Malcolm X, called for critical examination of American racial politics by the international community.

King's assessment of the historical context in which he would increasingly play a critical role captured the paradox that Bandung presented to the Department of State and other U.S. policy makers. Could the United States come to terms with a world of color in which whites were both a minority and a target of opprobrium? The Bandung Conference forced it to confront the reality of Communist Chinese influence in Asia, based upon China's ability to exploit both nationalist and anti-Western sentiment in the region. In Korea and Vietnam, the PRC had demonstrated its ability to foil the U.S. search for victory in Asia and had helped foster Asian nationalism.

Just as important, Bandung represented another obstacle to American pre-eminence in Asia. The failure of the U.S. effort to abort the conference, and the subsequent strategy of using it to engage the PRC and build an anticom-munist coalition among its allies and dependents simultaneously, demonstrated the limits of U.S. influence in the region. Asian assertiveness had redefined the terms of the U.S. engagement in Asia, and thereafter the legitimacy of its policies in the region would be dependent on its skill at wooing its allies.

Bandung also provoked a fundamental reassessment of European colonial influence in Africa. It was implicated in disputes over Israel's legitimacy as a Middle Eastern state, and the Western search for partners in constructing a viable anticommunist military pact in that region. Nasser's determination to distance himself from Western strategy, the broader Arab assault on French colonial rule, and the Saudi willingness to go to Bandung all pointed to an ex-panding opposition to the desired Pax Americana in the Middle East.

Finally, the Bandung Conference highlighted the intersection of race in American domestic politics and foreign policy. Dulles's frustration with the increasing rejection of white supremacy in the international system mirrored the unsettling effects of the *Brown* decision at home. While the major crises of the civil rights struggle were yet to unfold, the Afro-Asian conference opened a window of vulnerability on race for the United States. The State Department's inability to prevent Adam Clayton Powell from attending re-vealed the administration's desperate wish that African Americans who went to Bandung, such as Carl Rowan, should further U.S. foreign policy goals. Powell was not an obvious candidate for such a role. There was irony in his defense of American racial reformism at the conference. It highlighted the Du Boisian "double-consciousness" that afflicted the individual who sought "to be both a Negro and an American, without being cursed and spit upon by his fellows, without having the doors of Opportunity closed roughly in his face."[53]

American ambivalence toward Bandung had opened the door for Powell to adopt an independent posture toward the Afro-Asian gathering, but it came at the price of his defense of an administration that had little enthusiasm for the process of racial change the *Brown* decision initiated. Powell's public de-fense of the U.S. record on race at Bandung mirrored his complex relation-ship with the Eisenhower administration. After his return from Bandung, Powell briefed a meeting of Overseas Writers on his trip, telling them, "The great winner at Bandung was the cause of democracy. The U.S. must prove that it is a democracy particularly by its action on colonialism and racism. The Conference will meet again in Cairo next year. If the U.S. continues to vote in favor of our colonial friends or even abstains on colonial votes in the UN, our friends will not be able to stand with us as firmly in Cairo as they did in Bandung. We have only one year of grace."[54]

Powell also told the gathering that the administration had persuaded liberal Democrat Chester Bowles to stay away from Bandung. Bowles, in February 1955, had called for a bipartisan foreign policy that would allow the United States to overcome its loss of ground to the communist powers. It was obvious that the Afro-Asian conference had become an arena of partisan conflict, with the Democrats using it to portray the Eisenhower administration as deficient in its handling of African and Asian nationalism. Powell's willingness to upstage the administration by attending, defending the Supreme Court's decision in *Brown*, and publicly criticizing the United States for its attitudes on race and colonialism indicated his free-spirited commitment to accelerating the pace of racial progress. His own party, the Democrats, and the Republican administration would find it difficult to contain his propensity for being a political maverick even as he championed racial reform. His eagerness to be a gadfly demonstrated his desire to be in the limelight and the political shrewdness that allowed him to transcend party loyalties on the volatile issue of race.

For Richard Wright, Bandung had triggered a sense of identification with the struggle against white supremacy in both its American and international dimensions. Wright correctly perceived that the search for liberation in the Third World had enormous consequences for American politics. Bandung had opened a crack in the "Color Curtain" that would usher in an era of accelerated decolonization in Asia and Africa and the flowering of the civil rights struggle in the United States. Bandung offered the promise of freedom from the burden of race that had been the essential handmaiden of the rise of Europe and its satellites in the international system. For Americans of every hue, Bandung had opened a window on the power of race as a factor in the shaping of domestic and international relations.

Notes

1. For earlier scholarly explorations of African American participation in the Bandung Conference, see Brenda Gayle Plummer, *Rising Wind: Black Americans and U.S. Foreign Affairs, 1935–1960* (Chapel Hill: University of North Carolina Press, 1996); and Penny Von Eschen, *Race against Empire: Black Americans and Anticolonialism, 1937–1957* (Ithaca: Cornell University Press, 1997). For personal accounts of their participation in the Bandung Conference, see Adam Clayton Powell Jr., *Adam by*

Adam: The Autobiography of Adam Clayton Powell, Jr. (New York: Dial Press, 1971); Carl Rowan, *The Pitiful and the Proud* (New York: Random House, 1956); and Richard Wright, *The Color Curtain: A Report on the Bandung Conference* (New York: World, 1956).

2. The text of the communiqué is found in Telegram, Underhill to Department of State, 3 Jan. 1955, 670.901/1-355, Department of State Central Decimal File, 1955–59, Record Group (RG) 59, National Archives (NA), Washington, D.C. (All references to State Department documents in this essay come from this group of documents unless otherwise stated.)

3. For a contemporary assessment of the conference sponsors' goals, see George McTurnan Kahin, *The Asian-African Conference* (Ithaca: Cornell University Press, 1956).

4. For a more extensive discussion of the limits of the bipolar paradigm in explaining the history of international relations since 1945, see Cary Fraser, "A Requiem for the Cold War: Reviewing the History of International Relations since 1945," in *Rethinking the Cold War*, ed. Allen Hunter (Philadelphia: Temple University Press, 1998).

5. Telegram, Cumming to Secretary of State, 2 Jan. 1955, 670.901/1-255, box 2668.

6. Memorandum, Young to Robertson, Sebald, and Baldwin, 4 Jan. 1955, 670.901/1-455, box 2668. Kuo-kang Shao, *Zhou Enlai and the Foundations of Chinese Foreign Policy* (New York: St. Martin's Press, 1996), 211–29, provides an insightful examination of the PRC's foreign policy in Asia at this time.

7. The U.S. image of the PRC as a pariah state had rallied domestic support for the anticommunist currents that engulfed American politics after 1945, but as the Korean War and the Geneva Conference on Indochina demonstrated, both the PRC and the United States were prepared to use the Soviet Union, Britain, and India as alternative channels of communication in the absence of direct negotiations. For various accounts of these "back-channel" contacts, see Bevin Alexander, *The Strange Connection: U.S. Intervention in China, 1944–1972* (Westport, Conn.: Greenwood, 1992); Gordon H. Chang, *Friends and Enemies: The United States, China, and the Soviet Union, 1948–1972* (Stanford: Stanford University Press, 1990); David Allan Mayers, *Cracking the Monolith: U.S. Policy against the Sino-Soviet Alliance, 1949–1955* (Baton Rouge: Louisiana State University Press, 1986); and Kenneth T. Young, *Negotiating with the Chinese Communists: The United States Experience, 1953–1967* (New York: McGraw-Hill, 1968).

8. Telegram, Allison to Secretary of State, 5 Jan. 1955, 670.901/1-555.

9. For an account of the primacy accorded the United States in postwar Japanese foreign policy, see Michael Schaller, "Altered States: The United States and Japan during the 1960s," in *The Diplomacy of the Crucial Decade: American Foreign Relations during the 1960s*, ed. Diane B. Kunz (New York: Columbia University Press, 1994), 251–82.

10. Telegram, Dulles to Chiefs of Mission, 7 Jan. 1955, 670.901/1-755.

11. Telegram, Dulles to American Embassy, London, 8 Jan. 1955, 670.901/1-855.

12. Memorandum of conversation, 14 Jan. 1955, Subject: Afro-Asian Conference, Secretary's Office, 3:00 P.M., 7 Jan. 1955, 670.901/1-1455.

13. Telegram, Cumming to Secretary of State, 14 Jan. 1955, 670.901/1-1455.

14. Telegram, Achilles to Secretary of State, 12 Jan. 1955, 670.901/1-1255.

15. The British government would later reverse its position on the possible participation of African colonies in the Bandung Conference. In the wake of the British de-

cision, the French approached the Americans to adopt a similar position. Memorandum of conversation, Subject: Afro-Asian Conference, 21 Jan. 1955, 670.901/1-2155.

16. Shullaw to the Department of State, 26 Jan. 1955, 670.901/1-2655.

17. Ibid.

18. Dispatch, Stein to the Department of State, 16 Jan. 1955, 670.901/1-1655.

19. The term is borrowed from Michael H. Hunt, *Ideology and U.S. Foreign Policy* (New Haven: Yale University Press, 1987). Hunt's book is an interesting exploration of race as a central construct of the ideology of American engagement with the world.

20. Dispatch, Drumright to the Department of State, 20 Jan. 1955, 670.901/1-2055.

21. Ibid.

22. Ibid.

23. The consul general's response to Rowan's conversation indicated that State Department officers in the regional bureaus and in the field had developed an appreciation of the shifting climate of Asian opinion—an awareness that may have been lacking in senior department officers, including Secretary Dulles.

24. Carl T. Rowan, *Breaking Barriers: A Memoir* (New York: HarperCollins, 1992), 128.

25. It was a role to which Rowan was not opposed, as he indicates in his autobiography: "Ah, yes, whichever Dulles telephoned Cowles knew damned well that while the advantages of being a black journalist were not universally great, they could be of real importance at an Asian-African conference." Ibid., 128–29.

26. Memorandum of conversation, Subject: Afro-Asian Conference, 27 Jan. 1955, 670.901/1-2755. Dulles, however, reversed course and instructed the U.S. missions in Ethiopia and Liberia not to dissuade those governments from participating in the Bandung Conference once their planned attendance was announced. Telegram, Dulles to Addis Ababa, 28 Jan. 1955, and Telegram, Dulles to Monrovia, 28 Jan. 1955, 670.901/1-2855.

27. Circular Telegram 401 (over signature of Dulles), 25 Jan. 1955, 670.901/1-2555.

28. Dispatch, Jones to Department of State, 19 Feb. 1955, 670.901/2-1955.

29. Circular Telegram, Hoover, 25 Feb. 1955, 670.901/2-2555.

30. Ibid.

31. Ibid.

32. One of the problems confronting the United States was that the PRC was a USSR ally, not a colony, and the other Asian states were quite aware of the difference. The USSR was, furthermore, a federal state with a strong central government that ruled over diverse populations, including Asian Muslims, Russians, and non-Russian Europeans. The PRC was a unitary state with relatively small minority populations. This suggests the absence of a single concept of state organization among the communist powers. Insofar as "white supremacy" was only abandoned as U.S. constitutional doctrine in 1954, and Hawaii, Alaska, and other U.S. colonies had been granted neither statehood, self-government, nor self-determination, the United States in early 1955 was not well placed to advert to Soviet colonialism.

33. Telegram, Tappin to Secretary of State, 28 Feb. 1955, 670.901/2-2855.

34. Dispatch, Henry A. Byroade to Department of State, 7 Mar. 1955, 670.901/3-755.

35. Telegram, Dulles to American Embassy, Cairo, 30 Mar. 1955, 670.901/3-1455.

36. Circular telegram, Dulles, 2 Apr. 1955, 670.901/4-255.

37. Memorandum of conversation, 6 Apr. 1955, 670.901/4-655, box 2668. Malik also suggested that Nasser's greater willingness to adopt a neutralist position resulted from his view that the United States was responsible for the crisis within the Arab League.

38. Ibid.

39. For an interesting exploration of the ways in which Zhou En-Lai, the architect of the PRC's foreign policy, adopted a parallel strategy in using the Bandung Conference to limit American influence on China's periphery, see Kuo-kang Shao, *Zhou Enlai and the Foundations of Chinese Foreign Policy*, 211–29.

40. Memorandum of conversation, 9 Apr. 1955, 670.901/4-955, box 2669.

41. Memorandum of conversation, 7 Apr. 1955, 670.901/4-755.

42. Ibid.

43. Memorandum of conversation between Baron Dhanis, Belgian Congo Affairs Attaché, and Henry S. Villard, 31 Mar. 1955, RG 59, 670.901/3-3155, box 2669.

44. Powell to Maxwell Rabb, 2 Feb. 1955.

45. Telegram, Dulles to American Embassy, Djakarta, 28 Mar. 1955, 670.901/3-2655.

46. Powell, *Adam by Adam*, 103–4.

47. Powell actively sought to intercede with Chou En-Lai to secure the release of U.S. pilots captured by the Chinese government in spite of his willingness to defy the administration on the issue of his attendance at the conference (ibid., 113–14). Perhaps to indicate administration approval of Powell's performance at Bandung and as a belated apology for their former opposition, President Eisenhower, CIA director Allen Dulles, and State Department officials met with him after his return from Bandung.

48. Wright, *The Color Curtain*, 13–14.

49. Ibid., 15, 12.

50. Ibid., 178–79.

51. Ibid., 176–77. Carl Rowan also mentioned in his account of his Asian travels the presence at Bandung of "a Negro named Jones from California, whom I never quite figured out." See Rowan, *The Pitiful and the Proud*, 388.

52. See "Facing the Challenge of a New Age" (1957), in Martin Luther King Jr., *I Have a Dream: Writings and Speeches That Changed the World*, ed. James Melvin Washington (San Francisco: Harper, 1992), 15–16.

53. W. E. B. Du Bois, *The Souls of Black Folk*, in *Three Negro Classics*, introd. John Hope Franklin (New York: Avon Books, 1965), 215.

54. Richard H. Sanger, Memorandum to Jones, 5 May 1955, RG 59, 670.901/5-555. Powell indicated in his autobiography that he told President Eisenhower personally at a White House meeting that "Bandung had stepped up the timetable for freedom, and that it was absolutely impossible for the United States to continue to hope for further support from the peoples of Africa and Asia if we continued to abstain before the United Nations on the question of colonialism." See Powell, *Adam by Adam*, 116.

Segregationists and the World
The Foreign Policy of the White Resistance

As he waited for his ride to Rockefeller Center, George Wallace was nervous. In his first term as governor of Alabama he had become the leading symbol of the white resistance to the civil rights movement and was considering running for the presidency in 1964. In a few days he would fulfill his campaign promise to "stand in the schoolhouse door" to prevent black students from enrolling at the University of Alabama. But first he faced a panel of journalists on NBC's nationally televised *Meet the Press.*

Wallace did not fear questions on race or segregation, but, as a potential presidential contender, was certain he would be asked his views on foreign affairs. In frustration, Wallace turned to aide Grover Hall: "They're going to want to know about my foreign policy. If I'm going to run for the presidency next year I've got to have a foreign policy!" Hall rummaged through some clippings on international issues from the *Wall Street Journal* and handed them to the governor. After his TV appearance, a smiling Wallace shouted to Hall: "I don't need a foreign policy! All they wanted to know about was niggers, and I'm the expert!"[1] Wallace was essentially correct. Opponents of the civil rights movement largely concentrated on the single issue of resisting racial equality. Despite this fundamental focus, segregationists eventually turned their attention to U.S. foreign policy in an effort to justify and to gain support for their battle to preserve white supremacy.

The foreign policy of the segregationists was never elaborate or comprehensive. They offered no detailed position papers on diplomatic issues or proposed any major policy initiatives. Their analysis of foreign affairs was a mixture of paranoia and pragmatism. They saw themselves as a besieged minority under attack by black demonstrators and a hostile government at home and by an alliance of antagonistic nations abroad. Resistance leaders argued that the source of this assault was an international conspiracy dedicated to inciting racial conflict to divide and weaken America. Their claim of a nefarious global plot against segregation was accompanied by a very practical decision that they could use Cold War anticommunism to gain support for their domestic agenda.

The segregationist critique of international issues began with an attempt to use the newly independent African nations as examples of black inferiority to buttress their defense of continued white political power in the American South. They also contended that U.S. foreign aid and support of the United Nations contributed directly to the growing assault on segregation. By 1964, as their battle against integration became more desperate, white supremacists made a more direct connection between foreign and domestic affairs by trying to link international communism with the civil rights movement. They established an informal alliance with existing right-wing groups in the hope of gaining national support for preserving segregation. George Wallace's campaigns for the presidency in 1964 and 1968 offered a national forum for the segregationist view of foreign affairs. The Vietnam War, however, showed conflicts among the white resistance and contradictions in their analysis of America and the world.

The first foreign policy issue to engage white supremacists was the surge to independence of Europe's African colonies in the late 1950s and early 1960s. Both sides in the battle over segregation noted that African independence coincided with increased challenges to white supremacy in the United States. In 1960 ("the Year of Africa") seventeen nations gained independence on the continent. In the same year, the new Student Nonviolent Coordinating Committee (SNCC) launched the sit-in movement and began its first voter registration campaigns. Civil rights organizers and the white resistance agreed that this was more than coincidence.

Ironically, decolonization served as an important example for both sides in the civil rights struggle. African American leaders saw Third World independence as a model of nonviolent change and argued the American campaign for equality was a part of a global battle against white rule. White supremacists, in contrast, claimed decolonization showed the disastrous results of black political power and demonstrated the need for continued white supremacy in America. Chaos in independent Africa illustrated the inability of the African for self-rule and, by extension, reaffirmed the need to maintain white political dominance in the United States.

To segregationists, African independence was a clear premonition of the calamity that would follow racial equality at home. Black rule in Africa was a model to be avoided, not duplicated. Their defense of segregation was based in part on the assertion of the biological inferiority of the black race, and white supremacists argued that independent Africa was a glaring example of the inability of nonwhites to exercise political power.

As African nations gained independence, segregationists were quick to publicize examples of turmoil on the continent. The *Citizen*, official publication of the Citizens Councils (the major organization of the white resistance), repeatedly ran accounts of violence and corruption in the new African nations and in 1962 devoted an entire issue to independent Africa. The journal maintained that Europe's abandonment of its African empire had been a cowardly retreat that handed power to a race incapable of self-government. Segregationists argued that the inferiority of Africans and African Americans made them unfit for governmental leadership. Decolonization thus led inevitably to chaos, black violence against the white minority, and conflict among ethnic groups. Africans were not just unprepared for independence; they were unable to govern themselves.[2]

To support its negative critique of Africa, the resistance relied heavily on the writings of Robert Ruark, author of the best-selling novels *Something of Value* and *Uhuru*. Ruark's fiction was critical of the rapid shift to black rule, and he openly mocked the ability of Africans to govern themselves. To Ruark, independent Africa was run "by boys in funny hats and monkey-skin coats" who were "still trying to solve the problem of pants." Africa was a political and economic disaster and illustrated the folly of granting political power to people incapable of its exercise. Ruark became the white resistance's "expert on Africa," and his writings were staples of segregationist publications.[3]

To support their view that Africans were unfit for political and economic leadership, segregationists distributed numerous racist cartoons ridiculing Africans and their leaders. They often depicted Africans dressed in European suits but with bones in their noses and carrying spears. Their leaders were portrayed lugging suitcases overflowing with foreign money as they tried to figure out how to use a telephone or read a street sign. Whites were shown being driven from their homes by black mobs or cooking in huge pots. The *Citizen* even ran a mock interview with a fictitious African leader who asked directions to Washington so he could collect U.S. dollars and meet white women.[4]

Their racist stereotype of independent Africa enabled segregationists to dismiss all African leaders as primitive savages. The *Southern Conservative* claimed the president of Gabon had just completed a four-year jail sentence for "eating his mother-in-law." When Kenya's prime minister Jomo Kenyatta criticized American segregation, George Wallace responded: "I guess he was leaning on his spear when he said it."[5]

The chaos in the former Belgian Congo following its independence in 1960 served as the perfect example to segregationists of the result of black political power in Africa and, by extension, at home. Repeated press accounts of black violence against the white minority became fodder for the white supremacists. In January 1961 Gerald L. K. Smith, head of the Christian National Crusade, published "A Report on Atrocities Committed by the Congolese Army against the White Population of the Congo" in his newsletter, *The Cross and the Flag.* The lengthy document, written by the Belgian government, claimed the rape of white nuns, the torture of white missionaries, and cannibalism of Europeans was common. The graphic account quickly became a centerpiece of segregationist propaganda that cited the Congo as an example of the inevitable horrors of black rule. One segregationist author concluded that the Congo proved that in Africa "Freedom is Rape; Independence is Murder."[6]

Ray Harris, president of the Citizens Councils, claimed the turmoil in the Congo proved black inferiority: "In America as in Africa, the negro's behavior is that of an immature and childish people." To Harris, the Congo illustrated the inescapable calamity that resulted from black rule over whites and confirmed the need for unyielding resistance to racial equality in the United States: "The minute you turn them [Africans] loose they go back to their old tribal customs of eating the enemy." Without continued white control, African Americans would imitate their African kin.[7]

Harris explained that segregation was necessary as "the people of Mississippi are determined not to transport to Mississippi the law of the jungle as it exists in the Congo." He claimed that in the Congo "the rape of white women became legal after independence." Similarly, Leander Perez, leader of the white resistance in Louisiana, told a segregationist rally that the Congo exposed to the world the true, violent nature of the black race. Without white restraint, black Americans would revert to similar savagery. "Don't wait for your daughters to be raped by these Congolese," he concluded. Segregationist speaker R. Carter Dillman of Georgia declared the only difference between blacks in America and in the Congo was "in the Congo they eat more white people."[8]

To the white resistance, the Congo proved that "in Africa they are preaching and practicing black supremacy and as soon as they are given their freedom they seek to drive the white race out or to subject it to their every wish." Southern whites also attempted to link the violence in the Congo with the "horrors" of Reconstruction. Ruth Alexander, writing in the *Citizen,* claimed that "atrocities, such as those described by eyewitnesses as occurring in the Congo today were commonplace throughout the South. Men were castrated, women raped, young girls ravished and mutilated, homes burned and pillaged, the very earth scorched and barren." If black Americans succeeded in gaining the vote, they, like the Congolese and their American ancestors after the Civil War, would exact vengeance on whites. White protesters in Alabama greeted Attorney General Robert Kennedy with signs reading "No Kennedy Congo Here!"[9]

When Moise Tshombe, aided by white mercenaries and advisers and financed by Belgian money, led Katanga Province in secession from the Congo,
segregationists rallied to his support. They contended that Tshombe, unlike
other black Africans, understood the need to keep whites in power to preserve
order. Southerners formed dozens of groups to support Katanga's independence and criticized the State Department for denying Tshombe a visa to visit
the United States.[10] In 1961 southern whites found a second example to bolster their disparaging view of Africans when Angolans launched a revolt to
gain independence from Portugal. Portugal knew of the southern condemnation of black rule in Africa and hired an American public relations firm, Selvage & Lee, to portray the Angolan revolt as communist-inspired and antiwhite. Martin Comanco, the director of the campaign, noted the frequent
segregationist use of the Congo example and argued that "the entire South
could be persuaded to side with Portugal." Selvage & Lee distributed thousands of pamphlets titled "The Communists and Angola" and "On the Morning of March 15" to groups such as the Citizens Councils, the National States
Rights Party, the John Birch Society, and Billy James Hargis's Christian Crusade. By 1962 Angola had joined the Congo as a focus of the white supremacist portrait of Africa.[11]

The violence in the Congo and Angola led to renewed southern support for
the last bastions of white control in Africa: South Africa and Rhodesia. Segregationists had long admired the apartheid regime in South Africa and
hailed the nation as a stable, anticommunist, white haven on a violent, cha-
otic, black continent. They argued that whites in the American South and in
South Africa were both battling outside forces trying to topple efforts to preserve civilization. Louis Hollis, secretary of the Mississippi Citizens Council,
claimed that "in South Africa whites would die before they surrender. I think
we would too."[12]

Pretoria was well aware of southern support and regularly provided free
trips to Africa for resistance leaders. Senator Allen Ellender of Louisiana
urged the U.S. government to support "the civilizing whites" of South Africa
as it was clear from the Congo and Angola that the black majority was "incapable of self-rule." In 1963 South Africa paid for Ellender to visit the nation
and the senator issued an 800-page report defending apartheid.[13]

William Simmons, editor of the Citizen, following a free trip to South
Africa, noted "the lack of racial tension in South Africa" in contrast with the
violence and anarchy in black-ruled nations. Pretoria also sponsored trips to
South Africa by Kenneth Tolliver, assistant to Mississippi senator James
Eastland, and numerous other segregationist politicians and ministers.[14]

When Ian Smith and the white minority in Rhodesia illegally declared its
independence from Britain in late 1965 to avoid majority rule, segregation-

ists rallied to their defense. They claimed Rhodesians had revolted against British tyranny to preserve their liberty just as America had done in 1776. Within six months more than a dozen U.S. organizations were lobbying for support of the white regime in Salisbury. The Friends of Rhodesia, formed with financial assistance from the Rhodesian government, established 122 branches and claimed 25,000 members, most in the segregated South. Rhodesia also persuaded anti-integrationist radio commentators such as Dan Smoot, Carl McIntyre, and Clarence Manion to champion the nation's independence. Edgar Bundy of the prosegregationist Church League of America invited Ian Smith to the United States to speak to his group. When the government denied the Rhodesian a visa, J. D. Vorster, brother of South Africa's prime minister, filled in.[15]

Segregationists in Congress also defended Rhodesia. In August 1966 Eastland introduced a resolution calling U.S. economic sanctions against Rhodesia "inhumane, illegal, arbitrary, unfair, harmful, and costly." Congressman Joe Wagonner of Louisiana contended that whites in Rhodesia and the American South had carved out a civilized land where "the natives were not capable of producing a semblance of what we call civilization." The Citizens Councils of America passed a unanimous resolution calling for U.S. recognition of the Smith government. In 1971 segregationists helped pass Virginia senator Harry Byrd's amendment exempting "strategic and critical materials" from the U.S. sanctions against Rhodesia.[16]

To the white resistance, the disasters of black rule in Africa not only demonstrated innate white supremacy, but also revealed the hypocrisy and lack of realism that characterized U.S. foreign policy. America was engaged in a worldwide battle against communism, but rather than supporting stable, Christian, pro-American nations such as South Africa and Rhodesia, Washington courted radical, anti-American black governments. America declared an arms embargo against South Africa and imposed sanctions on Rhodesia but gave millions of dollars to black African nations incapable of preserving order and unwilling to stand up against Moscow. Washington rewarded its enemies while punishing those who supported the battle against communism. To segregationists, a prime example of this lack of diplomatic realism was the disastrous results of U.S. foreign aid.

American conservatives and isolationists had long denounced foreign aid as wasteful and a drain on the U.S. economy, but the white resistance developed a new criticism: it claimed foreign aid not only squandered taxpayers' money but indirectly contributed to the plot to destroy American segregation. Segregationists argued that the United States gave economic aid to Third World nations to induce them to join the battle against communism, but Africans and Asians wanted more than dollars. Their hatred of whites led them to demand that the U.S. government abolish segregation. To purchase support against Moscow, Washington had to agree to promote civil rights at home. The State Department gave antiwhite African and Asian nations not only money but indirect control over U.S. domestic policy.[17]

Such an argument seemed convoluted and lacked any direct documentation, but many white leaders and organizations tried to make the case that Washington's support for the civil rights movement stemmed directly from the pressure of Third World nations. Senator Richard Russell of Georgia argued that foreign aid not only helped the Soviet Union "bleed America white" but also encouraged anti-American nations to attack segregation. In an effort to buy allies against communism, the State Department gave money to "any country on the face of the globe," even those that criticized American foreign policy and dictated domestic racial policies. Wallace declared it was hypocritical of foreign nations to accept U.S. dollars and then assail American race relations. When a reporter from India asked about segregation, Wallace reminded him that his nation had received "billions of dollars in U.S. tax-payers money" and suggested he "go home to India and work to end the rigid caste system before you criticize my part of the United States." Hargis argued foreign aid was unconstitutional as it gave foreign countries control of America's racial policies.[18]

The argument that America had sold its sovereignty to foreign nations through economic aid was accompanied by vigorous segregationist attacks on the United Nations. Again, white supremacists gave a racial interpretation to traditional conservative hostility toward the organization. Many right-wing groups had long denounced the UN as a communist plot, an organized network of spies, or "the anti-Christ" fulfilling biblical prophecy of a one-world government. The John Birch Society even claimed the UN operated a secret military base in Georgia.[19]

Segregationists generally rejected such extreme conspiracy theories. Their assault on the UN had a more direct racial emphasis that mirrored their criticism of foreign aid policies. They argued that decolonization gave control of the UN to Third World nations with an ingrained hatred of whites. The General Assembly was stacked with African countries, many of them "hardly out of savagery" obsessed with revenge against Caucasians. As with foreign aid, U.S. diplomats were so concerned with maintaining votes against communism that they gave into Third World demands that segregation be ended. The civil rights movement was designed to appease "a rabble rousing minority of American negroes and the black nations of the world." The South was being sacrificed to appease undemocratic, anti-American, and insignificant nations that dominated the UN. Bureaucrats in Washington had given control of the nation's internal affairs to fanatically antiwhite countries dedicated to imposing black rule on America.[20]

Attacks on the UN quickly joined the assault on foreign aid among resistance leaders. To Wallace, the UN was a "diplomatic tower of Babel" that was "consistently anti-American" and illegally meddled in U.S. politics by attacking segregation. Hargis claimed that Africans "only slightly removed from cannibalism" dominated the organization. These blacks could not control their own nations but were telling the United States how to run its domestic affairs. Ruark dismissed the UN as a group of "left-leaning hog-wallow and mangrove-swamp nations" that inflicted terror on their white population while preaching to America about race relations.[21]

To segregationists, Third World nations were incapable of preserving order in their own countries, had an ingrained hatred of whites, and did not support the global battle with communism. Despite this, liberals in Washington were so eager to harvest their votes in the UN that they agreed to a war against white rule in the American South. The UN's efforts to prevent Katanga's secession, its condemnation of Portugal's war in Angola, and its sanctions against South Africa and Rhodesia confirmed the southern view that the organization was both anti-American and antiwhite. Most galling, the United States paid most of the costs of the UN, including intervention in the Congo against Katanga. To segregationists, American taxpayers were financing a global war against white civilization.[22]

Their indictments of independent Africa, foreign aid, and the UN were the first attempts of white supremacists to try to connect the domestic campaign against segregation with international affairs. As the civil rights movement intensified and gained political support in 1963 and 1964, segregationists became increasingly desperate. To revitalize the resistance to equality and to try to gain support from outside the South, they began to focus more directly on Cold War anticommunism in an attempt to reach out to older, extremist groups. The result was a new alliance: the American radical right began a new concentration on racial issues while segregationists embraced much of the agenda of existing anticommunist groups. By 1965 organizations such as the John Birch Society, Smith's Christian National Crusade, the Liberty Lobby, Hargis's Christian Crusade, and Fred Schwarz's Christian Anti-Communist Crusade began to focus their attention on the civil rights movement. At the same time, southern whites actively courted such organizations by claiming American black protest was part of a global communist conspiracy.

The white resistance had long charged that the American Communist Party was involved in the civil rights movement. In 1955 the attorney general of Georgia charged that the National Association for the Advancement of Colored People (NAACP) was a communist front. In the late 1950s the Citizens Councils distributed a pamphlet titled *The Kiss of Death*, which contended that communists encouraged civil rights to promote miscegenation to destroy the white race and weaken America's ability to fight communism. In 1958 the House Un-American Activities Committee held hearings on alleged communist involvement in the campaign against segregation.[23]

Until 1964, however, allegations of direct foreign control of the civil rights movement were rarely a major focus. More often the resistance relied on legal defenses of states' rights and racial arguments of black inferiority. This changed dramatically in 1964 as southern whites played the anticommunist card in hopes of revitalizing and expanding the campaign to preserve segregation by enticing existing right-wing organizations to the cause.[24]

The coalition between the militant right and white supremacists was a marriage of convenience. Established right-wing organizations recognized the potential for support of their agenda among white southerners opposed to racial equality. The white resistance was aware of the financial power of the right and saw an opportunity to make the battle against civil rights a national rather than a regional campaign.

Leander Perez was among the first southern leaders to urge a more direct focus on anticommunism as a way to enlist northerners in the fight to preserve white supremacy. To Perez, linking civil rights with Cold War anticommunism "held the potential to attract support from outside the South, to nationalize the opposition to civil rights which was giving the South a bad name."[25]

The Citizens Councils agreed. When civil rights groups announced plans for a 1964 Mississippi Freedom Summer, the councils launched a massive publicity effort to show international communist involvement in the movement. They claimed foreign revolutionaries had gained control of the civil rights movement and were using it to divide the nation and cripple America in its global battle with Marxism. In early 1964 the Louisiana Committee on Un-American Activities charged that "SNICK [*sic*] is substantially under the control of the Communist Party" and hoped to incite violence during the Mississippi Freedom Summer so "the federal government would take over the state of Mississippi."[26]

As they tried to connect African American protest with international Marxism, the Citizens Councils also began to embrace many of the tenets of extreme right-wing thought, including conspiracy theories of communism within the U.S. government. As Neil McMillen observed in his study of the organization: "Racism remained the nucleus of its thought, but the Council's

ideological circumference expanded to encompass the politico-economic characteristic of conservatism."[27]

To support their new orientation, segregationists tried to document direct
communist influence within civil rights organizations. Eastland compiled extensive lists of "known communists" active in the movement and distributed
them to segregationist publications. Posters and pamphlets naming communist advisers to Martin Luther King and other civil rights leaders followed.
The director of the Citizens Council of Louisiana claimed to have copies of di-
rectives from Moscow to the NAACP orchestrating racial protests. The Ku
Klux Klan also reprinted articles "proving" foreign communist control of the
civil rights movement.[28]

Other southern politicians followed the Citizens Council's lead and shifted
their rhetoric from states' rights and biological arguments for black inferiority to a new emphasis on resisting international communism. As Dan Carter
noted, even Wallace tempered "the traditional southern campaign chorus of
'Nigger-Nigger-Nigger'" and "substituted the Cold War battle cry: 'Commie-
Commie-Commie.'" The Alabama governor began to attack the media for
not exposing Moscow's control of the civil rights movement. The same reporters who "told us Castro was a good Democratic soul and that Mao Tse
Tung was only an agrarian reformer" now covered up communist influence
in the South. At a 1964 rally organized by Lester Maddox of Georgia, Wallace charged that the proposed Civil Rights Act "came straight out of the
Communist Manifesto."[29]

The new anticommunist emphasis succeeded in attracting support from
right-wing groups. In early 1965 Robert Welch, president of the John Birch
Society, announced his group would shift its focus from government subver-
sion to "an all-out drive against the civil rights movement." In May, Welch
published a pamphlet called *The Revolution at Home* that charged that the
onslaught against segregation was part of a massive Soviet campaign to use
the UN, the American Communist Party, and radical African governments to
weaken the United States in preparation for a communist takeover. Welch argued that if you "fully expose the 'civil rights' fraud you will break the back
of the communist conspiracy." The Birch Society immediately began to
reprint segregationist articles charging international communist control of
the civil rights movement.[30]

Birchers also claimed that the Watts riot in August 1965 was the "next
step" in communist strategy. Having successfully divided the United States
over southern integration, Russian, Cuban, and African agents now were
guiding black Americans in direct attacks on white people and property. The
group distributed 500,000 copies of a pamphlet titled *Two Revolutions at*

Once, which claimed the urban riots were controlled by Cuba and Moscow. It also launched Operation TACT (Truth about Civil Turmoil) to provide speakers and films to prove that attacks on segregation were part of a global communist conspiracy. The organization even hired Jim Clark, former sheriff of Selma, Alabama, as a lecturer on racial issues.[31]

Following the Birch Society's lead, other anticommunist groups began to concentrate on the civil rights movement. Gerald L. K. Smith had long argued that Jews were behind the battle against segregation but shifted his argument to emphasize foreign communist influence. Ultraconservative Dan Smoot followed suit by claiming Josef Stalin had planned the campaign against segregation to encourage conflict between white and black and between the North and South. "The so-called civil rights movement in the United States is a communist creation, and has largely been manipulated by communists since it was created," he asserted.[32]

Billy James Hargis also initiated a direct assault on the civil rights movement and its leaders. He claimed that "God ordained segregation" and in 1964 began a major campaign to show black protests were controlled by Moscow. He distributed lists of communists in the movement and told his followers that the proposed civil rights act "fulfills many of the demands of Karl Marx's 'Communist Manifesto.'" To Hargis, Mississippi Freedom Summer was part of a foreign plot to launch "a bloody race war" that would divide America and lead to UN intervention. Hargis noted that his new attack on the civil rights movement led to a dramatic increase in contributions to his Christian Crusade.[33]

Hargis's conclusion seemed accurate as the merger of race and anticommunism led to a surge in both membership and financial support for nearly all the right-wing groups that made opposition to civil rights their new priority. The six largest anticommunist organizations had total revenues of $1.3 million in 1960; in 1964 they raised $8.4 million. Much of this new support came from the segregated South. As former Mississippi congressman Frank Smith concluded in 1964, "The espousal of segregation by right-wing groups has won them membership and support in the South far beyond their due."[34]

Despite the Republican nomination of conservative Barry Goldwater (who voted against the Civil Rights Act), much of the anticommunist right threw its support to Wallace's 1964 presidential campaign. Bunker Hunt, a financial supporter of numerous right-wing groups, personally donated $250,000 to Wallace's primary campaigns. The Ku Klux Klan distributed 2.5 million cartons of matchbooks with "Draft Wallace in 1964" on the cover.[35]

Anticommunist groups also provided volunteers for the Alabama governor. In several states, over half the staff of the Wallace organization also belonged to the John Birch Society. When asked about support from the Birchers and the KKK, Wallace responded, "I have no objection to anyone who is anti-Communist."[36]

Four years later, Wallace called a meeting of advisers at the Woodbury Country Club in Montgomery to plan another run for the presidency. The group symbolized the new coalition of traditional segregationists and the anticommunist right. Aside from former Mississippi governor Ross Barnett, Leander Perez, and William Simmons of the Citizens Councils, Wallace also invited representatives from the John Birch Society and the Liberty Lobby. A sign of the merger of the white resistance and right-wing groups was a meeting between Asa Carter, a Wallace aide and former KKK organizer, and Willis Carto, head of the ultraconservative Liberty Lobby and publisher of *American Mercury*. Together they produced a pamphlet supporting Wallace for president in 1968. Carto distributed over 175,000 copies to members of the Liberty Lobby and other conservative groups in the North.[37]

The union of segregationists and the anticommunist right provoked a minor split within the white supremacist movement. Richard Morpheau, publicity director of the Citizens Councils of America, warned that resistance to integration was being weakened by "side issues" such as right-wing conspiracy theories about the Federal Reserve system and fluoridation of water. He argued that the movement needed to regain its focus on preventing integration rather than the more expansive right-wing agenda.[38]

Despite such warnings, by late 1964 the alliance of the white South and the national anticommunist movement was firmly established. Segregationists were willing to tolerate the often bizarre ideas of other groups in exchange for their support in the fight against equality. Despite the conspiratorial fantasies of many anticommunist organizations, the white resistance saw them, in the words of former congressman Smith, as dedicated "to saving the American way of life, and that boils down to segregation." When reporters asked Wallace about some of the more eccentric ideas of his far right allies, he replied, "The other side has more kooks than we do. Besides, kooks got the right to vote too."[39] As right-wing organizations joined the campaign against the civil rights movement, the Citizens Councils announced plans to expand nationwide. Having embraced national groups such as the Birch Society, they attempted to extend their organization into the North to show opposition to racial equality was not just a regional issue. In August 1964 they opened a branch in California and a month later established five chapters in the Washington, D.C., area. The group claimed there was "a lot of interest" in "the Pacific Northwest, Missouri, Wisconsin and Indiana" and announced a goal of forming chapters in all fifty states.[40]

George Wallace in
1968. (National
Archives)

The efforts to shift resistance to integration from a regional to a national
issue had its strongest expression in Wallace's 1964 and 1968 presidential
campaigns. His surprising strength in Democratic primaries in both years
showed resistance to civil rights and centralized government was not limited
to the South. Wallace's campaigns also demonstrated deep hostility toward
American foreign policy. He not only attacked civil rights legislation and the
power of Washington but also criticized America's weakness in the Cold War
and the elitism of policy makers. As an indication of his reach for a national
audience and a new emphasis on foreign policy, Wallace altered his guberna-
torial slogan of "Stand Up for Alabama!" to "Stand Up for America!" As part
of his campaign to "Stand Up for America," Wallace articulated many of the
foreign policy themes of the southern white resistance. He repeatedly denounced Third World influence on U.S. domestic issues, attacked the UN and
foreign aid, and tried to link international communism and the civil rights
movement.[41]

Wallace also criticized the strategists who shaped America's foreign policy, claiming that the same liberals who tried to force integration on the South were the architects of the nation's weak and ineffective diplomacy that was losing the Cold War battle. To Wallace, foreign policy was controlled by "experts" out of touch with the American people and unable to distinguish the nation's friends from its enemies. They had led the United States into "four wars in the last 50 years" and directly financed radical, anti-American governments. "We've spent $132 billion of our money and we've got less friends than we had when we started," he concluded.[42]

To Wallace, diplomacy was not as complex and difficult as the media and foreign policy specialists claimed. There was no need to rely on overeducated experts in the State Department, as the average American knew far better than the "intellectual morons" in Washington what was good for the nation. "Any man with a second grade education knew Castro was bad just by looking at his picture and reading what he said," Wallace argued, and "any cab driver in Montgomery" knew more about Vietnam "than a Yale professor."[43]

Rather than relying on common sense and the will of the people, the Washington "experts" lived in an unrealistic world of abstract ideas and convoluted theories. To restore America's place in the world, Wallace suggested, "we've got to get all this theory out of things." Wallace argued foreign policy decisions did not require specialists: "Maybe a fellow just ought to advise himself from the seat of his pants, just what his common sense tells him." When asked in his 1964 primary campaign in Indiana about his lack of experience in foreign policy, Wallace acknowledged, "I have no experience," but maintained this was an asset. Given the dismal state of U.S. diplomacy, "what we need in Washington is a little experience!"[44] Wallace's repeated attacks on "bureaucrats who can't even park their bicycles straight" were often directed at the foreign policy establishment. If elected, he promised to go to the State Department and "take away their briefcases and throw them in the Potomac River!"[45]

Wallace also attacked Washington for not being militant enough in its efforts against communism at home and abroad. When asked who he would select as his secretary of state, Wallace said he would not pick a Dean Acheson or Dean Rusk, but someone "like John Foster Dulles" who recognized the communist danger. "The Communists are dedicated to the overthrow of our form of government," he argued. "They are dedicated to the destruction of the concept of private property . . . to the object of destroying religion" and "to putting all resources under the control of the central government." Despite this threat, the nation's leaders were afraid to confront communists and communist nations. To Wallace, this weakness was in part the result of Moscow's creation of the civil rights movement that divided and distracted America from the global Cold War.[46]

As an example of the nation's timidity, Wallace claimed it was proved that Cuba had organized the urban riots "at a conference of world guerilla warfare chieftains in Havana," but Washington did nothing in response. The United States should "arm the underground patriots in Cuba" and let them "get rid of Castro."[47] To show American toughness, he urged an end of foreign aid to any country that did not support the United States on international issues or meddled in America's domestic policies and suggested the United States consider withdrawing from the UN "in the not too distant future." Wallace also charged that Washington was too sensitive to criticism from foreign nations, particularly on racial issues: "It's about time we quit worrying what they think of us and let them start worrying about what we think of them. . . . We don't have to apologize for America. We have more civil rights per square inch here than they have in a square mile behind the Iron Curtain."[48]

Wallace's anticommunism led him into a dilemma as the nation's involvement in Vietnam escalated. In 1964 he was free to attack America's lack of "toughness" overseas, but in 1968 the war forced him to define the term. Many of Wallace's supporters were isolationist but strongly promilitary. In a 1968 survey 64 percent of those who voted for the Alabama governor felt the United States should have "stayed out of Vietnam," but 67 percent thought the nation should take a "stronger stance" to win the war. Much of the white resistance showed a similar duality on the war.[49] Segregationists were deeply divided on Vietnam. Many saw the conflict as a prime example of the folly of internationalism and reliance on establishment "experts." As early as 1965 the John Birch Society called for a complete American withdrawal from the war. Other right-wing and white supremacist groups also condemned the war as a costly distraction from domestic racial problems and communist infiltration.[50]

Despite this dissent, most segregationists passionately hated the antiwar movement and many argued they needed to show their patriotism by supporting U.S. troops. Richard Russell, for example, privately opposed the war but felt "national honor" required him to publicly support the military. South Carolina senator Strom Thurmond spoke out on the war only after African American groups and leaders voiced their opposition. When SNCC became the first civil rights group to criticize involvement in Vietnam, Thurmond accused the organization of being "part of a worldwide communist strategy to incite insurrection and revolution." He later condemned Martin Luther King's public opposition to the war, claiming: "In attempting to link the war in Vietnam with the civil rights movement, King demeans his race."[51]

In 1967 the *Citizen* devoted an entire issue to Vietnam and displayed the conflicts among its members. William K. Shearer judged the war "a propaganda trap" by the communists to divide America and concluded: "We must stop attempting to play policeman for the entire world, and we can start by withdrawing from Vietnam." Medford Evans admitted that withdrawal would lead to a communist victory but contended that remaining in Vietnam would force America to occupy the entire nation and become a colonial power. It was best to leave and "fight communism on ground of our own choosing" in Cuba, Rhodesia, and within the United States. Retired General William Walker, a favorite of right-wing and segregationist groups, countered by claiming that liberal politicians who did not listen to the military were losing the war.[52]

David Duke, later a leader of the Ku Klux Klan, was a college student at Louisiana State University during the war and already active in the white supremacy movement. Like many other segregationists, he thought Vietnam was a blunder, but "since we had made a commitment . . . we should support our troops 100 percent." Wearing a shirt with a swastika on the pocket, he organized picketing of antiwar speakers and demonstrations.[53]

Wallace repeatedly faced the Vietnam dilemma during his 1968 presidential campaign. At times he expressed doubts about the war but attacked those who protested against it. He admitted, "I'm not sure we should be there, but as long as our service men are there we must give them our full support to win the war." On other occasions, he called for giving the military a free hand: "Just turn it over to the Joint Chiefs of Staff, ask them what they need to win and get on with doing it . . . we've got to pour it on. We've got to win this war. If that means stepping-up the bombing, step it up. If it means block off Haiphong, block her off."[54]

Wallace, while admitting doubts about U.S. involvement, never questioned the need to prosecute vigorously antiwar protesters who engaged in violence or supported the enemy. "To oppose the war was dissent—to advocate victory for the enemy was treason," Wallace maintained. "I know there's good people here tonight who sincerely believe we should not be involved in Vietnam," he explained in a 1968 campaign speech. "I respect their opinion. I believe in the right of dissent. But when somebody advocates a Communist victory, he's advocating killing of American boys and that's treason. He ought to be drug before a grand jury and put *under* a Federal jail." When asked about the Ku Klux Klan, Wallace responded: "At least a Klansman will fight for his country. He don't tear up his draft card."[55]

Support of U.S. troops and a hard line against protesters were part of Wallace's national appeal. He recognized, however, that many of his supporters, although appalled by the antiwar movement, thought involvement in Vietnam was a mistake. Wallace had to walk a fine line between total support of the war and recognition that many of his followers thought the war a blunder. In 1968 Wallace picked former air force general Curtis LeMay as his running mate to show his support for the American military, but the strategy immediately backfired. At the press conference announcing the general's selection, LeMay suggested nuclear weapons might be necessary to win the war. Despite earlier pledges to "pour it on" in Vietnam, Wallace was furious. He physically forced LeMay away from the microphone and disassociated himself from his running mate's comments. Critics, however, immediately labeled Wallace and LeMay "the Bombsey Twins."[56] After the 1968 election, Wallace visited Vietnam and returned with a solution to the war designed to appeal to both hawks and isolationists. He proposed giving the military unlimited resources and men for ninety days to win the war. If they did not succeed, he would immediately withdraw all U.S. forces.[57]

Wallace's 1968 campaign was one of the last gasps of the organized white resistance. The Civil Rights Act of 1964 and the Voting Rights Act of 1965 did not eradicate white racism, but they marked the beginning of the end of legalized segregation. White supremacist groups survived the overthrow of segregation but showed little sustained interest in foreign affairs after 1968. The only issue that generated persistent attention was perceived Jewish influence on U.S. diplomacy and Washington's support of Israel. Ku Klux Klan leader Robert Shelton, for example, endorsed the Palestine Liberation Organization's use of violence, asking, "What's wrong with Arabs killing a few people to protect their land?" David Duke, Wallace's successor as the most influential spokesman for white supremacy, repeatedly complained that U.S. policy was slanted toward Israel due to Jewish control of the media and called Henry Kissinger a tool of the Zionist lobby.[58]

Several scholars have argued that the white resistance's ceaseless criticism of the power of Washington and its demand for states' rights helped pave the way for Richard Nixon's "new federalism," Jimmy Carter's election as a Washington "outsider," and Ronald Reagan's campaigns against big government. Analysts have also concluded that their disillusionment with the Democratic Party helped shift the South into a Republican stronghold.[59] Their impact on U.S. diplomacy is more ambiguous. Segregationists were clearly unsuccessful in their efforts to use independent Africa as an example of the disasters of black political power in America. Their argument that U.S. foreign aid and UN policies were controlled by foreign states eager to force the nation to end segregation also had minimal impact. The alliance of segregationists and right-wing, anticommunist groups may have helped in their efforts to discredit the civil rights movement but did little to prevent the end of legalized discrimination. Wallace's impressive vote totals in 1964 and 1968 may have been due in part to his criticism of U.S. foreign policy, but his campaigns did not significantly alter Cold War diplomacy or Vietnam policy.

One reason for their lack of impact was that segregationists used selected international issues largely to gain support for their major domestic goal of defeating the civil rights movement. Foreign policy was always supplementary to the larger issue of domestic racial relations. When legal segregation ended, there was little incentive to continue a focus on foreign policy. The issues that later engaged their attention, such as affirmative action, busing, and racial quotas, seemed to have little connection to foreign affairs.

Segregationists may have exerted little influence on U.S. foreign policy, but their venture into international relations had a major effect on them. Ironically, they learned their major lesson from their opponents. Nearly all the leaders of the civil rights movement of the 1960s saw themselves as part of a global struggle against white supremacy and urged international unity among nonwhites. The remnants of the white supremacy movement borrowed this global emphasis and stress on international racial unity from their enemy. Nearly all U.S. white supremacist groups now emphasize the international significance of race and the need for global white unity. Many of the slogans of white racist groups in the 1990s urging international racial solidarity echoed those of the black leaders they so hated three decades earlier. The New Order of the Knights of the Ku Klux Klan, for example, proclaimed on a web page: "We are INTERNATIONAL in Scope. . . . We STRIVE for TOTAL ARYAN UNITY throughout [sic] the World! Not limited to the United States alone." The Aryan Nation published its material in six languages under the title "Different Tongues/One Elect Race," and the White Power Party has adopted the slogan "White Pride, Worldwide." Duke claimed the major mistake in the 1960s was a narrow focus on America, rather than the global issue of racial identity, and claims that white groups now recognize the international nature of their struggle. Similarly, Louis Bean of the Aryan Nation explained: "We do not advocate segregation. That was a temporary measure that is long past." The goal now is to unite "ALL those countries which have traditionally been considered White lands."[60]

It is paradoxical that a movement that was occasionally jingoistic, often isolationist, and always scornful of the rest of the world now proclaims global solidarity and international white unity. Like many civil rights activists of the 1960s, its leaders now argue that race is more important than nationality and claim that they share a common bond with people in other countries. "Stand Up for America" has been replaced by international racial unity. Having failed to maintain segregation at home, they now urge white unity throughout the world.

Notes

1. Wayne Greenhaw, *Watch Out for George Wallace* (Englewood Cliffs, N.J.: Prentice-Hall, 1976), 2–3; Dan T. Carter, *The Politics of Rage: George Wallace, the Origins of the New Conservatism, and the Transformation of American Politics* (Baton Rouge: Louisiana State University Press, 1995), 135–38.

2. See *Citizen* 7 (Nov. 1962), especially John B. Trevor, "Segregation: An Old African Custom," 9–10. Segregationists first used Africa to illustrate the result of black rule following the Mau Mau revolt in Kenya in the early 1950s. See, for example, "Stop Mau Mau or Die!," *White Men's News* (Sept. 1955): 172.

3. Robert Ruark, "Africa 'Emerging'—Its a Crazy World!," *White Men's News* (Sept. 1955): 13–14; "African Nations Emerging into Idiocy," ibid. 8 (Oct. 1964), 15–16.

4. See, for example, cartoons in *American Mercury* 91 (Nov. 1960): 80; 93 (Jan. 1962): 19, 22; Timeweek Interview: "An African Premier," *Citizen* 9 (Jan. 1965): 12–14.

5. Quoted in Robert Morris, "The Rush to Dismember the West," *American Standard* 1 (Mar. 1962), 4–5. See also George Jordon, "African Witches Brew Concocted in Moscow," *American Mercury* 92 (Jan. 1961): 19–21; Carter, *The Politics of Rage*, 237.

6. "The Congo," *The Cross and the Flag* 21 (Jan. 1961); *Dan Smoot Report*, 3 Oct. 1960, 1; "Rape of White Women Legal after Independence," *Augusta Courier* (Georgia), 20 June 1960, 4. Roy Harris, president of the Citizens Councils, was the editor of the *Augusta Courier*. See also Mark Sherwin, *The Extremists* (New York: St. Martin's Press, 1963), 103–4.

7. Roy Harris, "A Time for Optimism," *Citizen* 7 (Jan. 1963): 7–12; Amos Koontz, "'Uhuru' Does Not Confer 'Equality,'" ibid. 8 (Nov. 1963): 6–10.

8. *Augusta Courier*, 20 June 1960, 1; James Graham Cook, *The Segregationists* (New York: Appleton-Century-Crofts, 1962), 113–14; William J. Turner, *Power on the Right* (Berkeley: Ramparts, 1971), 32.

9. *The Cross and the Flag* 21 (Feb. 1963): 23–24; Ruth Alexander, "Violence in the Congo Is Reminiscent of Tragedy of Reconstruction in the South," *Citizen* 7 (Nov. 1962): 11–12; Carter, *The Politics of Rage*, 120.

10. Richard D. Mahoney, *JFK: Ordeal in Africa* (New York: Oxford University Press, 1983), 119, 135–37, and Stephen Weissman, *American Foreign Policy in the Congo, 1960–1964* (Ithaca: Cornell University Press, 1974), 168–69; Ernest van den Haag, *The War in Katanga* (New York: American Committee for Aid to Katanga Freedom Fighters, 1962), often quoted in segregationist publications.

11. Thomas J. Noer, *Cold War and Black Liberation: The United States and White Rule in Africa, 1948–1968* (Columbia: University of Missouri Press, 1985), 74–76; "The Case for Portugal," *Weekly Crusader* 3 (7 Sept. 1962); Daniel M. Friedenberg, "The Public Relations of Colonialism: Salazar's Mouthpiece in the U.S.," *Africa Today* 9 (Apr. 1972): 4–16.

12. John Trevor, "Facts vs. Fiction in South Africa," *Citizen* 11 (Jan. 1965): 7–8; Cook, *Segregationists*, 81.

13. *New York Times*, 6 Dec. 1962, 9; 8 Mar. 1963, 8. See also Colin Gonze, "With Ellender in Africa," *Africa Today* 10 (May 1963): 4–6.

14. William Simmons, "Report on a Trip to Southern Africa," *Citizen* 10 (July–Aug. 1966): 4–14; Kenneth Tolliver, "Traveler's Report on Southern Africa," ibid. 11 (July–Aug. 1967): 4–13.

15. Anthony Lake, *The "Tar Baby" Option: American Policy toward Southern Rhodesia* (New York: Columbia University Press, 1976), 109–12; "And Now Rhodesia," *Dan Smoot Report*, 10 Jan. 1966, 1; "Is Rhodesia an Enemy of Freedom?," *Weekly Crusader* 5 (25 Mar. 1966): 1–7.

16. Lake, *The "Tar Baby" Option*, 118; Noer, *Cold War and Black Liberation*, 222–25; Calvin Trillin, "Letter from Salisbury," *New Yorker* 12 (Nov. 1966): 139.

17. For early attempts to link foreign aid with the campaign against segregation, see the Citizens' Foreign Aid Committee newsletter, *Facts on Foreign Aid*, 1959–60; Eugene W. Castle, "Foreign Aid Follies," *American Mercury* 89 (June 1959): 26–35; and "Foreign Aid Is Killing America," *Dan Smoot Report*, 21 Oct. 1963, 1–3.

18. Gilbert Fite, *Richard B. Russell, Jr.: Senator from Georgia* (Chapel Hill: University of North Carolina Press, 1991), 248–52, 384; George Wallace, *Stand-Up for America* (Garden City, N.Y.: Doubleday, 1976), 85; John H. Redekop, *The American Far Right: A Case Study of Billy James Hargis and the Christian Crusade* (Grand Rapids, Mich.: Eerdmans, 1968), 56–57.

19. Gerald Schomp, *Birchism Was My Business* (New York: Macmillan, 1970), 117; Jonathan Martin Kolkey, *The New Right, 1960–1968* (Washington, D.C.: University Press of America), 134–35; Ralph E. Ellsworth and Sarah M. Harris, *The American Right Wing* (Washington, D.C.: Public Affairs Press, 1962), 27–30; and Hillary Grey, "U.N.: The New Cominform," *American Mercury* 89 (June 1959): 16–24.

20. Kolkey, *The New Right*, 134–35; Robert Morris, "And Still They Say It Can't Be True!," *American Standard*, May 1962, 13; *Alert!*, 24 Oct. 1966, 1–2.

21. Wallace, *Stand-Up*, 125; Redekop, *The American Far Right*, 70–71; Ruark, "Africa 'Emerging,'" 14.

22. John Bartlow Martin, *The Deep South Says "Never"* (New York: Ballantine Books, 1957), 113; Roy Harris, "Will Kennedy Ditch Whites for Black Africans?," *Augusta Courier*, 16 Jan. 1961, 4; Clarence Manion, *The Conservative American: His Fight for National Independence and Constitutional Government* (New York: Devin-Adair, 1964), 145; "United Nations: A Soviet Apparatus," *Dan Smoot Report*, 3 Aug. 1964, 1–3.

23. Eugene Cook, *The Ugly Truth about the NAACP* (Jackson, Miss.: Citizens Councils of America, 1955); Cook, *Segregationists*, 59; U.S. Congress, House of Representatives, House Un-American Activities Committee, *Communist Activities in the South*, 85th Cong., 2nd sess., 1958; George Weaver, "Liberation: Red Bait for Negroes," *American Mercury* 89 (Nov. 1958): 32–39.

24. Michael W. Miles, "The New South," in *The Odyssey of the American Right*, 267–82 (New York: Oxford University Press, 1980).

25. Liva Baker, *The Second Battle of New Orleans: The Hundred-Year Struggle to Integrate the Schools* (New York: HarperCollins, 1996), 220–21.

26. "Communism in the Civil Rights Movement," *Dan Smoot Report*, 1 June 1964, 1. See also Hurst B. Amyz, "Reds Want Summer of Violence and Chaos," *Citizen* 8 (Jan. 1964): 12–13.

27. Neil R. McMillen, *The Citizens' Council: Organizing Resistance to the Second Reconstruction, 1954–1964* (Champaign: University of Illinois Press, 1971), 191.

28. "Senator Eastland Reveals the Proof of Communist Influence in the Mississippi Invasion," *Citizen* 9 (Apr. 1975): 16–36; Sherwin, *The Extremists*, 105; "Communist Influence in the So-Called Civil Rights Movement," *Fiery Cross*, Aug. 1964, 1.

29. Carter, *The Politics of Rage*, 328, 161, 217.

30. Benjamin R. Epstein and Arnold Forster, *Report on the John Birch Society* (New York: Random House, 1967), 7–15; Medford Evans, "Why the Reds Say Mississippi Must Go," *American Opinion* 8 (Apr. 1965): 15–23; Jim Lucier, "Civil Rites," ibid. (June 1965): 17–20.

31. Alan Stang, "The King and His Communists," *American Opinion* 8 (Oct. 1965), 1–11; Epstein and Forster, *Report on the John Birch Society*, 7; Schomp, *Birchism Was My Business*, 134–35, 166.

32. Gerald Jeansonne, *Gerald L. K. Smith: Minister of Hate* (New Haven: Yale University Press, 1967), 115–29; "Reds, Race, Riots, and Revolution," *Christian Anti-Communist Crusade Newsletter*, 24 Aug. 1965, 1; "Communism in the Civil Rights Movement," *Dan Smoot Report*, 1 June 1964, 1: "Civil Rights or Civil War?," ibid., 22 Feb. 1965, 57–63.

33. Harry Overstreet and Bonaro Overstreet, *The Strange Tactics of Extremism* (New York: W. W. Norton, 1964), 194–97; Redekop, *The American Far Right*, 22.

34. Carter, *The Politics of Rage*, 296; Frank Smith, *Congressman from Mississippi* (New York: Pantheon Books, 1964), 125.

35. Smith, *Congressman from Mississippi*, 336–37; Patsy Simms, *The Klan* (Lexington: University of Kentucky Press, 1996), 100.

36. Jody Carlson, *George C. Wallace and the Politics of Powerlessness: The Wallace Campaign for the Presidency, 1964–1972* (New Brunswick, N.J.: Transaction Books, 1981), 130; Roy Jenkins, "George Wallace Figures to Win Even If He Loses," *New York Times Magazine*, 7 Apr. 1968, 26–27.

37. Carter, *The Politics of Rage*, 294–97.

38. McMillen, *The Citizens' Council*, 199.

39. Smith, *Congressman from Mississippi*, 125; Carter, *The Politics of Rage*, 298.

40. *New York Times*, 5 Aug. 1964, 36; 14 Sept. 1964, 75.

41. Carter and Carlson do the best analyses of the Wallace campaigns. See also James L. Canfield, *A Case of Third Party Activism: The George Wallace Campaign Workers and the American Independent Party* (Washington, D.C.: University Press of America, 1984); Margaret Conway, "The White Backlash Re-Examined: Wallace and the 1964 Primaries," *Social Science Quarterly* 49 (Dec. 1968): 111–26; Richard Haney, "Wallace in Wisconsin," *Wisconsin Magazine of History* 61 (Summer 1978): 259–78.

42. Carter, *The Politics of Rage*, 425; Carlson, *George C. Wallace and the Politics of Powerlessness*, 130.

43. Tom Wicker, "George Wallace: A Good and Simple Heart," *Harpers* 234 (Apr. 1967): 41–49.

44. Wallace, *Stand-Up*, 125; Kolkey, *The New Right*, 182; Carter, *The Politics of Rage*, 425.

45. Greenhaw, *Watch Out for George Wallace*, 30.

46. "Wallace Answers Unsparing Questions," *Richmond News-Leader*, 8 May 1967, reprinted in *Citizen* 11 (June 1967): 4–25; Greenhaw, *Watch Out for George Wallace*, 153–54.

47. Haney, "Wallace in Wisconsin," 267; Carter, *The Politics of Rage*, 315.

48. "Wallace Answers," 22; Wallace, *Stand-Up*, 90.

49. Carlson, *George C. Wallace and the Politics of Powerlessness*, 91–93.

50. *John Birch Society Bulletin* (Aug. 1965): 18–20; Frank P. Mintz, *The Liberty Lobby and the American Right: Race, Conspiracy and Culture* (Westport, Conn.: Greenwood Press, 1985), 102–3; Kolkey, *The New Right*, 221–44.

51. Fite, *Senator from Georgia*, 438–39; Nadine Cohadas, *Strom Thurmond and the Politics of Southern Change* (New York: Simon and Schuster, 1995), 386–87.

52. William Shearer, "Is U.S. Involvement in Vietnam Necessary?," *Citizen* 11 (Mar. 1967): 4–7; Medford Evans, "Global Perspectives on the Trap in Vietnam," ibid., 11–13; William A. Walker, "The Politicians' War in Vietnam," ibid., 8–10.

53. Michael Zatarain, *David Duke: Evolution of a Klansman* (Gretna, La.: Pelican Publications, 1990), 118.

54. Wallace, *Stand-Up*, 126; Phillip Grass, *The Wallace Factor* (New York: Mason/Charter, 1976), 95–96.

55. Jenkins, "George Wallace Figures to Win," 26; Wicker, "George Wallace," 46.

56. Carter, *The Politics of Rage*, 358–60.

57. Stephen Lesher, *George Wallace: American Populist* (New York: Addison-Wesley, 1993), 434–35.

58. Simms, *The Klan*, 103; Zatarain, *David Duke*, 119.

59. Carter concluded Wallace was "the most influential loser in twentieth century American politics." Carter, *The Politics of Rage*, 468; Kevin Phillips, *The Emerging Republican Majority* (New Rochelle, N.Y.: Arlington House, 1969), esp. 31–35, 206–8.

60. As of May 2002, the Aryan Nation maintained a web page at ‹www.nidlink. com/aryanvic›, and David Duke at ‹www.duke.org›. Because of the constantly changing nature of the Internet, the exact texts of these statements may no longer be publicly available. Loretta Ross, "White Supremacy in the 1990s," in *Eyes Right: Challenging the Right Wing Backlash*, ed. Chip Berlet (Boston: South End Press, 1995), 166–81.

The Unwelcome Mat

African Diplomats in Washington, D.C., during the Kennedy Years

Anyone who picked up a copy of the late 1960 edition of *Trends in Housing,* published by the National Committee against Discrimination in Housing (NCDH), would have been surprised to learn that many African diplomats characterized Washington, D.C., as a "hardship post." A front-page story suggested that America's housing problem extended into the international arena, noting, "African Diplomats Hit Race Barriers; Housing Problem Acute." The report that followed recounted a litany of complaints from African diplomats in Washington who faced constant discrimination and, in particular, problems in securing decent and affordable housing. The same publication boasted another front-page story that linked race and housing. A banner headline announced "Kennedy Committed to End Govt. Housing Bias; Executive Order Anticipated." The president-elect had pledged to abolish discrimination in federal housing "by a stroke of a pen." NCDH chairman of the board Algernon D. Black happily anticipated "a new frontier in housing."[1]

Neither the seriousness of the situation concerning African diplomats in Washington nor the relationship between that situation and the larger issues of domestic racial discrimination and housing problems was lost on the new Kennedy administration. According to historian Thomas Noer, Kennedy viewed Africa as "an arena of significant Cold War rivalry." In addition, African nations were coming to play a much more significant role in the United Nations. In 1945 there were only four African countries in the UN; five more joined during the 1950s. Between 1960 and the end of 1963, however, twenty-four new African nations became members of the UN; fifteen of those had joined in 1960, just a year before Kennedy came into office.[2]

Instances of racial discrimination against African diplomats in Washington would hardly win the United States allies or UN votes. At home, Kennedy had vigorously courted the black vote in the 1960 election, an election that he won by the narrowest of margins. Part of his success in securing the black vote was due to promises such as that dealing with discrimination in housing.[3]

Embarrassing and very public incidents involving African diplomats being denied housing in the nation's capital could only accentuate Kennedy's inability to keep to his campaign promise. Frederick G. Dutton, one of the new president's special assistants, urged Press Secretary Pierre Salinger to consider the implications of "preventing discrimination against African and Asian visitors." Such prevention was "but a part, though an important part, of the Administration's concern for civil rights." African and Asian nations were "judging American society [not] so much on the basis of what may happen individually to one of their diplomats as how much respect is really shown in this country for the American doctrine of human equality and equal protection of the laws." As such, instances of racial discrimination against African and Asian diplomats were extremely significant, for "they lie astride exactly where U.S. foreign problems and domestic circumstances converge."[4]

A closer examination of discrimination against African diplomats in Washington, D.C., during the early 1960s reveals that such a "convergence" was really made up of a number of important conflicts: the conflict between America's pronouncements of its commitment to civil rights and equality and the reality of its highly segregated society; the conflict between the African American and official U.S. viewpoints concerning the relationship between the domestic race situation and the nation's diplomacy; and, overarching all of this, the conflict resulting from America's attempt to fight a two-front war— against racism at home and communism abroad.

At first glance, the issue of African diplomats in Washington seemed to be one on which both African Americans and U.S. foreign policy officials could agree. That would certainly mark a distinct break with the general pattern of the post–World War II years in which the African American viewpoint on U.S. foreign relations was generally dismissed, suppressed, or ignored by the Department of State. Yet, on this occasion at least, there was widespread agreement that the discrimination faced by the African diplomats in the nation's capital was resulting in a foreign policy disaster for the United States.

It was hardly surprising that African Americans were so harshly critical of the situation in Washington. In the years since World War II the civil rights movement had taken on a life of its own, propelled by leaders such as A. Philip Randolph, W. E. B. Du Bois, Walter White, and Martin Luther King Jr. In addition, the African American community began to take an increased interest in U.S. foreign relations, particularly the interconnections between their own struggle for civil rights at home and the colonial battles for freedom being waged in Africa and Asia. The black-white conflict, they argued, was at least as significant as the East-West contest. Their concern with African issues, in particular, was quite high.[5]

In addition to their interest in foreign affairs, African Americans had a long and hard experience in American discrimination and segregation. No doubt, some remembered an event that took place when the Truman administration tried to recruit Ralph Bunche as an assistant secretary of state. Bunche demurred, angrily announcing in an interview with the *Pittsburgh Courier* that he would not subject his children to the Jim Crow atmosphere of Washington.[6]

Now, in 1960, African diplomats were getting a firsthand view of what Bunche was talking about. In May the United States had to apologize to Ghana's Assistant Commissioner of Labor William E. Annan, who was turned away from a boardinghouse in Washington because it "had a policy of not accepting Negro guests." An article in the *Norfolk Journal and Guide* claimed that African diplomats viewed Washington as a "hardship post," partly because of the expense of living there, but mainly because of the "racial barriers which still exist here. . . . Dark-skinned representatives, from ambassadors on down, have trouble finding decent homes in respectable neighborhoods— and even finding embassy sites." A State Department official opined that the Africans, many of whom had lived for long periods in Europe, were "'shocked' by their contact with prejudice here. 'America is underdeveloped in some ways too.'"[7]

The late 1960 *Trends in Housing* article recounted a list of horror stories from African diplomats seeking homes in Washington. One official had to "camp on the top floor of his chancery for three years because he was unable to obtain adequate housing." Another had found a home, but "anonymous phone calls, many of them threatening violence," finally drove him from his "'white' neighborhood." Those who were fortunate enough to secure housing usually paid "premiums up to 50 per cent above what their white counterparts pay." The situation would only get worse, as it was expected that more than 200 African diplomats from twenty nations would be arriving in Washington within a year. Words of regret from the Department of State would no longer suffice. As one African diplomat observed, "We have a big file of apologies from the State Department. . . . What good does it do us?" The damage done to the prestige and reputation of the United States was incalculable for, as another African official put it, "Racism as it is practiced in the United States . . . touches us at our rawest spot."[8]

The trenchant commentary from various African American quarters continued as the Kennedy team took office in 1961. An editorial from the *Pittsburgh Courier* bluntly concluded, "America 'Aint [sic] Ready.'" The string of complaints from African diplomats "poses the question whether Americans are quite ready for the role of world leadership in a world predominantly colored." That these officials had to suffer such indignities as "being passed up by taxis drivers, being seated in remote and obscure parts of dining rooms, being gypped on real estate rentals and sales, and being rudely treated by service employees" was "intolerable," and was "more eloquent than pious protestations by U.S. officials that such conduct is exceptional." The *Crisis*, official organ of the National Association for the Advancement of Colored People, noted the continuing insults to African dignitaries. What these officials learned was that America's "'democratic freedoms' do not apply to persons with dark skins. As a world power and the leader of the 'Free World' we can no longer afford the luxury of jim-crow, segregation, and second-class citizenship." America must grasp the international implications of its "'Negro problem,'" since "The world looks to see if our democratic preachments are also our practices."[9]

It was stunning to many African Americans, therefore, that discriminatory acts toward African diplomats continued unabated. The *New York Amsterdam News* ran a front-page story about a Nigerian representative who was refused service at two restaurants and hotels in Maryland and an unidentified African ambassador who was turned away from a Maryland restaurant. The latter had requested that the episode be kept out of the press and "expressed his sorrow for the U.S." And in Washington, the housing problem remained unresolved. A story in the *Courier* revealed that less than half of the seventy-five African diplomats and their families had been able to "secure suitable housing." This was not surprising, since "only eight of 211 luxury apartments in the Northwest Washington area were accepting African diplomats as tenants."[10]

The African American press was unanimous in its opinion that the incidents of racial bias suffered by African diplomats were wreaking havoc on America's foreign policy. Perhaps because of its proximity to the scene of so many of these incidents, the *Baltimore Afro-American* was particularly keen on making this point. A series of articles from 1961 publicized the "headache" the episodes posed for the Department of State and the fact that the "snubs" suffered by African diplomats in Maryland were "wrecking U.S. foreign policy." An article that appeared in May, entitled "Race Issue International 'Time-Bomb,'" tried to put the domestic incidents into a global framework. America, it claimed, was "sorely handicapped in its life-death struggle with the Sino-Soviet bloc by incidents of racial discrimination." In such an atmosphere, acts of discrimination against African diplomats in the United States did "untold damage." On the same page was an article discussing a recent proposal by Representative Adam Clayton Powell "making it a federal offense to insult foreign diplomats."[11]

While African Americans were often the first to comment on the situation affecting African diplomats in the United States, the incoming Kennedy administration quickly realized the seriousness of the incidents in Washington and elsewhere. Two reports to Assistant Secretary of State for African Affairs G. Mennen Williams dealt with specific acts of discrimination against African (and Asian and Caribbean) diplomats. A West African diplomat had been "insulted in the most foul and abusive language" at a drive-in restaurant near Washington; another had driven with his family hundreds of miles through a number of different states without stopping: "they were unable to find accommodations, food, or a rest room during the entire trip." One African ambassador felt "a little bit like a hunted criminal" as a result of racist humiliations he and his compatriots suffered. The Malian and Cameroonian ambassadors viewed it as "impossible for them and their families to travel freely throughout the U.S." Both wished to tour the country and learn more about Americans, but "this was physically impossible so long as the possibility continued to exist of their being slighted and ignored and insulted in public places because they were Negroes."[12]

The Department of State's Office of Protocol in February 1961 prepared the most detailed study of the problems facing diplomats from nations of color in the Washington area. While the focus was on African diplomats, the report noted that representatives from Asia, the Middle East, and Latin America also presented "a special kind of problem." Twenty-eight new nations had just set up diplomatic missions in Washington or were about to do so. Twenty-two other mostly Asian and Middle Eastern nations had already set up embassies; Latin American nations accounted for another seventeen missions. Yet, it was not simply the sheer number of new missions that made for a "special problem"; it was the fact that "an act of discrimination against a diplomat from one of them" was taken as a "slight to all of them, since, as far as discrimination is concerned, they constitute a special group. Discrimination against a Togolese diplomat infuriates the Cameroonians as much as it does the Togolese."

While diplomats from the Middle East, Asia, and Latin America were mentioned in the report, the focus was very definitely on the African representatives in Washington. That city, the study continued, had made "great progress . . . in the field of Civil Rights," but there was no doubt that the nation's capital had "a long way to go before anything like social equality is accepted by all." Moreover, civil rights progress in neighboring Maryland and Virginia was much slower. In particular, African diplomats faced difficulties in finding appropriate housing; socializing in Washington; being served at various businesses such as restaurants and barber shops; and obtaining satisfactory educational opportunities for their children. The housing situation was the "most embarrassing," as well as the "most urgent problem." The report estimated that "less than ten per cent of the landlords in the white areas in Washington are willing to lease living quarters to Negro diplomatic personnel of lesser rank than Ambassador."

The report also explained that the impact of such discrimination extended far beyond the individual foreign representative. Because the "so-called 'ruling classes' of these new nations are closely knit groups," any act that "affects one or more members of these groups is likely to have a strong influence on the opinions and attitudes of their governments." Hence, "If the French Ambassador in Washington feels that he is being mistreated, this is not likely to affect United States–French relations in a radical way. But, if the Nigerian Ambassador in Washington is consistently mistreated, his reactions may influence the nature of United States–Nigerian relations to a considerable degree."[13]

And as Kennedy administration officials were well aware, African nations were keeping a close eye on the civil rights situation in the United States and were alive to every instance of discrimination toward their diplomatic representatives. A Department of State report summarized some of the most recent press coverage in African newspapers. *L'Unité* (Cameroon) noted the "'indignities' suffered by African diplomats while searching for suitable lodgings in Washington" and added that "many African representatives in Washington remain unconvinced that racial incidents do not represent the true attitude of the American people." The *Lagos Daily Times* (Nigeria) expressed its "horror and dismay" over the "continued practice of racial discrimination in a country supposed to uphold and practice the rule of law and the observance of fundamental human rights and which claims to champion the cause of the Western democracies based on Christian principles." The Nigerian daily *West African Pilot*, commenting on a racial insult to a Nigerian diplomat, quoted one of the country's major political parties as saying, "A country devoid of respect for human dignity, a country with a completely bankrupt racial policy, a country which still lives in the Dark Ages, has no claim to the leadership of free men." The *Lagos Daily Mail* went even further, arguing that "U.S. policy for Africa might be laudable on paper, but a people suffering from the bite of the bug of Negrophobism cannot often impress us. It is to be seen how a nation of Ku Klux Klan officials can bring world peace. The qualities of Abraham Lincoln and Jefferson are non-existent any more in America."[14]

As Pedro Sanjuan of Protocol noted, these stories were but the tip of the iceberg. Referring specifically to another piece that had appeared in the *West African Pilot*, Sanjuan admitted, "There have been close to ninety major incidents involving African diplomats brought to our attention in the past two years. Through our efforts, almost all of them have been kept out of the pages of the newspapers. This article is based largely on those few incidents (seven) which could not be kept out. I think it illustrates the need to continue preventive measures that will insure in the future a similar degree of success."[15]

Whatever success these "preventive measures" might have had in keeping some stories out of the newspapers, it was apparent that Africans resented the discrimination their diplomatic representatives faced in the United States and that such resentments were hurting U.S. relations with Africa. A State Department study made clear the anger brewing among the African representatives. In general, they believed that they were residing in a country "where racial separation is an accepted practice and, therefore, where dark skinned diplomats are considered inferior to other diplomats." They put little faith in action by the U.S. government, because civil rights efforts were "not politically expedient." While admitting that the United States had made some progress, the African diplomats were "critical of what they consider to be the Government's policy of evading the issue." Apologies after the fact did not alleviate the resentment of the African officials, "primarily because they know that discrimination is not directed at them as representatives of certain foreign countries but as members of a race. They feel that this is an offense against their dignity as human beings." They became especially incensed when the United States attempted to "whitewash incidents," or when it was argued that "they should be treated differently than negro-Americans just for the sake of U.S. prestige in Africa."[16]

Acting Secretary of State Chester Bowles issued a press release in September 1961 decrying the recent spate of incidents in which African diplomats had been refused service in restaurants in the Washington area and stressing the harmful impact they had on U.S.-African relations. Episodes such as these were "not only morally wrong but have most unfortunate repercussions abroad." "We should not allow discriminatory practices to work to the detriment of our foreign policy," Bowles admonished. "It is the duty and the opportunity of every American to demonstrate to all foreign visitors that our democratic ideals 'are by no means hypocrisy.'"[17]

It was clear that African Americans and U.S. officials were nearly unanimous in their view that the discrimination against African diplomats in Washington and surrounding areas was damaging to the nation, both domestically and internationally. The calls for action—from African American newspapers, from civil rights groups, and from the Department of State—were therefore treated with some urgency. And so during the next few years the Kennedy administration looked for solutions to this "special problem." Some were a bit bizarre, such as the suggestion from a member of State's Bureau of African Affairs that "a suitable unique type of pin or button to be worn" should be distributed to the African diplomats. The federal government would inform the states about "the insignia worn by diplomats and that the bearer of such insignia must be accorded every right and privilege accorded to any citizen of the U.S."[18]

Fortunately, nothing ever came of this idea to "tag" foreign diplomats. More rational and well-organized efforts centered on the housing situation in Washington and the numerous complaints of discrimination against African diplomats in restaurants along Route 40 in Maryland. Action to alleviate the housing problem for African diplomats actually began shortly before Kennedy took office. In August 1960, State's Chief of Protocol Wiley Buchanan wrote to the president of the Washington Real Estate Board asking for his organization's assistance. A short time later, officials from the Bureau of African Affairs met with representatives of the Real Estate Board, which gave its assurances that help would be forthcoming in finding African diplomats suitable housing. In November, State Department officials, representatives from the Real Estate Board, and the Washington, D.C., Board of Commissioners met to expand the effort and to discuss zoning changes in the district to facilitate the construction of chanceries for the new African nations.[19]

These efforts continued under the Kennedy administration. The Office of Protocol worked directly with the Real Estate Board and various large real-estate firms to find "suitable housing in Washington for African and other diplomats." Protocol would now keep lists of realtors willing to find housing for the diplomats and would inform the realtors when new African officials arrived in town. The office would also work closely with local organizations such as the Urban League Housing Group, the National Capital Clearing House for Neighborhood Democracy, and the African American Institute, as well as continue its contacts with the Board of Commissioners.[20]

Problems along Route 40 were also addressed by the Kennedy administration. Restaurants along the highway had become constant targets of complaints from African diplomats (usually traveling between Washington and New York) who had been refused service. Once again, the Office of Protocol was at the forefront, meeting with the governor of Maryland, local newspaper editors, groups of Maryland citizens, and the restaurant owners. At the governor's request, the State Department had given its support to a public accommodations bill then pending in the Maryland Legislative Council. The program of "voluntary cooperation" resulted in thirty-five Maryland restaurant owners agreeing to desegregate their businesses.[21]

The convergence of domestic and international affairs had apparently re-

John F. Kennedy passes civil rights protesters as he attends a 14 November 1963 cere-
mony to open the Northeast Expressway connecting New York and Washington, D.C. Incidents of discrimination against African diplomats along highways in the D.C. corridor
led the State Department to put pressure on local governments. (Bettmann/Corbis)

sulted in a mutually satisfactory conclusion: some small progress had been
made on the civil rights front, while international (particularly African) criticism of American society would be blunted. In many ways, however, these
victories were illusory. The meeting between America's civil rights problem
and Cold War diplomacy that took place around the issue of African diplomats in Washington revealed some significant conflicts that no amount of
meetings, lists, or "voluntary cooperation" could overcome.

State's efforts to convince African diplomats (and the world) that America's
statements concerning freedom, equality, and human rights were more than
mere "hypocrisy," as Bowles had put it, inevitably ran into an insurmount-
able problem: America continued to be a highly segregated society. An August 1963 Harris poll provided an interesting insight into this conflict. It
found that nearly 80 percent of white Americans believed that racial discrimination in their nation was hurting the country's image abroad. However, this view was "tempered rather sharply when white people talk about
their own willingness to have greater contact with Negroes in their own personal lives." More than 50 percent of whites polled indicated that they would
object to living next door to African Americans; nearly a third did not want
their children going to school with black children. And one-fourth to one-
fifth of those surveyed would not want to attend church with or work next to
African Americans.[22]

Thus, efforts by the Office of Protocol to explain to African diplomats that "remarkable changes are taking place in our country" and that acts of discrimination were merely "vestiges of a form of social stupidity which is rapidly disappearing from the scene" were undercut by the fact that the forces of segregation still exerted tremendous influence in America. The "successes" in terms of housing in Washington and problems along Route 40 were never as far-reaching as the State Department would have the African diplomats believe. The NCDH reported in early 1962 that, although Washington realtors had assured the State Department that "housing equity could be accomplished within two or three years through quiet, unpublicized efforts," little had changed. In 1961 only 8 of 211 buildings in Northwest Washington would accept nonwhite tenants; a year later, only 9 of 214 buildings accepted African diplomats. One reason for this lack of success was suggested by the organization: "The Washington Board of Realtors has never admitted a Negro member." By early 1963 even the Office of Protocol had to admit failure. The problem of finding rentals for African diplomats remained "almost insoluble," with Protocol "powerless" to help. The office had received forty-two requests for assistance from African diplomats in the past year; in each case, the diplomats had "been insulted at some point in their search by a manager or owner who has told them that nonwhites are not permitted in this or that building." The "effort to secure apartments resulted in failure."[23]

The Route 40 campaign was not entirely ineffectual, but still fell far short of its promises. The Maryland public accommodations law that the State Department pushed for in 1961 was not passed until nearly two years later. The Office of Protocol claimed that it was a "great step forward," but then admitted that it was a "weak law." It did refine a trespass law whereby individuals could be jailed for refusal to leave a public establishment after being asked. This could still occur but not "on the basis of a person's color." Still, the law would have effect only in "the more progressive counties of Maryland," though it was hoped that it would have a "strong moral effect in bringing about the eventual inclusion of the counties which so far have exempted themselves from its jurisdiction."[24]

The issue of African diplomats in Washington also illuminated the conflict between the African American and official State Department viewpoints concerning America's civil rights problem and international relations. For many African Americans race and civil rights were at the center of their thinking concerning the nation's diplomacy, and for both domestic and international reasons they called for direct and decisive action to end segregation in America. Black Americans consistently pointed out the connections between racial segregation in the United States and the struggles for freedom in Africa.

Journalist Ethel Payne wrote in 1960 that "the events in Africa and particularly, the Congo crisis are making colored Americans more aware of international relations and the reciprocal effect upon their own struggle for full citizenship." The American Negro Leadership Conference on Africa (ANLCA), formed in 1962 with a membership made up of many of the leading African Americans of the nation, echoed that theme, stating that "Negroes are of necessity deeply concerned with developments in Africa because of the moral issues involved and because the struggle here at home to achieve in our time equality without respect to race or color is made easier to the extent that equality and freedom are achieved everywhere." According to one of the ANLCA members, Whitney Young, the "decision to link the integration struggle in the United States with the fate of the sub-Saharan African states would represent a new phase in the civil rights struggle."[25]

The situation with African diplomats in Washington provided one such "link." African Americans were convinced that the discrimination against African officials was not only stark evidence of the segregation that they themselves faced each and every day, but also a decidedly negative factor in the nation's diplomatic efforts in Africa. Efforts to put out a symbolic welcome mat for African diplomats would not suffice; only an aggressive civil rights stance by the federal government could meet the cries for reform at home and the criticisms from abroad. An editorial in the Crisis had more than a note of impatience when it stated, "While we commend the efforts of State Department officials and others to take steps to end the racial incidents involving African envoys, we must also remind these same officials that they must likewise take steps to free America of the racist attitudes which create incidents for her own colored citizens." Journalist Louis Lautier was more pointed. The programs to help the African diplomats were "laudable" and "praiseworthy," but even if they were successful "the dropping of such bars would hardly breach the walls of racial discrimination and segregation against all colored peoples in the nation's capital—native or foreign-born." Lautier then got to the core of his argument:

If the Kennedy administration would do something tangible about segregation and discrimination in housing and improve the image of the United States in the minds of Africans and dark-skinned peoples the world over, it should begin with colored Americans. Early in his Administration, President Kennedy promised to study the powers of the executive and determine whether he had the authority to issue an executive order banning racial segregation in federally assisted housing. Not a peep has been heard from him since he made this promise nearly six months ago.

A cartoon accompanying Lautier's editorial portrayed a well-dressed "African" dressing a black "American" in traditional African garb. "There!" the African announced. "Now you can get an apartment in your own country!"[26]

Three reporters from the *Baltimore Afro-American* took things a bit farther to demonstrate the absurdity of the government's approach to the problems faced by African diplomats. Posing as African dignitaries from "Goban," the three made a 125-mile trip along Route 40, ending with dinner in a segregated restaurant in Baltimore. Two restaurants along the highway served them, while one turned them away, claiming, "They ain't no Africans." In Baltimore, they dined at one of the city's "most discriminating downtown restaurants."[27]

The Department of State did not share the African American viewpoint on race, civil rights, and U.S. foreign policy. First and foremost, the department was decidedly uneasy with and ill equipped to handle issues of race and civil rights. In the years since World War II, State had been buffeted by criticisms of America's racial problems from both friend and foe abroad and by demands for action to help alleviate those problems from African Americans at home. Its responses had never been particularly effective. As to the international denunciations, the department took three main approaches: ignore them, decry them as communist-inspired propaganda, and/or create counterpropaganda that generally whitewashed the racial situation in America. To the African American criticisms that State was not showing proper attention to the issues of race and civil rights, the answer was consistent: token appointments of a handful of African Americans to well-publicized (but virtually powerless) foreign-policy-making positions.[28]

Despite the fact that during the Kennedy administration Department of State figures such as Secretary Dean Rusk made a number of public pronouncements concerning the adverse impact of the civil rights problem on U.S. diplomacy (including Rusk's testimony before Congress in 1963 supporting a public transportation bill outlawing discrimination), the department's response to the incidents concerning African diplomats in Washington indicated that its basic approach to both foreign criticism and domestic demands concerning civil rights had not changed very much.[29]

By 1961 the State Department could no longer ignore the civil rights issue when dealing with incidents of discrimination against African diplomats. Too many African nations were watching, and the civil rights movement at home was becoming too powerful. However, it could still rely on its other approaches to the issue: claiming that communist propaganda was "distorting" the civil rights problem in America, and attempting to counter that propaganda by putting a more favorable spin on events.

United States officials were well aware that communist propagandists were having a field day with each new incident involving an African diplomat. Assistant Secretary Williams, speaking to a gathering of states' representatives in 1961, charged that "one percent—that sounds like a small percentage but, nonetheless, it is large in all of the various items—one percent of all of the Communist propaganda is dedicated to this one failure on our part to handle our relationships with the individuals over here from foreign countries." The Soviet press claimed that the State Department was going to "organize 'a diplomatic ghetto' because it could not 'guarantee the security' of African diplomats." Another article speculated on a "need [for] a 'special quarter in Washington for African diplomats—somewhat in the manner of Indian reservations.'" Communist China also took advantage of the situation, and considered "these incidents as major propaganda windfalls which as 'a nation of color' can be utilized by the Red Chinese with particular effect in Africa and Asia."[30]

With this as their starting point, U.S. officials moved on to suggest that the problems such as those surrounding African diplomats in America were largely ones of perceptions: the distorted perceptions being promulgated by America's enemies, and the desired perceptions that needed to be molded and guided through U.S. counterpropaganda. Deputy Assistant Secretary of State for Public Affairs Carl Rowan (one of the high-profile African American appointees in State) urged his listeners in a 1961 speech to put America's race problems "in perspective. We must show that the picture is not one of whites vs. Negroes, as our enemies would depict it, but of the vast majority of whites and Negroes striving together for progress." Chief of Protocol Angier Biddle Duke even went so far as to blame some of the African diplomats, who were "representatives of African governments which are desirous of creating incidents. These incidents can be used to distort social conditions in the United States and to cripple our diplomatic efforts to win the friendship of the African continent." In a truly astonishing piece of reasoning, Duke suggested that part of the problem was that the African diplomats really could not be expected to act with "forbearance" and "understanding" when "exposed to affronts." This was in contrast to African Americans who, "after years of experience, can develop the psychological maturity that affords some degree of immunity." These Americans "may adjust to these limitations of what should be the most cherished rights of any man any where. . . . They adjust because they know the laws of the land are in the process of being applied more and more equally." Duke's solution was to accentuate the positive: "help the African diplomats and their staffs in their everyday problems, and . . . present to them the brighter aspects of American life and, perhaps more im-

portantly, the majority will in the United States for change." (The Harris poll
indicating that the "majority will" of the American people was somewhat less
bright than Duke might wish was two years in the future.) And, in a tip of
the hat to tokenism, he asked that "an intelligent and energetic Negro" be ap-
pointed to Protocol, one who could advise "as to the sources of the friction."
Such an appointment would also "be an example in diplomatic circles generally of the earnest desire of this administration to use its human resources in
an efficient and friendly manner."[31]

With such perceptions, it is small wonder that in contrast to the African
American demand for forceful action on the civil rights front, State preferred
quiet and voluntary efforts; indeed, aggressive action on the part of African
Americans alarmed some officials. Pedro Sanjuan's suggestion that "preventive measures" needed to be increased in order to keep stories about incidents
involving African diplomats out of the press was only part of the picture.
Secretary Rusk, writing to Attorney General Robert Kennedy about these incidents, indicated that the United States faced a "far larger and more complex
problem of relationships in a city which has a slight majority of negro citizens and the frictions arising therefrom." Yet Rusk also cautioned, "The matter is one which seems to me to require a compassionate regard for the origins of the difficulty and the deep-rooted feelings which surround it. It will
require a considerable amount of quiet, patient and persistent effort if we are
to achieve enduring results." He suggested that the administration "work
unobtrusively" with local civic leaders to see that acts of racial discrimination
were "reduced to the minimum." Citing his earlier interest with the "segregation problem" while serving with the Rockefeller Foundation, he observed that
"the most constructive efforts were those which were made without fanfare
and in a reasonable atmosphere not inflamed by violent public controversy."[32]

Assistant Secretary Williams was equally "compassionate" when he addressed a gathering of states' representatives concerning the problem of African diplomats. He was "quite conscious that in many states we have a problem because in these states there is a public opinion which doesn't completely
accept the idea of the equality of races for our own citizens." Happily, "these
happen to be states which, I think in the history of our country, have demonstrated a kind of patriotism that has been the kind that all of the other states
would seek to emulate, and here is a challenge to their patriotism of a special
and perhaps unique kind." He hoped that "we would find some way of resolving this internal problem they have in order to meet a problem that touches
us in a national way."[33]

In assessing the success of the Route 40 campaign, Pedro Sanjuan cited the
atmosphere of "voluntary cooperation" that led to "voluntary desegregation"

in some of the restaurants along the highway. The "Federal Government and the Maryland authorities" had arranged a "definite step forward." He noted in passing that the Congress of Racial Equality had threatened a "large protest all along that route" if the restaurant owners did not comply. Fortunately, the organization showed "sensible moderation . . . in accepting the partial fulfillment" of its demands.[34]

In the early 1960s, America's "foreign problems" and "domestic circumstances" had converged around the issue of discrimination against African diplomats. Because most African Americans and State Department officials agreed that this particular problem was a direct result of those circumstances, it seemed obvious that forceful action on housing discrimination in Washington and in the area of public accommodations in Maryland would have both international and domestic benefits. By the time of Kennedy's assassination in 1963, however, little had changed in Washington and its surrounding areas concerning incidents involving African diplomats: efforts to secure housing in Washington had met near "total failure"; a "weak law" barring discrimination in Maryland restaurants had been passed. Many African Americans threw sarcastic jibes at the U.S. government's well-publicized (but mostly ineffectual) attempts to come to the aid of the African visitors, while real civil rights progress for the millions of America's black citizens languished.

At least partially, of course, this record of failure was due to the very strong forces of racial prejudice and segregation still at work in American society. Yet, it was also due to reluctance on the part of the Department of State (as well as other agencies and personnel of the Kennedy administration) to take a stronger stand on the issue of civil rights. Perhaps not surprisingly, officials at State perceived the civil rights problem through the lens of the Cold War. Through this perspective, international criticisms were often dismissed as communist propaganda or distorted misunderstandings; answers to such criticisms, therefore, did not involve consistent or forceful support for substantive change or reform, but merely the fine-tuning of perceptions; and the necessity for keeping a domestic Cold War coalition intact meant that watered-down appeals for "volunteerism" to recalcitrant southerners were combined with deep suspicions concerning any "violent public controversy" on the part of African Americans. The convergence of a Cold War mind-set and a civil rights ideology, therefore, resulted in few victories either at home or abroad.

Notes

1. *Trends in Housing* 4, 5 (Sept.–Oct. 1960): 1–2.
2. Thomas J. Noer, "New Frontiers and Old Priorities in Africa," in *Kennedy's Quest for Victory: American Foreign Policy, 1961–1963*, ed. Thomas G. Paterson

(New York: Oxford University Press, 1989), 256–58. For more on Kennedy's policies toward Africa, see Thomas J. Noer, *Cold War and Black Liberation: The United States and White Rule in Africa, 1948–1968* (Columbia: University of Missouri Press, 1985); Richard D. Mahoney, *JFK: Ordeal in Africa* (New York: Oxford University Press, 1983); and Gerald E. Thomas, "The Black Revolt: The United States and Africa in the 1960s," in *The Diplomacy of the Crucial Decade: American Foreign Relations in the 1960s,* ed. Diane B. Kunz (New York: Columbia University Press, 1994), 320–60. Data on dates of entry of African nations into the United Nations is found on the UN web site ‹www.un.org/overview/unmember.html›.

3. On Kennedy, civil rights, and the 1960 election, see Mark Stern, *Calculating Visions: Kennedy, Johnson, and Civil Rights* (New Brunswick, N.J.: Rutgers University Press, 1992); James L. Sundquist and Brookings Institution, *Politics and Policy: The Eisenhower, Kennedy, and Johnson Years* (Washington, D.C.: Brookings Institution, 1968); Irving Bernstein, *Promises Kept: John F. Kennedy's New Frontier* (New York: Oxford University Press, 1991); Carl M. Brauer, *John F. Kennedy and the Second Reconstruction* (New York: Columbia University Press, 1977).

4. Frederick G. Dutton to Pierre Salinger, 10 Aug. 1961, White House Central Subject Files (WHCSF), HU2/CO, box 365, John F. Kennedy Library, Boston (JFKL).

5. For African Americans and U.S. foreign policy after World War II, see Thomas Borstelmann, *Apartheid's Reluctant Uncle: The United States and Southern Africa in the Early Cold War* (New York: Oxford University Press, 1993); Gerald Horne, *Black and Red: W. E. B. Du Bois and the Afro-American Response to the Cold War* (Albany: SUNY Press, 1986); Michael L. Krenn, *Black Diplomacy: African Americans and the State Department, 1945–1969* (Armonk, N.Y.: M. E. Sharpe, 1999); Hollis R. Lynch, *Black American Radicals and the Liberation of Africa: The Council on African Affairs, 1937–1955* (Ithaca: Cornell University Press, 1978); Brenda Gayle Plummer, *Rising Wind: Black Americans and U.S. Foreign Affairs, 1935–1960* (Chapel Hill: University of North Carolina Press, 1996); Penny Von Eschen, *Race against Empire: Black Americans and Anticolonialism, 1937–1957* (Ithaca: Cornell University Press, 1997).

6. "Bunche Blasts D.C. Jim Crow," *Pittsburgh Courier,* 11 June 1949, 1, 4, 13.

7. "U.S. Apology to Ghana for Insult to Envoy," *Pittsburgh Courier,* 7 May 1960, 6; "Washington Is 'Hardship Post' Say African Envoys," *Norfolk Journal and Guide,* 26 Nov. 1960, 12.

8. "African Diplomats Hit Race Barrier," *Trends in Housing* 4, 5 (Sept.–Oct. 1960): 1.

9. "America 'Aint Ready,'" *Pittsburgh Courier,* 2 Feb. 1961, 2:8; "African Envoys in U.S.A.," *Crisis* 70 (Oct. 1963): 499.

10. "Another African Diplomat Insulted," *Amsterdam News,* 19 May 1962, 1; "Suitable Housing for Only Half of African Diplomats," *Pittsburgh Courier,* 8 Aug. 1961, 2:2.

11. "U.S. Treatment of Africans Gives State Dept. Headache," 3 June 1961, 3; "Maryland-D.C. 'Snubs' Are Wrecking U.S. Foreign Policy," 26 Aug. 1961, 2; "Race Issue International 'Time-Bomb,'" 6 May 1961, 9; "Rep. Powell Presents Bill to Protect Foreign Envoys," 6 May 1961, 9, all in *Baltimore Afro-American.*

12. "Incidents for Governor Williams," attached to J. T. A. [John T. Abernethy] to Williams, 27 Apr. 1961; Donald Dumont to Williams, 6 Sept. 1961, Record Group 59, Papers of G. Mennen Williams (RG 59, Williams Papers), Administrative-Office Files (A-O), box 2, Discrimination—African Visitors folder, National Archives (NA).

13. Department of State, Office of Protocol, "Living Conditions of New Diplomats

in Washington and Vicinity and Suggestions for Easing of Tensions by the Office of Protocol," 23 Feb. 1961, Papers of Pedro Sanjuan, box 1, Living Conditions, New Diplomats, 2/23/61, JFKL.

14. "Representative African Reaction to Recent Incidents in the U.S. Involving African Diplomats," enclosed in Donald M. Wilson to Frederick G. Dutton, 27 Apr. 1961, RG 59, Williams Papers, A–O, box 2, Discrimination—African Visitors, NA.

15. Pedro Sanjuan to Robert Kennedy, 17 Dec. 1962, Papers of Robert F. Kennedy (RFK Papers), Attorney General Papers (AG), General Correspondence (GC), box 51, Sanjuan, Pedro: 9/1962–12/1962, JFKL.

16. "Latent Hostility of African Diplomats towards the United States," 1 June 1961, attachment to "Briefing for the Undersecretary on Diplomats in Washington," 2 June 1961, Sanjuan Papers, box 1, "Briefing, African Diplomats in Washington, 6/2/61," JFKL.

17. "Statement by Acting Secretary of State Chester Bowles," 19 Sept. 1961, RFK Papers, AG, GC, box 51, Sanjuan, Pedro: 9/1961, JFKL.

18. Dumont to Williams, 6 Sept. 1961, RG 59, Williams Papers, A–O, box 2, Discrimination—African Visitors file, NA.

19. J. C. Satterthwaite to Loy W. Henderson, 5 Jan. 1961, White House Staff Files of Harris Wofford (WHSF-Wofford), box 2, Civil Rights—Misc., 1960–1/62, JFKL.

20. "Living Conditions of New Diplomats in Washington and Vicinity and Suggestions for Easing of Tensions by the Office of Protocol," 23 Feb. 1961, Sanjuan Papers, box 1, "Living Conditions, New Diplomats, 2/23/61," JFKL.

21. Sanjuan to Chief of Protocol, 9 Nov. 1961, WHCSF, HU2/CO, box 365, JFKL.

22. "Majority of Whites on Discrimination: It Hurts Abroad; Housing Is Big Issue," Washington Post, 26 Aug. 1963, A1–A2.

23. "State Dept. Calls for FH Law in U.S. Capital," Trends in Housing 6, 1 (Jan.–Feb. 1962): 1, 4; Progress Report, Special Protocol Service Section, Office of the Chief of Protocol, 1 Feb. 1963, attachment to Sanjuan to James W. Symington, n.d., RFK Papers, AG, GC, box 58, State Dept., 1/1963–5/1963, JFKL.

24. Sanjuan to Robert Kennedy, 13 Mar. 1963, RFK Papers, AG, GC, box 51, Sanjuan, Pedro: 1/1963–3/1963, JFKL.

25. Ethel Payne to Louis E. Martin, 3 Aug. 1960, Records of the Democratic National Committee, box 145, 1960 Campaign, Civil Rights Division (Louis Martin), Foreign Policy (Africa) 8-3-60–10-25-60, undated file, JFKL; A. Philip Randolph, Roy Wilkins, Martin Luther King Jr., and others, form letter, 21 Aug. 1962, Papers of the NAACP, Group III, box A198, American Negro Leadership Council (ANLC) on Africa, 1962 file, Library of Congress, Washington, D.C.; "U.S. Negroes Link Aid to Sub-Sahara African Nations with Rights Struggle," New York Times, 25 Nov. 1962, 8.

26. "African Envoys in U.S.A.," Crisis 68 (Oct. 1961): 499; "Project to House Africans 'Laudable,'" Baltimore Afro-American, 22 July 1961, 5.

27. "Negroes Pose as Foreigners, Fool Restaurant," Pittsburgh Courier, 2 Sept. 1961, 2:2; "State Dept. Calls Hoax 'Great Show,'" Baltimore Afro-American, 9 Sept. 1961, 8.

28. For analysis of the relationship between the Department of State and African Americans in the postwar years, see Krenn, Black Diplomacy.

29. See "Statement of Secretary of State Dean Rusk before the Committee on Commerce Regarding S. 1732," attached to Sanjuan to Robert Kennedy, 28 June 1963, RFK Papers, AG, GC, box 51, Sanjuan, Pedro, 6/1963, JFKL.

30. "Meeting with Representatives of State Governments," 27 Apr. 1961, Sanjuan

Papers, box 1, Meeting with Representatives of State Governors, 4/27/61 file, JFKL; "Recent Moscow Comment," attached to Donald Wilson to Frederick Dutton, 27 Apr. 1961, RG 59, Williams Papers, A-O, box 2, Discrimination—African Visitors file, NA.

31. Remarks by Carl T. Rowan, "Fourth Regional Operations Conference," Lima, Peru, 10 Oct. 1961, President's Office File, Departments and Agencies, box 88, State 10/61–12/61 file, JFKL; Angier Biddle Duke to Secretary of State, 27 Jan. 1961, Papers of Chester Bowles, box 299, folder 515, Yale University Library, New Haven.

32. Sanjuan to Robert Kennedy, 17 Dec. 1962, RFK Papers, AG, GC, box 51, Sanjuan, Pedro: 9/1962–12/1962; Rusk to Robert Kennedy, 31 Jan. 1961, WHCSF, HU2/FG, box 365, JFKL.

33. Comments of G. Mennen Williams, "Meeting with Representatives of State Governments," 27 Apr. 1961, Sanjuan Papers, box 1, Meeting with Representatives of State Governors, 4/27/61 file, JFKL.

34. Sanjuan to Chief of Protocol, 9 Nov. 1961, WHCSF, HU2/CO, box 365, JFKL.

Birmingham, Addis Ababa, and the Image of America

International Influence on
U.S. Civil Rights Politics in the
Kennedy Administration

On 22 May 1963 Emperor Haile Selassie of Ethiopia convened the Conference of African Heads of States and Governments. Gathered in Addis Ababa, Ethiopia, were heads of state and other representatives of all but two independent African nations. This was a moment, Selassie told the assembled leaders, "without parallel in history." "We stand today on the stage of world affairs, before the audience of world Opinion," he intoned. "Africa is today in mid-course, in transition from the Africa of Yesterday to the Africa of Tomorrow. . . . The task on which we have embarked—the making of Africa, will not wait. We must act to shape and mould the future and leave our imprint on events as they pass into history." The mission of the conference was charting the future of African politics, and the Organization of African Unity resulted from its labors. Selassie hoped that the gathering, and the foundation it laid, would ultimately bear fruit in the formation of a unified Africa, operating as an integrated political entity like the United States of America or the USSR.[1] Over the next few days, African leaders worked together to produce a series of resolutions embodying their common goals and aspirations. As they did so, the focus of their deliberations would stray far from the shores of Africa. These heads of state believed that their own interests were implicated in a dramatic conflict many miles away.

During the weeks leading up to Addis Ababa, civil rights protest had come to a head in Birmingham, Alabama. On 3 May more than 1,000 African American children and teenagers embarked on a civil rights march. Birmingham's jails were already filled with protesters, so it was Police Commissioner Eugene "Bull" Connor's objective to deter the demonstrators without arresting them. To do that, he used fire hoses. The strength of the city's high-pressure hoses knocked down protesters. Police dogs lunging at demonstrators backed up water guns.[2] While the police tactics did not deter Birmingham's determined civil rights movement, they had a widespread impact. Dramatic photographs in newspapers throughout the country captured the nation's attention, focusing concern on the need for civil rights reform. News coverage throughout the world underscored international concerns about racial injustice in America.[3]

The news of Birmingham was fresh in the minds of African leaders as they gathered later that May in Addis Ababa. On the second day of the conference, Prime Minister Milton Obote of Uganda released an open letter to President John F. Kennedy protesting the treatment of African American demonstrators in Birmingham. "The Negroes who, even while the conference was in session, have been subjected to the most inhuman treatment, who have been blasted with fire hoses cranked up to such pressure that the water could strip bark off trees, at whom the police have deliberately set snarling dogs, are our own kith and kin," Obote wrote. "The only offences which these people have committed are that they are black and that they have demanded the right to be free and to hold their heads up as equal citizens of the United States."[4]

These matters were of relevance to African leaders, for "the tasks before us of effecting closer union of African states both in the political and economic fields necessarily include the emancipation of the people of dark races, and . . . colonialism and race discrimination are one of the fundamental issues for the future of our civilization." Obote believed that "nothing is more paradoxical than that these events should take place in the United States and at a time when that country is anxious to project its image before the world screen as the archtype [sic] of democracy and the champion of freedom." Africans, who had "borne the white-man's burden for . . . centuries . . . feel that our own freedom and independence would be a mere sham if our black brethren elsewhere in Africa and in the United States still remain in political, social and economic bondage." Obote told President Kennedy that "the eyes and ears of the world are concentrated on events in Alabama and it is the duty of the free world and more so of the countries that hold themselves up as the leaders of that free world to see that all of their citizens, regardless of the colour of their skin, are free."[5] Reflecting Obote's concerns, the Addis Ababa conference went on to consider the impact of Birmingham on U.S.-African relations.

The focus of discussion at Addis Ababa—the impact of race discrimination on U.S. relations with other nations—was an important topic but not a new one. Following World War II, the Truman administration recognized the importance of civil rights to U.S. foreign relations. As the Soviet Union came to feature U.S. racial problems as a principal anti-U.S. propaganda theme in the late 1940s, the nation's allies expressed concerns about the impact of this issue on the ability of the United States to provide leadership in the Cold

War. Why was democracy a model for other governments to follow, many asked, when discrimination and disenfranchisement occurred in the leading democratic nation? In this context, Truman's President's Committee on Civil Rights issued a report in 1947 arguing that one of three critical reasons that the administration had to take action on civil rights was the fact that race discrimination harmed U.S. foreign relations.[6]

Meanwhile, the U.S. Information Agency (USIA) and the State Department took steps to portray a positive image of American democracy to the world. U.S. propaganda turned the story of race in America into a story of the superiority of democracy as a system of government in achieving social change and celebrating individual freedom. This construction of race in America was greatly aided by *Brown v. Board of Education*. The news was broadcast to the world as evidence of the greatness of the American system of government.[7]

The image of American democracy as a just system of government for peoples of color assumed even greater importance as decolonization took hold, and as newly independent African and Asian nations contemplated both the structure of their own governments and their alignments in Cold War world politics. At the same time, this image of America was on unstable ground. Threats to the nation's image in the world were seen as threats to the U.S. position in the Cold War. In this context, when President Eisenhower sent federal troops to Little Rock, Arkansas, to enforce a school desegregation order in 1957 during the Little Rock Crisis, it was not out of a commitment to *Brown*, a ruling Eisenhower disagreed with. Instead it was because he hoped, in his words, that his effort would "restore the image of America."[8] While the Truman years were a period of coming to terms with the impact of civil rights on Cold War foreign affairs, the initial construction of a "Cold War imperative" for civil rights reform, the Eisenhower years were an era of safekeeping. *Brown* had provided the State Department with the sort of concrete progress needed for its reconstruction of race in America. During the rest of the 1950s, the Eisenhower administration did not move the civil rights agenda forward but rather took steps to protect against challenges to the reconstructed image of America, in part by responding forcefully in Little Rock.

When John F. Kennedy took office in 1961, his own aides considered him to be rather uninterested in civil rights. Harris Wofford, Kennedy's adviser on civil rights during the 1960 presidential campaign, was later asked whether, at that time, he "had any feeling . . . that the President had a particular interest in the problem of civil rights or did he recognize it as a political problem?" Wofford answered, "the latter." Wofford felt that during this period "rights was not a high priority for Kennedy." Instead, "his chief concern then and very possibly . . . to the end of his life, was foreign policy and peace and relations with the Soviet Union." According to Wofford, such issues "always seemed to be the dominant issues for him."[9]

During the campaign, Kennedy realized that he had "a problem" with black voters and called in Wofford to figure out how to resolve it. Carrying out his advice, Kennedy promised to end discrimination in federal housing programs "with the stroke of a pen," since that action could be taken by executive order. However, at the end of his first year in office, with no order in sight, civil rights activists sent thousands of pens to the White House to pressure the president to fulfill his promise. According to Carl Brauer, "In his first year in office, President Kennedy had done little that regular Southern Democrats could not tolerate." Civil rights leaders were dissatisfied with Kennedy. Facing an election year, liberal Democratic senators urged the president to back civil rights legislation in 1962, but the president declined. The justification for his inaction in the face of increasing pressure from the civil rights movement and from some members of his own staff and party was that moving forward on civil rights would jeopardize the president's initiatives in Congress.[10]

This is, of course, not to say that the administration was uninvolved in civil rights. An increasingly active civil rights movement placed crises on Kennedy's doorstep, and the administration played a role in managing them. Arrests of sit-in protesters and brutal violence against Freedom Riders provoked public outcry and called for a response. Attorney General Robert F. Kennedy, Justice Department officials, and sometimes the president himself were heavily involved in efforts to resolve these crises. A visible federal role in managing civil rights crises was something the civil rights movement demanded of the president.[11] Greater federal visibility also helped with a problem the president cared deeply about: the impact of discrimination on U.S. foreign affairs. Carl Brauer noted in his 1977 book, *John F. Kennedy and the Second Reconstruction*, that Kennedy saw American society as "a goldfish bowl before the world."[12] Brauer's important book was written long before the records to explore fully the impact of foreign affairs on civil rights were declassified or otherwise made public. As a result, an issue that Brauer recognized, but was unable to completely develop, remains to be more fully considered using the diplomatic and other materials made available in the years since his work was published.

When James Meredith was denied admission to the University of Mississippi, in 1962, USIA reports crossed the president's desk detailing the widespread international media coverage of the Mississippi crisis. Kennedy was concerned about the impact of Mississippi on the U.S. image abroad. The federal government stepped in, and after weeks of turmoil, after rioting and two deaths, including the death of a French news reporter, Meredith was registered as a student. In the aftermath of this crisis, the president wondered how Mississippi compared with Little Rock. What had been the impact of the crisis on international opinion? In which circumstance had U.S. prestige suffered more? And how did the world react to the administration's handling of the crisis, as compared with the reaction to Eisenhower's action in Little Rock?[13]

As it turned out, President Kennedy could take satisfaction in the world reaction to Mississippi. The president's handling of the Mississippi crisis, for example, impressed the former governor general of India, who told Chester Bowles that "as far as he knows this is the first time in the history of the world that any nation has ever demonstrated so dramatically its respect for law. Where else," he asked, "could we expect to see a government throw thousands of men and huge resources behind the application of a single individual to enter a university because the law said he had a right to be there?" Such reactions convinced Bowles that the United States had now dramatized that racial discrimination was illegal, and that the federal government was committed to opposing it. Bowles believed that the Meredith situation could be "a turning point not only in our struggle against segregation in this country, but in our efforts to make the people of Asia, Africa and Latin America understand what we are trying to do."[14]

Yet as long as discrimination and disenfranchisement plagued the nation, the image of democracy would be at risk. And the rank and file of the civil rights movement did not shy away from protest actions out of fear of harming the nation's image abroad. Instead, the movement questioned the truth of American rhetoric. As protest actions met with violent resistance, the movement kept the gaze of the international media focused on race in America.

In the early 1960s, as many nations in Africa gained their independence, the U.S. State Department was greatly troubled by the implications of discrimination for U.S. national security. One concern—an issue motivating the government since the late 1940s—was how race discrimination in the United States would affect Cold War alignments. Would race discrimination make it less likely that African and Asian nations would ally themselves with the United States and against the Soviet Union? There were practical consequences for UN politics as well. Would race discrimination make it more difficult for the United States to gain support for its positions in the UN from African and Asian nations? Would that affect the usefulness of the UN as a forum for the nation to further its interests in the global community?

Although the impact of race in America on the nation's diplomatic interests was of concern during the Truman and Eisenhower years, during the Kennedy administration the issue took on even greater importance. "Racism and discrimination . . . had a major impact on my life as secretary of state," noted Dean Rusk. "Stories of racial discrimination in the United States and discriminatory treatment accorded diplomats from the many newly independent countries of the old colonial empires began to undermine our relations with these countries."[15]

Secretary Rusk's concerns stemmed, of course, from the more deeply textured experiences the administration had in handling the problem of race discrimination, and not only from the particularly newsworthy incidents like those at the University of Mississippi and in Birmingham. It was particularly awkward when discriminatory practices were directed at black foreign diplomats. This would happen with increasing frequency as UN delegates from newly independent nations came to the United States. Dean Rusk recalled one incident when "early in the Kennedy years a black delegate to the United Nations landed in Miami on his way to New York. When the passengers disembarked for lunch, the white passengers were taken to the airport restaurant; the black delegate received a folding canvas stool in a corner of the hangar and a sandwich wrapped with waxed paper. He then flew on to New York, where our delegation asked for his vote on human rights issues."[16] Rusk believed that incidents like this were "a severe barrier to cordial relations with many foreign states." He charged the State Department Protocol Office with handling difficulties faced by foreign diplomats, but quickly discovered that the problems were deep-seated and "depended on racial progress throughout Washington and indeed the entire country. We could not expect an African diplomat to gain privileges and services denied black Americans. Nor could we expect him to display his diplomatic passport every time he wanted to eat or get a haircut." For these reasons, as well as, Rusk said, "the simple rightness of the cause," the State Department worked on antisegregation efforts, throwing "its full weight behind the Civil Rights Acts of 1964 and 1965, and especially legislation dealing with public accommodations."[17]

Although it lacked the drama and the level of brutality of Birmingham, a highway in Maryland was a source of great concern during the Kennedy years. Highway 40 was a route taken by many diplomats on the drive from the United Nations in New York City to the nation's capital. Yet time after time, when African diplomats stopped for a bite to eat, they were refused service at Maryland restaurants. On 26 June 1961, for example, Ambassador Malick Sow of Chad was on his way to Washington, D.C., to present his credentials to President Kennedy. The ambassador stopped for gas. When he tried to order of cup of coffee, he was refused service.[18] Incidents like this upset the diplomats, and generated a hostile press reaction in their home country. The implications of discrimination for U.S. relations with these countries concerned Kennedy administration staffers. As Chester Bowles remarked, "Now you have some 20 new nations in Africa. You have, of course, all the new nations of Asia. The UN has grown from 50 nations in the last few years to a hundred. They are all coming to the United States because the UN is here and because they look on this as a country of great promise. . . . And . . . of course, some of them get into all kinds of difficulties with some of our own ways of doing things. And they go home, a lot of them, pretty upset individuals."[19]

Upon hearing of these incidents, President Kennedy's initial reaction was that African ambassadors should not be driving on Highway 40. "It's a hell of a road," he said. "I used to drive it years ago, but why would anybody want to drive it today when you can fly? Tell these ambassadors I wouldn't think of driving from New York to Washington. Tell them to fly!"[20]

The seriousness of the problem, however, would require a more systematic response. The administration established a new Office of Special Protocol Services in the State Department to focus on such matters. Pedro Sanjuan was its director. While he was charged with handling the vast array of problems of discrimination against foreign diplomats throughout the country, a particular focus of Sanjuan's work was Route 40. When a bill prohibiting discrimination in public accommodations was introduced in the Maryland state legislature, Sanjuan testified in favor of the bill on behalf of the Department of State. Acknowledging that some people might wonder "why the Department of State is interested in what may appear to some to be an internal matter within the State of Maryland," Sanjuan recast his appearance as "a request by the Department of State for the assistance of the State of Maryland in insuring the success of the foreign policy of the United States." The State Department strongly supported the bill because it would "eliminate a source of embarrassment that greatly damages our relations with not only the neutral nations of the world, but many nations which are stoutly with us in the fight for freedom."[21]

Sanjuan drew an analogy between this request for assistance and the U.S. government's appeal to private industry to help by building better weapons during World War II. This time the war was a cold war, and the weapons required were different. "GIVE US THE WEAPONS TO CONDUCT THIS WAR OF HUMAN DIGNITY," he urged. "The fight for decency against Communism is everyone's war in America." After an initial setback, the Maryland public accommodations bill was passed by the state legislature in January 1963.[22]

Beyond the treatment of foreign diplomats, Rusk believed that race relations in the nation as a whole in the 1960s "had a profound impact on the world's view of the United States and, therefore, on our foreign relations."

He testified before Congress that "racial discrimination in the United States had great significance for our foreign policy and that our failure to live up to our proclaimed ideals at home was widely noted abroad. We had to recognize that the breakup of the old colonial empires and the emergence of newly independent nations were one of the epochal developments of our time and that these newly independent peoples, mostly-nonwhite, arrived on the scene determined to eradicate every vestige of colonialism and white supremacy."[23]

The impact of race in America on international politics came to a head in the spring of 1963, as the nation's critics quickly took up Birmingham. On 14 May 1963 the USIA reported that the Soviet Union had "stepped up its propaganda on Birmingham over the weekend to campaign proportions, devoting about one fifth of its radio output to the subject." Propaganda was more extensive than during the Meredith dispute, when in 1962 the presence of federal troops guaranteed that black student James H. Meredith would be able to attend the University of Mississippi. In most other countries, with the exception of African nations, "coverage has been unexpectedly moderate and factual, except in the Communist and leftist press." Nevertheless, "the damaging pictures of dogs and fire hoses have been extremely widely used." In Lagos, Nigeria, for example, "substantial improvement over past two years in Nigerian public understanding of progress in U.S. race relations is being rapidly eroded by reports, photographs and TV coverage from Alabama." It seemed to outside observers that violence in Birmingham was out of control. "Growing adverse local reactions in marked contrast situation at time Meredith case when strong stand Federal Government widely understood and applauded." In Kenya, police dogs and fire hoses were featured on television, and front-page newspaper stories featured headlines such as "Riots Flare in U.S. South—Infants Sent to Jail."[24]

Kennedy had called a meeting of his top advisers on 3 May. According to Burke Marshall, the reason for the meeting was that Birmingham "was a matter of national and international concern at the time because of the mass of demonstrations." The administration was under pressure to take action, yet the course of federal involvement was unclear. As Marshall remembered it, "Those pictures of the police dogs and fire hoses going throughout the country stirred the feelings of every Negro in the country, most whites in the country, and I suppose particularly colored persons throughout the world. And all of that emotion was directed at President Kennedy." The concern about Birmingham's impact would lead the administration to play a key role in resolving the crisis. Kennedy dispatched Marshall to the city, and Marshall helped manage negotiations that led to an agreement between the Southern Christian Leadership Conference (SCLC), the local government,

and the business community. Under the pact, steps would be taken to desegregate facilities in large department stores, redress employment discrimination, and release jailed civil rights demonstrators. Yet once Birmingham had
focused the world's attention on racial brutality in America, resolving problems on the local level would not fully end the crisis. As with so many civil
rights crises in the 1960s, Birmingham required a global, as well as local,
response.[25]

Then, in Addis Ababa, the diplomatic consequences of discrimination
reached a particularly dramatic level. African leaders engaged in a lengthy
discussion of Birmingham and debated the proper way to express concern over
the incidents in their joint resolutions. According to Reuters, they drafted a
resolution that, in its original form, could precipitate a rupture in U.S. relations with African states. Other news agencies reported the objections to such
a step from some delegations, "and in the end all agreed on substituting the
word 'deterioration' for 'break.'" Agence France Presse claimed that some
delegates suggested that other nations be "black-listed" as well. This was rejected as ineffective. The result was a milder resolution that mentioned only
the United States. The French wire service called it a "well-balanced plan
adopted after long debate and painful compromise."[26]

The resolution's final version indicated that the conference "expresses the
deep concern aroused in all African peoples and governments by the measures of racial discrimination taken against communities of African origin
living outside the continent and particularly in the United States of America.
Expresses appreciation for the efforts of the Federal Government of the United
States of America to put an end to these intolerable practices which are likely
seriously to deteriorate relations between the African peoples and governments on the one hand and the people and government of the United States of
America on the other."[27]

The State Department's reaction was that the resolution on discrimination
was "appreciably better from our standpoint, than the preliminary proposal."
According to a State Department memorandum for the White House, U.S.
ambassador to Ethiopia Edward M. Korry thought it was "as good an outcome as possible." The adoption of the watered-down version "was a remarkable tribute to the United States Government, considering the depth of
African feeling about the Alabama incidents." This achievement was "tangible evidence of the international impact of local incidents, and in the context
of our African relations reinforces the wisdom of Federal policy." From the
State Department's perspective, the federal government's role in resolving the
Birmingham crisis had had concrete and beneficial effects on U.S. foreign relations. This perspective was reinforced in post–Addis Ababa correspondence

African National Congress leader Oliver Tambo (center) greets Harlem residents in
1963. (Courtesy of Klytus Smith)

with African leaders. For example, President Nyerere of Tanganyika wrote to
Kennedy that he "appreciated your efforts in connection with the reinvigo-
rated demand by the Negro Citizens of America for full equal rights." Nyerere had confidence that Kennedy would "find a solution which gives justice
to all American citizens. In doing so you will be making a great contribution
to the cause of non-racialism throughout the world."[28]

Yet there was another reason for the turnabout in Addis Ababa. President
Youlou of the Congo wrote to Kennedy on the eve of the conference. Knowing that Birmingham would be on the minds of participants, Youlou noted,
"Certainly you can measure better than anyone else the repercussions which
the events in Birmingham are having in Africa." However Youlou would not
support a reaction to Birmingham at Addis Ababa. He had argued against
UN intervention in his own country and believed that problems in Africa
could be solved without the involvement of those outside the continent.
"This is the same argument I shall give to those who would like to see me
take a position on the events in Alabama," Youlou wrote. "I believe that the
American Negroes are Americans, and that, at the present stage of your difficulties, they do not yet have any aspiration for national independence. It is
your government that either will or will not be able to keep them in the
United States, or else make foreigners of them. But it is, first of all, *among
Americans* that the solution must be sought."[29] After the conference, President Kennedy replied to Youlou, noting his pleasure that the resolution on

discrimination in the United States mentioned the progress made by the government to abolish segregation. He also indicated that he appreciated Youlou's "concern that any intervention in African affairs by non-Africans might encourage a counter-reaction involving the United States' own affairs." Each nation, it was clear, had an interest in handling its domestic matters on its own.[30]

A crisis was averted in Addis Ababa. A "break" in U.S.-African relations was no longer contemplated. Yet following the meeting much work remained to be done. Secretary of State Dean Rusk sent a circular on race and foreign relations to all American diplomatic and consular posts. Rusk emphasized that the Kennedy administration was "keenly aware of [the] impact of [the] domestic race problem on [the] US image overseas and on achievement [of] US foreign policy objectives." Rusk felt that "there should be no illusions as to [the] seriousness of [the] situation." Foreign reaction to race in the United States was a "source of great concern. Evidence from all parts of [the] world indicates that racial incidents have produced extremely negative reactions." The reaction of African heads of state at Addis Ababa was just one example illustrating the "depth of emotional feeling" throughout the world. Such incidents suggested that "we have a certain amount of time before our racial problem will impinge even more seriously upon our policies and objectives." "Under these circumstances," Rusk continued, "we recognize there is no effective substitute for decisive action on [the] part of [the] United States Government. This will include a special Presidential message to Congress today, Administration-backed legislation, and a continued series of positive Federal actions throughout [the] country."[31]

The need for positive federal action would present itself yet again, as Alabama governor George Wallace stood in the schoolhouse door to block the integration of the University of Alabama. The Kennedy administration stepped in to resolve this new crisis, and finally the president took a strong, public stand on civil rights. He called for landmark civil rights legislation, explaining his course of action in a televised address to the nation. It was the president's most dramatic and heartfelt statement on civil rights. He asked all Americans to examine their conscience on the subject of race discrimination. "When Americans are sent to Viet-Nam or West Berlin," he reminded citizens, "we do not ask for whites only. It ought to be possible, therefore, for American students of any color to attend any public institution they select without having to be backed up by troops."[32]

Kennedy called civil rights "a moral issue . . . as old as the scriptures and . . . as clear as the American Constitution." He believed that "the heart of the question is whether we are going to treat our fellow Americans as we want to be treated." While Kennedy presented the issue as a question of morality, its resolution would protect the freedom of all Americans, for "this Nation . . . will not fully be free until all its citizens are free. We preach freedom around the world, and we mean it, and we cherish our freedom here at home, but are we to say to the world, and much more importantly, to each other that this is a land of the free except for the Negroes; that we have no second-class citizens except Negroes; that we have no class or caste system, no ghettoes, no master race except with respect to Negroes?" The president described an ambitious civil rights agenda that would depend not only on congressional action, executive branch enforcement efforts, and court orders. He called on every American "in every community across our country" to join together in a national commitment to equality.[33] While he spoke most directly to the American people, President Kennedy's target audience was much broader. The speech was distributed to all U.S. diplomatic posts with directions from the secretary of state and the president himself regarding how the speech should be used, and why this issue was of such importance.[34]

World reaction to the speech was highly favorable. U.S. ambassador to Ethiopia Edward M. Korry wrote to President Kennedy about the "quick turnaround in attitudes" that his civil rights statements had caused in Ethiopia. Emperor Haile Selassie thought the statements were "masterpieces." In addition to Ethiopian royalty, "student leaders, the up-and-coming educated middle bureaucrats and the younger Army elite" discussed Kennedy's actions "without a trace of the sensitivity that reportedly characterized their remarks in years gone by." Korry sent the president an editorial published in the *Ethiopian Herald* that called him "the Abraham Lincoln of the Democratic Party," and lauded the fact that the U.S. government, in the person of John F. Kennedy, "has at long last come out in defence of the Constitution." Predictably, in the Soviet Union, the speech was virtually ignored, as Soviet broadcasting continued a barrage at an unprecedented level, criticizing racism in America as an inevitable consequence of capitalism, and as an illustration of "the hypocrisy of US claims to leadership of the free world."[35]

Then, when the Kennedy administration's civil rights bill came before the Senate Commerce Committee, the president asked Rusk to lead off administration testimony with a discussion of the impact of discrimination on U.S. foreign affairs. The Civil Rights Act of 1963, as proposed by the Kennedy administration, would address a range of problems. Proposals included enabling the Justice Department to bring school desegregation lawsuits, creation of an Equal Employment Opportunity Commission, some protection of the right to vote and authority to deny federal funding to programs that discriminated on the basis of race in hiring. Of particular interest to the secretary of state was Title II of the bill that prohibited discrimination in public accommodations. Lobbying on behalf of the civil rights bill was an extension of State Department efforts to address the embarrassment that discrimination in housing, restaurants, theaters, and hotels had caused the administration. As Pedro Sanjuan had stressed, there was only so much the federal government could do to protect foreign diplomats from discrimination when American persons of color were segregated. If the public accommodations section became law, a foreign passport would not be a prerequisite to equal treatment.[36]

Due to incidents like that in Birmingham, Secretary Rusk believed that race relations in the nation as a whole in the 1960s "had a profound impact on the world's view of the United States and, therefore, on our foreign relations." He told the Commerce Committee that the "primary reason why we must attack the problems of discrimination" was not foreign affairs but because racism was "incompatible with the great ideals to which our democratic society is dedicated. If the realities at home are as they should be, we shan't have to worry about our image abroad." All was not as it should be, however, and as a result, "racial discrimination here at home has important effects on our foreign relations." Racial and ethnic discrimination existed elsewhere in the world, he told the senators. "But the United States is widely regarded as the home of democracy and the leader of the struggle for freedom, for human rights, for human dignity. We are expected to be the model. . . . So our failure to live up to our proclaimed ideals are noted—and magnified and distorted."[37]

International developments had crystallized the importance of this issue. According to Rusk, "one of the epochal developments of our time" was decolonization. "The vast majority of these newly independent peoples are nonwhite, and they are determined to eradicate every vestige of the notion that the white race is superior or entitled to special privileges because of race." The United States was engaged in a world struggle for freedom, against the forces of communism. Rusk warned, "In waging this world struggle we are seriously handicapped by racial or religious discrimination in the United States. . . . In their efforts to enhance their influence among the nonwhite peoples and to alienate them from us, the Communists clearly regard racial discrimination in the United States as one of their most valuable assets."[38]

This problem facing the nation would be worse, Rusk argued, if it were not for the progress made to overcome discrimination, and for the role played by the federal government, particularly the executive branch and the judiciary, to protect civil rights. To illustrate the importance of federal action, Rusk cited one example: "The recent meeting of African heads of state at Addis Ababa, condemned racial discrimination 'especially in the United States,' then approved the role of U.S. Federal authorities in attempting to combat it." Further action was now crucial. Rusk continued: "If progress should stop, if Congress should not approve legislation designed to remove remaining discriminatory practices, questions would inevitably arise in many parts of the world as to the real convictions of the American people. In that event, hostile propaganda might be expected to hurt us more than it has hurt us until now."[39]

For earlier secretaries of state, discrimination was a problem to be managed to safeguard the nation's image, and civil rights activism was a threat because it called attention to the nation's Achilles' heel. For Dean Rusk, however, the civil rights movement was to be embraced. The moral power of the movement could not be denied. In addition, civil rights activists presented the nation with an opportunity. As each crisis broke, it provided the federal government with a chance to demonstrate the nation's resolve. As long as the story told overseas could be one of U.S. government action against injustice, then civil rights crises provided occasions to demonstrate that American democracy sided with the champions of justice, and that the U.S. government would use its power in battles, small and large, between freedom and tyranny. In that sense, civil rights crises provided a stage upon which the United States could act out in symbolic form its Cold War commitments.

This issue would have salience, both with Congress and with the American people. By August 1963 a Harris Poll reported that 78 percent of white Americans surveyed thought that race discrimination in the United States harmed the nation abroad. Twenty-three percent of respondents volunteered that the primary reason discrimination harmed the United States abroad was that it gave the communists a valuable propaganda weapon. The second major reason was that it generally gave the country a bad name. As a Kingsport, Tennessee, lawyer put it, "The pictures of dogs attacking colored people in Birmingham have been sent abroad and you know what kind of opinion that gives them about us."[40]

Internationally, there were both progress and the need for continued vigilance. On 9 July 1963 Assistant Secretary of State G. Mennen Williams returned from a trip to Africa and reported that, on one hand, the nation's position in Africa was "strong because of our past policy and President Kennedy's image." On the other hand, it was "precarious because of the need to realize the promise of the President's civil rights program."[41] That program would not be realized under the aegis of John F. Kennedy. His assassination on 22 November 1963 cut short his civil rights efforts. By late 1963, his own aides and scholars have suggested, the president had been personally moved and affected by the events of the year. Carl M. Brauer suggests that there were several factors that influenced Kennedy's change in civil rights policy.

Intellectually Kennedy had long believed in the principle of racial equality, but the disturbing events of the spring added an emotional dimension to that belief. With Birmingham, American race relations seemed to be entering a period of crisis, yet the federal government lacked the necessary tools to deal with it. Thousands of blacks were taking to the streets to demand their rights— rights no federal law guaranteed. When local authorities proved obdurate and arrested or repulsed the demonstrators, a situation was created that both soiled America's reputation abroad and bred violence and extremism among blacks at home. Most important, in Brauer's view, was Kennedy's "perception of himself as a decisive leader." Birmingham "fostered an atmosphere in which he could only weakly respond to events rather than direct and shape them. It cast him in a weak and defensive position when his personality and view of the Presidency called for decisive leadership and a measure of control over events."[42]

In light of the mix of motivations that inform presidential action, it is difficult to separate out the relative weight of a particular issue over others. It can at least be said that President Kennedy's strengthened commitment to civil rights came at a time when international criticism was heightened, and the goodwill developed from the Meredith affair had been undermined. Further, if Brauer is right that Kennedy's sense of himself as a leader was at stake, then surely his sense of himself as a world statesman, as well as a national leader, was implicated. If Kennedy's push for a new civil rights bill in 1963 partly reflected a strengthened personal commitment and his concern with disorder in the South and his sense of his own presidential mission, it was surely also powerfully affected by his long-standing concern with the U.S. image abroad and the palpable impact discrimination had on U.S. relations with Africa.

Yet, paradoxically, the seeds of change lay at Addis Ababa. The sovereignty of individual African states and their political autonomy were principles central to the new Organization of African Unity. There were so many differences between African nations that they were ultimately held together by the Cold War, and their commitment to nonalignment. But within this framework, national differences underscored the need for genuine self-rule. As President Youlou had suggested to President Kennedy, to protect their own independence these nations would take less of an interest in social reform in another land.[43] Outside pressure for change had been one component of the Cold War imperative. At Addis Ababa, the stakes were raised as virtually an entire continent contemplated a break with the United States. In stepping back from the brink, African leaders helped chart a new path. Long before the Cold War was over, the Cold War imperative was losing strength as a factor influencing U.S. civil rights reform.[44]

Notes

1. *Keesing's Contemporary Archives (KCA)* (London: Longman, 1963–64), 14:19463; Brubeck to Bundy, 27 May 1963, folder: Africa, General, 6/63, box 3, National Security Files—Countries—Africa, John F. Kennedy Library, Boston. King Hassan II of Morocco was absent from the meeting out of concern that his presence would be construed as recognition of Mauritania. Mauritania's president was present at the meeting, and Morocco had previously claimed sovereignty over Mauritanian territory. According to *KCA*, Togo's president was absent because "no agreement had been reached on the question of his country's admission." South Africa was not invited to the meeting.

2. Taylor Branch, *Parting the Waters: America in the King Years, 1954–63* (New York: Simon and Schuster, 1988), 758–63.

3. Ibid., 764–65; David J. Garrow, *Bearing the Cross: Martin Luther King, Jr., and the Southern Christian Leadership Conference* (New York: Vintage Books, 1986), 267–68; United States Information Agency (USIA), "Reaction to Racial Tension in Birmingham, Alabama," 13 May 1963, R-85-63, Record Group (RG) 306, National Archives (NA); John Walton Cotman, *Birmingham, JFK, and the Civil Rights Act of 1963: Implications for Elite Theory* (New York: P. Lang, 1989), 100–102.

4. Addis Ababa to Secretary of State, 23 May 1963, folder: Civil Rights, 6/19/63–7/9/63, National Security Files, Subjects, box 295, Kennedy Library (quoting Obote letter); *KCA*, 14:19465. At the State Department's urging, President Kennedy had sent a congratulatory message to the conference. It was expected that many other nations, including the Soviet Union, would send such communications. Obote's letter was in response to Kennedy's message. See Brubeck to Bundy, 11 May 1963, folder: Africa, General, 5/63, box 3, National Security Files—Countries—Africa, Kennedy Library; Department of State to American embassy, Addis Ababa, 17 May 1963, folder: Africa, General, 5/63, box 3, National Security Files—Countries—Africa, Kennedy Library.

5. Addis Ababa to Secretary of State, 23 May 1963, quoting Obote letter.

6. Mary L. Dudziak, "Desegregation as a Cold War Imperative," *Stanford Law Review* 41 (Nov. 1988): 61–120; President's Committee for Civil Rights, *To Secure These Rights* (Washington, D.C.: U.S. Government Printing Office, 1947).

7. Mary L. Dudziak, *Cold War Civil Rights: Race and the Image of American Democracy* (Princeton: Princeton University Press, 2000), 47–78.

8. Dwight D. Eisenhower, "Radio and Television Address to the American People on the Situation in Little Rock, September 24, 1957," *Public Papers of the Presidents of the United States: Dwight D. Eisenhower, 1957* (Washington, D.C.: U.S. Government Printing Office, 1958), 694; Dwight D. Eisenhower, *Waging Peace, 1959–1961: The White House Years* (New York: Doubleday, 1965), 172; Mary L. Dudziak, "The Little Rock Crisis and Foreign Affairs: Race, Resistance, and the Image of American Democracy," *Southern California Law Review* 70 (Sept. 1997): 1641–1716. In his memoirs, Eisenhower noted that one of the reasons for his action in Little Rock was the need to protect the nation's international image. Eisenhower, *Waging Peace*. Other factors included the need to maintain the rule of law in the context of challenges to federal authority. See Robert F. Burk, *The Eisenhower Administration and Black Civil Rights* (Knoxville: University of Tennessee Press, 1984), 185–86; James C. Duram, *A Moderate among Extremists: Dwight D. Eisenhower and the School Desegregation Crisis* (Chicago: Nelson-Hall, 1981), 143–72. For a broad-based approach to the Little Rock crisis, addressing the importance of grassroots activism,

class, gender, religion, and foreign affairs, see David L. Chappell, ed., "Special Issue: 40th Anniversary of the Little Rock School Crisis," *Arkansas Historical Quarterly* 56 (1997): 257.

9. Harris Wofford, recorded interview by Berl Bernhard, 29 Nov. 1965, p. 7, John F. Kennedy Library Oral History Program. Carl M. Brauer describes Kennedy's posture toward civil rights during his Senate years as that of a moderate. Kennedy supported the Civil Rights Act of 1957 but also voted for an amendment favored by Southern Democrats that weakened the act. The African American press criticized him for this and similar votes. During the same period, Kennedy, asked about school desegregation while speaking in Mississippi, responded that "he accepted it as the law of the land." According to Brauer, "Kennedy's moderate stand on civil rights allowed and even encouraged Southern politicians to embrace him" in the era before his presidency. Carl M. Brauer, *John F. Kennedy and the Second Reconstruction* (New York: Columbia University Press, 1977), 20–23.

10. Brauer, *John F. Kennedy and the Second Reconstruction*, 43, 127, 205–13; Branch, *Parting the Waters*, 586–87; Harris Wofford, *Of Kennedys and Kings* (New York: Farrar, Straus, Giroux, 1980), 124.

11. Clayborne Carson, *In Struggle: SNCC and the Black Awakening of the 1960s* (Cambridge, Mass.: Harvard University Press, 1981).

12. Brauer, *John F. Kennedy and the Second Reconstruction*, 44.

13. USIA, Media Comment on the Mississippi Crisis, 5 Oct. 1962, folder: R-109-62, RG 306, Records of the USIA, Office of Research, Reports, 1960–63, box 10, NA; USIA, Racial Prejudice Mars the American Image, 17 Oct. 1962, folder: R-136-62, RG 306, Records of the USIA, Office of Research, Reports, 1960–63, box 5, NA; Arthur Schlesinger, *A Thousand Days* (Boston: Houghton Mifflin, 1965), 858–59, 866; Richard Reeves, *President Kennedy: Profile of Power* (New York: Simon and Schuster, 1994), 354–64.

14. Bowles to Robert F. Kennedy, 10 Oct. 1962, Bowles, Chester, 10/62–11/62, Papers of Robert F. Kennedy, Attorney General's General Correspondence, Kennedy Library. Long after the crisis was resolved, James Meredith remained on the minds of peoples around the world. When Chester Bowles later traveled through thirteen African countries, in each, one question was inevitable, urgent, and recurrent: what about James Meredith at the University of Mississippi? Chester Bowles, *Emancipation: The Record and the Challenge*, 15 Feb. 1963, folder: Bowles, Chester, 1963, Papers of Robert F. Kennedy, Attorney General's General Correspondence, box 6, Kennedy Library.

15. Dean Rusk, *As I Saw It* (New York: W. W. Norton, 1990), 579–92. The importance of civil rights to Rusk is illustrated by the fact that he devoted an entire chapter of his memoir to the issue.

16. Ibid., 582.

17. Ibid., 583–84.

18. Report of Incident Involving Ambassador Malick Sow of Chad (undated), folder: Chad, General, 1961–62, Papers of President Kennedy, President's Office Files, Countries, box 113a, Kennedy Library; Battle to O'Donnell, 19 June 1961, folder: Chad, General, 1961–62, Papers of President Kennedy, President's Office Files, Countries, box 113a, Kennedy Library; Wofford, *Of Kennedys and Kings*, 126–28.

19. Meeting with Representatives of State Governors (transcript), p. A-5, 16 June 1961; Second Meeting with Representatives of State Governors, Papers of Pedro Sanjuan, MS 78-21, Kennedy Library.

20. Wofford, *Of Kennedys and Kings*, 127–28. See also Wofford oral history. Ac-

cording to Harris Wofford, Kennedy's reaction led the State Department chief of protocol to wonder if the president was behind his office's efforts to end discrimination on Route 40. Brauer maintains that because Kennedy "wanted to improve America's image in the Third World and had served as chairman of a Senate subcommittee on Africa, he came to office disposed to be especially sensitive to this problem." Brauer, *John F. Kennedy and the Second Reconstruction,* 77.

21. Pedro Sanjuan, "Address to the Legislative Council for the General Assembly of Maryland," 13 Sept. 1961, folder: Campaign in Maryland for Passage of Public Accommodations Bill, 9/1/61, Papers of Pedro Sanjuan, MS 78-21, Kennedy Library; Renee Romano, "No Diplomatic Immunity: African Diplomats, the State Department, and Civil Rights, 1961–1964," *Journal of American History* 87 (Sept. 2000): 546–80; Timothy P. Maga, "Battling the Ugly American at Home: The Special Protocol Service and the New Frontier, 1961–63," *Diplomacy and Statecraft* 3 (1993): 126–42.

22. Pedro Sanjuan, "Address to the Legislative Council for the General Assembly of Maryland," 13 Sept. 1961; Progress Report, 2 Apr. 1962, folder: Progress Report, 4/2/62, Papers of Pedro Sanjuan, Kennedy Library; Progress Report, 16 June 1963, p. 6, folder: Progress Report, 6/16/63, Papers of Pedro Sanjuan, Kennedy Library; Robert F. Kennedy to Sanjuan, 28 Mar. 1963, folder: Sanjuan, Pedro: 9/1961, Papers of Robert F. Kennedy, Attorney General's General Correspondence, box 51, Kennedy Library.

23. Rusk, *As I Saw It,* 586–88; U.S. Senate Committee on Commerce, *Hearings on S. 1732: A Bill to Eliminate Discrimination in Public Accommodations Affecting Interstate Commerce,* 88th Cong., 1st sess., 1963.

24. Wilson to John F. Kennedy, 14 May 1963, folder: USIA (Classified) 1/63–11/63, box 133, Papers of Pierre Salinger, Background Briefing Material, Kennedy Library; Accra to Secretary of State, 17 May 1963, RG 59, Central Foreign Policy File 1963, SOC 14-1 US, NA; Richard Lentz, "Snarls Echoing 'Round the World: The 1963 Birmingham Civil Rights Campaign on the World Stage," *American Journalism* (forthcoming).

25. Burke Marshall, Oral History Interview, Kennedy Library; Cotman, *Birmingham, JFK, and the Civil Rights Act,* 21–60.

26. Quoted in Monrovia to Secretary of State, 22 May 1963, folder: Africa, General, 5/63, box 3, National Security Files—Countries—Africa, Kennedy Library.

27. Addis Ababa Resolutions, p. 5, folder: Africa, General, 6/63, box 99, National Security Files—Countries—Ghana, Kennedy Library.

28. Brubeck to Bundy, 27 May 1963, folder: Africa, General, 6/63, box 3, National Security Files—Countries—Africa, Kennedy Library; Nyerere to John F. Kennedy, 18 June 1963, folder: Tanganyika, 1961–64, box 124a, Papers of President Kennedy, President's Office Files, Countries, Kennedy Library.

29. Youlou to John F. Kennedy, 17 May 1963, folder: Congo, General, 1963, box 114, Papers of President Kennedy, President's Office Files, Countries, Kennedy Library.

30. John F. Kennedy to Youlou, 4 June 1963, folder: Congo, General, 1963, box 114, Papers of President Kennedy, President's Office Files, Countries, Kennedy Library.

31. Rusk to All American Diplomatic and Consular Posts, Circular 2177, 19 June 1963, folder: Civil Rights, 6/19/63–7/9/63, National Security Files, Subjects, box 295, Kennedy Library; Rusk, *As I Saw It.*

32. John F. Kennedy, "Radio and Television Report to the American People on Civil

Rights," 11 June 1963, *Public Papers of the Presidents of the United States: John F. Kennedy, 1963* (Washington, D.C.: U.S. Government Printing Office, 1964), 468.

33. Ibid., 469–70.

34. Read to Bundy, 7 July 1963, folder: African, General 7/63, box 3, National Security Files—Countries—Africa, Kennedy Library.

35. Korry to John F. Kennedy, 28 June 1963; Addis Ababa to Department of State, 29 June 1963, folder: Africa, General, 7/63, box 3, National Security Files—Countries—Africa, Kennedy Library. *Ethiopian Herald*, 25 June 1963, in folder: Africa, General, 7/63, box 3, National Security Files—Countries—Africa, Kennedy Library; "Soviet Media Coverage of Current US Racial Crisis," 14 June 1963; USIA to John F. Kennedy, 14 June 1963, folder: Civil Rights, 6/11/63–6/14/63, National Security Files, Subjects, box 295, Kennedy Library.

36. Rusk, *As I Saw It*, 586; U.S. Senate Committee on Commerce, *Hearings on S. 1732*; Reeves, *President Kennedy*, 527–28; Hugh D. Graham, *The Civil Rights Era: Origins and Development of National Policy* (New York: Oxford University Press, 1990), 125–52.

37. U.S. Senate Committee on Commerce, *Hearings on S. 1732*, 281; Rusk, *As I Saw It*, 586.

38. U.S. Senate Committee on Commerce, *Hearings on S. 1732*, 281–82.

39. Ibid., 282–83.

40. *Washington Post*, 26 Aug. 1963, 1, attached to Sanjuan to Robert F. Kennedy, 26 Aug. 1963, folder: Sanjuan, Pedro: 8/1963, 10/1963, box 51, Personal Papers of Robert F. Kennedy, Attorney General's Papers, General Correspondence, Kennedy Library.

41. Memo for Bundy, Status Report of African Reactions to Civil Rights in the United States, Week Ending 7/12/63, folder: Africa, General, 7/63, Status Report of African Reactions to Civil Rights in the United States, box 99, National Security Files, Countries, Kennedy Library.

42. Wofford, Oral History Interview, 50, 63; Brauer, *John F. Kennedy and the Second Reconstruction*, 246–47.

43. Amadu Sesay, "The OAU and Continental Order," in *Africa and the International Political System*, ed. Timothy M. Shaw and Sola Ojo (Washington, D.C.: University Press of America for the Dept. of International Relations, University of Ife, Ile-Ife, Nigeria, 1982), 168–77; W. Scott Thompson and I. William Zartman, "The Development of Norms in the African System," in *The Organization of African Unity after Ten Years: Comparative*, ed. Yassin El-Ayouty (New York: Praeger, 1975), 3–24.

44. There were many other factors affecting the decline of the Cold War imperative, including the positive effect of 1960s civil rights legislation on U.S. foreign relations, and the impact of Vietnam on domestic and international politics. See Dudziak, *Cold War Civil Rights*, 203–48.

Antiwar Aztlán

The Chicano Movement Opposes
U.S. Intervention in Vietnam

On 20 December 1969 a contingent of some seventy Brown Berets, a militant Mexican American youth group, marched in formation and in full-dress uniform—berets, army jackets, and dark pants for the men, brown skirts for the women—down Michigan Avenue in an unincorporated section of East Los Angeles.[1] Following the Berets, six young men acted as pallbearers and carried a replica of a coffin in a procession that organizers had labeled a "March against Death." Behind the mock funeral, another group held upright a large painting of a bloodied Chicano soldier, with the rank of private, who had been given the Chicano common name J. J. Montez. Both painting and coffin were meant to symbolize all Mexican Americans who had died in Vietnam. Several hundred more marchers followed this dramatic vanguard. As they traveled the narrow, residential street that was Michigan Avenue, demonstrators at the front of the line shouted, "Raza Si!" prompting those behind to thunder in return, "Vietnam No!" The call-and-response captured the most central theme of Chicano antiwar protest, that Chicanos and Chicanas should struggle at home for their *raza*, their fellow Mexican Americans, not fight and die in a war in Vietnam.[2]

The first large-scale antiwar protest by Mexican Americans in the Los Angeles area, the December 1969 march also was the first of more than a dozen Chicano Movement antiwar demonstrations that took place across the Southwest in the following months under the auspices of an organization called the National Chicano Moratorium against the Vietnam War.[3] The ethnic antiwar campaign culminated on 29 August 1970, when between 20,000 and 30,000 people gathered in East Los Angeles to protest the Vietnam War and its domestic consequences.[4] The march was the largest demonstration to occur during the course of the Chicano Movement, which remains the most intense epoch of Mexican American political and cultural protest to date. Although members of the ethnic group had long sought equal treatment, beginning in the 1960s, thousands of mostly young people combined demonstrative politics and cultural affirmation in a dynamic endeavor to address such social injustices as poor educational opportunity, lack of political representation, poverty, and discrimination.[5] As U.S. military involvement in Southeast Asia deepened and casualties mounted, the number of Mexican American dead and wounded was a growing concern. By the turn of the decade, international and domestic matters had become profoundly intertwined for Chicano Movement participants.

In an era that saw the advent of black, red, yellow, and brown power and the emergence of massive opposition to the war in Vietnam, Chicano Movement participants were hardly the only minority activists to condemn U.S. involvement in Southeast Asia. African American and Asian American activists also protested, and blacks, in particular, expressed concern about casualty rates.[6] Mexican Americans nevertheless stood alone among U.S. minorities in conducting a sustained campaign against U.S. policy toward Vietnam. Chicanos and Chicanas who protested the war were moreover forsaking a venerable Mexican American civil rights tradition that had emphasized patriotism in the hopes of obtaining first-class citizenship.

Since before World War II, many ethnic group leaders had pursued a civil rights strategy that was both sincere and effective. They had voiced strong support for American engagements abroad and highlighted Mexican American military contributions. By accentuating battlefield accomplishments, activists emphasized that members of the group had demonstrated the ultimate proof of patriotism: a willingness to risk one's life for one's country. They simultaneously promoted an archetypal Mexican American who met key standards of full citizenship first enshrined in the U.S. Constitution in 1789 and sanctioned in the political, legal, and popular culture ever since. Through two centuries of U.S. history, the ideal citizen was white, male, and willing to serve his country during wartime. These designations were self-reinforcing, as military service was not only an important marker of masculinity but, throughout the long era of segregation, an important marker of whiteness as well. Indeed, the U.S. military consistently categorized Mexican Americans as "white," a racial classification that ethnic activists strove to protect in times of peace as well as war.

Chicanos and Chicanas broke apart such narrow conceptions of citizenship to offer an alternative view of their past and present, and of their role within the United States and beyond the borders of the country. Refusing to conform to long-established hierarchies of race and gender, Chicano Movement participants instead crafted a new understanding of themselves as a people of color, as a colonized people, and as women and men who together had struggled against oppression for centuries. In the creation of each of these new conceptions, moreover, movement activists gained critical inspiration and

Antiwar poster emphasizing solidarity between Chicanos and Vietnamese, with the word "Fuera" (get out) the principal text element. (Courtesy of Malaquias Montoya)

confirmation by examining the conflict in Vietnam. Most important, as they both reclaimed and created a militant Chicano and Chicana identity, movement participants repeatedly identified with the Vietnamese men and women fighting against the U.S. military effort. Thus, just as recent works on African American responses to foreign affairs have provided a more nuanced portrait of black civil right efforts, an examination of Mexican American responses toward the war in Vietnam allows a much greater understanding of the Chicano Movement overall.[7] Like no other issue, antiwar activism crystallized the Chicano Movement's fundamental challenge to popular assumptions about American citizenship and national belonging.

Ironically, the December 1969 march's beginning and ending points had paid tribute to earlier notions of minority inclusion. The demonstration had started at a memorial built just after World War II to commemorate Mexican American soldiers who had died during that conflict and ended at Eugene A.

Obregón Park, named after a Mexican American marine who had lost his life in Korea.[8] The monument and park served as reminders that people of Mexican descent had served the country well as citizen-soldiers. Mexican Americans were understandably proud of this military record. During both World War II and the Korean conflict, the regular appearance of Spanish surnames on casualty and awards lists across the Southwest confirmed widespread Mexican American military participation. The long list of Mexican American soldiers receiving Congressional Medals of Honor, including Eugene Obregón, nineteen, who was granted the award posthumously, provided further uncontestable evidence of battlefield valor.[9] Beyond a source of pride, however, Mexican American soldiering was powerful proof that members of the ethnic group had shown themselves to be legitimate and patriotic citizens. Just as they commemorated past heroism, the war memorial and park's name made implicit demands for the recognition and full inclusion of Mexican Americans within the contemporary American polity. Beginning in the 1940s and continuing into the 1950s, Mexican American veterans and their families moved to the forefront of an invigorated civil rights effort.

Their work built on the foundational struggles of prewar Mexican American civil rights organizations, notably the League of United Latin American Citizens (LULAC) in Texas. Historians of the Mexican American experience have written extensively on LULAC, in no small part because of the organization's rich documentary record.[10] Of particular concern here, however, is the fundamental role the league played in promoting an understanding of people of Mexican descent as Americans. As much a part of the South as the Southwest, Texas was the site of some of the most severe prejudicial treatment directed toward people of Mexican descent. To combat this prejudice, the founders of the league, many of whom came from centuries-old Tejano families, encouraged Mexican Americans to present themselves as, in the words of the organization's 1929 founding document, "the best, purest and most perfect type of true and loyal citizen of the United States of America."[11]

LULAC members understood, moreover, that the "best" Americans were those whose claims of national belonging rested upon that citizenship tripod. Several founding members were proud veterans of World War I. All of the league's early members were men. Not until 1933 did women become voting members of LULAC and, even then, most women participated through ladies' auxiliaries that concentrated on charitable and social works instead of civil rights activism.[12] Via the organization's publications, letters of protest to elected politicians, and press announcements, league members constantly maintained that Mexican Americans, albeit of mixed indigenous and European background, were "white." By embracing and promoting a white and masculinist citizenship, the league sowed the seeds of a civil rights strategy that reached fruition after the Second World War.

The timing for this broader civil rights effort was largely the result of changing demographics. Whereas in the 1920s the U.S. population of Mexican descent was mostly an immigrant one, by 1940 the estimated 2 million people of Mexican parentage within the United States were almost twice as likely to have been born north of the Rio Grande than south of it. With the advent of the Second World War, more Mexican Americans entered the military than ever before. Once the war ended, these citizen-soldiers took advantage of the nation's renewed commitment to equal rights in the wake of the horrors of the Nazi Holocaust. Not only did LULAC see a boost in membership after 1945, but World War II veterans founded another influential and long-lasting Mexican American civil rights organization: the American G.I. Forum.[13]

Like the league, the forum advocated—through both its reform efforts and its organizational framework—the idealized American citizen. Certainly as a veterans' organization, the forum broadcast the patriotism of Mexican American men. Meanwhile, forum women, like female LULAC members, mainly participated via ladies' auxiliaries.[14] Throughout the 1950s, moreover, the American G.I. Forum joined forces with LULAC to argue successfully against the segregation of Mexican-descended people on the grounds that they were "white." Instead of mounting an attack on segregation itself, these organizations asserted that segregation should not apply to Mexican Americans. Cognizant that the United States historically had recognized but one great racial divide between black and white, these ethnic activists continued to insist that Mexican Americans, especially in view of their wartime sacrifices, belonged to the racial category that had access to full citizenship.[15]

Although alternative visions of inclusion exempt from specific racial, military, or even birthplace requirements did emerge during the twentieth century, they were short-lived. As early as 1903, for example, Mexican sugar beet workers in Oxnard, California, favored a continuing union alliance with their Japanese "brothers" in the field over membership as "whites" within the American Federation of Labor (AFL). Once denied AFL support, however, the Japanese-Mexican Labor Association soon faded.[16]

Certain activists attempted to construct solidarity between Mexican Americans and Mexican nationals. El Congreso de Pueblo Habla Española (The Congress of Spanish-Speaking Peoples), launched in 1939 in Los Angeles with the apparent help of the Communist Party of the United States, refused to draw a sharp divide between immigrant and U.S.-born people of Mexican descent. Until it disbanded for the sake of home front unity during World

War II, the congress vigorously pressed for an end to such civil rights abuses as police brutality and housing discrimination as well as an end to race and gender discrimination.[17]

After the war, the Asociación Nacional México-Americana, or ANMA, assumed the radical mantle. Like El Congreso and with some of the same members, ANMA broadly advocated civil rights. The association's most controversial position by far, however, was labeling the Korean War "unjust and unnecessary." Making an accusation that Chicano antiwar activists were to echo during the Vietnam War, ANMA members complained that Mexican American soldiers were being used as "cannon fodder." Such opinions were dangerous during the height of the domestic Cold War. In addition, a few ANMA members were also Communist Party members, although according to one of the most prominent ANMA activists in California, the party's influence upon the organization was "negligible." In 1954 the U.S. attorney general listed ANMA as a subversive organization. By then, the Immigration and Naturalization Service's persistent harassment of members—including deportation—already had fatally weakened it.[18]

In contrast, mainstream Mexican American organizations not only survived but also thrived. Membership was one indicator. ANMA at its height boasted a few thousand members in the five states of the Southwest. With even fewer members, El Congreso never organized beyond southern California. Yet by 1960 150 LULAC councils had been founded across the country.[19] The influx of Korean War veterans, meanwhile, similarly swelled the forum's ranks to an estimated 25,000 members in eighteen states by the turn of the decade.[20] Whereas radical organizations struggled against a tide of anti-Red hysteria, the G.I. Forum and LULAC, both staunchly anticommunist in any case, enjoyed a kind of protective cover. Their ready patriotism and strong endorsement of an accepted brand of citizenship made their civil rights demands less suspect. Banding together, the league and forum won several landmark court cases in Texas and California during the 1950s that all but dismantled the segregation of people of Mexican descent in schools and other public places.

The strategic foundation for these domestic successes, however, was unequivocal support for United States foreign policy. This tendency probably reached its most ludicrous height in October 1965 when a California group passed a resolution that both requested greater federal attention to the problems of Mexican Americans and cast Spanish-speaking Californians as dedicated U.S. allies in the Cold War since the early 1800s. As the resolution sponsored by California's Mexican American Political Association (MAPA) asserted, "Over 150 years ago, Spanish speaking Mexican Americans stopped the Russian colonial advance and conquest from Siberia and Alaska, and preserved the Western portion of the United States for our country."[21] State representatives from LULAC and the California G.I. Forum also signed the declaration, ignoring its historical inaccuracies in favor of the resolution's retrospective claim that Mexican Americans were always staunch defenders of the United States—even against tsarist aggression. The declaration epitomized the determination of civil rights organizations well into the 1960s to present their constituents as stalwart backers of the U.S. international agenda, and as the ultimate Cold Warriors.

This emphasis on military service and patriotism served to curb criticism within Mexican American civil rights organizations regarding the war in Vietnam. Early on, the American G.I. Forum voiced its strong approval of U.S. military intervention. Indeed, in 1965 and 1966, local chapters of the American G.I. Forum went so far as to organize marches in support of U.S. troops and the aim of helping the "South Vietnamese Remain Free."[22] Similarly, in 1964, certain members of the Mexican American Political Association introduced a resolution at the annual state convention expressing "unconditional support for President Johnson's war in Vietnam."[23] Others, however, were more sympathetic to the intensifying public concern over the war's morality, efficacy, and costs, and the 1964 resolution was tabled. Two years later, an antiwar resolution by the organization's liberal executive board encountered similar, effective resistance. In sum, tradition served to silence criticism: not until 1968 did the association publicly declare its opposition to the war in Vietnam.[24] Incredibly, the same year, a loose coalition of organizations called La Raza Unida, specifically founded to express Mexican American frustration with President Lyndon B. Johnson, also sidestepped the war issue. "Speaking of war," the conference proceedings of the 1968 Raza Unida gathering in San Antonio noted, "thoughtful reasons have been advanced for and against this involvement."[25]

The reticence of conference participants to directly engage the war issue was even more surprising given that by 1968 the war's impact upon Mexican Americans was a source of grave concern for many. The year before, Rafael Guzmán, a political scientist with the Ford Foundation's Mexican-American Study Project, released a report comparing the percentage of Spanish-surnamed Vietnam War dead from the five southwestern states to the percentage of Spanish-surnamed men of military age living in the U.S. Southwest. Widely publicized in Chicano Movement newspapers, his conclusion was stark: "American servicemen of Mexican descent have a higher death rate in Vietnam than all other G.I.s."[26] Although the number of Mexican American dead was soon to become a central indictment put forth by movement antiwar protesters, the San Antonio group preferred to use the same evidence to bolster their civil rights cause. As the conference proceedings advised, whenever Mexican Americans confronted "insensitive and stupid people" who questioned their loyalty, "the best answer we can possibly give them is to point to the disproportional number of Mexican-American casualties in the war in Vietnam."[27] Once again, activists embraced the notion of massive ethnic group sacrifice in battle, even though this war was becoming extremely unpopular. To do otherwise was to risk unraveling a previously successful civil rights strategy premised upon a white, masculinist, and militaristic citizenship.

During the turbulent era of the 1960s, however, Mexican Americans increasingly confronted the limits of that strategy. Just as the war in Vietnam raised questions about the aims of American foreign policy and the value of military service, the civil rights movement and the quest for black power undermined several long-standing ethnic group assumptions about race. Facing many of the same socioeconomic hurdles as African Americans, for example, Mexican Americans as "whites" initially received little attention from policy makers constructing Johnson's Great Society.[28] Ironically, what had once been a successful civil rights strategy now appeared to promote not only silence on international questions but also group exclusion from the benefits of domestic reform.

Under these circumstances, the aggressive tactics and militant speech of emerging Chicano Movement heroes held a tremendous appeal to many young Mexican Americans eager to be part of the decade's impulse toward protest and reform. The United Farm Workers, for example, led by Cesar Chavez and Dolores Huerta, marched, picketed, and organized a national boycott in support of the union's five-year strike against grape growers. One result was a union contract. Another was extraordinary public attention to the plight of Mexican Americans in general.[29] In New Mexico, meanwhile, Reies López Tijerina and members of the organization he led, La Alianza Federal de Mercedes Reales (The Federal Alliance of Royal Land Grants), were staging spectacular—and sometimes violent—protests to restore Spanish and Mexican land grants to the descendants of the original grantees.[30] Finally, the poetry, plays, and speeches of Rodolfo "Corky" Gonzales, founder of a Denver-based organization called the Crusade for Justice, were a particular inspiration for young, urban Chicanos and Chicanas.[31] In 1969 the Crusade hosted a Chicano youth conference that issued the premier document of Chicano cultural nationalism, or Chicanismo, El plan espiritual de Aztlán. Rejecting assimilation, the plan advocated Chicano autonomy in the realms of education, culture, and politics as a means of obtaining "total liberation from oppression, exploitation, and racism."[32]

The same document, however, made only one indirect reference to the then raging Vietnam War when it endorsed Chicano control over "the utilization of our bodies for war."[33] That the topic received scant mention was not so surprising. Although Chavez, Huerta, Tijerina, and Gonzales were each early opponents of the war, at first other issues dominated the Chicano Movement agenda. Inspired by events in California, for example, farm workers in the Southwest and Midwest, typically with student support, likewise organized and went on strike. Issues of economic justice also occupied Tijerina's Alianza, which headed the Southwest contingent to the 1969 Poor People's Campaign in Washington, D.C.[34] Elsewhere Chicano Movement participants sought an end to police brutality, the establishment of an independent political party, and, above all, improved education. Starting in 1968, thousands of Chicano high school students in California, Arizona, Colorado, and Texas launched a series of strikes to protest racist teachers, shoddy campuses, and a lack of culturally significant coursework. Mexican Americans on college campuses meanwhile pushed for Chicano Studies programs and greater minority enrollments.[35]

As they energetically advanced demands to increase the Mexican American presence on campus, however, Chicano activists raced against the looming specter of war. Precisely because they were not enrolled in college, the vast majority of draft-age Mexican Americans were ineligible for student deferments, one of the most common exemptions from military service. In 1967, for example, only seventy Mexican American students were enrolled at the University of California, Los Angeles. At the time, Los Angeles was home to the largest population of Mexican-descended people in the country. Chicano college enrollees and graduates were similarly scarce across the Southwest, while high school dropouts abounded. According to the 1960 census, about half the Mexican American population had less than eight years of schooling. This low educational achievement, moreover, characterized a population that was, by 1960, overwhelmingly U.S.–born and raised. Chicano Movement activists argued, however, that students did not so much drop out of school as were pushed out by second-rate facilities, culturally insensitive curricula, and hostile staff. All too often, they protested, young men who left school fell into the arms of eager army recruiters who purposefully sought out working-class youth.[36]

As pockets of Chicano antiwar activism began to emerge in 1968 and 1969, the Selective Service System and the egregious class biases of the draft were immediate concerns. Even the founder of the American G.I. Forum found the process inequitable and complained in a series of letters to President Johnson and his representatives about the complete absence of Mexican Americans on south Texas draft boards.[37] A more pervasive concern was that few Mexican Americans understood the draft or its exemptions. Certainly Rosalío Muñoz, a draft resister and former UCLA student body president who later chaired the National Chicano Moratorium, noticed an immense gap in opportunity and savvy between Anglo-American campus friends and the young Mexican American men whom he met in his 1969 job as a college recruiter. While the first group prided themselves on the outrageous means they had devised to escape the draft, Muñoz remembered, Mexican Americans from California's interior agricultural valleys simply assumed they would be going to Vietnam. They told Muñoz that they were not bothering to continue their education.[38]

Likewise, Lea Ybarra and Nina Genera, who together operated a Bay Area organization called Chicano Draft Help during the war, saw firsthand how poverty and minimal education contributed to a perception of inevitability. The two women, both college students with brothers in Vietnam (and, in Ybarra's case, eighteen cousins), literally ran interference at the Oakland Army Induction Center for months on end during 1969 and 1970.[39] On those mornings that buses from the agricultural towns of Watsonville and Salinas arrived, Ybarra and Genera greeted the new arrivals, who were overwhelmingly of Mexican descent, and pleaded with the young men to at least examine their available options. Although the vast majority always entered the building, some turned around. Years later, Ybarra remembered how she was able to obtain conscientious objector status for one young man who, although philosophically a pacifist, had had no idea what "conscientious objector" meant. In a like manner, Nina Genera recalled securing a medical deferment for another Mexican American with a severe back ailment. From a poor family, he had never seen a doctor until after Genera convinced him to delay reporting for duty.

By the turn of the decade, Chicano antidraft activism was in full bloom. Chicano Draft Help was one of the longest-running counseling centers, continuing until 1972. Yet similar draft counseling efforts also opened in New Mexico, south Texas, and especially southern California. Nor was Muñoz's status as a Chicano draft resister entirely unique. A recognized student leader, Muñoz had received substantial media attention when he declared his independence from the Selective Service System on 16 September 1969. Yet he was joining perhaps a half dozen Chicanos who already had publicly announced their decision to refuse induction as well as untold others who had taken the same step quietly.[40] Momentum against the draft was visible even in Texas, the home state of the American G.I. Forum and LULAC. Once members of a Chicano political party gained majority control of the Crystal City school board in 1970, the town's sole high school became a sanctuary of sorts. Chicano school board members hired a campus draft counselor, barred army recruiters from visiting the school, and prohibited any district employee from serving as a registrar for the Selective Service System.[41]

The turn of the decade also marked the launch of the Chicano moratorium campaign. Although Rosalío Muñoz and others had worked against the draft, the idea for a large antiwar campaign took root after Chicano activists from Los Angeles attended the massive New Mobilization against the War demonstration in San Francisco's Golden Gate Park on 15 November 1969. While the gathering of perhaps as many as 250,000 people impressed these Chicano activists with the saliency of the war issue, racism within the national antiwar movement also convinced them to work independently. They resented being treated as second-class protesters by the event's organizers and as second-class thinkers by representatives of the sectarian left. The future leaders of the moratorium campaign also perceived a distinct lack of concern within a movement dominated by whites regarding the war's cost to minorities. In a later interview, Muñoz, then the moratorium's chair, labeled the national antiwar movement "institutionally racist" for this reason. As Muñoz explained to a radical journalist, attending the New Mobe helped convince him that "the main thing the white peace groups were doing was keeping whites out of the service. That means only one thing: More Chicanos are in."[42]

By 1970 the Chicano Movement's opposition to the Vietnam War, including the nascent moratorium effort, broadened beyond a strict emphasis on who was serving and dying to disputing the war's aims and the value of military service. A telling example was a bilingual pamphlet called *La batalla está aquí* (The battle is here) that Ybarra and Genera coauthored in 1970. The major portion of the pamphlet featured "Legal Ways to Stay Out of the Military," a detailed listing in English and Spanish regarding what deferments were available. Yet the publication was also an antiwar manifesto. Ybarra and Genera made an emotional appeal to the entire Mexican American community, "young and old, male and female," to turn against what they considered an immoral war. Featuring several horrific photographs of dead and wounded Vietnamese children, all victims of American bombs, the booklet aimed to compel Mexican Americans to consider the suffering of the Vietnamese as much as the danger faced by their relatives in combat. In the light of the American war machine's awesome destructive capability, the authors dismissed military service as an avenue of ethnic group uplift. By supporting the killing and maiming of countless Vietnamese men, women, and especially children, they wrote, Mexican Americans "only lose—our men and our own honor and our pride." Representing a dramatic break with earlier attempts to claim citizenship because of military service and wartime sacrifice,

Ybarra and Genera challenged Mexican Americans to reconsider what truly made a man "courageous and honorable."[43]

No doubt the greatest challenge the two women offered, however, was a sweeping reexamination of the Mexican American experience that emphasized a shared history of oppression and invasion with the Vietnamese. According to Ybarra and Genera, injustice and suffering rendered by "the same imperialist system" inextricably linked the Chicano—and indigenous—past to the Vietnamese present. In advancing this alternative reading of the Chicano past, furthermore, Ybarra and Genera, on behalf of all people of Mexican descent, laid claim to the region that was now the American Southwest. "Just as the North Vietnamese are accused of 'invading' a city in their own country" whenever they crossed the seventeenth parallel dividing Vietnam into north and south, they wrote, "so are Chicanos considered foreigners in our own country—the land that originally belonged to our forefathers."[44]

Denoting the powerful merger between international and domestic affairs within the Chicano Movement, La batalla está aquí also made clear that Chicano antiwar activists had imbibed deeply the era's brew of protest politics. During the 1960s leftist critiques flourished within the national antiwar movement and elsewhere. Chicanismo in particular drew inspiration from the black power movement and its insistence on race pride, political liberation, and recapturing one's cultural identity. Just as important, Chicano Movement participants looked to their own ethnic group's long history of struggle on the North American continent. One of the appeals of Tijerina's land grant movement in New Mexico, for example, was in reminding both Mexican Americans and Anglo-Americans that Spanish-speaking and indigenous people had inhabited and cultivated the U.S. Southwest for centuries before 1848. Less noted by scholars, however, is that Chicano Movement participants also looked to events in Vietnam to develop and reinforce their sense of themselves as a people who had long struggled for self-determination. The result was more than a Mexican American echo of other groups' protest politics.

Chicano antiwar activism advanced a revolutionary vision of race within the ethnic group, of the potential contributions of men and women within the movement, and of Mexican Americans within the United States. Whereas a previous generation of activists had insisted that Mexican Americans were white, Chicano Movement participants contended that they were brown-skinned—just like the Vietnamese. Whereas American citizenship had placed males in the foreground, Chicano Movement participants carved out a new role for men and women alike within their cultural nationalist movement. Both could be partners in advancing la causa—just as women as well as men served as National Liberation Front soldiers, diplomats, and supporters. Most important, by drawing parallels between the American conquest of Mexico's northern territories in 1848 to the U.S. military effort in Southeast Asia, Chicano antiwar activism embraced and promoted the radical thesis that Chicanos and Vietnamese were together a "Third World" people facing a common enemy. Thus did Chicano protest against the war exemplify the essential boldness of Chicano cultural nationalism overall. In refusing to render support to the U.S. military effort in Southeast Asia, activists completely rejected the tripod of white, masculinist, and military-based citizenship. Engaged in a vibrant nationalist project, they sought instead to reclaim and create a Chicano cultural, and perhaps even political, homeland called Aztlán.

Labeled Chicano cultural nationalism's "most brilliant political maneuver" by one scholar, the adoption and prominence of the concept of Aztlán underscored the extent to which Chicano Movement participants were intent upon celebrating and reclaiming their indigenous heritage.[45] Shrouded in myth even before the Spanish conquest, Aztlán was the ancient place of origin of the Aztecs before they migrated southward to build their capital of Tenochtitlán, present-day Mexico City. Within the Chicano Movement, Aztlán, literally meaning in Nahuatl "the lands to the north," became geographically synonymous with the U.S. Southwest.[46] Equally important, the word referred to a people with deep ties to this region, the Mexican Americans. As the participants at the 1969 Denver Youth Conference proudly proclaimed, "We are Aztlán."[47] In both cases, Chicano Movement activists were striking a new claim for legitimacy that rested not upon their willingness to die in battle but upon their status as natives to the continent.

This racial repositioning had profound implications for how Chicano Movement participants saw themselves and their national allegiances. "We are so brainwashed. We keep thinking we are a minority . . . and . . . we are not," one of the leading movement columnists, Enriqueta Vásquez y Longeaux, explained in a 1970 newspaper interview. "We are a majority in this hemisphere." Chicano activists claimed a special relationship not only to their "Brown brothers" in Latin America as a result of their indigenous heritage, but to the Vietnamese as well.[48] The connection even became biological for some activists. As early as 1968, David Sanchez, one of the founders of the Brown Berets, a Chicano paramilitary group, and an early member of the Chicano moratorium committee, argued that "since Chicanos came down through the Bering Straits part Oriental, and that honkie, what's his name? Cortez, came across over and raped our women, so we're half mongoloid and half causcasoid, that makes the Viet Cong our brothers."[49] As "Orientals," Sanchez implied, the Vietnamese were not "white." As mestizos, a racially mixed people, he and other activists insisted, neither were Chicanos.

Embedded in Sanchez's comments, however, was a celebration of the masculinity and patriarchy—the Viet Cong were brothers, women belonged to men—that the Chicano Movement certainly embraced. Many of the earliest cultural productions of the movement were uncritical presentations of male supremacy. The male warrior, an archetype that originated with the glorious Aztecs and extended to contemporary Chicano GIs, recurred in movement literature and art. Movement participants sympathized with this icon even as they protested the war. Also abounding as image and metaphor was the concept of *la familia de la raza*. The idea implied not only that all Chicanos were family, but also that the family unit—headed by the father—was the cultural and political foundation of Chicanismo. Chicanas thus were most important as the caretakers of present-day activists and mothers of future revolutionaries. In its most extreme incarnation, such nationalism even opposed birth control as yet another way of limiting the Mexican American population: similar to, but cheaper than, sending soldiers off to Vietnam.[50] At best, the movement's dominant cultural nationalist motifs relegated Chicanas to a fixed, lesser role. At worst, they ignored movement women altogether.

Many Chicanas, however, actively resisted subordinate status by revising the movement's cultural nationalist imagery to better fit them. Even as the movement esteemed such heroes of the Mexican Revolution as Pancho Villa and Emiliano Zapata, women activists began to portray themselves as modern Adelitas, the *soldaderas* who fought beside male troops in that long war.[51] Similarly, in her regular columns for New Mexico's *El Grito del Norte*, Vásquez y Longeaux continually reframed the notion of la familia de la raza to include an equal, if not starring, role for la Chicana.[52] As a woman who had survived extreme poverty during her youth (five of her eleven siblings died in childhood), who had raised two children on her own as a divorced parent, and who had encountered blatant job discrimination, Vásquez y Longeaux was impatient with any implied subordination.[53] Instead, she insisted that the Chicano family "must come up together." The role for a woman in the movement was not behind a man, she declared, but "alongside him, leading."[54] Turning to the Mexican past as well as their own experiences as mothers, wives, and daughters, activists like Vásquez y Longeaux helped promote an understanding of Chicanas as defenders of their people, as equal partners in struggle.

As the Chicano Movement became increasingly radicalized, Chicanas began to look to Vietnamese women as role models. From the Chicana standpoint, here were tenacious, brave, and, above all, womanly warriors and leaders. A 1971 meeting that took place between Indo-Chinese women and Third World women in Vancouver, Canada, was for Chicana participants an occasion to record their positive impressions of their Vietnamese counterparts.

According to one Chicana attendee, the Vietnamese were physically delicate, "small, about five feet tall," but extraordinarily gracious, "humble and kind." Yet their apparent gentleness and fragility did not in any way compromise their political resolve. "One sister from South Vietnam . . . had been an ordinary housewife when she was arrested," the same participant noted. "When she was finally released (six years later) she became a dedicated fighter for her people."[55] To Chicanas, Vietnamese women appeared to be both feminine and, as fearless contributors to their struggle, equal to men. Perhaps that is why Vásquez y Longeaux, in a 1971 attempt to persuade Chicanas that their first loyalties remained to the Chicano Movement and not to "the white women's liberation movement," again depicted the Vietnamese woman as an exemplar. Exaggerating to make her point, she wrote, in a column entitled "Soy Chicana Primero" (I am first a Chicana), "We have seen the Vietnamese woman fight for survival with a gun in one hand and a child sucking on her breast on the other arm."[56] Notable for their acceptance of many traditional values, Chicana activists were going to be motherly, feminine, and heterosexual. These early writings by Chicanas nevertheless carved a space for women within a deeply patriarchal movement.

As women activists forcefully challenged their exclusion from the Chicano Movement's mainstream, moreover, their questioning inevitably extended to men's roles and ultimately demanded a revision of both machismo and patriotism. In a typical article, a Chicana college student flatly declared, "'machismo' is not proven by joining the armed forces." In the service, and especially in Vietnam, she wrote, the presumed fearlessness of Mexican Americans only awaited exploitation. The problem was not "machismo" per se, Corinne Sanchez argued, but where that male energy had been directed. She encouraged women in particular to persuade Chicanos that "manliness is a beautiful cultural concept that should be utilized for the betterment of our people not for the destruction of another people." At home, she wrote, men and women could work together to change "those institutions in this country that have oppressed our people."[57] The argument soon had male adherents. A male writer, dismayed at the injustices he confronted everyday in the barrio, likewise rejected the notion that Chicanos could prove themselves to be "real men" in the military. "You're not much of a man if you let your own people go hungry, live in poverty and get ripped off by this country," he asserted. "Our people need you to fight for our freedom right here." No longer willing to be a soldier, the writer furthermore wondered why the United States apparently valued him only in that role. "Dig man, something's wrong when you live in a country that offers people a better life in the Army than at home," he wrote.[58]

For Chicano activists, the domestic and international spheres had become inextricably connected. Protest against the Vietnam War strengthened an emerging anticolonial, anti-imperialist perspective among Chicano Movement participants that was rooted in their own experiences within the United States as well as their view of the world at large. As a pioneering historian of the Chicano experience pronounced in 1972, Chicanos constituted "a colonized people." Like other members of the Third World, like the Vietnamese, they had survived conquest, invasion, repression, and subsequent political and economic powerlessness.[59] Here was a radical revision of the relationship between Mexican Americans and majority society that contended that the ethnic group suffered second-rate citizenship, not as the result of any inherent shortcomings but as the logical consequence of Anglo-American racism, exploitation, and oppression. Therefore the burden did not fall upon people of Mexican descent to prove themselves worthy of first-class citizenship. To the contrary, by examining their plight in the American Southwest in relation to the war in Southeast Asia, Chicano Movement participants began to articulate criticisms about their status within the United States and that of Chicanas in relation to Chicanos. These reflections all but unraveled long-held notions of legitimacy based upon military service, whiteness, and masculinity.

As powerful as that tripod had been for earlier civil rights efforts, the Chicano Movement and, in particular, Chicano antiwar activism offered an alternative. The distance Chicanos and Chicanas had traveled politically was perhaps best captured again by Enriqueta Vásquez y Longeaux in a piece that was part of a special antiwar edition of *El Grito del Norte*. Published to coincide with the 29 August 1970 Chicano Moratorium demonstration, members of the newspaper staff brought several hundred copies of the paper to Los Angeles and distributed them among the thousands of Chicanos and Chicanas who had gathered to protest the war that day. In her antiwar article, Vásquez y Longeaux offered a new take on gender roles and patriotism. She urged men to fight for their *raza* in Aztlán, not Vietnam; she gave notice that Chicanas were no longer willing to suffer silently. Indicating the ethnic group's changing view on patriotism, she referred as much to the American invasion of Mexico as to the conflict in Vietnam. "We hear the first line of the Marine hymn . . . 'from the Halls of Moctezuma,'" she explained. "And we stop to wonder, 'What the hell were the Marines doing in the Halls of Moctezuma?'"[60]

Notes

1. The Brown Berets, founded in Los Angeles in 1967, were similar to the Black Panthers in endorsing paramilitary means to secure social change. The group became one of the most popular Chicano organizations, with dozens of chapters soon appearing across the country. Unlike the Panthers, who eventually espoused a revolutionary

socialism, the Brown Berets remained overwhelmingly cultural nationalist in orientation and saw protecting barrio residents from police abuse as one of their primary concerns.

2. *People's World*, 27 Dec. 1969, 1. I reserve the words "Chicano," "Chicana," and their respective plurals to describe participants in the movement and use "Mexican American" as a more general term. "Chicanas" always refers to women only, while "Chicanos" usually refers to men alone and, more rarely, to a mixed group of men and women. The word "Chicano" also appears as an adjective, as in "Chicano moratorium."

3. A partial list derived from Chicano press reports includes San Diego, Santa Barbara, San Francisco, Oakland, San Bernardino, Fresno, and Riverside, California; San Antonio, Austin, and Houston, Texas; and New York, Chicago, Denver, and the tiny border town of Douglas, Arizona.

4. The *Los Angeles Times*, 30 Aug. 1970, reported the lower figure, which apparently was based on police reports. Higher estimates appeared in *Regeneración* (Los Angeles), Dec. 1970, inside-page editorial "The Time Is Now," and *El Gallo* (Denver), Aug. 1970, date incorrectly listed as June 1970, p. 1. All Chicano Movement newspapers cited are on microfilm in the Ethnic Studies Library, University of California, Berkeley.

5. On the Chicano Movement, see Ignacio M. García, *Chicanismo: The Forging of a Militant Ethos among Mexican Americans* (Tucson: University of Arizona Press, 1997); Carlos Muñoz Jr., *Youth Identity and Power* (London: Verso, 1989); Marguerite V. Marin, *Social Protest in an Urban Barrio: A Study of the Chicano Movement* (Lanham, Md.: University Press of America, 1991); and Armando Navarro, *Mexican American Youth Organization: Avant-Garde of the Chicano Movement in Texas* (Austin: University of Texas Press, 1995). For an examination of the Chicano Movement in Los Angeles, see Ernesto Chavez, "Creating Aztlán: The Chicano Movement in Los Angeles" (Ph.D. diss., University of California, Los Angeles, 1994). An anthology of war-era writings edited and introduced by George Mariscal, *Aztlán and Viet Nam, Chicano and Chicana Experiences of the War* (Berkeley: University of California Press, 1999), is critical to understanding the Chicano experience at home and in Vietnam.

6. Martin Luther King Jr.'s 1967 speech "Beyond Vietnam" most famously captured African American concerns about the war. A copy of "Beyond Vietnam" can be found in box 1, folder 24, Social Protest Collection, Bancroft Library, University of California, Berkeley. For Asian American antiwar protest, see William Wei, *The Asian American Movement* (Philadelphia: Temple University Press, 1993), 38–41.

7. Mary L. Dudziak, "Josephine Baker, Racial Protest, and the Cold War," *Journal of American History* 81 (Sept. 1994): 543–71; Michael L. Krenn, *Black Diplomacy: African Americans and the State Department, 1945–1969* (Armonk, N.Y.: M. E. Sharpe, 1999); Brenda Gayle Plummer, *Rising Wind: Black Americans and U.S. Foreign Affairs, 1935–1960* (Chapel Hill: University of North Carolina Press, 1996); and Penny Von Eschen, *Race against Empire: Black Americans and Anticolonialism, 1937–1957* (Ithaca: Cornell University Press, 1997). The academic journal *Diplomatic History* 20 (Fall 1996) featured a symposium on "African American Affairs and U.S. Foreign Relations."

8. On the World War II monument's construction, see George Sánchez, *Becoming Mexican American* (New York: Oxford University Press, 1993), 274. For more information on Eugene Obregón, see Raul Morin, *Among the Valiant: Mexican-Americans in World War II and Korea* (Los Angeles: Borden Publishing, 1963), 260–61.

9. A list of Spanish-surnamed recipients, the vast majority of whom are of Mexican descent, includes twelve Congressional Medal of Honor recipients during World War II and eight Korean conflict recipients. *Hispanics in America's Defense* (Washington, D.C.: U.S. Department of Defense, 1990), 52–61.

10. Including Benjamin Márquez, *LULAC: The Evolution of a Mexican American Political Organization* (Austin: University of Texas Press, 1993); Mario T. García, *Mexican Americans: Leadership, Ideology, and Identity* (New Haven: Yale University Press, 1989), 25–61; Richard A. García, *Rise of the Mexican American Middle Class: San Antonio, 1929–1941* (College Station: Texas A&M University Press, 1991); and Cynthia E. Orozco, "The Origins of the League of United Latin American Citizens (LULAC) and the Mexican American Civil Rights Movement in Texas with an Analysis of Women's Political Participation in a Gendered Context, 1910–1929" (Ph.D. diss., University of California, Los Angeles, 1992).

11. Douglas Weeks, "The League of United Latin-American Citizens: A Texas-Mexican Civic Organization," *Southwestern Political and Social Science Quarterly* 10 (Dec. 1929): 264.

12. Cynthia E. Orozco, "Alice Dickerson Montemayor: Feminism and Mexican American Politics in the 1930s," in *Writing the Range: Race, Class, and Culture in the American Women's West*, ed. Elizabeth Jameson and Susan Armitage (Norman: University of Oklahoma Press, 1997), 436.

13. José Hernández Alvárez, *A Demographic Profile of the Mexican Immigration to the United States, 1910–1950* (Berkeley: International Population and Urban Research, 1966), 477; Carl Allsup, *The American G.I. Forum* (Austin: Center for Mexican American Studies, University of Texas, 1982); Henry A. J. Ramos, *The American GI Forum: In Pursuit of the Dream, 1948–1983* (Houston, Tex.: Arte Público Press, 1998).

14. Ramos, *The American GI Forum*, 6.

15. For an incisive critique of this strategy, see Neil Foley, "Becoming Hispanic: Mexican Americans and the Faustian Pact with Whiteness," in *Reflexiones 1997: New Directions in Mexican American Studies*, ed. Neil Foley (Austin: Center for Mexican American Studies, University of Texas, 1998).

16. Tomás Almaguer, *Racial Fault Lines: The Historical Origins of White Supremacy in California* (Berkeley: University of California Press, 1994), 189–202.

17. Mario T. García, *Mexican Americans*, 209–10; Sánchez, *Becoming Mexican American*, 245–49.

18. Mario T. García, *Mexican Americans*, 199–227; Mario T. García, *Memories of Chicano History: The Life and Narrative of Bert Corona* (Berkeley: University of California Press, 1994), 169–92.

19. Juan Gómez-Quiñones, *Chicano Politics: Reality and Promise* (Albuquerque: University of New Mexico Press, 1990), 63.

20. Allsup, *The American G.I. Forum*, 98. Ramos's estimates are higher; *The American GI Forum*, 28.

21. *Carta Editorial* (Los Angeles), 12 Oct. 1965, 4–5.

22. Plans for the 1965 march are mentioned in *Carta Editorial*, 23 Nov. 1965, 3. Newspaper clippings on the 1966 march from the *San Antonio Express News*, 2 July 1966, and *Corpus Christi Caller*, 3 July 1966, can be found in box 8, scrapbook 8.3, Dr. Hector P. Garcia Collection, Special Collections, Library, Texas A&M University, Corpus Christi.

23. *Carta Editorial*, 10 Aug. 1965, 1.

24. Mario T. García, *Memories of Chicano History*, 274.

25. "Mexican American United Conference: LA RAZA UNIDA," in box 13, folder 13, Ernesto Galarza Collection, Department of Special Collections, Stanford University, Stanford, Calif.

26. Guzmán's findings were published in *La Raza Yearbook* (Los Angeles), no. 13 (1968): 33, but were circulated among Mexican American and Chicano activists beforehand. A copy of Guzmán's report with the accompanying data can be found in box 2, folder 38, Social Protest Collection.

27. "Mexican American United Conference: LA RAZA UNIDA."

28. Julie Leininger Pycior, *LBJ and Mexican Americans: The Paradox of Power* (Austin: University of Texas Press, 1997), 154.

29. A dozen or so books, most by journalists, have been written about Cesar Chavez and the farm workers' struggle. One of the most recent is Susan Ferriss and Ricardo Sandoval, *The Fight in the Fields* (New York: Harcourt Brace, 1997). The Ferriss and Sandoval book is the companion volume to the 1997 film documentary of the same name produced by Rick Tejada-Flores and Ray Telles.

30. Peter Nabokov, *Tijerina and the Courthouse Raid* (Albuquerque: University of New Mexico Press, 1969); Richard Gardner, *Grito! Reies Tijerina and the New Mexico Land Grant War of 1967* (Indianapolis: Bobbs-Merrill Company, 1970).

31. Christine Marín, *A Spokesman of the Mexican American Movement: Rodolfo "Corky" Gonzales and the Fight for Chicano Liberation, 1966–1972* (San Francisco: R and E Research Associates, 1977).

32. The full text of *El plan espiritual de Aztlán* appears in F. Chris García, *Chicano Politics: Readings* (New York: MSS Information Corporation, 1973), 170–73. It is also available on line at ‹www.panam.edu/orgs/mecha/aztlan.html›, May 2002.

33. Ibid., 173.

34. Manuel G. Gonzales, *Mexicanos: A History of Mexicans in the United States* (Bloomington: Indiana University Press, 1999), 199; a 1968 oral history interview with Tijerina concerning his role in the Poor People's Campaign, labeled RJB 194, can be found in the Ralph J. Bunche Collection, Oral History Department of the Moorland-Spingarn Research Center, Howard University, Washington, D.C.

35. On the Chicano Movement and educational goals, see Muñoz, *Youth Identity and Power*. On third-party efforts, especially in Texas, see Ignacio M. García, *United We Win: The Rise and Fall of the Raza Unida Party* (Tucson: Mexican American Studies and Research Center, University of Arizona, 1989); Armando Navarro, *The Cristal Experiment: A Chicano Struggle for Community Control* (Madison: University of Wisconsin Press, 1998).

36. Lawrence M. Baskir and William A. Strauss, *Chance and Circumstance: The Draft, the War, and the Vietnam Generation* (New York: Knopf, 1978), 30–31; "Education and the Mexican American Community in Los Angeles County" (Sacramento: A Report of the California State Advisory Committee to the U.S. Commission on Civil Rights, Apr. 1968), 4. According to the 1960 census, the ethnic Mexican population in the United States in 1960 was 85 percent native-born. Leo Grebler, Joan W. Moore, and Ralph Guzmán, *The Mexican-American People: The Nation's Second Largest Minority* (New York: Macmillan, 1970), 117, 16, 30. Christian G. Appy, *Working-Class War* (Chapel Hill: University of North Carolina Press, 1993), 11–37.

37. Draft of a letter written to Lyndon Johnson, n.d., and letter written to Colonel Morris Schwartz, 9 July 1967, both in box 129, folder 61, Garcia Collection.

38. Author's oral interview with Rosalío U. Muñoz, Los Angeles, 15 and 28 May 1993, in the author's possession.

39. Author's oral history interview with Lea Ybarra, Fresno, Calif., 19 Jan. 1993, in

the author's possession; author's oral history interview with Nina Genera, Hayward, Calif., 12 Mar. 1997, in the author's possession. On Ybarra's eighteen cousins, see Gonzales, *Mexicanos*, 212.

40. Locations gathered and estimates obtained from Chicano Movement newspapers.

41. John Staples Shockley, *Chicano Revolt in a Texas Town* (Notre Dame: University of Notre Dame Press, 1974), 164.

42. Lorena Oropeza, "La batalla está aquí: Chicanos Oppose the War in Vietnam" (Ph.D. diss., Cornell University, 1996), 221–23; *Hard Times* (Washington, D.C.), 24–31 Aug. 1970, 1. Copy in author's possession.

43. Lea Ybarra and Nina Genera, *La batalla está aquí! Chicanos and the War* (El Cerrito, Calif.: Chicano Draft Help, 1970), 6–7.

44. Ibid., 6.

45. J. Jorge Klor de Alva, "Aztlán, Borinquen and Hispanic Nationalism," in *Aztlán: Essays on the Chicano Homeland*, ed. Rudolfo A. Anaya and Francisco Lomelí (Albuquerque, N.Mex.: Academia/El Norte Publications, 1989), 148.

46. *El plan espiritual de Aztlán* offers this translation.

47. From the preamble of *El plan espiritual de Aztlán*.

48. *Militant*, 24 July 1970, 7.

49. Rona M. Fields and Charles J. Fox, "The Brown Berets," in F. Chris García, *Chicano Politics: Readings*, 212.

50. *La Causa* (Los Angeles), 28 Feb. 1970, 9. For an in-depth exploration of the crossroads between nationalism and gender within the Chicano Movement, see Dionne Espinoza, "Pedagogies of Nationalism and Gender: Cultural Resistance in Selected Representational Practices of Chicana/o Movement Activists, 1967–1972" (Ph.D. diss., Cornell University, 1996). In a section entitled "'Concerned Chicanas' on Abortion," Espinoza examines several moments in which the Brown Beret paper, *La Causa*, addressed birth control.

51. Norma Cantú, "Women, Then and Now: An Analysis of the Adelita Image versus the Chicana as Political Writer and Philosopher," in *Chicana Voices: Intersections of Class, Race, and Gender*, ed. Teresa Córdova et al. (Austin: Center for Mexican American Studies, University of Texas, 1986); Elizabeth Salas, *Soldaderas in the Mexican Military: Myth and History* (Austin: University of Texas Press, 1990).

52. Espinoza argued that Vásquez y Longeaux sought "to place women at the center of the popular struggle." "Pedagogies of Nationalism and Gender," 169.

53. Author's oral history interview with Enriqueta Vásquez y Longeaux, San Cristobal, N.Mex., 28 June 1997.

54. "The Mexican-American Woman," reprinted in Robin Morgan, *Sisterhood Is Powerful* (New York: Random House, 1970), 432.

55. *El Grito del Norte* (Española, N.Mex.), 5 June 1971, p. K.

56. Ibid., 26 Apr. 1971, 11, 14.

57. *El Alacrán* (Long Beach, Calif.), 15 June 1970, 4.

58. "From El Barrio to Viet Nam," *El Barrio*, 1970.

59. Rodolfo Acuña, *Occupied America: The Chicano's Struggle for Liberation* (San Francisco: Canfield Press, 1972), 1–3.

60. *El Grito del Norte*, 29 Aug. 1970, 2.

From Cold War to Global Interdependence

The Political Economy of African
American Antiapartheid
Activism, 1968–1988

For most of the post–World War II era diverse groups of African Americans contested U.S. collusion with white supremacist regimes in southern Africa. Yet, scholarly analysis of those movements emphasizes black efforts to influence U.S. policy in response to crisis events such as the 1960 Sharpeville massacre and the Soweto uprisings in 1976. The focus on specific episodes in foreign policy management obscures how the long-term maintenance of apartheid relied on a matrix of international economic, social, political, and ideological arrangements, and how the fragility of those relationships presented new obstacles, opportunities, and resources for opposition movements.

This essay explores African American mobilization against apartheid and its response to structural transformations in advanced capitalist society. It contends that major societal changes created new opportunities to challenge state and corporate policy and to develop better explanations of U.S. connections to the production and distribution of wealth and poverty in southern Africa. Favorable circumstances helped expand possibilities for transnational citizen activism.

For more than a decade, scholars across a range of disciplines have devoted considerable attention to African American efforts to influence foreign affairs.[1] This trend counters perspectives that confine the study of transnational political activities by black Americans to "back-to-Africa" or "cultural identity" movements. Recent studies have identified a considerable and sustained African American group interest in the world beyond America's shores,[2] but much of the research concentrates on the first half of the twentieth century. Little assessment has been made of how increased levels of global interdependence since the early 1970s have shaped the direction of black American foreign affairs endeavors.

This essay explores major changes in African American politicization over southern Africa from the early 1970s through the mid-1980s. Growing awareness of southern African issues was not only a function of transition in conventional U.S. politics, but was also the outcome of a process wherein increased global interdependence accelerated postindustrial economic restructuring and set in motion new resources, actors, and goals for mobilization.

For more than a century, small groups of citizens with civil rights and humanitarian concerns organized to challenge the collaboration of the federal government and U.S. business enterprises with the brutal racist system in South Africa.[3] These groups were unable, however, to sustain protest campaigns or gain more than symbolic access to policy-making arenas until the mid-1970s. Their failures were due primarily to a lack of resources and access. Dominant economic and political power relationships effectively confined racial equality issues, whether originating at home or abroad, to the margins of policy-making processes. The U.S. interest articulation system, consisting of not only the institutions of government but also political parties, interest groups, and attentive publics, provided little, if any, space for civil rights and humanitarian concerns to penetrate policy-making venues. In a society deeply immersed in racial hierarchy, black efforts to inject African diaspora issues met with harsh resistance.

Even after World War II, when demands for racial equality acquired a degree of sustained public visibility, a succession of African crisis events failed to gain policy or protest momentum. The 1948 South African elections that brought the Nationalist Party to power and rigidly institutionalized racial inequality, the 1953 Defiance Campaign, and the Sharpeville massacre of unarmed black protesters in 1960 barely made ripples beyond the small Africanist community in the United States. Growing but largely invisible economic, political, ideological, and strategic relationships between the United States and South Africa effectively kept antiapartheid protest from entering the policy-making process.[4]

The 1960s, a decade characterized by worldwide social and political turmoil, was a major turning point for African American antiapartheid activism. Following passage of the Civil Rights Act of 1964 and the Voting Rights Act of 1965, civil rights activists increasingly turned their attention from the rural South to the urban North, and toward economic opportunity. A discourse that brought in the larger nation often invited comparisons with Third World societies. By 1965 Student Nonviolent Coordinating Committee (SNCC) activists had already begun to mobilize opposition to U.S. involvement in Southeast Asia, and by 1967 Southern Christian Leadership Conference (SCLC) director Martin Luther King Jr. publicly announced his opposition to the war in Vietnam. On the one hand, new concerns gained entry through established mechanisms such as political parties, legislative bodies, and administrative agencies at the federal, state, and local levels. On the other hand, new spaces opened as social movement behavior became varied and increasingly emulated the marketing practices of established civic organizations, charities, and other special interest groups. Protest organizations also began to engage mainstream society on the terrain of culture through the conventional routes of picketing, lobbying, and boycott.[5]

In the 1970s Americans faced the global energy crisis and other widely experienced economic uncertainties in what sociologist Anthony Giddens refers to as "world time," shared cross-national experiences that illuminate how actions taken in one country have rapid effects elsewhere.[6] Disruptions arising from external security commitments, dependence on imported oil, and industrial decline heightened awareness of internationally linked concerns. Daily experiences of travel, information, educational exchange, and entertainment refined a consciousness of global interdependence, while simultaneously raising questions about the U.S. role in it. Interdependence heightened the salience of African problems and shaped the temporal opportunities available for activism in American politics. By hastening the collapse of barriers between domestic and foreign politics, the process enhanced the power and legitimacy of African American group interaction with international issues.[7]

The post–World War II welfare state apparatus had provided a foundation for the stabilization of major conflicts that had previously disrupted capitalist production.[8] The enlarged reach of the state, however, seldom proceeded without challenge or interruption. Administrative and fiscal requirements for optimizing private capital accumulation while simultaneously providing for basic needs and maintaining formal democratic traditions invariably stimulated public debate about the collective means and ends. The state is consequently illuminated as a critical "site of contestation."[9] The power of the state after 1945 lay less in traditional instruments of control, such as a monopoly on the use of force and violence, but increasingly on "soft power," or the capacity to legitimate the claims of other actors, and preserve and extend its own legitimacy.[10] The antiapartheid movement emerged within the context of complex state-society interactions that responded to postindustrial transformation and global interdependence. Three elements of this process bear close examination: structural economic changes that magnified the value of critical expertise, the expansion of the sociodemographic base of activism, and the diffusion of resources and constituencies across national borders.

Scholars widely acknowledge the impact of scientific and technological advances on economic growth, but only recently have they devoted significant attention to how these developments affect group and social movement formation. Mayer Zald contends that the rise of the environmental protection and antinuclear movements responds to the negative externalities of industrial growth.[11] Karl-Werner Brand maintains that cultural critiques of modernity, which historically accompany periods of modernization, have multiplied in post–World War II Western societies.[12] Similarly, Timothy Luke argues that critical intellectuals play vital roles in information-based society.[13] These studies suggest that the politicization of expertise, whether in the form of extensive knowledge of subjects unfamiliar to laypersons, or the ability to define issues and evaluate facts, or intervention skills that can disrupt conventional decision making, enhances alternative group efforts to gain access to public forums and policy-making arenas.

The development of African studies in the United States illustrates how critical expertise develops linkages to a social movement. The postwar revitalization of area studies, largely funded by major foundations and the U.S. government, evolved from the need to improve U.S. institutional capacity to address rapid decolonization. Graduate programs, fellowships, curriculum revision, research and travel funds, conferences, professional associations, and journal outlets created and sustained networks of professional Africanists. The field included scholars from a range of social science disciplines, the humanities, and applied sciences. Africanists helped make Americans aware of Africa and provided empirical corroboration of the claims that antiapartheid activists made.[14]

The major growth stage of African studies programs occurred between 1960 and 1970, an era that preceded the proliferation of southern African liberation movements. By 1970 more than thirty programs offered advanced degrees in African studies, and nearly fifty other institutions provided undergraduate majors or concentrations in African studies.[15] The growth of the field, and the heightened visibility of African development as a policy issue, established an identity for professional Africanists that distinguished them from earlier generations of Americans with interests in Africa.[16] While the field produced no consensus about the mission of African studies in the United States, its intellectual vitality was an essential cause of the Africanist constituency's growing credibility with officialdom.[17]

Africanists began to experience regular opportunities for applying their critical expertise to policy issues in 1969 when Michigan representative Charles Diggs assumed the chair of the House Subcommittee on Africa. His leadership, chiefly evident in hearings that focused on U.S. policy toward southern Africa, provided a crucial opportunity for antiapartheid advocates to develop stronger links with those segments of the policy-making community that opposed the Nixon administration's rapprochement with the settler-dominated states in the region. Congressional hearings provided an occasion for newly minted experts to express their views and demonstrate the policy salience of their proficiency. The subcommittee became more active after 1969 and expanded the range of witnesses whose testimony it heard. Antiapartheid groups and academic Africanists especially benefited from this opening.

The changing character of the witness pool also reflects the enhanced role of committee staff, a result of the congressional reorganization of the early 1970s. Since 1973, the staff director of the Subcommittee on Africa and the majority of the five-person staff have been academically trained Africanists.[18] The evolution of the subcommittee's posture from passive to active provided a site for expanding the policy audience and increasing the perceived legitimacy of antiapartheid perspectives.[19]

The increased visibility of human rights groups in the policy-making community coincided with the unfolding of specific crises in U.S. relations with southern African countries and augmented the human rights component of antiapartheid activism. In addition to offering their testimony at congressional committee hearings, human rights groups provided legal assistance to southern African refugees seeking political asylum in the United States. They channeled financial and legal resources to attorneys representing South African political dissidents, challenged the legality of the South African government's commercial ventures in the United States, and initiated litigation to force U.S. courts to recognize international human rights laws.[20]

While Africanist human rights advocacy can be traced to the late nineteenth century in the United States, its growing social acceptance and political influence can be traced to the postwar growth of higher education, especially in fields such as area studies and international law. This provided the foundation for the professionalization of advocacy groups that continues to the present. Employment of graduates of African studies programs generated concentrations of skilled professional internationalists, in close proximity to policy-making institutions in Washington, D.C., and New York City, and near state capitals and college communities nationwide.[21]

The expansion of the sociodemographic base of social movements also derives from the character of the postindustrial, globally interdependent political economy. Traditionally, social movement scholars focused on "at risk" populations as the base for social movement formation. At-risk groups consisted of those segments of the population perceived as most vulnerable to fluctuations in the economy, or those experiencing low levels of social mobility and assimilation. Social scientists also distinguished between beneficiary constituencies—those who would benefit directly from the achievement of movement objectives—and conscience constituencies, supportive participants motivated by the desire to alleviate the suffering of aggrieved populations.[22] Three major sociodemographic changes contributed to the blurring of distinctions between these constituencies and thus extended the number of people who could be mobilized for social movement activity. These changes caused a shift in the racial-ethnic character of the population, increased rates of female participation in the labor force and in higher education, and led to the breakdown of the linear life course.[23]

The changing racial composition of postwar society significantly abetted the efforts of previously marginalized minorities such as African Americans, Latinos, Asian Americans, and Native Americans to legitimate their social and cultural claims and gain access to the ballot and other forms of political power. The politicization of racial-ethnic minorities, especially in urban areas and in regions with significant concentrations of non-European immigrants, led to the creation of new coalitions and collective self-definitions.[24] Groups emerged within those communities that claimed affinity with their countries of origin. African Americans, for example, used the electoral gains of the civil rights era to form organizations focused on African and Caribbean affairs.[25]

Women's increasing involvement in the labor force and in higher education brought activities, conflicts, and concerns previously confined to the margins of the economy to the center. The women's movement contested traditional patterns of exclusion in professional, clerical, and blue-collar workplaces.[26] Women joined and assisted in the redefinition of workplace agendas and the creation of new norms and standards of behavior in many of these settings. Women's ample representation as leaders in antiapartheid organizations from campus divestment groups to research and policy organizations, and the staff of the House Subcommittee on Africa, demonstrates how gender concerns penetrated movement constituencies.[27]

Changes in linear life course expectations of men and women furnished additional possibilities for enlarging the base of social movements. The one-career, one-marriage imperative, long identified as fundamental to industrial society, became problematic when new professional, social, and personal growth opportunities failed to synchronize smoothly with established custom. Prolonged and interrupted career preparation; delayed or altered family formation; reliance on part-time, temporary, or cyclical employment; flexible work and leisure time; and greater concentrations of skilled urban workers and professionals increased the potential membership base for social movements just when the American workplace was adjusting to changes wrought by globalization.[28] New demands in the workplace and at home enabled substantial segments of the population to channel more time into nonelectoral political activity.

One of the most significant by-products of global interdependence is the cross-fertilization of social movements. As such problems as economic and social inequality, human rights abuse, and environmental degradation assumed global dimensions, social movements in different parts of the world experienced greater opportunities to share ideas, resources, strategies, and symbols.[29] Technological developments in media and information dissemination make it possible for movements in one nation to have demonstration effects on citizens in other countries, and to reinforce relationships and networks that emerge from professional, educational, cultural, and political interactions.[30] U.S. antiapartheid activists relied heavily on long-term relationships with southern African liberation movements, as well as alliances with European antiapartheid organizations.[31] More recently, technological innovations played a substantial role in facilitating social movement growth as organizations adopted new techniques of fund-raising and constituency identification. The use of professional fund-raisers, canvassers, and telephone solicitation increased the potential base of support. The computer revolution facilitated use of mass-marketing techniques and enhanced the capacity to target appeals to specific audiences.[32]

These changes have led social scientists to revise the way they study social movements and have encouraged a shift from viewing them as isolated phenomena to analyzing the totality of group activity in society. Garner and Zald argue that overlapping and interrelated social movements in advanced industrial societies constitute a social movement sector.[33] It is clear that antiapartheid activism did not emerge in a vacuum. Major structural changes within the global system gave new groups and interests access to the international community.

It is ironic that the presidency of Richard Nixon coincides with one of the most critical growth stages of the African American constituency for southern Africa. Nixon had campaigned on the restoration of "law and order" at home and abroad. His administration empowered domestic law enforcement agencies to more rigorously control dissent. Nixon enacted a "Southern strategy" of reduced civil rights enforcement while simultaneously escalating the war in Southeast Asia.[34] He incorporated Africa more completely in his version of containment policy with National Security Study Memorandum

(NSSM) no. 39, secretly labeled the "Tar Baby" option. This policy advocated closer ties to the white settler governments in South Africa and Rhodesia, and with the Portuguese colonial governments of Angola and Mozambique.

Nixon's presidential victory represented a substantial obstacle to anti-apartheid activists, but the 1968 congressional elections created more favorable opportunities for them in two key areas. The first occurred when the 91st Congress opened and Michigan Democrat Charles C. Diggs became chair of the House Subcommittee on Africa. Diggs, the first African American to head the subcommittee, aggressively used it as a forum where antiapartheid issues could develop. He called numerous hearings on issues such as UN sanctions against Rhodesia, U.S. business involvement in South Africa, and political repression in both states. As chair, Diggs conducted fact-finding missions in southern Africa and regularly invited antiapartheid groups, civil rights and human rights organizations, Africanist scholars, and African liberation groups to participate in subcommittee proceedings.

The second area was the formation of the Congressional Black Caucus (CBC) in 1971, which institutionalized the black presence in Congress. African American congressional representation jumped from four members in 1960 to thirteen in 1971. Although domestic policy concerns dominated the CBC's agenda, its participation in the multiplying constituency for Africa further legitimated the foreign policy interests of African Americans. The establishment of the CBC coincided with a series of reforms in the congressional committee system that increased professional staff size and resources and improved support services such as the Congressional Research Service. These changes enabled legislators to challenge more effectively the powers of the executive branch.[35]

One of the most effective antiapartheid mobilization campaigns emanating from the African American community unfolded in 1970 when black employees at the Polaroid Corporation headquarters in Cambridge, Massachusetts, formed the Polaroid Revolutionary Workers' Movement (PRWM). Black employees had discovered that Polaroid produced and processed the film that the South African government used to photograph Africans for the internal passports that all blacks had to carry. PRWM exposed the company's segregated labor practices in South Africa and organized a boycott of Polaroid products. The organization succeeded at pressuring Polaroid to improve working conditions at its South African plants and offer 500 scholarships to black South African students.[36]

Southern Africa appeared prominently on the agenda of numerous black organizations in the early 1970s, including the Congress of African People, the Africa Information Service, the African American Scholars Council, the

African Heritage Studies Association, and the Pan-African Liberation Committee.[37] The National Black Political Convention, held in Gary, Indiana, in March 1972, devoted considerable attention to U.S. policy toward South Africa. The convention produced an uneasy coalition between black elected officials, particularly the CBC, and black nationalist and community-based activists. The African Liberation Support Committee (ALSC), which organized African Liberation Day marches in Washington, D.C., and thirty other cities around the nation in 1972 and 1973, originated from the convention.[38]

Black dockworkers played an active role in mobilizing opposition to U.S. collaboration with the colonial states in southern Africa during this period. In 1972 dockworkers, with students from Southern University, led demonstrations in Burnside, Louisiana, against the unloading of ships carrying Rhodesian chrome. Similar actions unfolded in Boston, New York, Philadelphia, and Baltimore from fall 1973 to spring 1974.[39] While many of these groups and efforts were short-lived, they organized the latent elements of the black constituency for Africa into a more expressive voice for policy change. Efforts to build a viable black foreign policy constituency benefited from Nixon's containment orientation in several ways. The administration's intolerance of liberal proposals in both domestic and foreign policy forced black elected officials and community-based activists to consolidate their resources to be more effective. Africa Day celebrations in the early 1970s and the African Liberation Support Committee resulted from such pressure.

Southern Africa mobilization coincided with dramatic increases in black student enrollment in higher education, growing black entry into the professions, and an explosion in public interest group activity. Each of these developments reinforced the base of potentially mobilizable persons whose age, education, occupation, and ideological outlook might incline them to examine critically U.S. foreign policy.[40] The administration's tilt toward the white settler states in southern Africa, though not immediately evident as a coherent strategy, additionally supplied a clear target for critics of Nixon's domestic and foreign policies.

Historically, American policy toward Africa has been confined to the margins of public discourse. For brief periods in the mid-1970s, however, southern Africa emerged as a surrogate arena of U.S.-Soviet rivalry. The collapse of the Portuguese dictatorship in early 1974 and the interim government's decision to dismantle its nearly 500-year hold on Angola and Mozambique unleashed a flurry of international activity that undermined Nixon administration assumptions about southern Africa's connection to U.S. global containment strategy. The eruption of civil wars in Angola and Mozambique, and the rise of a credible threat to the white settler government in Rhodesia, combined with the Soweto uprisings in South Africa, brought unprecedented public and official attention to the region. Better policies on southern Africa were clearly needed.[41]

Political turmoil in Africa unexpectedly penetrated the 1976 presidential campaign and forced candidates from the two major parties to address it. Both parties attempted to cultivate a black foreign policy audience. In the Republican primaries, incumbent President Gerald Ford faced a major challenge from former California governor Ronald Reagan. Reagan exploited conservative anxieties about racial conflict in southern Africa to revive his faltering campaign during a series of primaries in southern states.[42] In fact, some analysts attributed Reagan's Texas primary victory to an electorate alarmed that the Ford administration had sacrificed the interests of Rhodesian whites.[43] While Ford eventually won the nomination in a close race, the ruptures that Reagan created between party moderates and conservatives reinforced a sense of urgency for the incumbent. It was against this backdrop of party division and declining popular support that Secretary of State Henry Kissinger attempted to attract a black foreign policy audience for President Ford by initiating a series of meetings with civil rights groups. Like John F. Kennedy's surrogate use of Africa in the 1960 campaign to entice black voters,[44] Kissinger delivered major speeches on Africa policy to the National Urban League and the Philadelphia-based Opportunities Industrial Corporation. He arranged private meetings with black leaders such as Reverend Jesse Jackson and Manhattan Borough president Percy Sutton. Just as the administration's belated arrival on the southern Africa scene handicapped its efforts to address regional complexities, however, appeals to black Americans lagged behind those of Democratic candidate Jimmy Carter.

The electoral salience of southern Africa's racial conflicts for the black electorate proved auspicious for Carter. Running as an outsider to the Washington establishment, the one-term Georgia governor did not develop substantial black support beyond his home state until midway through the primaries. The turning point came in Florida as black voters mobilized to derail the campaign of former Alabama governor and arch-segregationist George Wallace. Carter defeated Wallace, and the overwhelming support he received from black voters led to refinements in his campaign strategy for appealing to African American communities.[45] Carter was endorsed by black southern politicians such as Congressman Andrew Young and Martin Luther King Sr., father of the slain civil rights activist, and strengthened his claim on the rhetoric of the civil rights movement and the New South simultaneously.[46]

A short-term strategy thus positioned Carter to exploit three critical elements that could influence the election outcome: a black electorate enlarged by the Voting Rights Act of 1965; greater black interest in foreign affairs; and Kissinger's continuing failure to reduce racial tensions in southern Africa. In the wake of Kissinger's miscalculated "realism," Carter's "moralism" in diplomacy captured the attention of those who were critical of past U.S. approaches to southern Africa.[47] In contrast to the Republican Party's reluctance to deal directly with race, Carter embraced the civil rights experience and black community interest in foreign affairs as tools for sharpening America's focus on Africa. "It would be a great help to this nation if people in public life were to be made aware of the problems of Africa through a significant Black interest in Africa," he claimed. "Americans might not have made the mistakes we made in Vietnam had there been an articulate Vietnamese minority in our midst."[48]

Overtures by the presidential candidates to the African American community followed a series of diverse measures undertaken by activists at the local and national levels to force change in policy toward southern Africa. A coalition of organizations, including ALSC, mobilized in support of the Angolan liberation movement forces. Groups of black public-sector employees across the country, especially in cities with majority black populations such as Detroit, Michigan, and Gary, Indiana, threatened to withdraw pension funds from financial institutions involved in South Africa to express their desire for divestment.[49]

The strongest organizational expression of African American interest in foreign affairs occurred in the fall of 1976 when the CBC convened the Black Leadership Conference on Southern Africa. More than 100 attendees represented black churches, civil rights and labor organizations, and elected officials. The group produced a document criticizing U.S. policy toward the region, and outlined an eleven-point plan for improvement of American–Southern African relations. Conferees laid the foundations for establishing TransAfrica, the first mass-based black foreign policy lobby, in July 1977.[50] TransAfrica provided an organizational presence, a research and lobbying staff, and improved access to congressional committees and the Washington, D.C., diplomatic community. Andrew Young, one of the founders, became U.S. ambassador to the United Nations during the Carter administration.

The first two Carter years heightened expectations that the foreign policy concerns of African Americans would become more thoroughly incorporated into the policy-making machinery. In addition to Andrew Young, the administration brought in African Americans with expertise on African decolonization issues as top officials. They included Donald McHenry, who was Young's deputy secretary; Goler Teal Butcher, director of the Africa Division of the Agency for International Development (AID); and George Moose, assistant secretary of state for Africa in the Department of State. The House reconvened the Subcommittee on Africa, with Charles Diggs as chair. The flurry of renewed activity on southern Africa during the first six months included a National Security Council review of Africa policy, meetings between Vice President Walter Mondale and South African prime minister John Vorster, Young's extensive African tour, and Secretary of State Cyrus Vance's speech at the annual National Association for the Advancement of Colored People meeting.[51]

Carter officials maintained a barrage of rhetoric on racial inequality in southern Africa, but few substantive changes in policy resulted. During the latter half of his term, the president's preoccupation with Soviet and Cuban support for Marxist regimes in Africa rationalized his accommodation to a more familiar Cold War containment approach to the region. Additionally, the Washington climate for reform on southern Africa policy began to erode as several liberal senators, most notably Dick Clark (D.-Iowa), were defeated in the midterm elections. Diggs was forced to resign as a result of a political scandal, and Carter dismissed Young after public revelations about his secret meetings with Palestine Liberation Organization (PLO) officials.[52]

In sharp contrast to Carter, who had campaigned in 1976 on the theme of greater openness to the international community, Reagan rode into the White House on a mandate to reassert U.S. military dominance and roll back the gains of Third World liberation forces. Unlike Young and McHenry, who devoted considerable effort to invalidating South Africa, Jeanne Kirkpatrick, Reagan's ambassador to the UN, advocated a positive relationship with Pretoria. She believed that the United States could not work with Marxist states, which she labeled totalitarian. South Africa, which she termed authoritarian, presented no such problem, as "racist dictatorship is not as bad as Marxist dictatorship."[53]

Chester Crocker, who had contributed to Nixon's NSSM no. 39, became assistant secretary of state for Africa, and authored its constructive engagement policy. He urged Americans to consider the needs and insecurities of whites before endorsing demands for majority rule.[54] In addition to accepting South Africa as an "authoritarian" state, the administration envisioned increasing Pretoria's role in the Western defense system.[55] From the Reagan administration's perspective, the existence of systematic racial discrimination was insufficient evidence for dismantling apartheid. Like Nixon's relaxed stance toward the settler states a decade earlier, Reagan's outlook saw white South Africans as a force of stability and of Western values and institutions.

From the latter half of Carter's term to the beginning of the Reagan administration, the depth and range of foreign policy access enjoyed by the

African American community declined significantly. In contrast to the early Nixon years, when the embryonic black constituency for Africa embraced a set of lobbying strategies designed to secure greater access to policy-making institutions, the hostility of the Reagan White House forced the channeling of energies back to the grass roots. TransAfrica, for example, began to work closely with black community groups in cities such as Chicago and Boston and to endorse their agendas on a range of domestic and foreign policy issues.[56] This electoral activism assisted in placing mayors such as Harold Washington of Chicago in office and refining the alliances among groups that favored a policy change in southern Africa.

Another potent tool in the antiapartheid arsenal was the entertainment industry. African American popular culture has enjoyed worldwide currency, and South Africa was no exception. The cultural boycott wing of the movement confronted South Africa's efforts to induce American athletes and entertainers to perform there. Booking agents working on behalf of the republic often targeted black artists specifically, for their presence seemingly offered a degree of legitimacy to the government's cosmetic reforms. Groups such as the Patrice Lumumba Coalition, African Jazz Artist Society and Studies (AJASS), and the United Nations Centre against Apartheid in New York City successfully countered this ploy by organizing domestic boycotts of artists who yielded to Pretoria's blandishments.

The publicity associated with entertainers helped spike black community interest in the antiapartheid movement. When large, guaranteed paychecks enticed popular recording artists such as Ray Charles, the O'Jays, the Temptations, Roberta Flack, and Stephanie Mills, boycott activists created the Coalition to End Cultural Collaboration with South Africa. Coalition leaders realized that the failure to exploit fully the cultural arm had restricted access to potentially significant constituencies. "We think this can be a very good organizing tool," Elombe Brath, cochair of the Patrice Lumumba Coalition, contended, "a process of raising people's consciousness about the situation in South Africa—to try to inform these musicians and the general public. We think this is very important, particularly in the case of youth, and most particularly in the case of Black youth, who often don't have a consciousness around South Africa. They worship these stars, know all about them, how much money they make, how many clothes they have, everything. When they come to a concert they see their particular star is being boycotted. About what? About South Africa? What's so wrong about South Africa? And they start to see."[57]

On the surface, the sheer magnitude of the entertainment industry made the tasks confronting the coalition overwhelming. Through a combination of

"No Apartheid in
Sports! Stop the
Fight!" Demonstra-
tors in New York City
protest NBC's telecast
of a Pretoria boxing
match in 1979. (From
Southern Africa,
1979)

assimilative and confrontational strategies, however, the coalition effectively
derailed efforts to marshal talent in the service of apartheid. It created an
artists' relations committee that worked with musicians, record companies,
and radio broadcasters to inform them about apartheid and the role that
African American performers were to play in it. Artists such as Roberta
Flack, Phyllis Hyman, Gladys Knight, and Third World canceled previously
scheduled engagements, while the O'Jays ended their brief tour early and
agreed to sponsor a conference encouraging others to join the boycott.

African American artists Ray Charles, Stephanie Mills, and Millie Jackson
resisted coalition appeals and honored their contractual obligations to South
Africa, thus becoming boycott targets. Boycotts focused on club rather than
concert hall performances because the former depended on selling food and
drink to patrons after the purchase of tickets, while the latter used advance
sales. Because club operators arranged performance schedules through re-

gional and national circuits, the coalition could identify and target specific venues as well as performers.[58]

One of the most innovative antiapartheid strategies was unveiled in late 1984, just weeks after Reagan's landslide reelection victory over Democratic challenger Walter Mondale. On 21 November TransAfrica launched the Free South Africa Movement (FSAM). The FSAM was a broad coalition of antiapartheid organizations, elected officials, labor unions, and student, civil rights, and church groups that successfully orchestrated a series of publicized arrests outside the South African Embassy and at other sites around the country. Over a five-month period, more than 3,000 Americans, including members of Congress, were arrested at these demonstrations. Nationwide collegiate divestment drives meanwhile provided a concrete focus that allowed the movement to capitalize on public concern over repression in South Africa. TransAfrica was a catalyst in appropriating civil rights movement tactics to arouse public memory of racial oppression, and linking the past to the current violence that Reagan administration foreign policies condoned and supported.

This essay has suggested that the African American constituency involved with southern Africa has evolved considerably over the past fifty years. The evolution is a product of the dynamic relationship between the black community's economic and political viability, the volatility of the domestic interest articulation structure, and official public interpretations of the salience of southern African problems to U.S. global interests. A more thorough understanding of this nexus can result from posing new questions that divert attention from single groups or individual activists. Instead, we might ask how increases in social-class stratification and geographical dispersion affect the African American community's organizational resources and prospects. How will the changing composition of the African American population, that is, the ratio of U.S.-born to Africa- or Caribbean-descended, alter perceptions of diaspora interests? How will the absence of threats clearly identifiable as racist influence activist strategies and tactics? In addressing these issues, we begin to understand how groups mobilize and explain victories and defeats. We can learn how change can sometimes occur even when unanticipated, and how activists can sometimes effect transformations in institutions and nations that lay beyond their direct reach.

Notes

1. Benjamin Bowser, "Blacks and U.S. Foreign Policy," *Sage Race Relations Abstracts* 12, 1 (Feb. 1987): 1–20; David Dickson, "American Society and the African American Foreign Policy Lobby: Constraints and Opportunities," *Journal of Black Studies* 27 (Nov. 1996): 139–51.

2. Brenda Gayle Plummer, *Rising Wind: Black Americans and U.S. Foreign Affairs, 1935–1960* (Chapel Hill: University of North Carolina Press, 1996); Charles P. Henry, *Foreign Policy and the Black (Inter)national Interest* (Albany: SUNY Press, 2000).

3. Elliott P. Skinner, *African Americans and U.S. Policy toward Africa, 1850–1924: In Defense of Black Nationality* (Washington, D.C.: Howard University Press, 1992); F. Chidozie Ogene, *Interest Groups and the Shaping of Foreign Policy: Four Case Studies of United States African Policy* (New York: St. Martin's Press, 1983).

4. Ogene, *Interest Groups and the Shaping of Foreign Policy.*

5. Michael McCann, *Taking Reform Seriously* (Ithaca: Cornell University Press, 1986).

6. Anthony Giddens, *The Constitution of Society* (Berkeley: University of California Press, 1984).

7. Warren Magnusson, "The Reification of Political Community," in *Contending Sovereignties: Redefining Political Community*, ed. R. B. J. Walker and Saul H. Mendlovitz (Boulder: Lynne Rienner, 1990), 52.

8. Fred Block, *Revising State Theory: Essays in Politics and Postindustrialism* (Philadelphia: Temple University Press, 1987).

9. Fred Block, *Postindustrial Possibilities: A Critique of Economic Discourse* (Berkeley: University of California Press, 1990).

10. Joseph Nye Jr., *Bound to Lead: The Changing Nature of American Power* (New York: Basic Books, 1990), chap. 6; Charles Tilly, *From Mobilization to Revolution* (Reading, Mass.: Addison-Wesley, 1978).

11. Mayer N. Zald, "The Trajectory of Social Movements in America," *Research in Social Movements, Conflicts and Change* 10 (1988): 25.

12. Karl-Werner Brand, "Cyclical Aspects of New Social Movements: Waves of Cultural Criticism and Mobilization Cycles of New Middle-Class Radicalism," in *Challenging the Political Order*, ed. Russell J. Dalton and Manfred Kuechler (New York: Oxford University Press, 1990), 23; Frances McCrea and Gerald Markle, "Atomic Scientists and Protests," *Research in Social Movements, Conflict and Change* 11 (1989): 219–33.

13. Timothy W. Luke, *Screens of Power: Ideology, Domination, and Resistance in Informational Society* (Urbana: University of Illinois Press, 1989), 207–39.

14. Kevin Danaher, *Beyond Safaris: A Guide to Building People-to-People Ties with Africa* (Trenton, N.J.: Africa World Press, 1991).

15. *Directory of African and Afro-American Studies Programs*, 7th ed. (Waltham, Mass.: Crossroads Press, 1987); Jane Guyer, *African Studies in the United States: A Perspective* (n.p.: African Studies Association Press, 1996).

16. Pearl T. Robinson and Elliott P. Skinner, eds., *Transformation and Resiliency in Africa* (Washington, D.C.: Howard University Press, 1983), 3–26.

17. Martin Staniland, "Who Needs African Studies?," *African Studies Review* 26 (Sept.–Dec. 1983): 77–97.

18. *Congressional Staff Directory* (Mt. Vernon, Va.: Congressional Staff Directory Limited, 1958–90).

19. James A. Thurber, "Dynamics of Policy Subsystems in American Politics," in *Interest Group Politics*, ed. Allan J. Cigler and Burdett A. Loomis, 3rd ed. (Washington, D.C.: Congressional Quarterly Press, 1991), 330–33.

20. Howard Tolley Jr., "Interest Group Litigation to Enforce Human Rights," *Political Science Quarterly* 105, 4 (1990–91): 620–23.

21. Edward Berman, *The Influence of the Carnegie, Ford, and Rockefeller Founda-*

tions on American Foreign Policy: The Ideology of Philanthropy (Albany: SUNY Press, 1983); Robert McCaughey, *International Studies and Academic Enclosure* (New York: Columbia University Press, 1984); McCann, *Taking Reform Seriously*.

22. John McCarthy and Mayer Zald, "Resource Mobilization and Social Movements: A Partial Theory," *American Journal of Sociology* 82 (May 1977): 1212–39.

23. Block, *Postindustrial Possibilities*, 10.

24. Zald, "The Trajectory of Social Movements," 28.

25. Elliott P. Skinner, "African American Perspectives on Foreign Policy," in *From Exclusion to Inclusion: The African American Struggle for Political Power*, ed. Linda F. Williams and Ralph Gomes (Westport, Conn.: Greenwood Press, 1992), 173–86.

26. Guida West and Rhoda Blumberg, *Women and Social Protest* (New York: Oxford University Press, 1990); Anne Costain, "Social Movements as Interest Groups: The Case of the Women's Movement," in *The Politics of Interests: Interest Groups Transformed*, ed. Mark P. Petracca (Boulder: Westview Press, 1992), 285–807.

27. African American women occupying leadership positions in antiapartheid organizations included Gay MacDougal, director, the Lawyers Committee for Civil Rights under Law; Jean Sindab, director, the Washington Office on Africa; and Anne Forrester Holloway, staff director, House Subcommittee on Africa.

28. Claus Offe, "New Social Movements: Changing Boundaries of the Political," *Social Research* 52 (1985): 832–38.

29. Bert Klandermans, "The Peace Movement and Social Movement Theory," in *International Social Movement Research*, vol. 3 (Greenwich, Conn.: JAI Press, 1991), 11–12.

30. Medea Benjamin and Andrea Freedman, *Bridging the Global Gap: A Handbook to Linking Citizens of the First and Third Worlds* (Cabin John, Md.: Seven Locks Press, 1989); Chadwick Alger, "Grassroots Perspectives on Global Policies for Development," *Journal of Peace Research* 27, 2 (1990): 155–68.

31. Abdul S. Minty, "The Antiapartheid Movement and Racism in Southern Africa," in *Pressure Groups in the Global System*, ed. Peter Willetts (New York: St. Martin's Press, 1982), 28–45; "Drive for Divestment Red Hot!," *Washington Notes on Africa* (Spring 1983): 6.

32. Jeffrey Berry, *The Interest Group Society*, 2nd ed. (New York: HarperCollins, 1989), 61–66; David Meyer, *A Winter of Discontent: The Nuclear Freeze and American Politics* (New York: Praeger, 1990), 182–83.

33. Roberta Garner and Mayer Zald, "The Political Economy of Social Movement Sectors," in *Social Movements in an Organizational Society: Selected Essays*, ed. Mayer N. Zald and John D. McCarthy (New Brunswick, N.J.: Transaction Books, 1987), 293–319.

34. Philip A. Klinkner with Rogers M. Smith, *The Unsteady March: The Rise and Decline of Racial Equality in America* (Chicago: University of Chicago Press, 1999), 291–93.

35. Jake Miller, "Black Legislators and African American Relations," *Journal of Black Studies* 20 (1979): 245–61.

36. Christopher Coker, "Collective Bargaining as an International Sanction: The Role of U.S. Corporations in South Africa," *Journal of Modern African Studies* 19, 4 (1981): 653–54.

37. Milfred C. Fierce, "Selected Black American Leaders and Organizations and South Africa, 1900–1977," *Journal of Black Studies* 17 (Mar. 1987): 305–26.

38. Francis A. Kornegay Jr., "Black Americans and U.S.–Southern African Rela-

tions," in *American–South African Relations: Bibliographic Essays,* ed. Mohamed El-Khawas and Francis A. Kornegay Jr. (Westport, Conn.: Greenwood Press, 1975), 149–60.

39. *Africa Today* 21 (July 1974): 3.

40. Henry F. Jackson, *U.S. Foreign Policy toward Africa since 1960* (New York: William Morrow, 1982), 57–91.

41. John Stockwell, *In Search of Enemies: A CIA Story* (New York: Norton, 1978).

42. In January 1974 South African lobbyists operating in the U.S. included Governor Reagan among a group of national leaders viewed as sympathetic to whites in southern Africa. Les de Villiers, *In Sight of Surrender: The U.S. Sanctions Campaign against South Africa, 1946–1993* (New York: Praeger, 1995), 37.

43. *New York Times,* 2 May 1976.

44. Richard D. Mahoney, *JFK: Ordeal in Africa* (New York: Oxford University Press, 1983), 30–31.

45. Ronald W. Walters, *Black Presidential Politics in America: A Strategic Approach* (Albany: SUNY Press, 1988), 33–34.

46. Donald R. Culverson, *Contesting Apartheid: U.S. Activism, 1960–1987* (Boulder: Westview Press, 1999), 81.

47. Jackson, *U.S. Foreign Policy toward Africa since 1960,* 77–83.

48. *Africa Report* 21 (May–June 1976): 20.

49. "City, State Actions Force Companies to Take Notice," *Africa News* 24 (20 May 1985): 19.

50. Steven Metz, "The Anti-Apartheid Movement and the Populist Instinct in American Politics," *Political Science Quarterly* 101, 3 (1986): 379–95.

51. Cyrus Vance, "U.S. Policy toward Africa," Department of State, Bureau of Public Affairs (1 July 1977), 2.

52. Jackson, *U.S. Foreign Policy toward Africa since 1960,* 160.

53. *Economist,* 29 Mar. 1981, 34.

54. Chester Crocker, *High Noon in Southern Africa: Making Peace in a Rough Neighborhood* (New York: W. W. Norton, 1992).

55. Lefever, head of the Human Rights Division at the Department of State, had testified in House Subcommittee on Africa hearings in 1979 that the U.S. should not be concerned with South Africa's racial policies, but should accept that nation as a full-fledged partner in the struggle against communism. *Public Papers of the Presidents of the United States: Ronald Reagan, 1981* (Washington, D.C.: U.S. Government Printing Office, 1982), 196–97.

56. James Jennings, *The Politics of Black Empowerment: The Transformation of Black Activism in Urban America* (Detroit: Wayne State University Press, 1992).

57. Mike Fleshman, "Building the Cultural Boycott," *Southern Africa* 16 (Jan.–Feb. 1983): 4.

58. Ibid., 5.

SELECTED BIBLIOGRAPHY

Allen, Ernest, Jr. "Satokata Takahashi and the Flowering of Black Messianic Nationalism." *Black Scholar* 24, 1 (1994): 29–31.

Allen, Theodore. *The Invention of the White Race.* London: Verso, 1994.

Almaguer, Tomás. *Racial Fault Lines: The Historical Origins of White Supremacy in California.* Berkeley: University of California Press, 1994.

Anderson, Carol. "From Hope to Disillusion: African Americans, the United Nations, and the Struggle for Human Rights, 1944–1947." *Diplomatic History* 20 (Fall 1996): 531–63.

Anderson, Jervis. *Bayard Rustin: Troubles I've Seen.* Berkeley: University of California Press, 1998.

Appy, Christian. *Working-Class War.* Chapel Hill: University of North Carolina Press, 1993.

———, ed. *Cold War Constructions: The Political Culture of United States Imperialism, 1945–1966.* Amherst: University of Massachusetts Press, 2000.

Back, Les. "The African Heritage of White Europeans." In *Invisible Europeans?: Black People in the "New Europe,"* edited by Les Back and Anoop Nayak, 23–49. Birmingham: AFFOR, 1993.

Bailey, Beth, and David Farber. *The First Strange Place: The Alchemy of Race and Sex in World War II Hawaii.* New York: Free Press, 1992.

Baskir, Lawrence M., and William A. Strauss. *Chance and Circumstance: The Draft, the War, and the Vietnam Generation.* New York: Knopf, 1978.

Beckman, Peter R., and Francine D'Amico, eds. *Women, Gender, and World Politics.* Westport, Conn.: Berin & Garvey, 1994.

Bellegarde-Smith, Patrick. *Haiti: The Breached Citadel.* Boulder: Westview Press, 1990.

Berman, Edward. *The Influence of the Carnegie, Ford, and Rockefeller Foundations on American Foreign Policy: The Ideology of Philanthropy.* Albany: SUNY Press, 1983.

Bernstein, Irving. *Promises Kept: John F. Kennedy's New Frontier.* New York: Oxford University Press, 1991.

Blackett, Richard. *Building an Anti-Slavery Wall: Black Americans in the Atlantic Abolitionist Movement, 1830–1860.* Baton Rouge: Louisiana State University Press, 1983.

———. "Pressure from Without: African Americans, British Public Opinion, and Civil War Diplomacy." In *The Union, the Confederacy, and the Atlantic Rim,* edited by Robert E. May. West Lafayette, Ind.: Purdue University Press, 1995.

Blakely, Allison. *Russia and the Negro: Blacks in Russian History and Thought.* Washington, D.C.: Howard University Press, 1986.

Borstelmann, Thomas. *Apartheid's Reluctant Uncle: The United States and Southern Africa in the Early Cold War.* New York: Oxford University Press, 1993.

———. "Jim Crow's Coming Out: Race Relations and American Foreign Policy in the Truman Years." *Presidential Studies Quarterly* 29, 3 (1999): 549–69.

Bowser, Benjamin. "Blacks and U.S. Foreign Policy." *Sage Race Relations Abstracts* 12, 1 (February 1987): 1–20.

Branch, Taylor. *Parting the Waters: America in the King Years, 1954–63*. New York: Simon and Schuster, 1988.

———. *Pillar of Fire: America in the King Years, 1963–65*. New York: Simon and Schuster, 1998.

Brands, H. W. *The Specter of Neutralism: The United States and the Emergence of the Third World, 1947–1960*. New York: Columbia University Press, 1989.

Brauer, Carl M. *John F. Kennedy and the Second Reconstruction*. New York: Columbia University Press, 1977.

Brennan, Mary C. *Turning Right in the Sixties: The Conservative Capture of the GOP*. Chapel Hill: University of North Carolina Press, 1995.

Brock, Lisa. "Questioning the Diaspora: Hegemony, Black Intellectuals and Doing International History from Below." *Issue* 24, 2 (1996): 9–13.

Burk, Robert F. *The Eisenhower Administration and Black Civil Rights*. Knoxville: University of Tennessee Press, 1984.

Carson, Clayborne. *In Struggle: SNCC and the Black Awakening of the 1960s*. Cambridge, Mass.: Harvard University Press, 1981.

Carter, Dan T. *From George Wallace to Newt Gingrich: Race and the Conservative Counter-Revolution, 1963–1994*. Baton Rouge: Louisiana State University Press, 1996.

———. *The Politics of Rage: George Wallace, the Origins of the New Conservatism, and the Transformation of American Politics*. Baton Rouge: Louisiana State University Press, 1995.

Cato, John David. "James Herman Robinson: Crossroads Africa and American Idealism, 1958–1972." *American Presbyterian* 68 (Summer 1990): 99–107.

Cell, John Whitson. *The Highest Stage of White Supremacy: The Origins of Segregation in South Africa and the American South*. Cambridge: Cambridge University Press, 1982.

Cheng, Charles. "Cold War and Black Liberation, Part 1." *Freedomways* 13, 3 (1973): 184–98.

———. "Cold War and Black Liberation, Part 2." *Freedomways* 13, 4 (1973): 281–92.

Clark, Wayne Addison. "An Analysis of the Relationship between Anti-Communism and Segregationist Thought in the Deep South, 1948–1964." Ph.D. diss., University of North Carolina, 1976.

Collum, Danny Duncan, ed. *African Americans in the Spanish Civil War: "This Ain't Ethiopia, but It'll Do."* New York: G. K. Hall, 1992.

Committee on Africa, the War, and Peace Aims. *The Atlantic Charter and Africa from an American Standpoint*. New York: n.p., 1942.

Cone, James H. "Martin Luther King, Jr., and the Third World." *Journal of American History* 74 (September 1987): 455–67.

Culverson, Donald R. *Contesting Apartheid: U.S. Activism, 1960–1987*. Boulder: Westview Press, 1999.

Daniels, Jessie. *White Lies: Race, Class, Gender and Sexuality in White Supremacist Discourse*. New York: Routledge, 1997.

Deconde, Alexander. *Ethnicity, Race, and American Foreign Policy: A History*. Boston: Northeastern University Press, 1992.

Delgado, Richard, and Jean Stefancic, eds. *Critical White Studies: Looking behind the Mirror*. Philadelphia: Temple University Press, 1997.

Dickson, David. "American Society and the African American Foreign Policy Lobby: Constraints and Opportunities." *Journal of Black Studies* 27 (November 1996): 139–51.

Dower, John. *War without Mercy: Race and Power in the Pacific War.* New York: Pantheon, 1986.

Du Bois, W. E. B. *The Souls of Black Folk.* Boston: Bedford Books, 1997.

———. *The World and Africa: An Inquiry into the Part Which Africa Has Played in World History.* New York: International Publishers, 1965.

Dudziak, Mary L. *Cold War Civil Rights: Race and the Image of American Democracy.* Princeton: Princeton University Press, 2000.

———. "Desegregation as a Cold War Imperative." *Stanford Law Review* 41 (November 1988): 61–120.

———. "The Little Rock Crisis and Foreign Affairs: Race, Resistance, and the Image of American Democracy." *Southern California Law Review* 70 (September 1997): 1641–1716.

Duster, Alfreda M., ed. *Crusade for Justice: The Autobiography of Ida B. Wells.* Chicago: University of Chicago Press, 1970.

Edmondson, Locksley. "Black America as a Mobilizing Diaspora: Some International Implications." In *Modern Diaspora in International Politics,* edited by Gabriel Sheffer, 164–211. London: Croom Helm, 1986.

———. "The Challenge of Race: From Entrenched White Power to Rising Black Power." *International Journal* 24 (Autumn 1968): 693–716.

———. "The Internationalization of Black Power: Historical and Contemporary Perspectives." *Mawazo* 1 (December 1968): 16–30.

Eisenhower, Dwight D. *Waging Peace, 1956–1961: The White House Years.* New York: Doubleday, 1965.

Enloe, Cynthia. *The Morning After: Sexual Politics at the End of the Cold War.* Berkeley: University of California Press, 1993.

Espinoza, Dionne. "Pedagogies of Nationalism and Gender: Cultural Resistance in Selected Representational Practices of Chicana/o Movement Activists, 1967–1972." Ph.D. diss., Cornell University, 1996.

Fairclough, Adam. "Martin Luther King, Jr., and the War in Vietnam." *Phylon* 45, 1 (1984): 19–39.

Farber, Beth Bailey, and David Farber. *The First Strange Place: The Alchemy of Race and Sex in World War II Hawaii.* New York: Free Press, 1992.

Feher, Michael. *Powerless by Design: The Age of the International Community.* Durham: Duke University Press, 2000.

Fierce, Milfred C. "Selected Black American Leaders and Organizations and South Africa, 1900–1977." *Journal of Black Studies* 17 (March 1987): 305–26.

Fine, Michelle, Lois Weis, Linda C. Powell, and L. Mun Wong, eds. *Off White: Readings on Race, Power, and Society.* New York: Routledge, 1997.

Foley, Neil. "Becoming Hispanic: Mexican Americans and the Faustian Pact with Whiteness." In *Reflexiones 1997: New Directions in Mexican American Studies,* edited by Neil Foley. Austin: Center for Mexican American Studies, University of Texas, 1998.

Fousek, John. *To Lead the Free World: American Nationalism and the Cultural Roots of the Cold War.* Chapel Hill: University of North Carolina Press, 2000.

Frankenberg, Ruth. *White Women, Race Matters: The Social Construction of Whiteness.* Minneapolis: University of Minnesota Press, 1993.

Fraser, Cary. *Ambivalent Anti-Colonialism: The United States and the Genesis of West Indian Independence, 1940–1964*. Westport, Conn.: Greenwood Press, 1994.

———. "Crossing the Color Line in Little Rock: The Eisenhower Administration and the Dilemma of Race." *Diplomatic History* 24 (Spring 2000): 233–66.

———. "In Defense of Allah's Realm: Religion and Statecraft in Saudi Foreign Policy Strategy." In *Transnational Religion and Fading States*, edited by Susanne H. Rudolph and James Piscatori, 212–40. Boulder: Westview Press, 1997.

———. "A Requiem for the Cold War: Reviewing the History of International Relations since 1945." In *Rethinking the Cold War*, edited by Allen Hunter, 93–115. Philadelphia: Temple University Press, 1998.

———. "Understanding American Policy toward the Decolonization of European Empires, 1945–64." *Diplomacy & Statecraft* 3, 1 (1992): 105–25.

Fredrickson, George M. *White Supremacy: A Comparative Study in American and South African History*. New York: Oxford University Press, 1981.

Fuchs, Lawrence H. "Minority Groups and Foreign Policy." In *American Ethnic Politics*, edited by Lawrence H. Fuchs. New York: Harper and Row, 1968.

Gabbard, Krin. "Louis Armstrong's Life as a Man." *Chronicle of Higher Education*, 30 June 2000, B9–10.

Gaines, Kevin. "From Black Power to Civil Rights: Julian Mayfield and African American Expatriates in Nkrumah's Ghana, 1957–1966." In *Cold War Constructions: The Political Culture of United States Imperialism, 1945–1966*, edited by Christian G. Appy, 257–69. Amherst: University of Massachusetts Press, 2000.

Gallicchio, Marc. *The African American Encounter with Japan and China*. Chapel Hill: University of North Carolina Press, 2000.

García, Ignacio M. *Chicanismo: The Forging of a Militant Ethos among Mexican Americans*. Tucson: University of Arizona Press, 1997.

Gibbs, David N. *The Political Economy of Third World Intervention: Mines, Money, and U.S. Policy in the Congo Crisis*. Chicago: University of Chicago Press, 1991.

Gill, Gerald R. "Afro-American Opposition to the United States' Wars of the Twentieth Century: Dissent, Discontent and Disinterest." Ph.D. diss., Howard University, 1985.

Gosse, Van. "The African-American Press Greets the Cuban Revolution." In *Between Race and Empire: African-Americans and Cubans before the Cuban Revolution*, edited by Lisa Brock and Digna Castañeda Fuertes, 266–80. Philadelphia: Temple University Press, 1998.

Gubar, Susan. *Racechanges: White Skin, Black Face in American Culture*. New York: Oxford University Press, 1997.

Hale, Grace Elizabeth. *Making Whiteness: The Culture of Segregation in the South, 1890–1940*. New York: Pantheon Books, 1998.

Haney-López, Ian. *White by Law: The Legal Construction of Race*. New York: New York University Press, 1996.

Harris, Joseph E. *African American Reactions to War in Ethiopia, 1936–1941*. Baton Rouge: Louisiana State University Press, 1994.

Harris, Robert L., Jr. "Racial Equality and the United Nations Charter." In *New Directions in Civil Rights Studies*, edited by Armstead L. Robinson and Patricia Sullivan, 126–48. Charlottesville: University Press of Virginia, 1991.

Hayashida, Cullen T. "Identity, Race and the Blood Ideology of Japan." Ph.D. diss., University of Washington, 1976.

Heald, Morrell, and Lawrence S. Kaplan. *Culture and Diplomacy*. Westport, Conn.: Greenwood Press, 1977.

Henry, Charles P. *Foreign Policy and the Black (Inter)national Interest*. Albany: SUNY Press, 2000.

———. *Ralph Bunche: Model Negro or American Other?* New York: New York University Press, 1999.

Hero, Alfred O. "American Negroes and U.S. Foreign Policy, 1937–1967." *Journal of Conflict Resolution* 13 (1969): 220–51.

Hogan, Michael J. *A Cross of Iron: Harry S. Truman and the Origins of the National Security State, 1945–1954*. Cambridge: Cambridge University Press, 1998.

———. *The End of the Cold War: Its Meaning and Implications*. Cambridge: Cambridge University Press, 1992.

———. *The Marshall Plan: America, Britain, and the Reconstruction of Western Europe, 1947–1952*. Cambridge: Cambridge University Press, 1987.

———. *Paths to Power: The Historiography of American Foreign Relations to 1941*. Cambridge: Cambridge University Press, 2000.

Hogan, Michael J., and Thomas G. Paterson. *Explaining the History of American Foreign Relations*. Cambridge: Cambridge University Press, 1991.

Horne, Gerald. *Black and Red: W. E. B. Du Bois and the Afro-American Response to the Cold War*. Albany: SUNY Press, 1986.

———. *Black Liberation/Red Scare: Ben Davis and the Communist Party*. Newark: University of Delaware Press, 1994.

———. *Communist Front? The Civil Rights Congress, 1946–1956*. Cranbury, N.J.: Associated University Presses, 1988.

———. *Fire This Time: The Watts Uprising and the 1960s*. New York: Da Capo Press, 1997.

———. *From the Barrel of a Gun: The U.S. and the War against Zimbabwe, 1965–1980*. Chapel Hill: University of North Carolina Press, 2001.

———. "Gangsters, 'Whiteness,' Reactionary Politics and the U.S.-Rhodesian Connection." *Southern Africa Political and Economic Monthly* 9, 2 (November 1995): 31–34.

———. "'Myth' and the Making of 'Malcolm X.'" *American Historical Review* (April 1993): 440–50.

Hunt, Michael H. *Ideology and U.S. Foreign Policy*. New Haven: Yale University Press, 1987.

———. "Internationalizing U.S. Diplomatic History: A Practical Agenda." *Diplomatic History* 15 (Winter 1991): 1–11.

Ignatiev, Noel. *How the Irish Became White*. New York: Routledge, 1995.

Isaacs, Harold. "American Race Relations and the United States Image in World Affairs." *Journal of Human Relations* 10 (1962): 266–80.

———. *The New World of Negro Americans*. New York: John Day, 1963.

———. "Race and Color in World Affairs." *Foreign Affairs* 48 (January 1969): 235–50.

———. "World Affairs and U.S. Race Relations." *Public Opinion Quarterly* 22 (Fall 1958): 364–70.

Jackson, Henry F. *From the Congo to Soweto: U.S. Foreign Policy toward Africa since 1960*. New York: William Morrow, 1982.

Jackson, Walter A. *Gunnar Myrdal and America's Conscience*. Chapel Hill: University of North Carolina Press, 1990.

Janken, Kenneth Robert. *Rayford W. Logan and the Dilemma of the African American Intellectual.* Amherst: University of Massachusetts Press, 1993.

Jeffords, Susan. "Culture and National Identity in U.S. Foreign Policy." *Diplomatic History* 18, 1 (Winter 1994): 91–96.

Johnson, Sterling. "Nation-State and Non-State Nations: The International Relations and Foreign Policies of Black America." Ph.D. diss., Ohio State University, 1979.

Kahin, George McTurnan. *The Asian-African Conference.* Ithaca: Cornell University Press, 1956.

Kalb, Madeleine G. *The Congo Cables: The Cold War in Africa—From Eisenhower to Kennedy.* New York: Macmillan, 1982.

Kearney, Reginald. *African American Views of the Japanese: Solidarity or Sedition?* Albany: SUNY Press, 1998.

Kelley, Robin D. G. *Race Rebels.* New York: Free Press, 1994.

———. "The World the Diaspora Made: C. L. R. James and the Politics of History." In *Rethinking C. L. R. James,* edited by Grant Farred, 103–30. Cambridge, Mass.: Blackwell, 1996.

Kincheloe, Joe L., Shirley R. Steinberg, Nelson M. Rodriguez, and Ronald E. Chennault, eds. *White Reign: Deploying Whiteness in America.* New York: St. Martin's Press, 1998.

Klinkner, Philip A., with Rogers M. Smith. *The Unsteady March: The Rise and Decline of Racial Equality in America.* Chicago: University of Chicago Press, 1999.

Klor de Alva, J. Jorge. "Aztlán, Borinquen and Hispanic Nationalism." In *Aztlán: Essays on the Chicano Homeland,* edited by Rudolfo A. Anaya and Francisco Lomelí, 135–63. Albuquerque, N.Mex.: Academia/El Norte Publications, 1989.

Kornegay, Francis A., Jr. "Black Americans and U.S.–Southern African Relations." In *American–South African Relations: Bibliographic Essays,* edited by Mohamed El-Khawas and Francis A. Kornegay Jr., 149–60. Westport, Conn.: Greenwood Press, 1975.

Krenn, Michael L. *Black Diplomacy: African Americans and the State Department, 1945–1969.* Armonk, N.Y.: M. E. Sharpe, 1999.

———. *The Impact of Race on U.S. Foreign Policy: A Reader.* New York: Garland, 1999.

———. "'Their Proper Share': The Changing Role of Racism in U.S. Foreign Policy since World War One." *Nature, Society, and Thought* 4, 1–2 (1991): 57–79.

Kühl, Stefan. *The Nazi Connection: Eugenics, American Racism, and German National Socialism.* New York: Oxford University Press, 1994.

Kunz, Diane B., ed. *The Diplomacy of the Crucial Decade: American Foreign Relations in the 1960s.* New York: Columbia University Press, 1994.

Lacey, Leslie Alexander. "Malcolm X in Ghana." In *Malcolm X, the Man and His Times,* edited by John Henrik Clark, 217–25. New York: Macmillan, 1969.

Lauren, Paul Gordon. *Diplomacy: New Approaches in History, Theory, and Policy.* New York: Free Press, 1979.

———. *The Evolution of International Human Rights: Visions Seen.* Philadelphia: University of Pennsylvania Press, 1998.

———. "First Principles of Racial Equality: History and the Politics and Diplomacy of Human Rights Provisions in the United Nations Charter." *Human Rights Quarterly* 5 (Winter 1983): 1–26.

———. *Power and Prejudice: The Politics and Diplomacy of Racial Discrimination.* 2nd ed. Boulder: Westview Press, 1996.

Lauren, Paul Gordon, and Raymond Finlay Wylie. *Destinies Shared: U.S.-Japanese Relations.* Boulder: Westview Press, 1989.

Layton, Azza Salama. "International Pressure and the U.S. Government's Response to Little Rock." *Arkansas Historical Quarterly* 56 (Autumn 1997): 257–72.

LeMelle, Tilden J. "Race, International Relations, U.S. Foreign Policy, and the African Liberation Struggle." *Journal of Black Studies* 3 (September 1972): 95–109.

Lie, John. "The State as Pimp: Prostitution and the Patriarchal State in Japan in the 1940s." *Sociological Quarterly* 38 (Spring 1997): 251–64.

Lilley, Charles R., and Michael H. Hunt. "On Social History, the State, and Foreign Relations: Commentary on the Cosmopolitan Connection." *Diplomatic History* 11 (Summer 1987).

Lincoln, C. Eric. "The Race Problem and International Relations." *New South* 21 (Fall 1966).

———. *Race, Religion, and the Continuing American Dilemma.* New York: Hill and Wang, 1999.

Lipsitz, George. *Rainbow at Midnight: Labor and Culture in the 1940s.* Urbana: University of Illinois Press, 1994.

Lloyd, David. "Nationalisms against the State." In *The Politics of Culture in the Shadow of Capital,* edited by Lisa Lowe and David Lloyd, 173–97. Durham: Duke University Press, 1997.

Lockwood, Bert, Jr. "The UN Charter and U.S. Civil Rights Litigation: 1946–1955." *Iowa Law Review* 69 (1984): 901–56.

Logan, Frenise A. "Racism and Indian-U.S. Relations, 1947–1953." *Pacific Historical Review* 54 (February 1985): 71–79.

Lott, Eric. "Double V, Double-Time: Bebop's Politics of Style." *Callaloo* 11, 3 (1988): 597–605.

Louis, William Roger. *Imperialism at Bay, 1941–1945: The United States and the Decolonization of the British Empire.* Oxford: Clarendon Press, 1977.

Love, Janice. *The U.S. Anti-Apartheid Movement: Local Activism in Global Politics.* New York: Praeger, 1985.

Lowe, Lisa, and David Lloyd, eds. *The Politics of Culture in the Shadow of Capital.* Durham: Duke University Press, 1997.

Luke, Timothy W. *Screens of Power: Ideology, Domination, and Resistance in Informational Society.* Urbana: University of Illinois Press, 1989.

Lynch, Hollis R. *Black American Radicals and the Liberation of Africa: The Council on African Affairs, 1937–1955.* Ithaca: Cornell University Press, 1978.

Maga, Timothy P. "Battling the Ugly American at Home: The Special Protocol Service and the New Frontier, 1961–63." *Diplomacy and Statecraft* 3 (1993): 126–42.

Mahoney, Richard D. *JFK: Ordeal in Africa.* New York: Oxford University Press, 1983.

Mariscal, George, ed. *Aztlán and Viet Nam, Chicano and Chicana Experiences of the War.* Berkeley: University of California Press, 1999.

Marks, George P. *The Black Press Views American Imperialism (1898–1900).* New York: Arno Press, 1971.

Marx, Anthony. *Making Race and Nation: A Comparison of the United States, South Africa and Brazil.* New York: Cambridge University Press, 1998.

Massaquoi, Hans J. *Destined to Witness: Growing Up Black in Nazi Germany.* New York: William Morrow, 1999.

Massie, Robert Kinloch. *Loosing the Bonds: The United States and South Africa in the Apartheid Years*. New York: Doubleday, 1997.

McAdam, Doug. "On the International Origins of Domestic Political Opportunities." In *Social Movements and American Political Institutions*, edited by Anne Costain and Andrew McFarland, 251–67. Lanham, Md.: Rowman & Littlefield, 1998.

McCaughey, Robert. *International Studies and Academic Enclosure*. New York: Columbia University Press, 1984.

McCoy, Donald R., and Richard T. Ruetten. *Quest and Response: Minority Rights and the Truman Administration*. Lawrence: University Press of Kansas, 1973.

McFerson, Hazel M. *The Racial Dimensions of American Overseas Colonial Policy*. Westport, Conn.: Greenwood Press, 1997.

Mealy, Rosemari. *Fidel and Malcolm X: Memories of a Meeting*. Melbourne: Ocean Press, 1993.

Metz, Steven. "The Anti-Apartheid Movement and the Populist Instinct in American Politics." *Political Science Quarterly* 101, 3 (1986): 379–95.

Miles, Robert. *Racism after "Race" Relations*. New York: Routledge, 1993.

Miller, Jake C. *The Black Presence in American Foreign Affairs*. Washington, D.C.: University Press of America, 1978.

Minty, Abdul S. "The Anti-Apartheid Movement and Racism in Southern Africa." In *Pressure Groups in the Global System*, edited by Peter Willetts, 28–45. New York: St. Martin's Press, 1982.

Mintz, Frank P. *The Liberty Lobby and the American Right: Race, Conspiracy and Culture*. Westport, Conn.: Greenwood Press, 1985.

Moon, Katharine H. S. *Sex among Allies: Military Prostitution in U.S.-Korean Relations*. New York: Columbia University Press, 1997.

Moore, Carlos. *Castro, the Blacks, and Africa*. Los Angeles: University of California, Center for Afro-American Studies, 1988.

Morris, Milton D. "Black Americans and the Foreign Policy Process: The Case of Africa." *Western Political Quarterly* 25 (1972): 451–63.

Myrdal, Gunnar. *An American Dilemma: The Negro Problem and Modern Democracy*. 2 vols. New York: Harper and Brothers, 1944.

Nelson, Keith L. "The 'Black Horror' on the Rhine: Race as a Factor in Post–World War I Diplomacy." *Journal of Modern History* 42, 4 (December 1970): 606–27.

Noer, Thomas J. *Cold War and Black Liberation: The United States and White Rule in Africa, 1948–1968*. Columbia: University of Missouri Press, 1985.

———. "New Frontiers and Old Priorities in Africa." In *Kennedy's Quest for Victory: American Foreign Policy, 1961–1963*, edited by Thomas G. Paterson, 253–83. New York: Oxford, 1989.

———. "Truman, Eisenhower, and South Africa: The 'Middle Road' and Apartheid." *Journal of Ethnic Studies* 11 (Spring 1983): 75–104.

Ogene, F. Chidozie. *Interest Groups and the Shaping of Foreign Policy: Four Case Studies of United States African Policy*. New York: St. Martin's Press, 1983.

Oguntoye, Katerine, and May Opitz. "Showing Our Colours! The Testimony of Two Afro German Women." In *Invisible Europeans? Black People in the "New Europe,"* edited by Les Back and Anoop Nayak, 94–119. Birmingham: AFFOR, 1993.

Omi, Michael, and Howard Winant. *Racial Formation in the United States*. 2nd ed. New York: Routledge, 1994.

Oropeza, Lorena. "La batalla está aquí: Chicanos Oppose the War in Vietnam." Ph.D. diss., Cornell University, 1996.

Packenham, Robert A. *Liberal America and the Third World*. Princeton: Princeton University Press, 1973.

Plummer, Brenda Gayle. "Castro in Harlem: A Cold War Watershed." In *Rethinking the Cold War: Essays on Its Dynamics, Meaning, and Morality*, edited by Allen Hunter, 133–53. Philadelphia: Temple University Press, 1998.

———. "Evolution of the Black Foreign Policy Constituency." *TransAfrica Forum* 6 (Spring–Summer 1989): 67–81.

———. *Rising Wind: Black Americans and U.S. Foreign Affairs, 1935–1960*. Chapel Hill: University of North Carolina Press, 1996.

Plummer, Brenda Gayle, and Donald R. Culverson. "Black Americans and Foreign Affairs: A Reassessment." *Sage Race Relations Abstracts* 12 (February 1987): 21–31.

Posner, David Braden. "Afro-America in West German Perspective, 1945–1966." Ph.D. diss., Yale University, 1997.

Powell, Adam Clayton, Jr. *Adam by Adam: The Autobiography of Adam Clayton Powell, Jr.* New York: Dial Press, 1971.

Pycior, Julie Leininger. *LBJ and Mexican Americans: The Paradox of Power*. Austin: University of Texas Press, 1997.

Ratcliffe, Peter, ed. *"Race," Ethnicity and Nation: International Perspectives on Social Conflict*. London: UCL Press, 1994.

Reddick, L. D. "Africa: Test of the Atlantic Charter." *Crisis* 50 (July 1943): 202–4, 217–18.

Roark, James L. "American Black Leaders: The Response of Colonialism and the Cold War." *African Historical Studies* 4, 2 (1971): 253–70.

Robinson, Cedric J. *Black Marxism: The Making of the Black Radical Tradition*. Chapel Hill: University of North Carolina Press, 2000.

———. *Black Movements in America*. New York: Routledge, 1997.

Robinson, Randall. *Defending the Spirit: A Black Life in America*. New York: Dutton, 1988.

Roediger, David R. *The Wages of Whiteness: Race and the Making of the American Working Class*. London: Verso, 1991.

Romano, Renee. "No Diplomatic Immunity: African Diplomats, the State Department, and Civil Rights, 1961–1964." *Journal of American History* 87 (September 2000): 546–80.

Rosenberg, Emily. "Foreign Affairs after World War II: Connecting Sexual and International Politics." *Diplomatic History* 18 (Winter 1994): 59–70.

Rowan, Carl T. *Breaking Barriers: A Memoir*. New York: HarperCollins, 1992.

———. *The Pitiful and the Proud*. New York: Random House, 1956.

Rusk, Dean. *As I Saw It*. New York: W. W. Norton, 1990.

Rustin, Bayard. *Down the Line: The Collected Writings of Bayard Rustin*. Chicago: Quadrangle Books, 1971.

Sale, Kirkpatrick. *Power Shift: The Rise of the Southern Rim and Its Challenge to the Eastern Establishment*. New York: Random House, 1975.

Sánchez, George. *Becoming Mexican American*. New York: Oxford University Press, 1993.

Savage, Barbara Dianne. *Broadcasting Freedom: Radio, War, and the Politics of Race, 1938–1948*. Chapel Hill: University of North Carolina Press, 1999.

Schaller, Michael, Virginia Scharff, and Robert D. Schulzinger. *Coming of Age: America in the Twentieth Century*. Boston: Houghton Mifflin, 1998.

Schlesinger, Arthur. *A Thousand Days*. Boston: Houghton Mifflin, 1965.

Schoenbaum, Thomas J. *Waging Peace and War*. New York: Simon and Schuster, 1988.

Schulzinger, Robert D. *A Time for War: The United States and Vietnam, 1941–1975*. New York: Oxford University Press, 1997.

Scott, William R. *The Sons of Sheba's Race: African Americans and the Italo-Ethiopian War, 1935–1941*. Bloomington: University of Indiana Press, 1993.

Segal, Ronald. *The Race War*. London: Jonathan Cape, 1966.

Shankman, Arnold. *Ambivalent Friends: Afro-Americans View the Immigrant*. Westport, Conn.: Greenwood Press, 1982.

Shepherd, George W., Jr. *Anti-Apartheid*. Westport, Conn.: Greenwood Press, 1977.

———. *Racial Influences on American Foreign Policy*. New York: Basic Books, 1970.

Shepherd, George W., and Tilden J. LeMelle. *Race among Nations*. Lexington, Mass.: Heath Lexington Books, 1970.

Sitkoff, Harvard. *Perspectives on Modern America: Making Sense of the Twentieth Century*. New York: Oxford University Press, 2001.

Skinner, Elliott P. "African American Perspectives on Foreign Policy." In *From Exclusion to Inclusion: The African American Struggle for Political Power*, edited by Linda F. Williams and Ralph Gomes, 173–86. Westport, Conn.: Greenwood Press, 1992.

———. *African Americans and U.S. Policy toward Africa, 1850–1924: In Defense of Black Nationality*. Washington, D.C.: Howard University Press, 1992.

Skrenty, John David. "The Effect of the Cold War on African American Civil Rights: America and the World Audience, 1945–1968." *Theory and Society* 27 (1998): 237–85.

Small, Melvin. *Democracy and Diplomacy: The Impact of Domestic Politics on U.S. Foreign Policy, 1789–1994*. Baltimore: Johns Hopkins University Press, 1996.

Smith, Graham. *When Jim Crow Met John Bull: Black American Soldiers in World War II Britain*. New York: St. Martin's Press, 1987.

Smith, Tony. *Foreign Attachments: The Power of Ethnic Groups in the Making of American Foreign Policy*. Cambridge, Mass.: Harvard University Press, 2000.

Sniderman, Paul, Philip Tetlock, and Edward Carmines, eds. *Prejudice, Politics, and the American Dilemma*. Stanford: Stanford University Press, 1993.

Solomon, Mark. "Black Critics of Colonialism and the Cold War." In *Cold War Critics*, edited by Thomas G. Paterson, 205–39. New York: Quadrangle Books, 1971.

Southern, David W. *Gunnar Myrdal and Black-White Relations: The Use and Abuse of An American Dilemma, 1944–1969*. Baton Rouge: Louisiana State University Press, 1987.

Stanfield, John H. *Philanthropy and Jim Crow in American Social Science*. Westport, Conn.: Greenwood Press, 1985.

Stanford, Karin L. *Beyond the Boundaries: Reverend Jesse Jackson in International Affairs*. Albany: SUNY Press, 1997.

Starr, S. Frederick. *Red and Hot: The Fate of Jazz in the Soviet Union, 1917–1980*. New York: Oxford University Press, 1983.

Stephanson, Anders. "Diplomatic History in the Expanded Field." *Diplomatic History* 22 (Fall 1998): 595–603.

Stern, Mark. *Calculating Visions: Kennedy, Johnson, and Civil Rights.* New Brunswick, N.J.: Rutgers University Press, 1992.

Streater, John Baxter. "The National Negro Congress, 1936–1947." Ph.D. diss., University of Cincinnati, 1981.

Sundquist, James L., and Brookings Institution. *Politics and Policy: The Eisenhower, Kennedy, and Johnson Years.* Washington, D.C.: Brookings Institution, 1968.

Tinker, Hugh. *Race, Conflict and International Order: From Empire to United Nations.* New York: St. Martin's Press, 1977.

Tobias, Channing. *World Implications of Race.* New York: n.p., 1944.

Trouillot, Michel-Rolph. *Silencing the Past: Power and the Production of History.* Boston: Beacon Press, 1995.

U.S. Congress. Senate. Committee on Foreign Relations. *Hearings on the Charter of the United Nations.* 79th Cong., 1st sess., 9–13 July 1945.

Urquhart, Brian. *Ralph Bunche—An American Life.* New York: W. W. Norton, 1993.

Villiers, Les de. *In Sight of Surrender: The U.S. Sanctions Campaign against South Africa, 1946–1993.* New York: Praeger, 1995.

Von Eschen, Penny. *Race against Empire: Black Americans and Anticolonialism, 1937–1957.* Ithaca: Cornell University Press, 1997.

———. "Who's the Real Ambassador? Exploding Cold War Racial Ideology." In *Cold War Constructions: The Political Culture of United States Imperialism, 1945–1966,* edited by Christian G. Appy, 110–31. Amherst: University of Massachusetts Press, 2000.

Wei, William. *The Asian American Movement.* Philadelphia: Temple University Press, 1993.

Weisbord, Robert. *Ebony Kinship: Africa, Africans and the Afro-Americans.* Westport, Conn.: Greenwood Press, 1973.

Weston, Rubin Francis. *Racism in U.S. Imperialism: The Influence of Racial Assumptions on American Foreign Policy, 1893–1946.* New York: Columbia University Press, 1972.

White, Walter. *A Rising Wind.* New York: Doubleday, Doran, 1945.

Wilkins, Roger. *A Man's Life.* New York: Simon and Schuster, 1982.

Williams, Yohuru R. "American Exported Black Nationalism: The Student Nonviolent Coordinating Committee, the Black Panther Party, and the Worldwide Freedom Struggle, 1967–1972." *Negro History Bulletin* 60 (July–September 1997): 13–20.

Wittner, Lawrence S. *Rebels against War: The American Peace Movement, 1933–1983.* Philadelphia: Temple University Press, 1984.

Wofford, Harris. *Of Kennedys and Kings.* New York: Farrar, Straus, Giroux, 1980.

Wright, Richard. *The Color Curtain: A Report on the Bandung Conference.* New York: World, 1956.

Carol Anderson is an Assistant Professor of History at the University of Missouri–Columbia. Her book, *Eyes Off the Prize: African Americans, the United Nations, and the Struggle for Human Rights, 1944–1955,* will be published by Cambridge University Press. Anderson is a Ford Fellow, an ACLS Fellow, a Center for International Cooperation (CIC) Fellow, and a recent recipient of the William T. Kemper Fellowship for Excellence in Teaching.

Donald R. Culverson is Professor of Political and Justice Studies at Governors State University in Illinois. He is the author of *Contesting Apartheid: U.S. Activism, 1960–1987.* Culverson's work has appeared in *Political Science Quarterly, TransAfrica Forum, Sage Race Relations Abstracts,* and other venues. His current research project examines the impact of globalization on U.S. domestic racial politics.

Mary L. Dudziak is Judge Edward J. and Ruey L. Guirado Professor of Law and History at the University of Southern California School of Law. She is the author of the pioneering and widely cited *Stanford Law Review* article "Desegregation as a Cold War Imperative." Dudziak most recently published *Cold War Civil Rights: Race and the Image of American Democracy.*

Cary Fraser teaches the history of American foreign policy and twentieth-century African American history at Penn State University. He has been a recipient of fellowships from the Social Science Research Council and the John D. and Catherine T. MacArthur Foundation. Fraser is the author of *Ambivalent Anti-Colonialism: The United States and the Genesis of West Indian Independence, 1940–1964.*

Gerald Horne teaches at the University of North Carolina–Chapel Hill and is the author, most recently, of *From the Barrel of a Gun: The United States and the War against Zimbabwe, Race Woman: The Lives of Shirley Graham Du Bois,* and *Race War! White Supremacy vs. Blacks and Asians in the Japanese Attack on Hong Kong and the British Empire, 1920–1950* (forthcoming).

Michael Krenn is currently serving as chair of the Department of History at Appalachian State University. He received his Ph.D. in 1985 from Rutgers University, where he studied under the guidance of Lloyd C. Gardner. His most recent book is entitled *Black Diplomacy: African Americans and the State Department, 1945–1969.* He is now at work on a manuscript about U.S. art exhibits sent overseas during the Cold War.

Paul Gordon Lauren is Regents Professor at the University of Montana. He is an internationally recognized scholar on diplomacy, human rights, and racial discrimination, having lectured before the United Nations and published eight books, including the award-winning *The Evolution of International Human Rights,* which was nominated for a Pulitzer Prize, and *Power and Prejudice: The Politics and Diplomacy of Racial Discrimination.*

Thomas Noer is Valor Distinguished Professor of Humanities at Carthage College in Kenosha, Wisconsin. *Choice* named his book *Briton, Boer, and Yankee* one of "the Ten Outstanding Books of the Year." His book *Cold War and Black Liberation* received the Society of Historians of American Foreign Relations' Stuart Bernath Prize. He is currently working on a biography of G. Mennen Williams.

Lorena Oropeza is an assistant professor in the History Department at the University of California, Davis. She is the author of "Making History: The Chicano Movement" in *Voices of a New Chicana/Chicano History* as well as a forthcoming book on Chicano protest and patriotism during the Vietnam War era. Her current research interests include the land-grant movement of New Mexico.

Brenda Gayle Plummer is a professor at the University of Wisconsin. She has received fellowships from the Social Science Research Council, the National Endowment for the Humanities, and the National Humanities Center. Plummer's books include *Rising Wind: Black Americans and U.S. Foreign Affairs, 1935–1960*, which won the Society of Historians of American Foreign Relations' Myrna Bernath Prize and was cowinner of the American Historical Association's Wesley-Logan Prize.